Dick
1905 F____, ___ ___
Prescott, AZ 86303
(928-443-9911)

An Unpredictable Gospel

An Unpredictable Gospel

American Evangelicals and World Christianity, 1812–1920

JAY RILEY CASE

OXFORD
UNIVERSITY PRESS

OXFORD
UNIVERSITY PRESS

Oxford University Press, Inc., publishes works that further
Oxford University's objective of excellence
in research, scholarship, and education.

Oxford   New York
Auckland   Cape Town   Dar es Salaam   Hong Kong   Karachi
Kuala Lumpur   Madrid   Melbourne   Mexico City   Nairobi
New Delhi   Shanghai   Taipei   Toronto

With offices in
Argentina   Austria   Brazil   Chile   Czech Republic   France   Greece
Guatemala   Hungary   Italy   Japan   Poland   Portugal   Singapore
South Korea   Switzerland   Thailand   Turkey   Ukraine   Vietnam

Copyright © 2012 by Oxford University Press, Inc.

Published by Oxford University Press, Inc.
198 Madison Avenue, New York, New York 10016

www.oup.com

Oxford is a registered trademark of Oxford University Press

All rights reserved. No part of this publication may be reproduced,
stored in a retrieval system, or transmitted, in any form or by any means,
electronic, mechanical, photocopying, recording, or otherwise,
without the prior permission of Oxford University Press.

Library of Congress Cataloging-in-Publication Data
Case, Jay Riley.
An unpredictable Gospel : American evangelicals and world
Christianity, 1812–1920 / Jay Riley Case.
p. cm.
Includes bibliographical references (p.   ) and index.
ISBN 978-0-19-977231-5 (pbk. : alk. paper)
ISBN 978-0-19-977232-2 (hardcover : alk. paper)
1. Missions, American—History—19th century.   2. Protestant churches—Missions—
History—19th century.   3. Christianity and culture—History—19th century.
4. Missions, American—History—20th century.   5. Protestant churches—Missions—
History—20th century.   6. Christianity and culture—History—20th century.   I. Title.
BV2410.C37 2012
266.00973'09034—dc22   2011016110

For Elisa,
Karin and Jon,
Brenna, and Kelsey

CONTENTS

Acknowledgments   ix

Introduction   3

PART ONE

1. American Baptists and the "Wild" Karen People of Burma   19
2. The Challenge of Karen Christianity   48
3. The Native Ministry in the United States   74

PART TWO

4. An Appalachian Revivalist in Queen Victoria's Colonies   103
5. The Circuit-Riding Missionary and Gilded Age Methodism   128

PART THREE

6. The African-American Great Awakening   159
7. The AME Church and South Africa   183

PART FOUR

8. Holiness Conversions   209
9. And Ever the Twain Shall Meet   231
Epilogue   256

Notes   261
Index   301

ACKNOWLEDGMENTS

I understand better than I once did how significant feedback, support, assistance, and conversations with others can be for what otherwise seems like the rather solitary business of historical research. This work was a long time in the making, so I am grateful to many people.

I have received valuable assistance from several archival staff members at the American Baptist Historical Society and Drew University. I am also thankful for the help given by Bonnie Houser at the Taylor University archives, David Himrod at the United Library of Garrett-Evangelical Theological Seminary, and William Kostlevy at the B. L. Fisher Library at Asbury Theological Seminary. Joyce Lee and every staff member I encountered at the Flower Pentecostal Heritage Center have been particularly helpful and gracious.

The origins of this work began many years ago in graduate school at the University of Notre Dame, where I found a particularly inspiring community in which to launch into historical scholarship. I regularly found myself discussing American religion and evangelicalism with many people, including Tom Bergler, Joe Creech, Darren Dochuk, Scott Flipse, Nicole Gothelf, Mike Hamilton, Randy Heinig, Fred Jordan, Tommy Kidd, Steve Nolt, Rick Ostrander, Kurt Peterson, Anita Specht, Kathleen Sprows Cummings, Bill Svelmoe, Peter Wallace, and John Wigger. Those who read and made valuable observations on early portions of the material in this book included Gail Bederman, Nathan Hatch, Walter Nugent, and Grant Wacker. I am thankful also for feedback from Jay Green, Bob Lay, and the late Gary McGee. Bob Woodberry not only broadened my understanding of the missionary movement but also located sources on Karen Christianity that I otherwise would not have found. Joel Carpenter has given particularly timely and incisive advice. I am also deeply grateful to Bill Ringenberg and Alan Winquist for inspiring me to head down the path of historical scholarship in the first place. George Marsden has been a formative influence all along the way on this project. His thoughtful analysis, dedication, high standards, insights, feedback, integrity, and friendship have made him a truly invaluable guide.

A Seminar in Christian Scholarship on "Christianity as a World Religion," hosted by Calvin College and led by Lamin Sanneh in the summer of 2000, reoriented my thinking in significant ways. The seminar added time to the work on this book by convincing me that I needed to take apart and reconstruct my dissertation. Perhaps there were better ways to go about pursuing this project, but I am grateful for that reorientation. Numerous discussions and sessions with participants at the Yale-Edinburgh Group on the History of the Missionary Movement and World Christianity further widened my understanding of world Christianity. Malone University has provided a rich and stimulating community that has aided the development of this project in several ways. A sabbatical semester and two summer research grants from Malone gave me the opportunity to conduct additional research. Jan Anderson and Stan Terhune at the Malone University library helped me track down a few obscure sources. David Yakley proved to be quite patient and gracious in helping me negotiate the mysterious world of managing images. The observations and reactions to portions of this work by students in my course on the history of the missionary movement helped me clarify several sections. The Malone Writers Group not only provided a thoroughly delightful way to spend an occasional Friday evening but also gave careful thought, insightful reflections, and valuable feedback on later versions of this book. This group has included Jim Brownlee, David Dixon, Georgia Eshelman, Bryan Hollon, Steve Jensen, Maria Lam, Matt Phelps, Nate Phinney, Ken Stolzfus, and Fred Thomas. I cannot say enough about the members of the History, Philosophy, and Social Science Department at Malone, whose members, among other things, have consistently renewed my enthusiasm for scholarship, teaching, and service. I am not sure why I am so fortunate to work at a place where I truly look forward to coming into the office on Monday morning. Several have been gracious enough to comment on sections or discuss ideas found in the work, including Geoff Bowden, Malcolm Gold, Jane Hoyt-Oliver, Greg Miller, Jeff Polet, Scott Waalkes, and Jacci Welling. Becky Albertson has helped with countless administrative details, displaying an efficiency and graciousness that I always find remarkable.

A research project like this inevitably spilled over into the lives of my family, who have been more than patient and encouraging. Typical of their support for my academic work over the years, Dwight and Karin Jessup offered to let me work in their newly constructed hideaway. My mother, Ruth Case, has patiently listened to me describe my latest efforts, while graciously adapting family events to busy academic schedules. My father, Riley B. Case, has taken a keen interest in my project, accompanying me on a research trip, loaning me Methodist sources, listening to my analysis, and happily offering up his own historical perspectives. He taught me to take ordinary Methodists seriously. Karin, Brenna, Kelsey, and, more recently, Jon have not only patiently endured times at home when I have been preoccupied but have also read and commented on sections of the work. More important, they have blessed me with lives that have helped to keep me grounded. Finally, I hardly know how to be properly grateful to my wife, Elisa. She has shared in my intellectual curiosity, she has listened to me process my thoughts aloud, and she has read, edited, and commented on all of my writing. Mostly, though, she has accompanied me throughout the years of this work with a love that has gone well beyond what I ever envisioned.

An Unpredictable Gospel

Introduction

The missionaries were excited about the revival, but they did not know what to make of the fire. For several months in 1905, a number of students at Mukti, a school for young women in India, had followed the lead of the headmistress, Pandita Ramabai, by praying for a revival and preaching in the surrounding villages. Then, one night in June, a girl awoke to the sight of a fire burning on the person of her roommate, who was at prayer. After her initial alarm, the girl decided it was actually a manifestation of the Holy Spirit, and she spread the news of what she had seen. That started a series of religious activities at the Mukti school that continued for more than a year, activities that eventually led to more than one thousand conversions, as well as reports of miraculous healings, casting out of demons, speaking in tongues, and additional incidents involving the fire sensation.[1]

Aware that lower-caste Hindu religious practice sometimes included spirit possession accompanied by a burning sensation, the evangelical missionaries hadn't expected this fire phenomenon to appear amidst a Christian revival. Fiery spirit possessions were not, of course, the sort of thing one usually found within the churches of the small towns in the U.S. midwest where many of these missionaries had been raised. So how would one make sense of the events at Mukti? If they were like most Americans in 1905, they would have agreed with the missionary from a different organization, who dismissed the events as "sensuous and superstitious...pure heathenism in Christian dress."[2]

But these missionaries came from the radical-holiness wing of evangelicalism. As such, they took a different path. True, some of them initially viewed the fire as a sort of exorcism for those who had been "idolators." But their suspicions began to wane when some of the young Indian women whom the missionaries regarded as "fully saved and sanctified" received the fire. Wandering into unknown territory, the missionaries decided that the fire was a sign of the baptism of the Holy Spirit, granting "power for service" to anyone who sought it. Following the logic of this theological path, they did more than simply approve of these surprising religious developments. Several of the missionaries became religious inquirers, seeking out the young lower-caste Asian women so that they could experience the fire sensation for themselves.[3]

And so the missionaries at Mukti did something that would not have even occurred to most Americans in 1905: they pitched the white man's burden out the window. They not only ignored the terminology of civilization to describe this missionary situation, but they also behaved in ways that confounded the very terms of the civilizing mission. Working at the height of Western imperialism, these American missionaries at a boarding school in colonial India turned to young Indian women in hopes of accessing a supernatural religious experience that seemed remarkably close to lower-caste Hindu practices.

They did not stop there. Radical-holiness missionaries believed that they needed to encourage others to embrace movements of the Spirit. Making effective use of the informal networks of the holiness missionary movement, one of these missionaries, Minnie Abrams, spread news of the Mukti revival, primarily by way of a booklet called *The Baptism of the Holy Ghost & Fire*. Unlike the common missionary report to those in "Christian civilization" who observed their missionaries promoting the steady march of progress in far-off "heathen lands," Abrams called on her readers to seek the Pentecostal experience that had fallen on these young women in India. True to its evangelistic purposes, the book provoked Pentecostal activity in many locations, most famously making its unlikely way from India to Chile, where it helped spark the first Pentecostal movement in Latin America.[4] But it also targeted North Americans. Accompanying reports of revivals elsewhere around the world, the news of the Mukti revival flowed to scores of towns and cities in the United States and Canada, to fan the flames of revivals and conversions in what many considered to be the heart of civilization.[5]

Judging by their publications, most missionaries had not really anticipated something quite like the Mukti revival when they set out for India. Missionaries expected to reap conversions and lead revivals themselves, but this movement began with recently "idolatrous" young Indian women, under the leadership of an Indian headmistress. Evangelical missionaries brought elements of Western civilization with them—the idea of establishing a school for widowed Indian females, for instance, owed much to missionary influence—but they never predicted that a vibrant revival would grow from ecstatic practices similar to Hindu worship. Hoping to spread Christianity in South Asia, missionaries did not expect a stirring revival in an obscure spot in India to sweep back to influence religious life in the United States.

Years later, the Mukti revival still surprises. Judging by scholarly and popular accounts of missionaries written in the last half of the twentieth century, the Mukti revival is not really what most scholars or evangelicals imagine when they set out to write about the history of missionaries. For many years, ordinary American evangelicals wrote popular accounts in which missionaries seemed to be the only important characters in the stories. Indigenous Christians stood passively in the background, except for brief moments when they accepted the

Gospel. Mainstream scholarship, meanwhile, had a different problem, even though it also tended to ignore indigenous Christianity. Following the rhetorical lead of prominent nineteenth-century Protestants who spoke of the march of Christian civilization, most scholarly works (not to mention textbooks and novels) have understood the missionary enterprise in terms of Western cultural imposition and non-Western resistance. Flatly stated, these works usually define missionaries as cultural imperialists.[6]

The cultural-imperialist narrative, however, has not yielded fruitful explanations for why non-Western resisters embraced Christianity with such confounding enthusiasm that they now outnumber the Western imposers.[7] As many scholars now recognize, Christianity's center of gravity has shifted from Europe and North America to Africa, Asia, and Latin America. The revival at Mukti represented a very small part of what may be the most significant religious development of the twentieth century. Christian bodies—evangelical and nonevangelical, Protestant and Catholic—have seen their numbers in the global South grow dramatically. Pentecostalism, the branch of evangelicalism most deeply influenced by the Mukti revival, claimed an estimated 425 million adherents by the year 2000, encompassing more than one-fourth of all Christians around the globe. If it has not happened already, our mental geography of religion needs to be redrawn.[8]

For most of the twentieth century, few people outside these religious communities in Asia, Africa, and Latin America paid attention to these movements, in part because they often grew on the margins of their societies. That is changing. One century and a seismic shift in global religion later, scholars have begun to sit up and take notice. Presenting a clearer sense of the dynamics of Christian movements on the ground in Africa, Asia, and Latin America, many scholars describe these bodies as different strands of a culturally diverse phenomenon known as world Christianity. Christians in Africa, Asia, and Latin America adapted to a variety of different cultural situations, produced new theological perspectives, and undercut assumptions that cast Christianity as a Western religion. Many scholars now consciously focus on the actions, practices, and theologies of non-Western Christianity, describing them in terms of indigenization, translation, or contextualization. In other words, Christians in Africa, Asia, and Latin America have not blindly and passively followed leaders from Europe and North America, nor were they unwillingly coerced into joining institutions they would rather avoid, but eagerly shaped Christianity according to terms and issues from their own cultures. The global shift, in fact, has provoked scholars to remind us that never in its two-thousand-year existence has Christianity been solely a religion of Europe and North America.[9]

It is becoming clear that African, Asian, and Latin American Christians played the primary role in spearheading and shaping the growth of new religious movements. And yet a female missionary from Minnesota, Minnie Abrams, keeps popping in and out of the story of the Mukti revival, raising questions about the role of missionaries in this process. Significantly, the narrative of Western cultural imperialism does not adequately explain Abrams. For one thing, she was out of step with several cultural trends that dominated modern America during the Progressive Era. Abrams exchanged the American love affair with "progress" for a "Latter Day" conviction that history was just about to end in a mighty worldwide apocalypse. Uninterested in the naturalistic claims of science or the power of technology, she saw supernatural forces pervading the revival. Indian girls, in Abrams's account, emerged as models of Christian dedication that unconverted and unsanctified Americans ought to listen to and emulate. This was during a decade when most white Americans doubted whether blacks, Asians, Native Americans, or immigrants were fit for full participation in American society. In the end, Abrams simply did not speak or act according to the terms of the superiority of Western civilization.

Abrams's holiness movement represented just one of many variations within the evangelical missionary movement. Even in 1905, when the "glories of civilization" thoroughly permeated American ways of thinking about the world, evangelical missionaries were anything but united in their views of how they should engage those outside their borders. As might be expected, a number of prominent evangelical spokespersons saw the cause of Christianity and the progress of Western civilization as much the same thing. Students of American history know that President William McKinley told fellow Methodist leaders in 1899 that he had decided that the United States should take imperial control of the Philippines in order, among other things, to "educate the Filipinos, and uplift and civilize and Christianize them, and by God's grace do the very best we could by them, as our fellow-men for whom Christ had died."[10] But many evangelicals were uncomfortable with this attempt to affix Christianity to the civilizing project. One Baptist spokesperson argued in 1895 that "civilization is a strange tree that brings forth both good and evil fruit; it blows hot and cold; it helps save some and it damns many whom it touches." That same year, the editor of the *Baptist Missionary Magazine* argued that the best missionaries did not seek "the imposition of civilization—even a Christian civilization—upon any people" but sought instead simply to evangelize "on lines which may be strictly national and natural to their environment." Abrams, meanwhile, ignored the concept of civilization altogether.[11]

Our mental conceptions of missionary engagement, therefore, also need to be revised. Mainstream scholarship has, at times, internalized myths and stereotypes of coercive missionaries that have filtered down into popular culture, such as the myth of the "missionary position."[12] To be sure, many missionaries attempted to impose their will on others, and themes of resistance may effectively describe those who did not accept the message brought by missionaries. However, the missionary encounter did not simply encompass imposition and resistance, as many scholars have painted it, or simple proclamation and acceptance, as many evangelicals have described it. New movements of world Christianity emerged from a complex process of engagement in which local Christians selectively took resources brought by missionaries and adapted them to their own cultural context. Since these movements often took off in unexpected directions, missionaries reacted in a range of different ways. Missionary engagement, then, also involved cooperation, negotiation, conversation, reassessment, and transformation, from all parties.

This book examines the missionary side of the American evangelical engagement with new movements of world Christianity in the nineteenth century. Little turned out exactly the way missionaries originally anticipated. Part of the reason for this resided in the very nature of evangelicalism itself. At the heart of evangelical missionary engagement lay paradoxes of power, culture, and influence. In power relations, new movements of world Christianity were more likely to emerge when missionaries operated from positions of weakness and less likely to thrive when missionaries attempted to exert control. Culturally, evangelicalism produced critiques of whatever culture it found itself in, be it the United States, Africa, Asia, or Latin America, but these cultural critiques gained vitality because they inevitably used elements of that same culture to make that critique. Finally, when evangelical missionaries sought to influence the rest of the world, they inadvertently built conduits by which influences from new movements of world Christianity circulated back to affect American evangelicalism.

The very characteristics of evangelicalism help to explain the nature of these missionary paradoxes. A definition, then, is in order. Evangelicalism is best defined as a Christian tradition with four components: a theological emphasis on the atoning work of Christ, the necessity of some sort of conversion experience (or conscious commitment to Christ), the belief in biblical authority, and devotion to the spreading of the Gospel.[13]

The paradox of missionary power relations begins with the evangelical goal of conversion and a reality that often has gone unnoticed: missionaries were almost always lousy at converting large numbers of non-Westerners. To be sure, missionaries often played critically essential roles in the birth of new movements of Christianity by establishing contact, facilitating the first few conversions, educating leaders, translating materials, and providing resources. But few nineteenth-century missionaries could point to more than a handful of individuals who converted under their preaching, despite dogged evangelistic efforts that sometimes lasted for decades. In fact, if conversion was a form of cultural imperialism, it proved to be a remarkably ineffective form of imperialism, at least compared with all of the other political, economic, social, and cultural encroachments of the West in the nineteenth century.[14] Conversion to Christianity may have been the easiest injunction from missionaries for non-Westerners to resist. Millions refused successfully.

And yet vibrant new movements of world Christianity still emerged, even in the nineteenth century. Indigenous Christians, not the missionaries, invariably harvested the bulk of this evangelistic fruit. Important cultural factors help explain this dynamic. Far better than missionaries, indigenous Christians understood their vernacular, the subtle but pervasive cultural structures of their life, the issues particular to their circumstances, and the challenges of their distinct social situation. In other words, when it came to dynamics of their own culture, indigenous Christians, not the missionaries, were the experts.[15]

This held important implications for power relations. Evangelical missionaries tended to believe that new movements of world Christianity would be most healthy under their guidance, direction, and control. But the more control missionaries exercised over new movements of world Christianity, the less these movements would unfold according to indigenous cultural patterns and local issues of concern. The less these movements unfolded according to indigenous patterns, the less evangelistically vibrant they were likely to be. Here, then, lay a paradox. Evangelical missionaries who clutched the political, social, or economic tools of power at hand were likely to undermine the very evangelistic movements they wanted to encourage. On the other hand, evangelistic success emerged more often when missionaries operated from positions of weakness. Some missionaries came to see this; others did not.

Indigenous leaders further undermined missionary attempts to control their movements. Ironically, non-Western Christians could do this because they adapted evangelical practices and polities presented to them by the missionaries. In the United States, evangelicalism had always been very weak at enforcing a centralized, hierarchical church polity beyond the local congregation. By inadvertently encouraging religious dissent and empowering marginalized Christians, American evangelicalism had a way of turning around and challenging its own established leaders.[16] A similar process unfolded in places such as Burma and South Africa. In the face of vibrant new movements, evangelical missionaries enjoyed far less control of the religious situation than they anticipated. This lack of missionary leverage not only gave indigenous Christians more space to maneuver, but it also sometimes compelled missionaries to give serious attention to issues they had never previously considered.

The paradox of power relations is closely related to a second theme of the evangelical missionary engagement. Evangelicalism displayed a persistent knack for using elements of the culture in which it was found to critique that same culture.[17] Baptists in the era of the early republic, for instance, employed a new characteristic of American culture, democratization, to challenge an older part of their culture, the religious establishment. In the missionary engagement, new movements of Christianity sometimes turned this cultural paradox back on the missionaries in unpredictable ways, adopting evangelical forms of democratization, for instance, to challenge Western claims that the "uncivilized" needed guidance from educated Westerners. Or they might use the tools of literacy brought by the missionaries to read the Bible in such a way as to affirm traditional cultural beliefs in the existence of supernatural activity. The list of cultural variations on this theme is endless, particularly since cultures borrow, adapt, and shift over time.

These cultural tensions emerged from the very components of evangelicalism itself.[18] For example, through the conversion experience, evangelicals saw themselves converting from "the world" to a new spiritual state, a state linked to a particular body of believers within their local community that was, paradoxically, shaped by the same culture from which they had converted. Biblicism infused evangelicalism with an optimistic, modern idea that literacy and education were critically important for ordinary individuals, while simultaneously leading evangelicals to grant sacred authority to an ancient text with its ancient cultural forms. The evangelical understanding of the atonement, in which God offered salvation to every person in the world, all of whom were created in God's image, assumed that all people were equally fallen and capable of transformation through Christ's work on the cross, regardless of their national, racial, ethnic, social, or cultural states. This conviction simultaneously assumed a certain level of sinfulness in one's own culture and potential for good in the cultures of others.[19] Finally, tensions with national or cultural identity emerged when evangelicals acted on their conviction to spread the Gospel beyond their own communities. New movements of world Christianity, for instance, presented American evangelicals with fellow believers from "uncivilized" societies, who claimed a shared identity with them. Evangelicals who took that shared identity seriously had to reconsider their assumptions about the superiority of American, white, or civilized identities.

This cultural ambivalence pushed open the door to a third theme: the missionary movement created conduits by which influences from new movements of world Christianity circulated back to affect American evangelicalism. Ripples from movements of world Christianity flowed back through missionary channels to Europe and North America, returned again in new forms to existing missionary fields, redirected themselves to new areas of the globe, or diverted themselves off in multiple directions, sometimes bypassing Europe and North America altogether. Among the more notable ways in which world Christianity influenced American evangelicalism in the nineteenth century was its challenge to Western conceptions of what it meant to be civilized or uncivilized.

Most nineteenth-century Americans and Europeans stored their cultural perceptions away in conceptual baggage that they called "civilization." Although the discourse of civilization carried a wide range of meanings and implications, it almost always assumed a process of historical development that placed "primitive" societies at the bottom end of a cultural ladder and "high" civilizations at the top. Modern Westerners tended to attribute characteristics of sophisticated technology, just government, productive economies, advanced intellectual knowledge, social flourishing, and even higher moral principles to the progress of civilization. Primitive, barbarian, or semicivilized societies, of course, fared poorly by comparison.[20]

The baggage of civilization contained, among other things, complicated problems related to race, disenchantment, and education. For instance, the concept of civilization could promote laudable ideals, but because it almost always carried racial connotations, it could also produce and reinforce pernicious ways of thinking and acting. Given the racial composition of those in power in Europe and North America, "advanced civilization" increasingly came to be associated with the white race. In essence, it was extremely difficult for most nineteenth-century Americans to speak about civilization without assuming that whites were in some way smarter, more productive, and more moral than other races around the world. Inevitably, missionaries carried these assumptions with them as part of their cultural baggage.

Missionaries then arrived in their new locales and began unpacking their baggage. When some of the civilizing concepts they brought with them did not work as anticipated, missionaries had to decide whether the problem lay with the race of the people they sought to evangelize or with the conceptual materials the missionaries had brought with them. Failure or success in evangelism shaped those decisions. Oddly, perhaps, evangelistic disappointment had less effect than evangelistic success in challenging the racist components of "civilization." Slow rates of conversion proved to be particularly puzzling and frustrating, making it easier for missionaries to maintain existing conceptions of nonwhites as "savage," "primitive," or "benighted." But many times, missionaries found themselves working alongside "uncivilized" Christians who effectively evangelized, displayed solid traits of piety, and persevered in their faith under difficult circumstances. The capabilities of these indigenous Christians simply did not fit with the racial assumptions underlying Western conceptions of civilization. Missionaries often responded by reconfiguring their conceptions of race. This was not an insignificant development. Arguably, world Christianity did more than academic theories of human difference to undermine racism in nineteenth-century America. More often than not, the academic trends of that era intensified racist thinking.[21]

Missionaries also struggled with the refusal of many Christians in Asia, Africa, or Latin America to accept a disenchanted conception of the world. Initially described by Max Weber, "disenchantment" refers to a characteristic of the modern world whereby materialistic and naturalistic forces appear to guide the daily routines of life, providing full explanations for how the cosmos operates.[22] Many evangelical missionaries arrived in Asia or Africa with a largely disenchanted understanding of the world, even though they believed that the Holy Spirit was still at work. When Asian or African Christians claimed not only that demons or spirits existed but also that they had real power, evangelical missionaries often pulled a piece of Enlightenment faith out of their cultural luggage to dismiss these beliefs as "superstition." Western civilization, it was thought, with its advances in science, technology, and bureaucratic systemization, had proven these ways of viewing the world to be relics of a primitive era. But then new movements of world Christianity often provoked these evangelical missionaries to reconsider their positions. Christians in Africa, Asia, and Latin America not only claimed biblical authority for their "enchanted" beliefs but also demonstrated evangelistic success by taking the spirit world seriously.

There were exceptions to the disenchanted missionaries, though. Many evangelicals, particularly within the holiness movement, became disenchanted with disenchantment. They sought out divine healing, miraculous events, and identifiable movements of the Spirit. In this critical way, they actually held more in common with Christians in Asia, Africa, or Latin America than they did with Christians in Europe and North America. Radical-holiness missionaries such as Minnie Abrams sent glowing reports back home of supernatural manifestations within evangelistic movements of world Christianity in India, South Africa, or Chile. At that point, world Christianity intensified radical-holiness revivals in America, whose advocates no longer cared about the machinations of civilization as much as they cared about the wondrous workings of the Spirit around the world.

And then there was education. Missionaries discovered that issues related to modern forms of education proved to be far more complicated than they seemed at first glance. In practice, modern academic systems were far less culturally adaptable and far more restrictive in leadership promotion than were the dynamics of evangelism. This created an odd cultural tension between evangelism and education. Even if they were preliterate or held a minimal level of Western education, Asian and African Christians demonstrated that they could be particularly adept at evangelism. Experts in their own vernacular and cultural dynamics, local preachers steeped in oral cultures effectively adapted Christianity to the sensibilities of their audiences. Many of these new Christians were not, however, extensively trained from childhood in the formal processes of engaging written texts, a fundamental component of modern education and nineteenth-century Western culture. Very often, though, new Christians in Asia and Africa desired to be trained in these modern forms of education. Thus, academic systems tended to shore up missionary power and authority at the same time that evangelistic systems shored up the authority of poorly educated but effective evangelists. That tension would not be easily resolved. Missionaries struggled to figure out how much formal, text-based education local Christians would need in order to be qualified to lead religious institutions.

This issue became particularly apparent after significant numbers of people from different cultures began to convert to Christianity. Evangelical missionaries instinctively promoted literacy among preliterate peoples because evangelical conceptions of a vibrant Christian life dictated that every individual read the Bible for himself or herself. But the relationship between higher education and evangelicalism was more complicated. Evangelical missionaries responded in different ways, in part because they were busy struggling with this issue in their home churches in America. Missionaries who were highly educated and closely connected to the American establishment tended to require Asian or African Christians seeking ministerial positions to meet very high requirements, which usually came attached to ideals of the "civilized" individual. Democratized Baptists and Methodists, however, came from traditions that promoted Americans to ministerial positions on the basis of their evangelistic effectiveness, not their academic qualifications. Democratized missionaries, then, had far fewer scruples about ordaining poorly educated or "uncivilized" Christians in Asia, Africa, and Latin America. Either way, new movements of world Christianity compelled missionaries to wrestle with the role of modern education in their efforts among uncivilized Christians.

World Christianity, then, made itself felt by confronting American evangelicalism with a host of unexpected issues tied to civilization. The influence of world Christianity, though, did not unfold in a uniform or inevitable manner. Some missionaries concluded that they would have to reconsider or readjust their conceptions of civilization and their ways of engaging the world if they were to encourage or replicate these movements. Others made adjustments without giving much thought to what was taking place. Some missionaries blazed ahead with their programs anyway, ignoring unsettling questions, making few adjustments, and gaining little understanding of what was unfolding around them. Nevertheless, when one finds evangelical missionaries who gained cultural insights or acted in ways that ran counter to the dominant trends of Western culture, one almost always finds previous activities by non-Western Christians lurking around in the background, having effectively thrown the missionaries back on their heels.

Unsurprisingly, evangelical missionaries engaged new movements of world Christianity in different ways. Evangelicals had always been too motley a collection of enthusiasts to agree fully with one another on most cultural issues anyway, despite many efforts to forge a united front. In the nineteenth century, American evangelicalism produced Calvinist presidents of Ivy League colleges, fiery circuit-riding frontier preachers, southern slave owners, enslaved African Americans, passionate abolitionists, working-class female evangelists, respectable businessmen in New York City, and holiness faith healers in small Midwestern towns.[23] These people did not suddenly draw up a common cultural blueprint once they launched themselves even further into the world. Yankee Baptist men and women in Burma, bureaucratic Methodists in India, stern New England

Calvinists in Hawaii, holiness women in Liberia, black nationalist preachers in South Africa, and Pentecostal advocates in Chile shared evangelical religious commitments but not a common textbook on cultural anthropology.

The complexity and diversity of this ragtag swarm of religious enthusiasts, then, might be better understood by keeping in mind tensions between formalists and antiformalists. These terms, which some evangelicals used in the early nineteenth century, represent two ends on a spectrum that describes particular ways in which American evangelicals engaged society. That continuum had existed since the First Great Awakening and persisted long after, indicating that these conflicting impulses seem to have been hardwired into evangelicalism from its birth. Evangelical missionaries carried both formalist and antiformalist impulses with them as they traveled the world.[24]

Evangelicals with formalist sensibilities believed not only that a loving God redeemed humanity through individual conversions and orderly revivals but also that Christians promoted the Kingdom of God through the structures of civil society. Passionately working to form what they believed to be a godly social order, these evangelicals published reams of written material, established countless denominational agencies, founded colleges by the dozens, launched reform movements, and created a dizzying array of voluntary societies. Understandably, then, formalist evangelicals have received a great deal of attention from scholars. Experts at building institutions, formalist evangelicals may have had their greatest missionary impact in the religious organizations, schools, and hospitals they established. Instinctively gravitating toward "civilizing" activities, formalist missionaries often assumed the superiority of Western civilization, which sometimes led them to align themselves with imperial powers. But these same formalist impulses could work against tendencies of cultural superiority. Since they internalized democratic ideals and tended to concern themselves with civil society, formalist evangelical missionaries sometimes launched efforts to oppose unjust institutions and structures, such as slavery, Indian removal, or imperialism.[25]

Evangelicals with antiformalist sensibilities, who have been studied far less, were fired primarily by a zeal for conversion. Displaying a greater knack for sparking movements, antiformalist evangelicals were quite willing to break or ignore cultural norms if by doing so they could reap more evangelical conversions. Drawing their energy from a democratized Christianity that found virtue in the abilities of the common, unsophisticated segments of society, antiformalist evangelicals maintained suspicions of elites who tried to utilize institutions and bureaucratic systems to Christianize society. Baptists and Methodists in the first half of the nineteenth century and holiness advocates at the end of the century, for instance, refused to view the clergy as a separate order of men and accepted the spiritual experiences of ordinary women and men at face value, without subjecting them to the scrutiny and authority of learned theologians.

INTRODUCTION

This recipe produced popular religious movements that were often enthusiastic in their character, highly adaptive to local situations, and effective at promoting marginalized people to leadership positions. Much more willing to disregard social conventions for the sake of evangelism, antiformalists sometimes adopted more radical stances toward the existing social order, particularly in regard to conceptions of race, gender, progress, and naturalistic workings of the world.[26]

In the missionary setting, the antiformalist disregard for social convention could lead its advocates to ignore existing conceptions of civilization. As a result, antiformalist missionaries often proved to be much more adaptable to non-Western cultures, which made them more likely to spark, encourage, and validate new movements of world Christianity. This is where antiformalist evangelicals may have had their greatest influence. Paradoxically, given their egalitarian impulses, antiformalist evangelicals were much less successful than formalist evangelicals in identifying and engaging structural injustices. Antiformalist evangelicals often remained apolitical, in part because the very characteristics that made them culturally adaptable also turned their attention away from a deep and sustained consideration of the structures of society.

The boundaries along the formalist-antiformalist spectrum were usually fluid, porous, and shifting. Individual evangelicals and entire evangelical denominations often displayed both impulses, depending on the situation. Evangelistic growth, for instance, often compelled antiformalist evangelicals to develop institutions, which moderated their more radical impulses. On the other hand, formalist evangelicalism contained democratized impulses that periodically gave birth to new antiformalist evangelical movements.

Because evangelicals insist on being diverse and complicated, this book attempts to tell the larger story of evangelical missionary engagement with world Christianity through four smaller interconnected and overlapping narratives. Part I examines the American Baptist men and women who ventured to Burma, a project that had a formative influence on that denomination's sense of its place in the world. Part II follows the peripatetic career of the globe-trotting Methodist evangelist William Taylor, who laid the groundwork for the radical-holiness missionary network. The two chapters of part III examine the peculiar situation of African-American evangelicals in the context of world Christianity, as they struggled to come to terms with the question of what it meant to be of African descent. Part IV examines the radical-holiness missionary movement, whose democratized, unsophisticated, and marginal position in American society helped give birth to the decentralized, culturally diverse worldwide movement of Pentecostalism.

With that it mind, it might be wise to indicate certain things that this book does not try to do. First, this is not a comprehensive overview of the nineteenth-century American missionary enterprise but, rather, a study of the dynamics within the movement, particularly as they related to cultural issues. A great deal more can be done on many other evangelical missionaries from this era, including southern white evangelical bodies, Calvinist agencies, missionary women on the formalist side of the movement, Canadian or British evangelicals, smaller evangelical denominations, or missionaries among the Native Americans, just to name a few. Second, although this book attempts to take into account how Christian movements in Africa, Latin America, or Asia affected American evangelicalism, it is primarily a study of American evangelicalism, rather than what happened on the ground around the world. Third, this book does not give an extensive examination of how evangelicals engaged non-Christians around the world and how that engagement affected American evangelicalism. While such a study would certainly be valuable and worthwhile, the reality seems to be that American evangelicalism was more deeply affected by world Christianity. Fourth, it should also be noted that while evangelical missionaries have undertaken a wide variety of important tasks—education, translation work, health care, and development work, for instance—the emergence of new movements of world Christianity steers this study primarily to questions of evangelism. Finally, while the most expansive movements of world Christianity flourished in the late twentieth century, their original cultural and religious patterns often took root in nineteenth-century interactions with missionaries, which explains the time frame of this work.

This book proceeds on the assumption that missionaries could not, as some twentieth-century schools of thought assumed, simply leave their cultural baggage at home and observe other people from an objectively neutral stance, completely detached from their own culture. With that in mind, I am also aware that this work cannot analyze the history of missionary engagement from an objectively neutral stance. I work from a particular cultural position, which provides me with both my own peculiar limitations and insights. Although careful readers will be able to determine those assumptions in the chapters that follow, if they have not spied them already, it might be helpful for me to add a brief comment about some of my own perspectives. I am shaped by evangelical convictions and sensibilities, although I also draw on ideas from a range of Christian and secular thought. In my understanding of the discipline of history and evangelicalism, I owe my greatest intellectual debt to the works of George Marsden and Nathan Hatch, while Andrew Walls and Lamin Sanneh have shaped my most fruitful thinking about the missionary movement and world Christianity. With that very brief intellectual biography in mind, I should say that I certainly do not expect all readers to agree with my conclusions and analysis, particularly those holding different theoretical or theological commitments. However, I do hope that, whatever the perspective of the reader, this work might help shed some light on the workings of the evangelical missionary movement and contribute to a productive and fruitful conversation about the themes addressed in this book.

PART ONE

1

American Baptists and the "Wild" Karen People of Burma

A-Pyah Thee had a book, but he could not read. For a religious leader of a village with an oral tradition promising that one day the power of a book would be available to his people, this was a problem. In fact, very few of A-Pyah Thee's people, the Karen, could read. A seminomadic minority in the early nineteenth century, they lived on the peripheries of Burmese society. Their oral tradition, which existed among many of the Karen villages, had several variations, but a common version held that the creator god, Y'wa, had given a book of life to an elder brother, the Karen. The elder brother had lost the book, causing him to lose favor with Y'wa, thereby plunging the brother into ignorance and misery. The oral tradition held out hope, however. A younger brother had departed with the book but would return someday to share the book with the elder brother, who would be restored to Y'wa if he obeyed the message of the book.[1]

Hope for the fulfillment of this prophecy had risen in A-Pyah Thee's village when a man, most likely another Karen, had brought a book to his village in the remote hills of southern Burma. The visitor, who had arrived sometime around 1818, had given the villagers the book and instructed them in a number of religious practices. After the man left, the village had divided over the significance of these teachings. One faction embraced the new teachings and followed the lead of the elderly A-Pyah Thee, who probably already held the status of prophet or "medicine teacher," a common religious position found among most traditional Karen villages. A-Pyah Thee and his followers took these new teachings quite seriously, holding on to the teachings and their book for more than a decade, even in the face of hostility and harassment by neighboring Burman people.[2]

When he got word that two foreign religious teachers had moved into the Burmese city of Tavoy in April 1828, A-Pyah Thee moved quickly. The British military had occupied Tavoy since 1825, after seizing a strip of southern Burma from the Burmese king. A-Pyah Thee apparently had not been interested in foreign soldiers, even though he knew their presence now allowed him to inquire about the books without harassment. Religious leaders, however, were a different matter.

And so, after just three weeks of living in Tavoy, two young American Baptist missionaries, George and Sarah Boardman, discovered a group of thirty Karen people on their doorstep. The Karen delegation had found its way to the house of the missionaries at the end of a three-day journey from A-Pyah Thee's village. Under instructions from A-Pyah Thee, who had remained in the village, members of the delegation talked with George Boardman for some time, relating their story to him and asking a number of questions about the missionary's religion. They also asked if the American teacher would visit their village or send an Asian Christian out to teach them more. George Boardman promised to visit them sometime in the future, gave them a religious tract written in Burmese, and encouraged them to find a person who could read it to them.[3]

Sarah and George Boardman were about to be surprised. They were not very interested in the Karen people that day in 1828 when the delegation left them. To the Boardmans, it seemed to make much more sense to target the Burman people, who dominated the land numerically, politically, economically, and religiously. Baptist missionaries, in fact, had already invested fifteen years of work attempting to spread the Gospel among the Burman, though with very little success. But the Boardmans did not know that Christianity would quickly emerge among the poor, preliterate, and marginalized Karen. Nor could they guess that Karen Christianity would have a significant effect on the American Baptist missionary movement itself, challenging American evangelicals to reconsider their perceptions of "uncivilized" people.

A-Pyah Thee was not about to lose contact with the missionaries. He apparently believed that his book held the key to a better life for the Karen, who lived in difficult circumstances in the rough hinterlands of Burma and Siam. The Karen sometimes spoke of themselves as "a worthless nation" and "a nation of slaves" who endured much suffering. Living in a region of endemic warfare, a scarcity of arable land, and periodic famine, many Karen hoped to achieve literacy, prosperity, and some sort of spiritual fulfillment. Since the mid-eighteenth century, large numbers of Karen had moved from relatively inaccessible areas of Burma and Siam into the lowlands, a move that created tensions with the dominant Burman and Siamese peoples. The literate Burman and Siamese viewed the Karen as a "wild" people and often mistreated them, particularly during times of political instability. During conflicts between the Burman and the Siamese, the Karen often faced enslavement, burdensome taxes, kidnapping, and attacks that wiped out entire villages.[4]

Most Karen tried to avoid inciting the Burman and Siamese people by distancing themselves from their neighbors. They remained in remote settlements where they could direct their traditional customs and religious beliefs on their own. A minority of Karen people tried to integrate themselves into Burmese society, learning from Burman teachers, adopting Buddhism, and joining Buddhist monasteries. A few who studied at the monasteries even achieved the status of merit, which in Theravada Buddhism signified that a better rebirth had been achieved in this life. But most of these Karen living among the Burman remained outsiders, lacking social status or economic opportunity.[5]

A-Pyah Thee lived apart from the Burman, but he may have provoked harassment by sending some of his villagers into neighboring Burman settlements to learn to read Burmese. Somehow, A-Pyah Thee's son had learned to read. When the newly literate son returned to the village, the villagers then discovered that their book was not written in Burmese. They did not know what language the book was written in, though. Waiting for the right opportunity to learn more about the contents of the book, A-Pyah Thee seemed convinced that if help came, it would come not from the Burman but from a foreign people, whom he apparently identified as the younger brother in the oral traditions.[6]

He apparently thought that the American missionaries might be the younger brother. When the delegation returned from Tavoy, the Burmese tract was read aloud to the village, probably by A-Pyah Thee's son. Something stirred within the aged A-Pyah Thee, who wept when it was read to him. He then traveled from home to home with his son, exhorting the villagers to embrace this new faith spoken of in the missionary tract. But A-Pyah Thee wanted more than just the tract and its teachings, so he sent three individuals back to Tavoy. Appearing at the Boardman house just twelve days after their first visit, the trio presented George Boardman with a gift of fourteen duck eggs.

Then the requests came. They asked Boardman if he would permit one of the three to stay with the missionary for two or three years to learn English so that he might better teach the principles of Christianity. They asked him, again, if he might visit their village to explain the Christian scriptures. As circumstances would have it, they also witnessed Boardman baptize Ko Tha Byu, a Karen Christian who had been living with American missionaries for several years. They responded to this strange new ceremony by asking the missionary if Ko Tha Byu might accompany them back to their village. And they asked Boardman, once again, if he would come to their village to see their book.[7]

The Karen trio clearly indicated that they would defer to Boardman's authority on the merits of the book. Demonstrating a respect for religious authority common to many traditional cultures, they said that if he declared it to be a bad book, they would burn it. The American missionary told them that he could not make the trip to their village during the rainy season, but he agreed to send Ko Tha Byu to their village at some point in the future. George and Sarah Boardman also agreed to take in one of the three messengers as a student. The other two Karen inquirers returned home, and word of the Christian faith spread beyond A-Pyah Thee's village. Over the next four months, some of the Karen who had originally visited the Boardmans took the tract George Boardman had given them and traveled to other villages, urging others to adopt Christianity. More

Karen inquirers appeared at the Boardman door, some of whom had not actually met any of A-Pyah Thee's evangelists but had gotten word about the foreign religious teachers through some sort of Karen grapevine. Ko Tha Byu, eager to carry news of this religion to the Karen, ventured out on several trips to the hinterlands himself.[8]

One Sunday evening in September, George Boardman returned to his home in Tavoy to discover, once again, a large delegation of Karen inquirers waiting for him. A-Pyah Thee had undertaken the trip to the city to meet the missionary himself, towing a large contingent of his villagers behind him. Boardman retired to another room to take his tea and then called the delegation in to ask what it was they wished. A-Pyah Thee stepped forward and explained that for several years, he and his followers had been trying to follow the Christian faith, which they believed was contained in the book, which he had brought with him. However, since they could not read this book, they did not know for sure whether it really did contain the truth. The old Karen teacher had now taken the long journey to Tavoy to ask the young missionary if he would tell them for sure. Boardman asked to see the book. A-Pyah Thee opened a large basket, extracted a package, unfolded wrapper after wrapper, and handed the sacred book to the American Baptist missionary to inspect. It was the Anglican *Book of Common Prayer*.[9]

Boardman told the delegation that although this was a good book, they must not worship the book itself but, rather, the God that it revealed. He also told A-Pyah Thee that his decade-long "worship" of the book did not signify that the old Karen had achieved any "claim to heaven." This seemed to disappoint the aged man. Yet if A-Pyah Thee seemed unsettled by the prospect that his efforts as a leader of the Christian faith had not been adequate, he showed that he was still determined to get it right. Perhaps personally wounded by Boardman's comments and worried that his authority among his villagers as a religious teacher had been undermined, A-Pyah Thee made a show the next morning of donning clothes that denoted his status as a Karen religious teacher. But one of the Asian Christians who lived with the Boardmans told A-Pyah Thee that the outfit did not grant him special standing, either. The old religious leader then pledged to throw the clothing into a stream if God was not pleased. He fulfilled this vow on the trip back to his village.[10]

The news, however, was out. Individuals from other Karen villages began flocking to the missionary house, requesting that George Boardman visit them. During the nine months following the Karen visit, at least twelve different contingents of Karen inquirers from various villages visited the Boardmans, making at least eight separate requests for American missionaries or Asian Christians to visit their villages. Ko Tha Byu made at least five separate tours of Karen villages, exhorting the Karen he met to adopt Christianity.

In January 1829, nine months after the first delegation had arrived at Tavoy, George Boardman finally ventured out for the first time to see for himself what he could do among the Karen villages. He preached seventeen times during his eleven-day journey, an evangelistic venture made more productive when he received requests for baptism from seven different people. One of these requests came from A-Pyah Thee, whom Boardman now referred to as "the old sorcerer." The missionary decided to "suspend judgment respecting them all till the morning," for he was unsure about whether these candidates qualified for baptism. The next morning, after "much reflection and prayer," Boardman announced that he was going to hold off on the baptisms. Old A-Pyah Thee would have to wait.[11]

A-Pyah Thee's name does not appear in the missionary records after this point, so it is not known if he ever received the baptism he sought. It is quite possible that he did, though, because missionaries later returned to his village and baptized scores of Karen converts. A-Pyah Thee might have been encouraged to know that he had played a key role in the birth of Karen Christianity. More than one thousand Karen from southern Burma received baptism during the 1830s. As evangelists such as Ko Tha Byu combed through further regions of Burma, the estimated number of conversions reached sixteen thousand by 1852.[12] A new movement of world Christianity had emerged from a marginalized people in Burma who doggedly pursued Western missionaries.

As Karen Christianity grew in Burma, George Boardman's fame grew among Baptists in America. Many evangelicals came to know "Boardman of Burma" as the pioneer missionary who first brought the Gospel to the Karen people. A 1940 biography of Boardman described him as "the human instrument used of God to initiate [the] transformation" of "the Karen people of Burma from a despised, down-trodden, backward race to a people with a prominent and honorable position in the life of Burma." As in many similar missionary stories, the account put "Boardman of Burma" at center stage while unnamed Karen Christians passively waited for him in the background.[13]

In reality, however, Boardman did not exactly pounce on the chance to transform the people who appeared on his doorstep in 1828. Karen exhorters, on the other hand, were anything but tentative, pulling an ambivalent "Boardman of Burma" into the kingdom of missionary hagiography. While Boardman remained in Tavoy, Karen evangelists ventured to remote villages with the news of the foreigner with the book, toting missionary tracts written in Burmese with them. It was an odd hesitancy for an evangelical missionary who had committed his life to the cause of spreading the Gospel in a foreign land. The hesitancy can be explained, in part, as an issue of power. If Boardman were to help the Karen, he would have to relinquish his existing vision, cooperate with the Karen, and allow the Karen inquirers to incorporate their desires into his missionary efforts.[14]

Figure 1.1. Ko Tha Byu preaching in a Karen house. Illustration in Francis Mason, *The Karen Apostle: Memoir of Ko Thah-Byu* (Boston: Gould, Kendall & Lincoln, 1843).

George Boardman had not expected anything quite like the Karen inquirers. Like many individuals shaped by the modern world, the twenty-seven-year-old missionary had formulated a plan for how his labor would proceed and believed that he could make that plan work. The plan just did not include the Karen. Twelve months previously, he and his young wife, Sarah, had arrived in the Burmese city of Moulmein to begin a life of evangelistic work among the Buddhist Burman people. The Boardmans had focused their energies on making contacts with the Burman people, studying the Burmese language, making observations about Buddhism, and adapting to Burmese culture, which was, of course, quite different from that of their Yankee homeland. When the Baptist missionary board had instructed them to branch out from the missionary base in Moulmein, the American couple had moved to Tavoy. Sticking to their plan, the Boardmans conversed regularly with Buddhist priests. They explored the religious sights of the city. They wrote about Tavoy to supporters in America. They described the gilded pagodas that ranged in size from six to one hundred fifty feet high, small bells in the temples that chimed in the slightest breeze, Burman women offering lilies to Buddhist images under banyan trees, and footpaths that wound through mango groves to sacred wells. When he discovered that pagodas were "solid monuments of brick or stone, without any cavity or internal apartments," Boardman had to change his prayers that Buddhist pagodas someday might be transformed into Christian churches.[15]

The Boardmans were following the lead of the missionary heroes Adoniram and Ann Judson, who had captured the imagination of American Baptists shortly after they had arrived in Burma fifteen years previously. The Judsons and the missionaries who followed them placed their hopes in the Burman people, who, in their judgment, exhibited several features of a civilized people. The Burman people had built cities, developed a complex system of government, and employed a well-regulated police force. Shaped by centuries of Buddhist practice, Burmese society produced not only a literate class of educated priests and government officials but also a sophisticated collection of religious poetry, philosophy, and science. Even though he perceived idolatry pervading the society, Adoniram Judson devoted many hours to the study of Burmese, grappled with Pali philosophy, engaged Buddhist priests in theological discussions, and instructed new converts in the finer points of Christian theology. Even his main mode of evangelism elicited civilized but Asian overtones of a settled ministry; he spent long hours in a *zayat*, a roadside structure that, in Buddhist fashion, accommodated travelers who stopped in for religious instruction and rest from their travels.[16]

The Boardmans envisioned similar sorts of missionary activity in Tavoy. George obtained use of an old *zayat*, which he began to repair. Sarah immediately began to establish a boarding school for Asian boys, starting with Burman boys from Moulmein who accompanied them to Tavoy. She also established a day school for Asian girls and hired an assistant to help her in her duties. If the Burman people appeared exotic and idolatrous to the Yankee way of thinking, they also, at least, displayed features of a fairly developed civilization.

They could not say the same about the Karen. Here is where Western conceptions of civilization clearly affected missionary perceptions. Like so many other aspects of life in Burma, the Karen puzzled the young missionaries. In his initial attempts to make sense of them, George Boardman reached into the cultural baggage he had brought with him from the United States and pulled out the closest ethnographic analogy that his upbringing in early-nineteenth-century Maine could provide him. He likened the Karen people to the "Aborigines of America." It was a cultural category fraught with uneasy connotations and missionary frustrations. From the early colonial era through recent conflicts such as the War of 1812, white Americans framed their violent clashes with Native Americans as battles between "civilized" societies and "savage" tribes. Other than a few "praying towns" in colonial New England and some scattered communities largely tied to Moravian work, Native Americans had been largely impervious to Protestant missionary efforts.[17]

The Native American analogy revealed that in George's mind, a wide chasm divided Christian civilization from Karen society. Three months before they had moved to Tavoy, Sarah had been entrusted with the care of four young Karen orphans in their boarding school at Moulmein. To George, the orphans embodied animalistic characteristics that white Americans regularly ascribed to Native Americans. "These boys are exceedingly wild," he wrote, "as though just caught in the jungle." Burman contacts reinforced this perception. "They are called by Burmans, 'Wild men,'" Boardman explained to his supporters "because they have no written language, no religion, avoid the cities and . . . dwell in the wilderness." The Karen people had not produced any of the "arts of civilization" in their small villages in the hinterland, such as writing, settled agriculture, or the "mechanical arts," let alone science or philosophy. The evidence for savagery looked quite conclusive.[18]

Initial interactions with Ko Tha Byu did little to refashion Boardman's conceptual baggage, either. Ko Tha Byu had lived a harsh life of robbery and murder in Burmese society before debt nearly landed him in slavery. Ko Shway-bay, a Burman Christian, had paid Ko Tha Byu's debt and taken him in as a servant. But Ko Tha Byu had proved to be so difficult to handle that Ko Shway-bay persuaded Adoniram and Ann Judson to take him on. Under their influence, Ko Tha Byu converted to Christianity, the first Karen individual to do so. But he seemed unlikely to contribute much to the missionary project. With a criminal record, a "wild" lineage, and affinities to "aborigine" races, Ko Tha Byu might even undermine the fledgling Christian body in Burma. The small congregation of Burman Christians at Moulmein, in fact, delayed his baptism, unconvinced that the former criminal had fully changed his ways. Boardman stood with the Burman Christians, arguing for a longer testing period of Ko Tha Byu's character before accepting him for baptism.[19]

Boardman's initial analysis of the "wild" Karen people contained a number of flaws. This is not surprising, given that he had barely one year of experience in Burma, held no knowledge whatsoever of the Karen people before that, and could not speak the Karen language. The young missionary explained to his evangelical supporters in America that the Karen were atheists who acknowledged "no being whatever, as an object of worship." He obviously knew nothing of the traditional Karen belief in Y'wa. Missionaries and Burmans alike also believed that the Karen had no laws or system of government; anthropological analysis had yet to develop tools to explain how preliterate and seminomadic peoples handed down oral traditions and formed social structures. Finally, Boardman's idea of "idolatry" led him to conclude that A-Pyah Thee "worshipped" the book in his possession. Boardman had not reconciled this judgment with the declaration by the Karen inquirers that they would burn the book if the missionary instructed them to, indicating that they sought a spiritual source that lay beyond the simple material properties of the book.[20]

Cross-cultural ignorance, theological complexities, and white American anxieties about uncivilized "aborigines" caused Boardman to hesitate in granting too much to Karen character. Evangelical theology simultaneously compelled him to hold out hope for the capabilities of the "wild" Karen people. "Perhaps God will be pleased to convert them," he had written in reference to the orphans at his school at Moulmein, "and send them as missionaries to their benighted countrymen." He placed hope in the fact that the Karen people in Burma were not Buddhist, writing that they might "more readily receive the Gospel" since "it is said by some, that they have no religion at all."[21]

Still, the Karen remained an evangelistic sidelight in the Boardmans' world during their first year at Tavoy. Even after seven different Karen delegations had visited Tavoy, making at least four different requests for George Boardman to visit them, he exhibited his Burman interests in a "Plan of Extended Operations in Education" submitted to Baptist missionary officials in the United States. Reflecting the institution-building impulses within American evangelicalism, his plan detailed his vision of directing a central school that would train teachers who would set up a string of schools in neighboring villages. Tavoy's location would make it likely that "Siamese, Daways, Karens, Taliengs, Burmans, Arracanese, and Chinese" would send their sons to this school, "and it is not too much to hope that some of the boys on their return home, will take with them the gospel." The process would involve years of instruction, tutelage, and careful oversight, but, like other evangelical missionaries who gravitated toward a "civilizing" model of missionary work, Boardman was optimistic about its eventual effectiveness. Most likely, he also believed that it promised a settled and relatively steady life in the city, in comparison with an unpredictable ministry among the Karen, which demanded precarious treks through the wilderness.[22]

The plan never materialized. In fact, the Boardmans' hopes for their work in Tavoy unraveled quickly. In 1829, George Boardman wrote that two Burman Christians "whom I had received, baptized, and spoken of in such high terms, had apostatized and disgraced the Christian profession." He confessed that his reputation as a "cautious, prudent, discerning missionary, would greatly suffer in the judgment of wise and good people." A few months earlier, "the last hopeful inquirer forsook me, and I felt the cause of Christ in Tavoy was lower than on the day of our arrival in the place." A series of personal tragedies deepened the Boardmans' discouragement. A young daughter died. George and Sarah had become quite ill. They lost some of their possessions in a boating accident. A failed Burmese revolt against the British troops forced the couple to flee Tavoy temporarily. Upon returning, they discovered that they had lost all of their remaining possessions. Their missionary prospects looked bleak.[23]

In the midst of these trials, the Karen inquirers managed to draw George off into the jungle, with his reservations in tow. Those reservations seemed, at first, to be well founded. The young missionary and his Karen companions traveled more than one hundred miles on foot, forded rivers, endured torrential rains, and slept in the open air. Revealing, perhaps, deep anxieties, Boardman reported that "insects and reptiles, the tiger, the rhinoceros, and the wild elephant, render our situation not a little uncomfortable and dangerous." It was here, far from the relative comforts of the Burmese city, that the "wild" Karen compelled Boardman to come to terms with his own ambivalence about responding to their requests.[24]

Evangelical piety, both his own and that of the Karen Christians, provided Boardman with self-examination, encouragement, and direction. Sitting around a fire in the midst of a drenching rainstorm at the end of the first day of the journey, Boardman and the new Karen Christians turned to "spiritual conversation" and prayer. Exposing a measure of guilt over his reluctance to make this journey, the young missionary later admitted that he did not measure up to the evangelical heights he set for himself. He wrote of his "unworthiness to be employed in carrying the tidings of salvation even to the wild men of the wilderness." Three days later, he pulled out a copy of the only book, other than the Bible, that he had carried with him on the trip. Authored by Jonathan Edwards, *The Life of David Brainerd* detailed the spiritual life of an eighteenth-century missionary working among, of all people, Native Americans. Probably feeling that he now had more in common with David Brainerd than he wished, Boardman turned to the work for devotional purposes. He confessed in his journal that his reading left him feeling "condemned and humbled" that he "had so little fervor of devotion, so little spiritual mindedness, so little, in fine, of all those qualifications required in a missionary to the heathen." With this confession in writing, he admitted that he did feel "a little compassion for the poor Karens" and prayed for more faith, love, and zeal.[25] If Boardman were to accomplish his evangelistic goals, he would have to rework his comfortable missionary plans drawn up under the protection of the British soldiers in the city and follow the Karen to their homes in the remote hill villages, where they resided in hardship and vulnerability.

Just as Boardman unexpectedly found himself far from the comforts of Tavoy, sitting in a tropical rain and discussing Christian spirituality with "wild" evangelists shortly removed from "atheism," American Baptist missionaries would find themselves negotiating a host of puzzling issues throughout the nineteenth century. These issues ranged from theology, educational theory, and church policy to race, class, gender, supernaturalism, and American conceptions of civilization. Karen Christians continually pulled American Baptists into unfamiliar conceptual territory because they did not fit the conceptions of civilization that missionaries had brought with them.

Those challenges had been in the works for fifteen years. Well before the A-Pyah Thee's first delegation arrived on the Boardman doorstep, the Baptist missionary conception of their work in Burma had been shaped by their interactions with the Buddhist Burman people. As they tried to make sense of Burma, the first generation of Baptist missionaries found themselves negotiating a number of conflicting cultural impulses in their enterprise. That task of making sense of Burma helps explain why Boardman initially focused all of his attention on the Burman of Tavoy.

Culture shock, far more intense than later generations faced, proved to be the first missionary challenge. The first two Baptist missionaries in Burma, Ann and Adoniram Judson, arrived in 1812 with very little cross-cultural experience, knowledge of Burmese society, or academic preparation in how to handle cultural differences. The Judsons, in fact, never planned to work in Burma. They had settled in India in 1812, but the British East India Company, which opposed missionary work within its spheres of colonial influence, issued orders to deport them to England. The Judsons spent six months casting about in an attempt to obtain permission from the authorities to settle just about anywhere outside Europe or North America. They gave serious consideration to Ceylon, Japan, Brazil, Madagascar, Malaysia, and Indonesia. Twice they evaded deportation orders by catching whatever ship happened to be heading to some other destination in the region, the first time sailing from Calcutta at midnight to take illegal passage on a ship bound for Mauritius. The second time, they fled arrest in Madras on the only available ship, which happened to be bound for Rangoon. They knew that English Baptists had tried and failed to establish a mission there five years earlier. That may be why Adoniram wrote that it was a location "we had been accustomed to regard with feelings of horror." And so they arrived in Burma.[26]

It is not clear that they would have been favorably disposed toward any Asian society, though. The Judsons' perceptions of Asia had been shaped by reports from English Baptist missionaries in India, whose accounts included descriptions of infanticide, widow immolation, and human sacrifice. Adoniram Judson's "feelings of horror" may have been further exacerbated by the weakness of the couple's political, social, and economic position. In India, the Judsons' cross-cultural adjustments had been eased by the presence of English missionaries and British colonists. But who knew what they would find in Burma without any local support from Westerners? "We had never before seen a place where European influence had not contributed to smooth and soften features of uncultivated nature," Adoniram Judson wrote shortly after arriving in Rangoon.[27]

As George Stocking has pointed out, early-nineteenth-century missionaries had to process a world containing much more radically differentiated cultures. The "sheer visual impact," Stocking writes, of trying to interpret a range of very different cultural practices that in some places included "cannibalism, widow-strangling, or infanticide" could lead "otherwise humane individuals to question common humanity."[28] American Baptist missionaries did not witness these particular practices in Burma, but they sometimes discovered in themselves a greater sense of shock and revulsion than they had expected. "I can truly say, I had no idea of a state of heathenism before I saw it," George Hough stated simply shortly after arriving in Burma in 1818.[29]

Evangelical missionary fund-raising practices fueled these bleak assessments. In the first two decades of the foreign-missionary enterprise, Baptist publicists in America intentionally emphasized the shocking aspects of other cultures in an attempt to raise sympathy and support for the fledgling foreign-missionary cause. Borrowing material from English Baptist missionaries in India, the early issues of the *American Baptist Magazine* produced a steady stream of references to infanticide, idol worship, human sacrifices to the Juggernaut, female oppression, robbery, filth, and despotism. An 1833 article entitled "Promotion of Missionary Spirit" explained that churches must be informed of the "actual miseries and degradation of the heathen" to fill members with "pain and sympathy." Pastors were encouraged to highlight the brutal treatment of women, the throwing of babies into the Ganges, the "trammeled and fettered" minds capable of such actions, along with a reminder that non-Christians ultimately faced judgment and damnation.[30]

The image of "fettered" minds fit with a particular conception of "idolatry" that missionaries drew on to explain Asian religion. Influenced by Enlightenment conceptions of "superstition," early Baptist missionaries thought of "idolatry" in India and Burma in terms of ignorance and rational errors. Missionaries believed that Asians worshipped material idols that held no spiritual power or reality, whether they were Hindus before the Juggernaut, Buddhists at pagodas, or A-Pyah Thee holding a religious book that he could not read. This modern conception of religion encouraged missionaries to see education as a tool that could enlighten Asian minds.[31]

Finally, discouragement colored Baptist perceptions of Burmese culture. Missionaries quickly discovered that their optimistic plans crashed against the rocks of Buddhist religious commitments. Adoniram Judson concluded that none of his visitors during his first two years of work asked about Christianity from a position "of sincere inquiry." He had discussed religious ideas with Buddhists numerous times, "preached the gospel to many," and received several Burman visitors who inquired about Christianity, but, aggravatingly, most of the Burman visitors seemed more interested in his "customs and manners" than in his religious faith. Buddhist priests who accepted the claims of Western science still did not abandon their Buddhist religious beliefs. Writing about a conversation with two Buddhists, Judson stated that even though he "so clearly refuted their system, in two or three instances, that they could not refrain from an involuntary expression of assent and approbation," they still stated that it was impossible for them to embrace a new religion. After the first ten years of work by a half-dozen missionaries, only eighteen Burman individuals had converted.[32] An

American Christian "would think a poor miserable idolater would leap for joy at the message of grace," missionary George Hough lamented in 1818. But most of the people the missionary talked to were "unconvinced by argument and unmoved by love."³³

These dark assessments form only part of the picture of Baptist missionary engagement, though. While some impulses pulled early Baptists toward self-righteous positions of superiority, different impulses simultaneously pulled missionaries toward egalitarian positions of common humanity. Evangelical conceptions of sin, atonement, and conversion played a key role in the latter. The missionary board, for instance, reminded its missionaries that they traveled to Asia because sin, salvation, repentance, and faith were "in all men essentially one in principle and character." After an absence of six months from a band of ten Burman converts who had gathered in Rangoon, Ann Judson returned in 1821 to find each still steadfast in the faith. She attributed this religious perseverance to the same effects of grace, humiliating knowledge of self, discovery of God, and hopes of eternity as those found in American evangelicals.³⁴ Jonathan Wade hopefully described a revival he conducted in a Burman school as being "of the same stamp as those we have seen in America." The *American Baptist Magazine* argued in 1828 that no difference could be found between domestic missions to nominal Christians in America and foreign missions to the heathen: "They are identical, in being the same means used on people of the same moral character, to produce the same moral effects." Daily interactions, relationships, and familiarity also changed attitudes. After seventeen years in Burma, James Haswell explained that "at first, we loathed them, but as we put forth our labors in their behalf, we came at length to love them."³⁵

Evangelical conceptions of conversion bound missionaries to their audiences. Conversion rested at the center of both the missionary goals for Burma and evangelical self-understanding, for evangelicals themselves had undergone the experience. Nineteenth-century evangelicals produced a sizable literature demonstrating their fascination with conversion. The conversion stories of Adoniram and Ann Hasseltine Judson, which were among the most prominent of these accounts, demonstrated that missionary conversion began not in Asia but at home with those who would later become missionaries.³⁶

The Judsons' spiritual narratives simultaneously affirmed and critiqued American culture. Ann Judson's narrative, grounded in her conversion experience as a young woman, stressed the preconversion influence of familial piety, academic pursuits, and a concern for the state of her soul, characteristics that had long shaped New England, where she grew up. But the narrative also noted that after her "change from sin to holiness," she left behind the temptations of "gay associates" and "relish for amusements" of her community to pursue new forms of religious labor.³⁷

Adoniram Judson, who grew up as the son of a Congregationalist minister, had been similarly formed by the Calvinist evangelicalism of New England. The young Judson read theology and matriculated to the newly established Andover Seminary. But even then, he had not been converted. The evangelical administrators at Andover, in fact, accepted him on a provisional basis, withholding full status until he made a public profession of faith. His process of conversion, which began with an academic study of religion before he had entered seminary, took a significant turn one memorable evening in a Connecticut inn. He was kept awake wondering about the state of the soul of a very ill young man in the next room, whose groans he could hear as the man was being attended to by others. When he discovered the next morning that the young man not only had died during the night but turned out to be an unconverted former classmate of his from college, he began earnestly to examine his own religious state. In the words of Francis Wayland, Judson soon "surrendered his whole soul to Christ as his atoning Savior." Judson's evangelical biographer pointedly explained that the minister's son had turned from earlier "vanity of worldly pursuits," characterized as self-serving dreams of literary and political ambition, ungodly dalliances with the theater, and the intellectual errors of deism.[38]

These conversion narratives hold important implications for the missionary stance toward culture. Well before they ever launched into the missionary enterprise, evangelical American missionaries, including those raised in evangelical churches as children, had undergone some sort of religious experience in which they saw both the darkness of sin and the light of the Gospel residing in the American culture in which they were converted. In terms of identity, American evangelicals did not convert from an Asian culture to a Western culture, or from Buddhism to Christianity, or from barbarism to civilization. Instead, evangelical converts internalized a conviction derived from the biblical injunction that one must be in the world but not of the world. Baptists wrote about the "heathen in our own state," referring to citizens of central New York who were as ignorant of "the plan of salvation" as the people of Burma. Although the term *heathen* came to carry connotations of cultural inferiority, especially in the late nineteenth century, many evangelicals employed the term for its earlier meaning, which referred to people who did not worship the Christian or Jewish God. In the evangelical way of thinking, Americans who did not undergo a conversion experience or attend church could fall into this category.[39]

Paradoxically, evangelicals zealously campaigned against a culture that deeply shaped their own evangelicalism. American culture granted evangelicals the liberty to pursue their goals of conversion, encouraged a spirit of voluntary choice, and provided evangelicals with economic resources to finance their movements and institutions. At the same time, however, deep concerns about American society always burst forth from evangelical exhortations. In addition to evangelistic campaigns designed to save individuals from personal sins, formalist evangelicals launched reform movements to counter numerous features of American culture, such as slavery, alcohol abuse, Native American removal, and market incursions on the Sabbath. Antiformalist evangelicals railed against elites who sought to use their established positions to guide society. In the evangelical understanding, sin still permeated an American culture that stood in need of redemption.[40]

Evangelicals extended the offer of conversion to everyone, whether or not they grew up in evangelical homes. "Missionary" efforts grew first from local evangelistic impulses and rapidly extended to anyone in the world who was within reach. Always a highly mobile and enthusiastic lot, nineteenth-century American evangelicals launched missionary enterprises among Yankee farmers in upstate New York, forty-niners in San Francisco, blacks in the American south, Native Americans on western reservations, immigrants in industrializing cities, and Europeans in "Old World" nations such as Sweden, Greece, Germany, and Italy. Foreign missionary ventures in Asia, Africa, the Pacific Islands, and Latin America, then, emerged as an extension of fervent efforts to evangelize fellow Americans.

But Burma was not Connecticut. Cultural differences and the unenthusiastic response by the Buddhists made it difficult to figure out how to replicate American evangelical practices. An 1835 missionary report concluded with genuine bewilderment: "Human nature indeed exists in the Burman, but it is human nature so peculiarly modified by vice and idolatry, that one must study long and profoundly before he can analize [sic] or explain it."[41] The reference to "human nature" here is instructive. Given the cultural complexities they faced, along with the impulses to make disparaging assessments of this "idolatrous" society, it would have been easy for missionaries simply to dismiss the Burman people as somehow less than human and not simply marred by sin, a trait common to all humanity in evangelical ways of thinking.

Evangelical missionary tasks compelled missionaries to try to figure out how a common human nature functioned in this very different culture. Bible translation may have been the most significant task in this process, not only in Burma but everywhere evangelical missionaries went in the nineteenth and twentieth centuries. Evangelicals believed that the ability to read the Bible for oneself was absolutely crucial. Missionaries faced a linguistic choice here. They could teach the Burman people English so that they could read existing Bibles, or they could translate the Bible into Burmese so that they could read it in their vernacular. Baptist missionaries in Burma chose the latter, a decision with far-reaching implications that nineteenth-century missionaries only dimly perceived.[42]

Language acquisition and biblical translation changed the missionaries. Instead of demanding that the Burmese engage the missionaries on American terms, the missionaries had to immerse themselves in the terms set by Burmese culture. Adoniram Judson discerned that unlike his experience in learning French, he could not simply find "terms" or "modes of expression" in Burmese that easily corresponded to meanings in English. Discovering that words and phrases in Burmese held nuances and complexities that reflected Burmese cultural perspectives, Judson wrote of the difficulty in mastering a language "spoken by a people on the other side of the earth, whose very thoughts run in channels diverse from ours, and whose modes of expression are consequently all new and uncouth."[43]

Over time, Judson formed cultural lessons from his language acquisition. When he published advice to missionary candidates in America, twenty years after he arrived in Burma, he warned prospective missionaries that some appearances would disappoint and disgust them. The veteran missionary recommended cultural immersion and language acquisition as the remedy for these initial negative reactions. Giving advice that may sound more like a product of twentieth-century concepts of cultural equality than the nineteenth-century missionary encounter, he declared that the new missionary should not judge the people without gaining a familiarity with their language. They should be aware that their initial reaction could build in them a "prejudice" against persons or places.[44]

The decision to translate the Bible into Burmese differed markedly from missionary decisions made among Native Americans. This helps explain why missionary engagement with Native Americans seems to have contained many more culturally coercive dynamics. The diverging missionary strategies stemmed less from any specific insight than from comparative differences in positions of power. Through the eighteenth and nineteenth centuries, whites vastly outnumbered Native Americans, achieved military superiority over Native American resistance, erected a political economy that overwhelmed traditional Native American systems, and successfully carried out demands to possess Native American lands. By the early nineteenth century, this position of power had produced a mind-set among most white Americans that the Native Americans faced a stark choice of either assimilating into white American culture or dying off completely. Few whites felt compelled to learn Native American languages. Evangelical missionaries largely followed these patterns. In 1862, after more than two centuries of extensive Protestant contact with hundreds of Native American languages, a complete translation of the Bible existed in only two of these languages. Strikingly, these meager translation efforts came amid a massive expansion of evangelical print media and a frenzy of Bible publishing in America. This lack of linguistic concern did not encourage missionaries, let alone white Americans, to immerse themselves in the complexities of Native American cultures.[45]

By contrast, a few dozen Baptist missionaries had translated the entire Bible into two languages and portions of the Bible into three others after just four decades of work in Burma.⁴⁶ The missionaries' political, economic, and cultural weakness played the key role here, a weakness they felt. "Instead of rejoicing, as we ought to have done, in having found a heathen land from which we were not immediately driven away," Adoniram Judson wrote upon arriving in Rangoon in 1813, "such were our weaknesses that we felt we had no portion left here below." Acutely aware that they could not hope to make the Bible available to millions of Burman people by teaching everyone English, Ann and Adoniram Judson immediately set to work learning the Burmese language and translating the Bible. The arrival of British colonialism, of course, would strengthen the political, economic, and cultural hand of the missionaries in Burma, but by that time, the translation principle had already been well established. It would be repeated, not only among the Karen in Burma but also by evangelical missionaries in many places around the world in the next two centuries.⁴⁷

Evangelism also pulled missionaries into further consideration of Burmese terms. Since evangelical conversion relied on persuasion, the first generation of missionaries to Burma began to search for culturally appropriate ways to communicate their message. Adoniram Judson did not initiate his evangelistic activities by building a New England church structure modeled after American architecture and Calvinist worship. After learning Burmese, studying the scholastic tenants of Buddhism, and interacting with the Burman people around him, he decided to initiate public evangelism by constructing a *zayat*, a bamboo shelter that Burmese Buddhist priests often built along the roadside to provide travelers with both rest and instruction. His "*zayat* preaching" became a central part of Baptist evangelistic work throughout the nineteenth century.⁴⁸

Back in the United States, the Baptist missionary board picked up on these themes, informing readers that effective evangelism only took place if the missionary immersed himself or herself in the cultural patterns of Asia, through "long habits of intimate acquaintance and intercourse." Long periods of cultural study should enable the missionaries to understand the Burmese people and identify with them. "The longer [the missionary] has been among them, the more fully he can enter into their wishes and feelings, the more likely will he be to find out the best way to approach them," the board declared "the more completely will he be identified with them in affection and interest." The missionary would then be able to "reciprocate with them, those expressions of confidence and esteem, which they naturally extend to each other." Language translation further encouraged the board to argue that Christianity would have to adapt to Burmese culture:

> Tracts prepared by Burman christians with a native's mastery of his own familiar idiom, and with a nice adaptation to the peculiar feelings,— the varied and flickering habits and fashions that distinguish each people from their neighbors, and which only one of themselves can

perfectly catch and successfully address;—translations polished with a skill in language which few can attain but in their own vernacular tongue;—and Burman pastors and evangelists trained by Burman teachers, are yet, we trust, to occupy and to bless the fair regions now resigned to the dreamy reign of Gaudama.[49]

Baptist missionaries had briefly stumbled upon an insight made by Andrew Walls more than a century later: because the Christian faith has been grounded in cultural translation from its very origins, "there can be no single Christian civilization."[50]

That cultural insight did not emerge as a dominant theory or policy, though. More commonly, missionaries sorted through perceptions of common humanity and cultural difference with analysis in which an abstract ideal of "civilization" tended to function as the key standard of measurement. Yankee missionaries identified positive features of Burmese government, family relations, religious practices, social relations, education, and medicine. Burmese laws, other than those dealing with religious freedom, were "wise, and pregnant with sound morality; and their police is better regulated than in most countries." The Burmese also compared favorably with the people of India in their treatment of women and the absence of a caste system.[51]

On the other hand, the missionaries reported that the Burman people lacked generosity and permitted a great deal of "idleness," polygamy, and prostitution. They fell victim to "superstitious" beliefs in evil spirits, ghosts, demon possessions, and charms, although they were "certainly not incapable of strong attachments, or of exercising the social virtues." Highest on the missionary list of criticisms, though, lay Buddhist beliefs and the restrictions on religious freedom felt by the missionaries under the Burmese government. American Baptists placed a particularly high priority on the value of religious freedom, since their own identity had been formed in disestablishment campaigns. "Could their public character be formed in a different mould from that in which their system of government has already cast it," George Hough wrote in 1826, "they would be found by no means destitute of those elementary principles which combine to form the happiness of civilized society."[52]

The resulting missionary conception tended to rank all cultures in hierarchical levels of "civilized society," although they all held egalitarian possibilities. Early missionaries wrote that the depth of sin and degradation in Asia stemmed from an absence of the ameliorating influences of Christian civilization but held confidence in the power of spiritual transformation and education. In a widely published address given during a brief return to the United States in 1822, Ann Judson asked her female audience, who lived in "the country favored by Heaven above most others," to develop compassion for the plight of our "tawny sisters [on] the other side of the world" who lived in "female wretchedness." Arguing that relations between husband and wife "distinguish civilized from heathen nations," she recited a litany of gender inequities facing women in less civilized societies, such as female segregation, arranged marriages, female illiteracy, female infanticide, the practice of settee, and husbands who commonly called their wives "my servant" or "my dog." Judson pointed out that Burman women enjoyed better status than Indian women, but husbands still disciplined wives as if they were children, and women were not given the chance to cultivate their minds. She exalted the activities of a Burman convert, Mahmen-la, as evidence that if properly educated, Asian females would equal the intellectual attainments of women in America. She closed by calling on her fellow American Christian women to join her in efforts "to raise, to refine, to elevate, and point to that Savior who has died equally for them as for us." Christ died for all equally, but all needed to be "elevated."[53]

Conceptions of civilization drew missionaries toward educational tasks, for several reasons. First, New Englanders dominated the Baptist missionary movement before the Civil War. As good Yankees, they believed that education played a crucial role in religious and civic life. Of the thirty-one males who had worked in Burma by 1844, twenty-one had attended college or seminary, a far higher percentage than from the rest of American society.[54] Education also lay at the center of missionary tasks taken on by evangelical women. Even though a college or seminary education had been denied to women of her era, Ann Judson had undertaken a vigorous program of self-study, reading Calvinist theology before she left America. As would the Baptist women who followed her, Judson established a school for girls in Burma, acting on a Yankee conviction that dated back to the Puritans, who assumed that girls, as much as boys, ought to be schooled in the rudiments of reading and religion. She arrived in Burma just when New Englanders began to believe that females could assume the role of schoolteacher.[55]

The Burman Buddhist refusal to convert in large numbers added fuel to the educational strategy. Schools, these missionaries figured, would provide them with the opportunity to spend years socializing Asian children and instructing adult inquirers in the truths of evangelical Christianity. It was a strategy built on a particularly modern set of assumptions. With the errors of idolatry exposed, Asian students might come to the point where they would voluntarily adopt the Christian faith. "Let the books used be such as will tend to elevate and enlarge the mind, inform the understanding, eradicate previously imbibed errors, and lay the foundation for a superstructure of Christian instruction," George Boardman had urged Baptist officials in America.[56] It was at that point that the Karen inquirers had begun to appear at his door, setting off a series of events that challenged conceptions of civilization and education embedded in their missionary plans.

"This poor Karen," the young Boardman wrote of the older Ko Tha Byu in March 1829, "who, to say the least, does not excel in intellectual endowment of human learning, is continually devising new and judicious plans of doing good." It was less than three weeks after the two of them had returned from their first evangelistic journey into the remote hills beyond Tavoy. Ko Tha Byu had pleaded with Boardman for permission to "declare the Gospel" to the Karen in a wide range of regions: "the districts of Pai and Palan...the province of Mergui," across the hills to Siam, and up north to the region near Rangoon, and in Bassein, his place of birth.[57]

Despite his earlier doubts about the character of the former criminal, Boardman granted Ko Tha Byu permission to launch a seven-week journey to the south of Tavoy, where he preached, in Boardman's words, to the "wild wanderers among his native mountains." After additional forays into Karen villages around Tavoy, Ko Tha Byu took a seven-day trip in December into Siam with two other Karen converts. Apparently, "this poor Karen" excelled in more than just planning and zeal. Eight years after his tours, when American missionaries made their first evangelistic forays to the villages south of Tavoy, they encountered many "wild wanderers" who promptly requested baptism, already counting themselves as Christians. The missionaries suddenly had to shift their expectations of their expedition, from a pioneer missionary exploration among uncivilized heathen to a sacramental ceremony of baptism among fellow Christians in the jungle. Several of these Karen Christians later went on to become, in the words of one missionary, "pillars of the church."[58]

As Boardman began to put more trust in Ko Tha Byu's zeal and piety, he also demonstrated a greater willingness to meet the Karen in their home territory. He embarked on two more arduous tours to remote Karen villages. Not only were his reports more encouraging, but they also displayed a greater sense of affection toward the Karen Christians, an affection expressed through moments of joyful fellowship. In a letter to Sarah from a remote Karen village in April 1830, Boardman described "a communion season as we never before had in Tavoy, either as to the number of communicants, or the feeling manifested by them." He went on to exclaim that "it was indeed, the house of God, and the gate of heaven. O that you had been present to partake of our unusual joy." Increasingly encouraged by the piety and zeal of the Karen Christians, he wrote of the "delightful employment" of spending the day listening to their "Christian experiences" and praying with them.[59]

The Karen Christians, Boardman reported, wanted to know the names of all of the Baptist missionaries "that they might pray for them distinctly." They also wanted specific terms for "the American Indians, of whom they had heard me speak as a people somewhat resembling the Karens," so that they might also pray for them. Boardman also began to place greater trust in the judgment of Karen evangelists when seven individuals requested baptism. He explained that he "had not that evidence which arises from a daily observation of their conduct," but he accepted testimony to their character from two baptized Karen

Christians, Moung Kyah and Moung Khway. And so the seven were baptized. The capabilities of these uncivilized Karen Christians were rising in the missionary's estimation.[60]

Boardman also changed his terminology for the Karen people, a shift that mirrored a larger American Baptist missionary shift in thinking in the 1830s. After the summer of 1830, Boardman stopped using the term *wild* to describe the Karen. Describing a group of Karen near Tavoy who "manifested but little interest" in what he said, he wrote that he felt "somewhat as David Brainerd did, when, in spite of all his remonstrances, the poor Indians *would* dance, and powwow, and use their various infernal arts."[61] The term *poor* pointed to the shift in Boardman's mind: the Karen were no longer a wicked and potentially dangerous group of idolators but a people more akin to ignorant children in need of guidance. This shift toward benevolent paternalism might have moved Baptist missionaries a bit closer to an accurate understanding of the Karen, but it still contained its problems. Just as the "wild aborigine" perception did not accurately describe the Karen, the image of dependent children held its flaws, too.

Karen Christians, for instance, displayed remarkable initiative and independence. With minimal missionary contact, thousands of Karen converted to Christianity in the 1830s and '40s, almost entirely at the hands of barely literate, "uncivilized" Asian evangelists such as Ko Tha Byu. The missionaries, with their seminary degrees, long-standing theological development, and formative upbringing in a "Christian civilization," were directly responsible for only a handful of these conversions. While Boardman agonized that he had failed to handle early converts in Tavoy correctly, many Karen converts maintained a steadfast devotion to their new religious commitments that lasted for years before they even met a missionary.

This was a puzzling situation. As the Karen evangelists combed the countryside, Baptist missionaries wondered how to make sense of what was unfolding before them. Somehow Christianity had taken root among the Karen for good, while in many other people, it remained on precarious footing. "It does sometimes happen, that missionaries labour for years, and have no apparent success," one missionary in Burma mused, "and it seems also to happen, that where none of them have sown the seeds, the ripened sheaves wait to be gathered to the garner."[62] Through the 1830s, Karen evangelists continued to strike off into the hinterlands of Burma while American Baptist missionaries scurried to follow along in their wake.

Boardman did not live to see much of this. By September 1830, he was suffering from illness that would take his life within a few months. Aware that he probably would not live much longer, he cemented his commitment to Karen Christianity and his place in American Baptist hagiography by agreeing to Karen requests to take one last trip to a distant village, even though he was not strong enough to walk long distances. Karen Christians carried Boardman on the entire twelve-day journey. He was accompanied by Sarah, his son George, and a new missionary named Francis Mason, who had arrived in Tavoy one week before the journey began. At a village that served as their main destination, Boardman gave a short address, and Mason, who had yet to learn the Karen language, baptized thirty-four people. Earlier, Sarah had asked whether his health had deteriorated to the point where they ought to return, but George told her not to ask him to return until "these poor Karens have been baptized." He died on the return journey, twelve miles from Tavoy and just three years after he first met A-Pyah Thee. Poignant stories of his death fueled his fame in America as a pioneer missionary.[63]

After her husband's death, Sarah Boardman ran the school in Tavoy. Ko Tha Byu, meanwhile, continued to do much of the same sort of evangelistic work that he had been doing the previous three years, unofficially assuming the spiritual leadership that George Boardman had held. Francis Mason later wrote that for more than a year, "the whole care of the [Karen] people when they visited town, the whole care of the church, and the instruction of the inquirers, devolved on Ko Tha Byu." In the spring of 1833, Ko Tha Byu left the British-controlled territory of southern Burma and traveled more than two hundred miles north with Cephas Bennett, a missionary printer, to Rangoon, which was still under the authority of the Burmese king. Bennett ventured a note of cautious optimism when Ko Tha Byu and a Burman Christian returned from an evangelistic

Figure 1.2. A dying George Boardman watching Karen baptisms. Illustration in G. Winfred Hervey, *The Story of Baptist Missions in Foreign Lands* (St. Louis: C. R. Barns, 1892).

foray among the Karen, "who are scattered in the wilderness." Most likely thinking that a few might come to the faith, he observed that the Karen audiences expressed some interest after initially being indisposed to "listen to his message."[64]

In October, the tide came in. While Ko Tha Byu was in another town taking care of his ill wife, Bennett found himself awash in a sea of Karen inquirers. "We are in distress and send to you for relief," he wrote anxiously to another missionary. "The Karens are thronging us from Dalla, Leing, Maubee, Kyadan, and many places I have not here named, men, women, and children, and all anxiously inquiring about the religion of Jesus." Ko Tha Byu, not Bennett's fellow missionaries, brought the relief. He returned to Rangoon; the Karen inquirers crammed into his small house to hear him speak. They explained that in their attempts to "practice according to the requirements of the Scriptures," they had been singing, praying, and reading daily from the tracts in Burmese that they had obtained. Then they asked for schools. The missionary printer, who could not speak Karen, clearly felt overwhelmed. "What shall we do?" Bennett wrote. "Ko Tha Byu is only one among a thousand." Several weeks later, Ko Tha Byu's bamboo house began to break down from the crowds of Karen inquirers that poured in during a festival. Bennett could only look on while the Karen evangelist preached from morning to night. Once again, Bennett asked the American board for more missionaries, pointing out that many of these Karen who sought out Ko Tha Byu had arrived without even having met him previously.[65]

This pattern continued for two more decades. Karen evangelists continued to promote conversion and literacy, while American missionaries scrambled along behind, trying to adapt their missionary machinery to a new movement of world Christianity. The ten Baptist missionaries who had learned the Karen language by 1841 simply could not keep pace with four dozen Karen evangelists and thousands of new converts scattered among villages in the distant hills. American missionaries, both male and female, occasionally conducted preaching tours through the Karen regions, accompanied by Karen evangelists, but they spent most of their time at mission stations far from Karen villages, building schools and translating biblical literature. The missionaries lost more contact with many Karen when tensions between the British and the king of southern Burma cut off American missionary presence altogether in the lower delta and upper river regions of Burma between 1839 and 1852. Christianity continued to spread among the Karen of those areas, though. When American missionaries returned to southern Burma after the Second Anglo-Burmese War, they encountered about five thousand new Karen Christians.[66]

It should be noted that most of the Karen did not convert to Christianity. Through the end of the twentieth century, a majority held to their traditional religious beliefs, while a small minority continued to assimilate with the Burman by adopting Buddhism. The non-Christian people of Burma responded to Karen

Christianity in a variety of ways. Karen Christians sometimes faced opposition from fellow Karen in their families or villages, and Karen chiefs occasionally appealed to Burman officials to clamp down on the movement. Meanwhile, some Burman individuals converted to Christianity and worked together with Karen evangelists to spread the movement among both the Karen and the Burman people, actions that challenged traditional animosities between the two groups. But Karen Christianity also challenged Burman dominance, a development that could intensify ethnic tensions. By the late nineteenth century, many non-Christian Karen joined Karen Christian leaders in a growing movement of Karen nationalism. The rise of Karen nationalism built on old conflicts between the Karen and Burman peoples, while providing new contexts through which those conflicts were played out, conflicts that would continue through the end of the twentieth century.[67]

The emergence of Karen Christianity displayed the evangelical missionary paradoxes of culture and power. The prophecy of the lost book served as just one of several points where Karen folk religion found continuities with the new evangelical faith. The use of the Karen name for God, Y'wa, as the name of the Christian God ensured that Karen converts filtered both the changes and the continuities of the new Christian faith through Karen culture. "Many of them listen with unfeigned astonishment as they hear for the first time the great truths of revealed religion, they seeming as it were to suggest something once known, but long since irrecoverably lost," wrote a missionary in 1852. "Their first inquiry almost is for Pwo books, and they will sit with evident delight, for a long while listening to the reading of a book in their *own* language."[68] For the Karen, the cultural implications of Bible translation meant that the Karen language, oral traditions, and folklore would be preserved in writing.

Traditional Karen culture and religion helped lay the groundwork for conversion. Songs from traditional Karen religion had extolled Y'wa as perfect, omniscient, omnipotent, omnipresent, unchangeable, and eternal. Under Christianity, Y'wa maintained these characteristics. Karen oral traditions included stories of creation, a male and a female placed in a garden, temptation, fall from Y'wa's favor, a flood, and future resurrection, which were adapted but reinforced by biblical authority. Karen Christians drew on the tradition of Karen teachers called Bukhos who had taught that the ways of Y'wa differed from those of *nats*, which were seen as evil spirits. Karen religious ethics extolled prayer, honor to parents, and love for one's enemies, while prohibiting theft, murder, idolatry, adultery, deception, and swearing. In fact, these Karen traditions resembled the biblical ideas so closely that several missionaries speculated that Karen must have derived them from contact with the Old Testament or the Jewish people at some point in ancient history.[69]

But Karen Christianity simultaneously transformed Karen life. Evangelical Christianity helped provide the framework for this cultural negotiation. Theologically, evangelical Christianity introduced the person of Jesus Christ into the religious world of the Karen converts, altering their understanding of their relationship to Y'wa. Literacy and education opened the Karen to wider and more complex engagement with other peoples. Karen Christians dropped their old Karen songs for new Christian hymns, although some of these hymns were sung to traditional melodies. Missionary education provided Karen students with literacy, bureaucratic skills, and the practices of modern political mobilization, tools that the Karen later used to negotiate conflicts peculiar to the modern world.[70]

Built on the foundation of the Karen vernacular, grafted onto Karen oral tradition, directed by indigenous leadership, and receiving vital missionary contributions but little missionary oversight, Christianity became translated into another culture. This pattern of cultural translation had existed for centuries, as Andrew Walls and Lamin Sanneh have demonstrated, dating back to the very foundations of Christianity.[71] The Baptist missionaries in Burma, however, did not anticipate or fully understand this process. Most confusingly, to these Baptist missionaries, Karen Christianity did not emerge from the virtues of "civilized society."

Missionaries played key roles but could not control Karen Christianity. In fact, even had they wished to impose all manners of Western culture on the Karen or place themselves in direct authority over these new converts, Baptist missionaries would have found it extremely difficult. The vast majority of the new converts had never even met an individual from the West. Baptist missionaries found themselves doing a much smaller share of the grassroots evangelism than they had anticipated. Vastly outnumbered, the missionaries found themselves interacting with a vibrant, decentralized movement scattered among remote regions.

American Baptist missionaries tried to compensate for their limited personal presence by printing as much written material as they could. The newly literate Karen Christians displayed a voracious appetite for the printed word. The Baptist missionaries responded to their requests with as much printed material as they could muster. In the 1830s and '40s, while Burman converts still numbered in the dozens, missionaries printed 21 million pages in the Karen language. Francis Mason began publishing the *Morning Star* in 1841, a Karen religious monthly that became Burma's longest-running vernacular newspaper, until it was forcibly shut down by the government more than a century later. By 1853, Karen Christians had snapped up all but seventy-four of the six thousand copies of the Karen New Testament that the missionaries had published between 1843 and 1851.[72]

Baptist missionaries sometimes found it strange how Karen evangelists adapted the Christian faith to traditional Karen culture. In 1852, a Karen evangelist and a missionary discussed the situation of a Karen Christian who had come down with an affliction. In the words of missionary Henry Van Meter, the afflicted person was "partially insane." The Karen evangelist described the problem in different terms. The nineteenth-century Karen believed that they lived in a world of demons and spirits, many of which could be called on by individuals with special powers to bring sickness or death to another person. The Karen evangelist explained that the affliction was caused by the influence of an evil spirit that had been sent by a Buddhist priest. Like a good Karen Christian, the evangelist attempted to help by calling on the power of Christ to deliver the man from the spirit. Like a good child of the Enlightenment, Van Meter attempted to help the afflicted man by trying to change the irrational thinking of the Karen evangelist. "It seems almost impossible to show them the absurdity of such a belief," he wrote.[73]

Van Meter's reaction illustrates how disenchantment shaped some evangelical missionaries as they negotiated questions of the natural and the supernatural. Highly educated American Christians from pre-Enlightenment eras, such as the Puritans, saw both natural and supernatural forces at work in physical and mental illnesses. In the wake of the Scientific Revolution and the Enlightenment, the modern societies of both Europe and America tended to divorce physical and mental illnesses from the spiritual realm, explaining causes and solutions largely in biological or natural terms. If it was suggested that demons or spirits were somehow involved in physical or mental illnesses, most of the Puritans' descendants in the mid-nineteenth century, be they of free-thinking, Transcendentalist, Unitarian, Episcopalian, Congregational, or Baptist convictions, would have regarded claims for demons and spirits as an illustration of superstition or insanity.[74]

Van Meter, however, unwittingly provided Karen Christians with evangelical resources to resist his argument. American Baptist seminaries did not exactly devote much of their curriculum to demonology, but educated missionaries had gone forth into Burma promoting evangelical convictions that the Karen people must be taught to read the Bible. Like good Baptists, Karen evangelists embraced this evangelical program and promptly interpreted the Bible within the framework of Karen culture. In this case, that meant upholding the presence and activities of spirits and demons. "When pressed upon such points," Van Meter wrote, "they reply by referring to the fact that such things are recognized by Scriptures, especially in connection with the miracles of Christ, e.g. in the case of the possessed of devils so frequently mentioned in the gospels."[75]

The issue of supernatural activity apparently surfaced with some regularity in missionary engagements. Missionaries did not write about it very often, perhaps because they were uncertain of the appropriate response.[76] Van Meter reported that once, when he and Elisha Abbott were "in the jungle with a large number of native preachers," Abbott preached from Romans 9 and stopped to ask the evangelists to interpret a passage. After considerable hesitation, one of the evangelists explained that his sister had become "insane—almost wild." In great agony, the evangelist had prayed and "begged of God to send him to hell—do anything with *him*—only save his sister from her dreadful insanity." The sister then recovered. The Karen evangelist concluded that this supernatural action of God illustrated the truth of the Bible verse. The American missionary was not so sure.[77]

The Karen evangelists may have been trying to suggest to their teachers that the missionaries had missed out on important aspects of the Christian faith. "Many...remarkable instances of answers to prayer, especially in case of the sick, are related by Karens," Van Meter wrote, "and not unfrequently do we hear them lament the loss of that faith which wrought such wonders in former times." Biblicism led Van Meter to suggest to his American supporters that perhaps there might be some merit to the Karen belief in the power of prayer. "This narrative reminds us of the age of miracles and apostolic labors," he wrote. "True or not true, things equally incredible are related by Karens at times; and they come so well attested that, however astonishing they may be, we can hardly find room for doubt."[78]

Karen Christianity stamped the image of Burma into the collective Baptist mind as the land of foreign missionary success. Even when the missionary enterprise took American Baptists to India, China, Japan, Africa, and Europe, Karen Christianity always hovered right at the surface of missionary consciousness. Reports on the Karen Christians appeared in virtually every issue of the *Baptist Missionary Magazine* from 1835 through the end of the century. More than one-fourth of all Baptist missionaries by 1845 had been appointed to Burma, while as late as 1897, no other country hosted more than half as many American Baptist missionaries. By 1892, at least thirty-five books devoted solely to the lives of missionaries to Burma or missionary work in Burma had been published in the United States. Burma "is almost synonymous, in popular speech, with the term *foreign missions*," wrote a Baptist missionary biographer in 1892. "It is the joy and pride of Baptists in America."[79]

Even non-Baptists conjured up the image of Burma to define the nature of missionary work. An agent for the nondenominational American Tract Society decided that he could generate support in 1838 for tract distribution in that strange land known as the western states of America by declaring that "the fact is, this field is about as much Missionary ground as Burmah."[80] When John Mott wanted to give proof to the delegates of the Ecumenical Missionary Conference in New York in 1900 that the world could be evangelized in one generation, he upheld the Karen as one of several "recent missionary achievements of the Church."[81]

The dynamic growth of this new movement also made heroes out of Baptist missionaries. Ann and Adoniram Judson practically created a cottage industry for a new genre of evangelical print media, the missionary biography. The couple alone accounted for fifteen biographies, at least three of which sold more than twenty-six thousand copies each during the 1850s. Dramatic missionary tales about the Judsons intensified evangelical themes of self-sacrifice, spiritual dedication, and religious activism. Adoniram Judson had been jailed in 1824 by Burmese authorities who were resisting encroachments by British imperialists. Ann Judson worked tirelessly to gain his release, generating stirring images of a lone and defenseless woman persisting bravely against an exotic but threatening autocracy, all for the cause of the Gospel. This story would be retold countless times in missionary literature. After she died two years later at the young age of thirty-six, writers and artists created a symbol of missionary sacrifice with the image of the hopia tree under which she and her daughter were buried. Adoniram Judson added fascinating domestic twists to themes of evangelical martyrdom in 1834 by marrying the newly famous missionary widow from Burma, Sarah Boardman. After her death in 1845, he married Emily Chubbock, a writer of popular evangelical female fiction who wrote under the name of Fanny Forester. A few years after this wedding, Fanny Forester wrote a biography of her new husband's former wife, Sarah Boardman Judson. The religious press of early Victorian America did not have to manufacture dramas when intriguing missionary celebrities like these were landing in their laps.[82]

In their excitement, American Baptists extended this wave of Judsoniana beyond the genre of biography. On through the twentieth century, poems, songs, churches, historical prints, church camps, commemorative medals, a denominational press, and several colleges were named in tribute to the Judsons. It is not known how many evangelical parents named their children after these missionary heroes, but a brief survey of genealogical records turns up more than one hundred nineteenth-century Americans named for Adoniram Judson.[83]

Judson's popularity would not have been nearly as widespread without the growth of Karen Christianity. Working primarily with the Burman people, he had minimal contact with the Karen, but this point was lost on most American evangelicals. The biggest wave of Judson biographies hit the market after he died in 1850, just after Karen Christianity had taken off in the 1830s and '40s. Baptists remained fascinated with Burma and the Judsons because, in the evangelical way of thinking, something seemed to work in this region of the world.[84]

Karen Christianity did more than make missionaries into celebrities. As the nineteenth century unfolded, developments in Western culture strengthened American beliefs in the superiority of Anglo civilization and the limited capabilities of nonwhites. The accomplishments of Karen evangelists ran counter to dominant assumptions about white civilization in anthropology, philosophy, science, politics, laissez-faire capitalism, and race relations, not to mention the imperialistic ventures of the United States and Great Britain. American Baptists could not accept these developments wholesale if they wanted to encourage Karen Christianity, the movement that embodied the success of Baptist missionary work. The question, then, became one of how to reconcile the vitality of Karen Christianity with these powerful forces in American culture.

2

The Challenge of Karen Christianity

In his initial evaluations of the Karen, George Boardman had commented on what he perceived to be their "credulity," declaring that "almost any religion, true or false, may be introduced among them." His analysis reflected an Enlightenment conceit that uneducated masses could be easily swayed by those gifted with more highly developed rational and rhetorical capabilities. These "simplest children of nature," Boardman declared, were "the most timid and irresolute" of any of the people of the world he had seen. But Karen Christians proved to be anything but "timid and irresolute." Even Boardman came to recognize the determination of inquirers who repeatedly negotiated jungle hardships that he himself had hesitated to face.[1]

Karen Christianity had a way of compelling Baptist missionaries to readjust their thinking. In a relatively short period of time in the 1830s, the missionary conception of the Karen had shifted from potentially dangerous and wild aborigines to a poor, docile, and childlike people. Then, in the 1840s, circumstances beyond their control cut the Baptist missionaries off from direct contact and supervision of most of these Karen Christians, much to the frustration of the Yankee evangelicals. New conceptions of the Karen emerged. Some Baptist missionaries saw the Karen as a people who, if they adopted the Christian faith, were fully capable of effective leadership, unregulated initiative, and mature judgment.

Then the debates cropped up. Could an uncivilized people truly embody these qualities? Or would a seminomadic people living in the jungles of Burma still need extensive educational guidance from the missionaries? Just how much authority were missionaries supposed to exercise? Some Baptist missionaries suddenly found themselves considering a strange idea: perhaps the best way missionaries could help this new movement of Christianity would be to give up some of their power.

Ten years after Boardman's death, Karen Christians deeply impressed another Baptist missionary, Elisha Abbott. Assigned to work among the Karen in 1835, Abbott witnessed Karen Christians doggedly promoting their faith under forms of oppression that white Christians of his generation in America did not face. From 1836 to 1838, the Burmese government was wracked by an internal power struggle, while simultaneously contending with renewed imperialistic encroachments from Great Britain, to which it had been forced to cede territory after the First Anglo-Burmese War. Because they had quashed a rebellion of Karen ten years earlier, many Burmese government officials viewed the emerging literate and Christian Karen as both an internal threat and a potential ally of the British. Several Karen Christians possessing books were beaten, jailed, and threatened with execution. Many were fined, and a number were forced to work in service for the Buddhist temple in Rangoon.[2]

By persevering amid these hardships, Karen Christians further destabilized the cultural perceptions held by the missionaries. Abbott described a conversation with a Karen convert who had recently been released from jail in Rangoon. Noticing his physically weakened state, Abbott asked the man how he felt while he was being beaten. When the Karen man replied that he prayed for the Burman official, Abbott asked whether he wasn't angry. "No," came the reply, "I told them they might beat me to death, if they wished, but they would not make me angry, and that I should live again at the resurrection."[3]

Timidity, if it were to be found anywhere, materialized in the cautious actions of the civilized missionary. Fearing for the safety of individual Karen who might be identified with the missionaries, Abbott urged Karen Christians to stay in the remote hills. He refrained from greeting them in public and refused to give them books for their return journeys. They responded by acting more boldly. After Abbott turned down a request from a group of five Karen to sneak out of Rangoon with "a few small tracts," the young converts waited until his attentions were directed elsewhere and took a number of books with them anyway. This zeal deeply impressed Abbott. "Their steadfastness under these trials indicates their strong attachment to the truth, and the genuineness of their Christian character," he wrote to American supporters.[4]

Imperial conflicts soon forced Abbott farther away from the Karen Christian communities. Until the end of 1838, he had stationed himself in Rangoon, in the southern delta region that had remained under Burmese control after the First Anglo-Burmese War. However, the Burmese authorities in Rangoon began restricting Abbott's movements, while Karen Christians reported more instances of harassment, heavy taxation, and imprisonment. Abbott decided that his presence only roused further persecution of Karen Christians. In fact, the rest of the Baptist missionaries had already evacuated the delta region of Burma. In late November 1838, Abbott and a fellow missionary left Rangoon for Sandoway, a city under British control near the west coast. Except for a brief visit to Rangoon in 1839, Abbott and his fellow missionaries were unable to return to the delta region of Burma until it fell to British conquest after the Second Anglo-Burmese War in 1852. The Burmese response to the pressures of British imperialism thus produced a situation in which all of the Karen converts in lower Burma lived out their new Christian faith in distant villages far from direct supervision of the missionaries. It did not slow down Karen evangelism. Preachers such as Mau Mway, Mau-koh, and Shway Sah continued to take the initiative to evangelize fellow Karen, while extending their efforts to Burmese regions.[5]

The terms of missionary engagement had shifted, though. Evangelists and ordinary Christians made long, surreptitious journeys over mountain passes from Burmese-controlled regions to Abbott's station at Sandoway "to get books and learn to read, and to be baptized." Abbott was amazed. "The eagerness of these people to procure books, leads them to undertake the most difficult enterprises, and to endure any hardships," he explained to American supporters. "It is astonishing how rapidly they learn to read, and how fast readers multiply." Far from enervated by his absence, the Karen Christians displayed an enthusiasm that reinforced Abbott's conviction that the locus of vital energy in evangelism resided among indigenous leaders. "The work of the Lord," he told the board, "is certainly going forward in the jungles through the instrumentality of the native assistants."[6]

The idea that "native assistants" would play a key role in the evangelical missionary movement was not a new one. American Baptist missionaries had encountered it in the writings of William Carey and the English Baptist missionaries who set off for India in 1793. Like the American Baptists in Burma, the English Baptists in India worked from a position of political, economic, and social weakness. A dozen missionaries could not, at that time, attempt to spread Christianity by dictating their wishes or overwhelming India numerically. Carey came to see that the meager number of European missionaries and their high cost precluded any chance that they alone could reach the vast numbers of Indians with the Christian faith. Carey also argued that missionaries needed to cultivate the gifts of indigenous converts, because they understood the vernacular and customs better than the missionary. By 1805, the Baptist Missionary Society in England had established a policy that sought to evangelize India by means of "native preachers." In 1818, it founded Serampore College to train Indian Christians to act as missionaries to their own people. Under this plan, the English missionary did not evangelize or serve as pastor of a local church but planted churches and resolved issues of discipline and doctrine.[7]

American Baptists drew on these examples, regularly expressing the hope that converts would actively evangelize and teach their own people.[8] When the annual report of the board in 1828 gave its blessing to Adoniram Judson's decision to send Moung Ing off to evangelize his fellow Burman people, it repeated Carey's arguments. Indigenous preachers possessed familiarity with the language, understood the "sentiments and habits of thinking" of their people, did not need to adjust to the climate, and could operate at a much lower cost than missionaries.[9]

Up to this point, this idea of a "native ministry" among American Baptists had existed as a supplemental goal for the future rather than a cornerstone for engagement or an organizing framework for missionary work. Consumed by pragmatic issues of evangelism, missionaries in Burma had not worked out when or under what terms congregational authority should be granted to indigenous leaders. But Karen Christians, with their Baptist dynamics, outran the Baptist missionaries. Of the six hundred to one thousand newly committed but inaccessible Christians in the delta region of Burma in 1839, only one had been baptized, a sacrament that, according to both American Baptist and Karen Christian doctrine, had to be conducted by an ordained minister. From his base in Sandoway, Abbott tried to keep up with demand by baptizing converts who traveled across the mountain range that separated Arracan from central Burma. Even though he had baptized four hundred wayfaring Karen by the end of 1840, Abbott acknowledged the system to be a far from ideal way to build a church. And it did not escape his attention that no females took such a trip. Since Baptists only counted baptized individuals as members, Abbott now faced a sizable community of converts composed mostly of individuals who could not become church members, despite their spiritual qualifications.[10]

Before 1840, only ordained missionaries had baptized Asian converts. The one exception had been Ko Tha-a, a Burman evangelist ordained by Adoniram Judson in 1829. But even Ko Tha-a achieved his ordination and authority to baptize by forcing the hand of the missionaries. Several Burman converts had asked the unordained Ko Tha-a to baptize them, and he had consented without seeking confirmation for his actions from the American missionaries. After discovering this, Judson and Jonathan Wade decided to give Ko Tha-a "the rights which he had assumed irregularly." In his report to the American churches, Judson retroactively granted his blessing to Ko Tha-a's ministerial status, explaining that Ko Tha-a had been "so evidently called of God to the ministry, that we have not felt at liberty to hesitate or deliberate about the matter." Still, American missionaries had looked on the ordination of Ko Tha-a as an exception rather than a precedent, reserving for themselves the right to baptize.[11]

Karen Christianity forced the issue. The first stage in this process arose with the question of who had the authority to judge a candidate's qualifications for baptism. Ever since the first Burman had converted to Christianity in 1819, Baptist missionaries had attempted to ascertain the spiritual condition of candidates before agreeing to baptize them. Influenced by Calvinist theology of total depravity, evangelical ministers in the Yankee Baptist tradition believed that the sin of pride could deceive candidates into thinking that they were converted when their hearts had not truly changed. Among Baptists in New England, ministers had the responsibility to observe the behavior of the candidate over several months' time and to examine the candidate to determine whether she or he adequately understood the fundamental doctrines of Christianity.[12] In Burma, conceptions of the "uncivilized" and "idolatrous" people of Burma made missionaries even more suspicious about the validity of Asians who professed faith. This is why George Boardman delayed the baptisms of converts such as "the old sorcerer" A-Pyah Thee and the "aborigine" Ko Tha Byu.[13]

The dedication of the Karen evangelists, however, led Elisha Abbott to abandon these suspicions of the uncivilized Karen character. In May 1840, thirty Karen arrived at his house in Sandoway, wracked with fever, exhaustion, and hunger after enduring a twelve-day journey from the delta region. A few weeks earlier, a group of six had reached Sandoway carrying on their shoulders several individuals who had collapsed from the heat of the journey. Shway Meing, a Karen evangelist, took a circuitous eleven-day journey through the jungle, a trip that usually took four days, because he had to avoid Burmese officials who had been arresting Karen who had learned to read. How could one worry about the lingering effects of "idolatry" when confronted with this commitment to the faith?[14]

Furthermore, Abbott's absence from central Burma compelled him to accept the evaluations of Karen evangelists. They regularly presented him with candidates for baptism whom he had never met. He could question these candidates on a few matters of doctrine, but he knew that he could not evaluate their character. As a result, Abbott relied almost wholly on the judgment of the evangelists when determining which of the candidates to baptize. In a letter to the American board in early 1843, he took pains to justify his faith in the assistants' judgment, conscious of concerns the board might raise. The evangelists "have all studied with me, and this subject has been dwelt upon *minutely and repeatedly*," he told the board. "Moreover, all have seen my example. Were the reception of candidates left to my judgment alone, I should often be at a loss what to do." In an assessment that revealed more than he probably realized about the educated Yankee faith in rationality as a reliable sign of spiritual character, Abbott added that "those who pass the best examination do not always make the best Christians."[15]

Abbott began to trust the Karen with additional pastoral duties. Not that he could have prevented this process. In May 1840, he wrote that "nearly all these assistants are at the head of large Christian congregations, and are, in fact pastors, except in administering the ordinances." The logic behind this analysis pointed to ordination. Accordingly, Abbott began to press upon these "uncivilized" evangelists the idea that they should strive for independent leadership. In February 1841, several Karen evangelists left Sandoway with a charge from Abbott. "During their stay I have endeavored to impress the truth upon their minds, that *they* are to *lead* the host of God in Burmah," Abbot wrote, "that they must not lean upon missionaries, but upon God," a circumstance that may have already existed more fully than either he or the evangelists had perceived. "I am looking forward to the time when some of them will be deemed worthy of ordination, that they may fully discharge the duties and obligations of pastors."[16]

And then, a curveball. The Karen Christians did not think this was such a good idea. Evangelists who had so enthusiastically spread the faith and established churches actually hesitated in the face of a directive that granted them independent pastoral authority. The Karen Christians seemed amenable to the idea of ordination, but not if they were to be the individuals who actually had to select the candidates. "I have been endeavoring to ascertain the wishes of the church-members, but it is not an easy matter," wrote a slightly frustrated Abbott. "They would consent to any thing 'the teacher' proposes, but I try to make them see that the ordination of a pastor particularly concerns *them*. Of course, the subject is all new to them; and they can only do as they have been taught, so far as form is concerned, which is just what people do all over the world." Abbott remained firm, though, telling the Karen evangelists that he would not choose the candidates for ordination but only the candidates the Karen church members requested.[17]

Abbott's decision to push the Karen Christians to select their own candidates for ordination can only be partially explained by the circumstances in Burma. The dynamics of American evangelicalism also made ordination a live option for Abbott, simultaneously contributing to his capacity to overcome the missionary suspicions of the lingering effects of "idolatry." During the era of the early republic, when the role of mediating elites diminished markedly within American evangelicalism, Baptists in the United States constructed polities in which ministerial candidates had to be proposed and approved by congregations. Increasingly infused with democratized concepts of authority, early-nineteenth-century American Baptist congregations demanded the right to select their own leaders and organize churches for themselves. In his decision on Karen ordination, Abbott drew on conceptions of democratized Christianity that were quite common among evangelicals in the region around his hometown near Syracuse, New York. In true fashion of democratized Christianity, Abbott sanctioned the ministerial status of Karen leaders who evangelized effectively, accepted the testimony of Karen evangelists at face value, and encouraged Karen Christians to organize and lead their own churches.[18]

It is more difficult to determine why the Karen evangelists were reluctant to select candidates for ordination, especially since traditional Karen villages seemed to have fairly democratic means of selecting religious leaders. It is possible that the Karen evangelists viewed Abbott as something like a Christian man of *pgho*, a religious leader with special abilities to communicate with Y'wa and the supernatural realm. They may have considered it to be some sort of religious violation to abandon deference to a man of *pgho*. Similarly, they may have understood Abbott to be so deeply tied to their Karen oral tradition about the lost book that they believed they needed his leadership to fulfill the Karen prophecies of literacy, prosperity, and reconciliation with Y'wa. Or they may have calculated that their selection of candidates for ordination would lead to a loss of contact with the missionaries, thereby cutting them off from their source of literacy and Christian education. Later events demonstrated that they had developed a deep affection for Abbott, so they may have been reluctant to take steps that might loosen that attachment. Finally, it is very possible that they feared that if the missionaries ordained Karen pastors, the missionaries would depart, and the Karen would fall into greater persecution by the Siamese and Burman people.[19]

Regardless, it was a puzzling situation. Missionary engagements had a way of exposing paradoxical power relationships within evangelicalism, often with unanticipated cross-cultural twists to them. How does one grant authority to individuals who do not wish to have it? In the end, Abbott could see no other way to implement democratic practices than to order the Asian evangelists to follow his instructions, while the Karen evangelists could see no other way to maintain deference to the religious authority of the American missionary than to agree to become more autonomous. In other words, the democratized missionary imposed a form of autonomy upon the Karen Christians, who accepted their independence out of deference to authority.

The Karen evangelists fulfilled Abbott's order a year later, handing him a letter in which they requested that he ordain Bleh Poh. "It was signed by several old men, and the request was concurred in and urged by all the assistants, which not only indicated his standing, but a good degree of the right kind of feeling among the assistants," Abbott explained. Even then, Bleh Poh declined the nomination, stating that he wanted to study with Abbott for at least one more year. The authoritarian pressure of the democratized missionary eventually won out, though, and the Karen assistant submitted to ordination and his own independent authority.[20]

Unfortunately, on the day that Bleh Poh was due to arrive in Sandoway for the ordination ceremony, Abbott received news that he had died of cholera. Bleh Poh's death saddened Abbott, but it did not deter him from pushing the Karen evangelists to submit more candidates for ordination. A short time later, Karen Christians proposed two more evangelists for ordination, Myat Kyau and Tway Poh. These two became the first Asians, other than the "irregular" Burman minister Ko Tha-a, to receive ordination under American Baptist auspices. It was a small event with far-reaching consequences.[21]

The issue involved more than Karen preachers. Abbott's proposal suggested a policy whereby missionaries gave up key powers that they had assumed. By arguing for the ordination of Karen evangelists, Abbott not only abandoned his claim to the supervision of Karen congregations but also implicitly invested Karen pastors with a status equal to that of missionaries. Traditional Baptist polity did not recognize any position of religious authority higher than ministerial ordination. The ordination of Karen evangelists, then, challenged the assumption that "uncivilized" people did not have the capabilities to wield congregational authority in place of "civilized" missionaries.

Abbot knew that he needed to convince his American supporters that Karen evangelists should be ordained, a process that would require him to overcome American racial and cultural anxieties. To that end, he published an obituary of Bleh Poh in the *American Baptist Magazine*, in which he highlighted commonalities of religious piety between Bleh Poh and American Baptists. Abbott began by praising Bleh Poh's steadfastness after his conversion in the face of opposition from relatives and Burmese officials. The obituary concluded with a description of Bleh Poh's perseverance in ministering to his village while he and many others suffered from cholera. In between, Abbott listed qualities of meekness, wisdom, simplicity, consistent piety, deep habits of prayer, and a self-sacrificing spirit. Since only the Gospels and the Book of Acts had been translated into the Karen language in 1842, Abbott conceded that Bleh Poh's knowledge of the Bible was necessarily limited. Nevertheless, Bleh Poh had a grasp of "fundamental truths," being "a man of *thought* and of studious habits," treasuring up "in his heart whatever came within his reach."[22]

Aware that Abbott's ordination of Karen evangelists could establish a precedent for Baptist missionary work, a sympathetic missionary official in the United States published Abbott's letters in the annual report of the Baptist General Convention for Foreign Missions and the *American Baptist Magazine*. "If these men are competent to preach the gospel" and qualified to "lead and instruct Christian congregations," Abbott argued in one letter, "why not recognize them as also competent to administer the ordinances?" Abbott did not think Karen converts should have to take a ten-to-fifteen-day journey to Sandoway to seek baptism. "Why not ordain their own pastors, under whose preaching they were converted, and under whose guidance they are to live? Why not allow their pastors to baptize them at their own homes?" Hundreds of Karen Christians had never seen a missionary, Abbott pointed out, and they never would, unless the Burmese monarchy were to fall.[23]

Abbott made a compelling argument, but Karen ordination inadvertently raised perplexing questions. His plea made sense in light of the evangelistic dynamics of Karen Christianity, but it did not address the exact relationship between Christianity and civilization. As a result, Karen ordination brought out tensions between antiformalist and formalist impulses within evangelicalism. It also represented another chapter in a debate that had emerged among missionaries in America and Britain in the first decades of the nineteenth century. That debate turned on whether civilization ought to precede Christianity or whether evangelism ought to come before civilization. By implying that Christianity could thrive among a people who were not civilized, Abbott drew on democratized impulses within evangelicalism that found formalist institutions unnecessary for effective evangelism.

The older American formalist missionary tradition, dating back to the Puritans, found it necessary to establish some form of civilization before evangelism could take hold. This approach, which appeared most often among evangelicals from Calvinist traditions, stemmed from societal arrangements based on religious establishments. Working from a theological tradition that emphasized the role of godly social structures in restraining sin and evil, evangelical Calvinists saw civilization as the human system that God used to establish just principles for society. When religious disestablishment spread through America during the era of the early republic, evangelical Calvinists transferred many of these older custodial instincts to their voluntary societies, which they saw as the means by which a moral social order could be maintained in a republic.[24]

Dr. Samuel Worcester, one of the founders of the American Board of Commissioners for Foreign Missions (ABCFM), declared in 1816 that the order of missionary tasks to be "civilizing and Christianizing." This position reinforced missionary power and tended to uphold Western culture as the standard that others should hope to attain. Worcester's policy shaped assimilationist practices by the ABCFM among Native Americans, whereby missionaries used boarding schools to teach the English language, "civilized" habits, and the "useful arts of life," a policy that the Boardmans employed in their educational plans in Burma. The removal of Native American or Burman children from the deleterious effects of their parents' culture, it was thought, would civilize them, enabling them to reach a point where, as they grew in knowledge and virtue, they could embrace the Christian faith. Many European evangelicals followed the similar theories of the Scottish Presbyterian missionary in India, Alexander Duff, who argued that missionaries ought to undermine non-Western systems of thought with scientific knowledge and English-language education, allowing Christianity to fill the vacuum. Deeply influenced by an Enlightenment conception of rationality, Duff believed that education would sweep away the religious errors and flaws that distorted the thinking of the elites in India, who would then convert to Christianity. These new Christian leaders would, in turn, establish Christian foundations for a progressively civilized society. The masses of people would respond by following the lead of these elites.[25]

"Civilization first" policies did not encourage missionaries to pay much attention to the cultures of "uncivilized" peoples. They tended to produce missionaries who expected Native American villages to end up looking like Boston, or at least Lowell. Yet the civilizing impulse, with its theological emphasis on the need to work toward a more godly and just social order, also directed missionary zeal toward structural evils or problems within American culture. The same civilizing instincts that animated the ABCFM infused a host of other voluntary societies that worked for social causes such as common school education, temperance, prison reform, and abolition. As a result, ABCFM missionaries to the Cherokee not only converted Native Americans and established schools but also assisted Cherokee leaders who opposed Indian removal. ABCFM missionaries provided Cherokee leaders with legal assistance in their Supreme

Court battles and published materials critiquing Indian removal policies. Reverend Samuel Worcester, nephew to the "civilization first" proponent Dr. Samuel Worcester, wrote vigorous antiremoval letters in 1831 to northern newspapers, the secretary of war, missionary supporters, and Cherokee readers, protesting the "highly unjust and oppressive" removal laws passed by the state of Georgia. Worcester, who was sentenced to hard labor for violating a new state law that prohibited whites from living with the Cherokee, invoked the old Puritan jeremiad that God would punish the nation if Americans allowed their politicians to continue their "covenant-breaking and oppression and robbery."[26]

American Baptists had always been torn between formalist impulses to establish civilizing institutions and antiformalist tendencies that encouraged them to break free from established institutions. Since the sixteenth century, American Baptists had fought strenuously for the separation of church and state, forging their identity in cultural battles against religious elites who had established themselves as the custodians of civilization. To Baptists, "civilization first" advocates such as Worcester sounded suspiciously like the type of Yankee cleric who claimed that Congregationalist ministers ought to lead a religious establishment in Massachusetts. In fact, Worcester was that kind of person.[27]

Moreover, antiformalist Baptists had experienced phenomenal growth as outsiders during the early republic, drawing their energy from a democratized Christianity that found virtue in the abilities of the common, unsophisticated segments of society. The most radical Baptists, such as John Leland, embraced ideas of liberal individualism and personal autonomy to the extent that they opposed any form of organized religion beyond the local congregation. From 1790 until his death in 1841, Leland campaigned against benevolent societies, seminaries, mission boards, and the New England conviction that schools and colleges promoted piety and morality. "Did many of the rulers believe in Christ when he was upon earth?" the Baptist populist wrote in 1791. "Were not the learned clergy [the scribes] his most inveterate enemies? . . . Is not a simple man, who makes nature and reason his study, a competent judge of things?" Similarly, many working-class Baptist women in the early republic disregarded established gender roles by launching careers as itinerant preachers.[28]

Several Baptist missionaries drew on themes of democratization to explain their efforts. Baptists knew precisely how to respond to the bastion of British literary sophistication, the *Quarterly Review*, when it criticized missionaries in 1826 for working among the disreputable segments of the foreign populations. Missionaries themselves, retorted a reviewer in the *American Baptist Magazine*, were humble, poor individuals who received their support almost entirely from the poor. The fact that Jesus Christ himself assumed the humblest position and chose disciples from among the humblest in society, the writer continued, ought to be an adequate reason to conduct missions in a similar manner. Evoking a fairly common missionary theme, the reviewer noted that missionaries operated from the principle that the souls of all individuals were of equal value to God. Just as in the political realm, where great changes in a nation always begin with the common people, so it goes in religion, the article continued. Converting chiefs might make for more proselytes, but it would not necessarily make more Christians.[29]

This brand of evangelical self-understanding as populist outsiders made missionaries willing to dispense with reigning cultural conceptions, if it furthered the evangelical cause. For instance, in their early decades in Burma, Baptist missionaries countered several conceptions of "proper" gender roles of middle-class America. Dana Robert has found that Baptist missionary wives in the early nineteenth century were much more likely to take on traditional male activities, such as translation work and preaching, than their evangelical counterparts in the ABCFM. Sarah Boardman did not simply stick to her boarding school in Tavoy after George died but set off into the hills several times with her young son, where she preached and led worship to several hundred Karen. Deborah Wade initially established a boarding school in Burma but launched into evangelism when she decided that "there was more urgent work than that of the school." Sometimes accompanying her husband into remote regions and sometimes itinerating separately, Wade often lived for weeks at a time among the sparse bamboo huts of the Karen, where she taught and evangelized. Calista Vinton not only itinerated among the Karen but also consciously considered preaching to be a key part of her missionary call. While the formalist missionary wives in the ABCFM saw their role as nurturers and protectors of the home, Baptist missionary publicists did not worry about maintaining the proper Victorian image for their missionary women. From 1835 until her death in 1840, Eleanor Macomber regularly published letters in the *American Baptist Magazine* describing her work in Burma. This single woman missionary told Baptist supporters that she led worship, preached daily, conducted religious instruction, itinerated among Karen villages, and supervised several Karen evangelists.[30]

But American culture has a peculiar way of embracing certain kinds of religious outsiders, making them victims of their own success. Democratized Christianity swept through such a large segment of American society that many Baptists began moving into positions of influence and respectability, particularly in regions of economic prosperity, such as the industrializing northeast. This achievement of reaching the American establishment blunted the antiformalist edges of the movement. The expansion of Baptist higher education, which grew from one institution of higher learning in 1800 to fifteen by 1850, represented a critical feature of this new economic prosperity and cultural respectability. Solidifying the link between rising economic fortunes and higher education, Baptists named institutions of higher education in honor of donations given by Baptist industrialists William Colgate, John Crozer, and William

Bucknell.[31] At the same time, women of the northeast, who outnumbered men in evangelical congregations, began to adopt new middle-class ideals of domesticity and female virtue as the basis for moral education. Through the influence of these women, northern Baptist churches increasingly joined other middle-class Yankees in situating education as the cornerstone of Christian civilization.[32]

As they increased in economic prosperity, established colleges, and blended their evangelical theology with republicanism, many Baptists embraced the Whiggish nation-building ethos of the antebellum era. Northern Baptists joined forces with evangelical Calvinists in promoting political causes ranging from antislavery and abolitionist movements to temperance, sabbatarianism, and anti-Catholic immigration restriction.[33] In 1843, the people of Massachusetts, who had been supporters of a Congregationalist religious establishment just a decade earlier, elected a Baptist and former Democrat, George N. Briggs, as the governor of their state, on the socially respectable and religiously activist Whig ticket. Continually hunting for influential Baptists to serve on its missionary board, the American Baptist Missionary Union then elected Briggs to its board of managers in 1846 and to the presidency of the entire organization from 1848 to 1859.[34]

The Baptist procession into the American establishment moved unevenly and ambivalently. This was evangelicalism, after all. Yankee Baptists debated whether prosperous churches that adopted Gothic architecture and trained choirs promoted or detracted from evangelical piety.[35] Most Baptists in the south and the west flatly refused to join the parade to elite respectability. African-American and female Baptists were not admitted to full status as insiders, even if they desired those positions.

The role of higher education, a cornerstone of the "civilizing" argument, proved to be especially perplexing. Those who wanted to establish theological seminaries for Baptist ministers had to convince large numbers of Baptists that at least some of their ministers ought to be highly educated and erudite. As late as 1851, that point was by no means a foregone conclusion. Only a handful of the seven thousand Baptist churches in America in 1853 were led by ministers who had been educated at one of the dozen modest Baptist seminaries.[36] A Baptist newspaper editor found it necessary to defend seminaries, explaining that they equipped students not only with increased intellect "but also with the means for a *higher* culture, in these opportunities for doing good which are so necessary to fit us for the responsible duties of life, either as pastors at home, or missionaries abroad."[37]

Terms such as *higher culture* provoked anxieties, though. Some Baptists worried that by promoting a refined and educated clergy, they were forsaking the Gospel for love of the world. Advocates of ministerial education, they argued, had framed their arguments in ways that undermined the work of uneducated ministers. "School girls can sneer at the appearance of an uneducated minister, and talk of his bad pronunciation," quipped one Baptist writer sarcastically. "They are following the example of the learned and great, and, of course, consider themselves on the highway to renown." But another Baptist argued that "instances are now exceedingly rare when even the most intelligent man . . . is justified in entering on the pastoral office without any preparation." The debate would not be resolved easily.[38]

Baptist missionaries carried these cultural, social, academic, and theological tensions with them to Burma. Through the 1830s and '40s, the Baptist missionary movement displayed characteristics of both democratized Christianity and the civilizing mission. So while Elisha Abbott sent home reports that lauded the abilities of the Karen evangelists, other missionaries offered evaluations of Karen Christians that painted a different picture.

Francis Mason, for instance, thought that Karen autonomy was a bad idea. Granted, Mason and Abbott were in agreement on several points. Mason often praised Karen evangelists. He authored a biography of Ko Tha Byu, the only book from the vast nineteenth-century Baptist missionary literature that had an Asian Christian rather than a missionary as its primary subject. Early in his career, after he had first visited a Karen Christian village that George Boardman had visited only once but Ko Tha Byu had visited a number of times, Mason could barely contain his enthusiasm. "I cry no longer, 'The horrors of heathenism!' but 'The blessings of missions,'" he wrote in his journal. "I date no longer from a heathen land. I am seated in the midst of a Christian village, surrounded by a people that love as Christians, converse as Christians, act as Christians, and look like Christians. . . . I eat the rice, and yams, and fruit cultivated by Christian hands; look on the fields of Christians, and see no dwellings but those inhabited by Christian families." The remote Karen village obviously did not display the trappings of "civilization," but as Mason saw it at that point, the village had become thoroughly Christian.[39]

This enthusiasm did not last. Ten years later, Mason wrote that although he once had been intent on ordaining assistants as quickly as possible, "further acquaintance with the native character has raised insuperable obstacles in my mind." He warned that new missionaries may "attach too much importance to native assistants as independent agents." The only reason he could see for ordaining an assistant would be if the circumstances were like those in the lower delta region of Burma, where an Asian assistant could go but a missionary could not.

Tellingly, Mason had cast his earlier enthusiasm in the terms of a "Christian village." His formalist and structural conception of Christianity, particularly as it led to institutions of higher education, led him to lower his expectations. In Mason's thinking, the problem with the "native character" lay in its lack of education and civilization. The Karen and the Burman people had the ability to learn, but in Mason's view, they had not yet been convinced about making the sacrifices necessary for mental discipline. The "one great hindrance to the spread of light in all heathen countries," Mason wrote, "is the extreme apathy of the people in regard to literary and scientific knowledge."[40]

Mason's background helps explain his frame of mind. Born in England, he had emigrated to America, converted in a Baptist church, and graduated from Newton Theological Institute. He arrived in Burma to work among the Karen in 1830, five years before Abbott. A member of the American Oriental Society, a regular contributor to scholarly journals such as the *Asiatic Society of Bengal*, and a missionary who found it fitting to begin a letter to his board with a quote from Lord Byron, Mason retained closer ties to the transatlantic scholarly community than most American Baptist missionaries.[41] Unlike Abbott, Mason settled into a region in southern Burma that had come under British imperial control, where he spent a great deal of his time in academic pursuits. Mason's closer identification with Western institutions of power most likely reinforced a civilizing mind-set.

True to his formalist instincts, Mason encouraged Karen converts to abandon their seminomadic lifestyle in favor of settled villages made up of Christians. These communities, Mason hoped, would help the Karen grow in Christian piety, build educational institutions, forge democratic decision-making processes, abstain from alcohol, adopt patterns of cleanliness, and develop economically prosperous practices of trade and agriculture. Mason tended to evaluate the "native character" on the basis of their accomplishments in the classroom rather than their evangelism in the hinterlands. In 1843, after quoting his own 1832 journal entry that had praised Ko Tha Byu's evangelistic efforts, Mason pointed out "a shade to the picture." Since Ko Tha Byu "was a man 'possessed of very ordinary abilities'" and had begun his studies late in life, "the great body of the church members, especially the younger portion, soon knew more than their teacher, and hence his labours with them became less and less acceptable." Apparently, Karen students did not need to take cues from schoolchildren in upstate New York in order to sneer at poorly educated ministers.[42]

In an 1842 *Baptist Missionary Magazine* article, Mason gave his audience in its "Christian and enlightened" country a sense of what he believed he was up against. To understand Asians, Mason explained, Americans had to take away all of their knowledge of the earth, history, astronomy, chemistry, geometry, navigation, and the first principles of arithmetic. They also had to eliminate their association with the arts, machinery, printing, agriculture, and medicine. This was only the beginning, for Americans also had to consider that Asians lacked the mental discipline needed for learning. Having hiked down this path of comparative civilizations, Mason unsurprisingly arrived at a type of paternalism that cast the missionary in the role of the adult caretaker. Echoing a theme that would continue to carry weight with Western intellectuals over the next century, Mason pointed to Karen belief in supernatural activity as evidence of their immature intellectual capabilities. "To say they are full grown children, is saying too much in favor of their intellectual character," he wrote, "because it throws into shade their demonology, and its thousand auxiliary superstitions with which their minds are crowded."[43]

Mason did not see that uneducated Karen evangelists held expertise in areas that educated missionaries did not match. Missionaries such as Mason probably found it hard to entertain such an idea because their own academic credentials seemed far more impressive by comparison. George Boardman, for instance, benefited from a common school education in New England, where he learned Latin. He then attended Colby College, where he studied Greek, Latin, mathematics, English composition, history, and philosophy, before matriculating at Andover Seminary, where he studied rhetoric, theology, metaphysics, biblical literature, and ecclesiastical history.[44] Ko Tha Byu, of course, who had achieved just a basic level of literacy, understood little, if anything, of these subjects. However, he knew the Karen language and understood Karen culture deeply, which gave him a decided advantage in the task of evangelism. In his biography of Ko Tha Byu, Mason revealed more than he understood when he quoted a Karen Christian who compared Ko Tha Byu's evangelistic efforts with those of the educated American missionary pioneer: "Teacher Boardman preached to me the words of God, and I understood a little, but not fully: Ko Tha-byu taught me in Karen so that I understood perfectly."[45]

Despite his claims that "the native character" lacked mental discipline, Mason argued that the key to a thriving Karen Christian community lay in Christian education. He published a translated letter written by Sau Nga-tau, a Karen evangelist, who explained that after his conversion, the Holy Spirit worked through his study with Mason to give him deeper holiness and an unshakable desire to preach. "Teacher, through thy teaching me the truth of God, I have obtained this much of a new heart," Sau Nga-tau wrote. "I never felt formerly as I do now. Because thou has enlightened mine eyes with the light of God, this much of a new heart have I obtained." Sau Nga-tau closed with a poem expressing a plea to God to give the teacher wisdom so that he might receive holiness and wisdom. Mason then turned his missionary zeal on the board in New England:

> Have you ever met . . . with pupils more interesting than such as these, civilized or uncivilized? Is it not cruel, then, to leave such pupils without teachers? And what is the reason that such pupils have not been multiplied tenfold, that our little churches might now be enjoying the advantages of enlightened and devoted native pastors? *The lack of teachers*; THE LACK OF TEACHERS.

To clinch his point, Mason related how one of the most effective assistants under his direction, who had been baptized more than a decade earlier, had recently asked him, "Paul, Paul, who was Paul? Was he a Christian?"[46] Now, there was an anecdote that would unsettle biblically minded evangelicals.

What was the typical Baptist supporter of missions to make of Karen Christians, then, as she paused in her Connecticut sitting room to reflect on Asia after reading the *American Baptist Magazine*? In April 1842, she would have read Francis Mason saying that calling them "full grown children" gave the Karen people too much credit. In July 1844, she would have read Elisha Abbott explaining that the Karen evangelists were "competent to preach the gospel," qualified to "lead and instruct Christian congregations," and ought to administer the ordinances.[47]

Board officials certainly wondered. The corresponding secretary of the ABMU, Solomon Peck, struggled to make a proper evaluation of the Karen ministry from his vantage point in Boston, describing the issue as one of "extreme delicacy and difficulty." On the one side, Abbott described Bleh Po in terms that would have qualified him for ordination in just about any Baptist church in America in the first half of the nineteenth century. Yet there was Francis Mason, arguing that "a mind without knowledge and without discipline is the mind of a child; and such is the most favored aspect under which the minds of the natives of this country appear."[48] Baptist congregations in America certainly would not ordain a pastor with the mind of a child.

Nobody in the Baptist missionary establishment denied the evangelistic abilities of Karen preachers, but nobody argued that education should stop at basic literacy, either. Most Baptists assumed that in order for a church to remain effective and healthy, ordinary Christians ought to have a solid knowledge of the Bible, and ministers ought to have at least some sort of education beyond that. The crucial issue of indigenous ordination could not be separate from the question of academic accomplishment. "It is worthy of serious question, how far it is *safe* to intrust to native teachers, in their present comparative ignorance, the powers of the Gospel ministry," the board reported. If the character of the Karen evangelists was like that of Bleh Po, the board mused, "the danger of improper admissions would not seem to be greatly increased, although placed beyond the personal observation of the missionary." On the other hand, "the opinion appears to have prevailed among the missionaries generally, who, it may be supposed, are best qualified to judge of the native character, that the time for ordaining a native ministry is not yet come." Did "native" characteristics hinder the moral development, ability for ecclesiastical authority, and capability for spiritual responsibility among Karen evangelists? Or did the standards of higher education unnecessarily withhold ordination from those who were entitled to it? Peck remained internally conflicted. He worried that the "case involves, on either hand, a fearful responsibility."[49]

Mason could be just as persuasive as Abbott. "But you will say, 'the assistants must help,'" he wrote. "Alas! they are very little in advance of the people they are set over; and one reason why help is so urgently requested, is, to instruct *them*." Only two of the native assistants in Mason's region, he reported, had as much as twelve months' schooling, and most had less than six.[50] With Karen Christians indeed eager for some sort of education, Mason challenged the assumption that evangelical faith, tied as it was to biblical authority, literacy, and education, could truly thrive without the influence of elite academics. Like Abbott's argument for ordination, Mason's argument for education also raised perplexing questions.

These questions turned on culturally laden evaluations of the "native character." Significant differences underlay the arguments by Abbott and Mason, of course, but they also shared some basic assumptions that may have been even more important in the long run. Karen Christians had convinced both missionaries that, regardless of the differences exemplified by the "native character," Asians were effective at evangelizing their own people. Mason's portrayal, to some degree, and Abbott's, in particular, displayed a faith in the capabilities of nonwhites that countered powerful racial trends in nineteenth-century American culture. Abbott's democratized ministry and Mason's civilized ministry both assumed that changeable, environmental factors explained human difference. These environmentally based missionary schools of thought crystallized in the 1840s, just at a time when influential trends in American society increasingly explained human differences in terms of inherent, unchanging characteristics of race. Biological explanations of race became even more powerful as the nineteenth century unfolded.

All Baptist missionaries agreed that the Karen were capable of both academic achievement and pastoral responsibilities equal to the missionaries. They debated just when or how those capabilities would be realized. The distinctive evangelical missionary assumptions underlying these convictions can only be fully appreciated when placed in the context of the racial ideas coursing through American culture in the nineteenth century. From the 1830s through the end of the century, a range of different racial frameworks socialized Americans, most of which discouraged ideas of nonwhite capability.

Few whites in the 1830s and '40s, north or south, thought that blacks were capable of playing productive roles as independent citizens in a republican society. An increasing number of white southerners saw slavery as a positive good instead of a necessary evil. Thomas Roderick Dew published a proslavery tract in 1837 in which he argued that the eventual Christianization and civilization of the black race, which would take a thousand years or so, could only occur under the paternalistic forces of the slave system.[51] Meanwhile, popular antislavery trends among northern whites gained much of their force from desires to keep economic opportunities open for whites, rather than visions of a nation of social equality among the races. When Congressman David Wilmot of Pennsylvania opened up the sectional conflict over western territories in 1846 by proposing that slavery be excluded from any land the United States acquired from Mexico, he explained that his proposal did not come from a "squeamish sensitiveness...nor morbid sympathy for the slave" but was an effort to "preserve for free white labor a fair country, a rich inheritance...where sons of toil, of my own race and own color, can live without the disgrace which association with negro slavery brings upon free labor."[52]

As an organizing framework, "civilization" could be used to explain the development of sound governmental systems, sophisticated intellectual trends, and ethical social structures, but it could also be used to justify any number of injustices inflicted by whites who held power. During the decades of the early republic, conceptions of civilization lay behind government policies toward Native Americans that perpetuated a long history of mistreatment and abuse. By 1830, Lewis Cass, the governor of the Michigan Territory and a widely regarded expert on Indian policy, employed ideas of civilization to justify a new policy of Indian removal. "Existing for two centuries in contact with a civilized people, they have resisted, and successfully too, every effort to meliorate their situation, or to introduce among them the most common arts of life," Cass explained. "Their moral and their intellectual condition have been equally stationary." Andrew Jackson adopted this Indian-removal policy, proclaiming in his 1830 State of the Union address that "the waves of population and civilization are rolling westward, and we now propose to acquire the countries occupied by the red men of the South and West by a fair exchange."[53]

The most popular visions of the American republic excluded Native Americans, even if Indians such as the Cherokee effectively demonstrated their ability to adapt to American civilization. Americans who indulged in the mania of Manifest Destiny not only justified territorial expansion by claiming providential sanction but also described their encounters with Native Americans, Asians, Mexicans, and African Americans in the terms of a republic in which whites occupied and dominated the land. When John L. O'Sullivan coined the term *Manifest Destiny*, he cast it in racial terms of the "irresistible army of Anglo-Saxon emigration." Senator Thomas Hart Benton saw "advancing Whites" bringing a superior civilization to "the Yellow race" in Asia, which ranked "far below the White" though well above the black, brown, and red races. Like these darker races, Asians "must receive an impression from the superior race" as they face "civilization, or extinction."[54]

Displaying a deep ambivalence about this form of American nationalism, Baptist missionary leaders attempted to reconfigure the blustery rhetoric of Manifest Destiny. Although they supported a certain kind of expansion, the Baptist Committee on Asiatic Missions in 1845 did not equate it with that of the American nation, market economics, or Western civilization. Neither did they tie evangelical expansion to the superiority of the white race. Admitting that "for centuries, the tide of colonization, conquest, civilization and evangelization, rolled from the East westward," the missionary committee criticized this form of expansion, except regarding how God might refashion these evil plans of humans for a greater good. God had made a "thousand discordant, unwitting or unfriendly influences, work together for his purposes," the report declared. Western merchants and colonizers, in their greed and sinfulness, fulfilled God's will in their expansion as unwitting tools for a higher purpose. The report declared bluntly that the selfish ambition of Warren Hastings, the first governor-general of British India, "was, in God's plan, making the way for the missionary zeal of William Carey," the first English missionary to India. Of course, by declaring that God used the evils of colonization to spread the Gospel, missionaries over time could lose sight of the sins of conquest and give blanket support for imperialism, as happened to some missionaries in the nineteenth century. Nevertheless, the missionary vision of the 1840s held that thinking in check among northern Baptists. And in rejecting the white superiority that infused colonial expansion, whose accomplishments did the Baptist committee uphold as the culmination of their reconfigured narrative of Manifest Destiny? The uncivilized seminomadic Karen evangelists, of course.[55]

Other Baptists were more direct. The *Christian Watchman and Reflector*, a leading Baptist newspaper in New England and a solid promoter of the Baptist missionary enterprise, offered something quite rare in mid-nineteenth-century America: an explicit critique of American imperialism. In August 1854, the editor, Hiram Graves, heard a rumor that a treaty was about to be signed whereby the king of Hawaii would cede power to the American government.[56] Since many Hawaiians had converted to Christianity through their engagement with the ABCFM, evangelical missionaries during the antebellum era considered Hawaii to be an example of successful missionary work and progress in civilization. Graves explained that a "Christian nation has sprung up from elements of the most savage and self-destructive heathenism," as he decried a proposed action by a "feeble sovereign" that would deny the Hawaiian people sovereignty. But Graves reserved his harshest criticism for the United States, turning his civilizing impulses on his own society. The Gospel had brought moral and spiritual triumph in the face of "indigenous paganism made more virulent" by the sinful actions of European and American residents who "have done their utmost to thwart and defame the mission." Graves's formalist evangelicalism contained a multicultural dimension, too, as he argued that the transfer of power to the Americans would cause the Hawaiians to be "denationalized and disfranchised." Graves closed by arguing that the governments of the United States and Great Britain should protect the independence of Hawaii, instead of seeking to make it "a new theatre of colonization and extermination."[57]

Graves's evangelical portrayal of Hawaiian Christian civilization faced stiff opposition from trends in anthropology and science at mid-century. Environmentalist explanations of human differences in academia rapidly lost ground to influential theories grounded in biological terms tied to race. An "American School" of ethnology emerged in the scientific circles of the United States in the late 1830s and 1840s, based on claims that craniology demonstrated critical racial differences. Some scientists argued for the existence of polygenesis, in which races represented different human species. Marshaling "scientific" measurements of the cranial capacities and facial angles of skulls that he had collected, Samuel George Morton published *Crania Americana* and *Crania Aegyptiaca* in 1839 and 1844, to argue that since the times of the ancient Egyptians, Caucasians had significantly larger brains than nonwhites. Morton distorted his evidence and reasoned in conflicted and selective ways, but he presented himself as a neutral scientist examining facts, uncommitted to any preconceived ideas or theories. His studies in craniology would continue to influence scientific racism for decades to follow. One phrenologist, for instance, wrote in 1839 that individuals and nations could be distinguished by the size of their brains, which explained why Native Americans "remain to the present hour enveloped in all their primitive savageness and ... have profited extremely little from the introduction amongst them of arts, sciences and philosophy."[58]

At that hour, in fact, Baptist missionaries were busy introducing the arts, sciences, and philosophy to the uncivilized Karen from the jungles of Burma. In 1845, Baptists built a seminary in Burma, declaring that they intended to provide the brightest of the Karen evangelists with a classical education so that these graduates could fill the most important posts in their churches and "give a literature to their nation." This was at a time when Louis Agassiz, the world-famous botanist and Harvard University professor, argued that history demonstrated that the "inferior races" needed different educational programs. "It seems to us to be mock-philanthropy and mock-philosophy to assume that all races have the same abilities, enjoy the same powers, and show the same natural dispositions," Agassiz explained, "and that in consequence of this equality they are entitled to the same position in human society."[59]

Some Americans in the 1830s, '40s, and '50s espoused Romantic racialism, a type of thinking that described white Americans in terms of Anglo-Saxonism. Inspired by the literature of Romanticism, highly literate Americans identified unchangeable features of nation, language, and race as the characteristics that distinguished the particular achievements of one people from another. Romantic racialists produced a diverse range of ideas. Blending Romanticism with Christian humanitarianism, some abolitionists critiqued American society by describing blacks as inherently meek, affectionate, and peaceable, in contrast with lamentable Caucasians, who were inherently aggressive, warlike, and domineering. Southern versions of Romantic racialism gloried in an Anglo-Saxon stock that produced a chivalric civilization built on military conquest, racial expansion, and slavery. Most Romantic racialists, though, like the Transcendentalist Ralph Waldo Emerson or the historian George Bancroft, dwelled less on other races than on extolling the virtues of liberty, resourcefulness, reasonable behavior, and national purpose found within the Germanic and Anglo-Saxon origins of the United States. Although Romantic racialists varied in their estimation of the role that environment played in shaping national characteristics, the thrust of the movement was to grant different races inherent characteristics.[60]

When it came to conceptions of race and civilization, abolitionists proved to be the closest cousins to the Baptist missionaries in Burma. This makes sense, because they drew from similar cultural sources. In fact, sometimes they were not just cousins but one and the same person, since many abolitionists were also evangelicals. A large number of evangelicals supported both antislavery and the missionary movement, although the majority of the antislavery evangelicals opposed immediate abolition. Shaped by liberal democratic ideals and Finneyite revivals that preached the possibility of social perfectionism, many abolitionists after 1830 held out hope that white Americans could be persuaded to eliminate slavery.

Still, distinctions are in order. Some abolitionists embraced ideas of immutable racial characteristics, while others argued that the environmental influences of slavery explained whatever degraded characteristics one could find among blacks. Garrisonian abolitionists differed from evangelical abolitionists in their conviction that evils in society did not emerge from spiritual forces as much as they did from political economy. William Lloyd Garrison, who had grown up in a Baptist household in New England, had abandoned evangelicalism after deciding that the Bible sanctioned slavery. For Garrison, free labor and republican education, not evangelical conversion and Christian education, would cure whatever deficiencies slavery had instilled in blacks. Similarly to civilizing missionaries, most abolitionists expressed faith in black capability, although Yankee culture usually served as the yardstick by which they measured that capability.[61]

Just as Abbott and Mason were divided on their understanding of the role that civilization played in missionary work, evangelical abolitionists debated whether one worked first for a just society in which Christianity could then flourish or whether one evangelized first, from which justice would emerge. Evangelical abolitionists such as the Tappan brothers and Theodore Dwight Weld pushed for abolitionist reforms while supporting revivalism and evangelistic efforts. Revivalists such as Charles Finney, who supported abolition, believed that evangelism should take primacy over reform. All of these evangelical abolitionists, however, supported Oberlin College as a means to produce preachers and teachers. In a racial engagement that mirrored Baptist faith in the abilities of Asian evangelists, Oberlin became the first school of higher education to admit both black and white students.[62]

Finally, a very small cadre of African-American thinkers in the 1830s and '40s began to address racism on a theoretical level. In 1837, an African Methodist

Episcopal minister from Connecticut named Hosea Easton published what may have been the most cogent analysis of race from this era. Easton drew on evangelical faith, natural history and the African-American experience to criticize conclusions drawn from polygenesis. Easton appealed to the Bible verse from Acts 17, "God hath made of one blood all nations," a reference widely used by nineteenth-century African Americans. Differences among human peoples, Easton argued, emerged from patterns of historical and cultural differences, not "natural" or biological characteristics. Because it violated the laws of nature, the "complicated disease" of slavery shaped African-American life through harmful and undeserved suffering, while it simultaneously "educated" whites into the distorted and abusive terms of prejudice. Unfortunately, very few white Americans read Easton's analysis of race or took black arguments seriously, although the arguments of free blacks did convince Garrisonians and white evangelical abolitionists to abandon colonization and gradual emancipation.[63]

Similarly to Hosea Easton and many other African-American writers, Baptist missionary spokespersons utilized Acts 17:26 to understand race. "God has made of one blood all nations of men to dwell on the face of the whole earth," proclaimed an 1847 article in the *Baptist Missionary Magazine*. The Gospel, the article declared, contained "one great code of moral duty, equally applicable to the learned and the ignorant, the polished and the rude, the civilized and the savage."[64] Yet Baptist missionaries in the 1840s did not address existing racial theories as forthrightly as Easton. More significant was that their models lacked Easton's recognition that social systems "educated" whites into the distorted and abusive terms of prejudice. Even though Adoniram Judson had pointed out this cross-cultural problem in earlier decades, Baptist missionaries had largely lost this insight by the 1840s.

None of these particular schools of thought on race influenced the missionary wing of evangelicalism nearly as much as missionary engagement with nonwhites. Most American evangelicals, however, did not think about race the way missionaries did. Because evangelicalism contained impulses to affirm their own culture, evangelicals could be found in most of the different camps of racial discourse. As a result, missionaries constantly battled racialized trends that pulled evangelicals in alternative directions.

Baptist missionaries did develop a relatively coherent school of thought about race. It is found in the concept of the "native ministry." During the 1840s and '50s, Abbott's democratized-ministry ideal and Mason's civilized-ministry ideal both influenced Baptist missionary policy, even as the tensions within these visions persisted. As they began to see the key to their evangelistic goals residing in Karen assistants and the ordination of Karen preachers, American Baptist missionary leaders merged these two visions into a "native ministry" ideal. Regardless of whether a missionary leaned toward the democratized mission or the civilizing mission, American Baptist missionaries agreed that the "native ministry" would play a key role in the spread of Christianity.

Abbott's ordination of Myat Kyau and Tway Poh established a significant precedent for the American Baptist missionary movement. In 1845, the Committee on Asiatic Missions of the ABMU pointed out that with the baptism of two thousand Karen during the previous year, the growth of the Karen church exceeded the resources of the American missionaries. The committee concluded that the key to missionary success lay with indigenous leadership: "Our main reliance here, as in every highly successful mission, must be upon the native evangelists and pastors God shall raise up and endow." Other missionaries working among the Karen acknowledged that the Karen themselves had been far more effective evangelists than the American missionaries. Realizing that effective missionary work simply could not be carried out without Karen preachers, missionaries ordained eight more Asians between 1841 and 1849. Through the rest of the century, American Baptists would ordain a significantly higher proportion of nonwhites than other missionary agencies.[65]

Baptist missionaries had not, however, worked through all of their questions about how to develop Asian ministers, particularly if they were "uncivilized." To many in the Baptist missionary establishment, a thriving, orderly evangelical movement depended on a seminary training that matched what was enjoyed by the male missionaries from America. With the specter looming before them of thousands of newly converted Karen Christians gathered under the leadership of minimally educated pastors, Baptist missionary leaders began to push for an educated native ministry.

Mason's pleas shaped policy by provoking new initiatives for education. In 1843, the ABMU formed a Committee on the Education of Native Teachers and Preachers. The committee noted the progress already made in evangelism but argued that the press, literacy, primary education, and an educated ministry were necessary for Christianity to maintain any permanency. "The men whom we send out to preach must themselves be taught, or else a most imperfect type of Christianity must be propagated among the nations, and they would, in the end, in all probability, relapse into heathenism," the committee reported. The board recommended that special attention be given to "diffusing among the Karens the blessings of education" and the establishment of theological education for the native assistants.[66]

The board then sent Joseph Binney to Burma for the express purpose of founding the Karen Theological Seminary. Born and raised in Boston, Binney had earned degrees from Yale and Newton, pastored three churches in America, and served as president of Columbian College in Washington, D.C. Given this academic pedigree, it is not surprising that Binney pushed for greater theological education for the Karen pastors. Posing the problem in terms that would resonate with many Yankee Baptists, Binney asked how American ministers could meet the needs of American churches if the most highly educated among them had not even attained an educational level above that of a freshman in college. Binney's version of the native ministry shaped Baptist missionary policies for years to come.⁶⁷

Binney built his seminary project into a vision for creating mediating elites among the Karen. While the "gradual improvement" of the people then under way may prepare teachers and preachers, his seminary would develop a "class of men more thoroughly disciplined and educated." Within ten years, they would fill the "important posts in the church and for the people, and... wield a controlling influence in their councils." According to Binney, a small class of Karen "children and youth" had to be identified and actively developed in a school before candidates entered seminary. Karen leaders could be developed by training "the most promising" children for a number of years "free from parental interference." Under the direction of a competent female missionary, these youths could be given a classical education, with English as the classical language.⁶⁸ A missionary board report echoed these goals in 1848, describing the Karen Normal School as a "nursery" that would supply preachers, teachers, and scholars who could "give a literature to their nation." Even those graduates who chose to pursue other avenues would be "useful" to their country. And since "it is impossible to elevate any people while the females are ignorant and degraded," the normal school, in good Yankee fashion, set aside one-third of its positions for girls. Ann Judson would have approved.⁶⁹

As with most projects tied to the civilizing mission, a strong element of paternalism infused Binney's cross-cultural academic vision. The best-educated assistants, Binney declared, currently lacked not only knowledge but also the character needed to carry out church discipline. Without "our constant care and frequent supervision," Karen leaders would pervert their knowledge and abuse their power. "Error is already spreading, and discipline,—kind, steady, but firm,—is even now required," since all converts were "babes." Of course, Binney added, this is not surprising, given the history of Christianity: "the *safety* of the church, its purity in doctrine, practice and experience, is *endangered* just in proportion as its numbers are increased."⁷⁰

This stance reflected Binney's understanding of America. Regularly comparing the condition of the Karen church with that of Baptists in the United States, Binney felt that the Karen lagged behind Americans in the area of higher education but declared them to be perfectly capable of closing the gap. Binney estimated that within ten years, they could develop Karen leaders who could supervise individual churches and schools designed for popular education. The theological seminary and the school for classical education would have to remain under the supervision of missionaries for a longer period of time, but Binney did not venture to estimate how long that would be.⁷¹

Figure 2.1. A Baptist missionary school for Karen teachers in Burma. Illustration in G. Winfred Hervey, *The Story of Baptist Missions in Foreign Lands* (St. Louis: C. R. Barns, 1892).

Elisha Abbott found no problem supporting Binney's plan for a "well-educated ministry." After a two-year absence, Abbott returned to Burma in 1847, gratified to find the Karen preachers "steadfast and immovable." Still, the ABMU needed to supply "a large number of school-teachers," and "all the pastors must, of course, study with us before receiving a regular appointment." After he visited Binney's theological seminary and normal school, Abbott came away impressed with Binney's system, giving the executive committee an endorsement of the plan to provide a "thorough English education" to a "select class" of Karen youth.[72]

Any plan that was good for the Karen, of course, would be good for the Germans. With characteristic evangelical enthusiasm, Baptists missionaries applied the native-ministry ideal to their efforts in Europe. Here we see how the dynamics of evangelicalism could rearrange conceptions of race, ethnicity, and nationality. Evangelicals not only found it necessary to hold revivals within the "Christian civilization" of the United States but also sent out foreign missionaries to Europe, the very birthplace of Western civilization and Christendom. In 1832, while Baptist missionaries were following the "wild" Karen evangelists into the hills of Burma, the missionary board also sent missionaries to France, Germany, and Greece. Drawing on themes of primitivism that ran deep in early-nineteenth-century evangelicalism, American Baptists saw their missionary efforts in Europe as efforts to purify a corrupt church and, by extension, a corrupted Christian civilization. With liberal use of the adjectives *apostolic* and *primitive*, the Committee on European Missions reported in 1844 that their efforts in Europe helped to bring the first-century and nineteenth-century churches together. Even in "the cradles of Protestantism," the committee explained, the church in Germany and Denmark had "almost by an inevitable necessity, corrupted into formalism and embittered into persecution" by choosing to ally itself with the government.[73]

American Baptists described the growth of evangelicalism in Europe as the work of the "native ministry." Applying the terminology originally designed to describe the Karen in Burma, the board reported that it had appointed twenty missionaries to Europe, accompanied by ten "native preachers and assistants" in France and seventeen in Germany. Baptist leaders saw no hope of reforming the Orthodox church in Greece, so they sent missionaries to form separate, autonomous Christian congregations in the nation that prided itself on giving birth to democracy, Western culture, and the first missionary successes of ancient Christianity. Using language that could have been written by Elisha Abbott in Burma, the Baptist board described its plan for evangelizing Greece: "A church composed only of hopeful converts, independent, and as far as man governs it, self-governed, is our view of the New Testament polity, and our scheme for modern missions." As enthusiastic evangelicals, the Baptist missionaries also carried their native-ministry ideal to other areas of the world. Shortly after arriving in Ningpo, China, in 1853, Josiah Goddard wrote that it took missionaries too much time to acquire "a knowledge of the language and customs of the people, which but few, after all, fully attain." Therefore, the Chinese people needed to be "supplied with pastors of their own."[74] The native-ministry pattern, in some form, would be replicated everywhere Baptist missionaries traveled in the nineteenth century. That would include the United States.

3

The Native Ministry in the United States

The Baptists in Rochester, New York, were abuzz on July 12, 1853. The president of Brown University, Francis Wayland, had arrived to give an address at the Second Baptist Church. So many people showed up that the event had to be moved to the twelve-hundred-seat Corinthian Hall, a venue used for various public functions, including weekly abolitionist lectures by Frederick Douglass. Just one year before, Douglass had drawn six hundred people to Corinthian Hall, where he gave his famous speech, "What to the Slave Is the Fourth of July?"[1]

On this day in 1853, however, it was not the national debate over slavery that generated the excitement among the people of Rochester. Instead, they were agitated about seminary education. The New York Baptist Union for Ministerial Education had invited Wayland to speak at a ceremony commemorating the birth of a new Baptist seminary. Anticipating a controversy, Wayland had invested an extra amount of time preparing his three-hour speech. If he had wanted to spark public debate, he was not disappointed. His address generated two books, a flurry of newspaper articles, and a two-year argument among Baptists that swept out from Rochester through the rest of the northeast. Wayland's presentation may mark the only time in history in which a commemorative speech on theological education by a university president generated both high drama and popular interest.[2]

In the eyes of those Baptists in Rochester, though, far more was at stake than the question of whether a Baptist minister could properly parse a Greek verb. Wayland's speech, "The Apostolic Ministry," spoke to larger issues of religious institutions, the structure of society, the direction of the cosmos, and, interestingly, the development of Karen Christianity. This obscure movement of Christianity in the hinterlands was beginning to make itself known in the United States, affecting northern Baptist self-understanding, missionary policies, and, eventually, African-American life. Baptist missionaries had gone out to influence the world. World Christianity was influencing them.

It was fitting that the debate began in Rochester. A restless boomtown that had not even existed four decades earlier, Rochester mirrored the expanding fortunes and accompanying growing pains of northern Baptists. The population of the young mill town exploded after the western terminus of the Erie Canal reached Rochester in 1821, expanding from fifteen hundred to twenty thousand in a little more than one decade. Wealthy eastern investors, young unmarried craftsmen, Yankee farming families, Irish Catholic boatmen, female domestic servants, aspiring clerks, free black laborers, and middle-class merchants flocked to Rochester, seeking economic opportunity. As a critical cog in the commercial and transportation revolution transforming the United States, the Erie Canal connected the western agricultural economy to the eastern seaboard, and Rochester emerged as the social and cultural center that linked the surrounding countryside of western New York to the wider religious and intellectual currents of the world.[3]

In its very short history, the competitive, market-driven society of Rochester had generated an intense swarm of political and religious movements, each propelled by its own newspaper or journal. Avid newspaper readers, the people in the state of New York were second only to Massachusetts in per capita subscription rates. Most of the people of Rochester and western New York subscribed to several different periodicals, and the city supported seven nondaily journals, totaling more than sixty-five thousand copies per issue. Religious periodicals alone, which represented more than one-fourth of the overall total, accounted for 4.2 copies per person in the state in 1850.[4]

This amounted to a lot of reading, but then, there had been a lot to read about. In 1828, a committee of city politicians formed the Anti-Masonic Party, based on widely held conspiracy theories that Masonic businessmen and politicians were using their connections to gain control of the state. In 1830, Charles Finney drew national attention with a series of popular evangelical revivals linked to the temperance movement. Antislavery and abolition causes found supporters and detractors in Rochester, where Douglass had moved in 1847 to argue his abolitionist cause. Between 1848 and 1851, a new fascination with spiritualism and séances swept the region, after newspapers reported that two teenage sisters communicated with a spirit through a series of "rappings" in their farmhouse near Rochester. Susan B. Anthony and Elizabeth Cady Stanton stirred passions at the first meeting of the Woman's State Temperance Society, held in Corinthian Hall in 1852, when Stanton demanded that women be given the right to divorce drunkard husbands. Sabbatarians, Millerite Adventists, Mormons, freethinkers, and Fourierists also all found enthusiastic audiences in the city.[5]

Baptist evangelism, missionary work, and church building thrived in this sort of environment. Since 1792, Baptist itinerants had accompanied Yankee migrants moving into western New York. The Massachusetts Baptist Missionary Society launched systematic efforts to evangelize upstate New York in 1802. The fires of the Second Great Awakening produced forty thousand Baptist members in the state by 1825, and the American Baptist Home Missionary Society (ABHMS) supported forty-eight churches and eighteen missionaries in western

New York in 1838. Baptist growth seemed to increase the farther west one went. One decade after its founding, Rochester counted several Baptists churches, a branch of the Baptist General Tract Society, and five of the twelve Sunday schools in the city.[6]

Baptist successes produced growing pains. Many of the Baptist missionaries and evangelists in upstate New York displayed democratized enthusiasms that ran afoul of the emerging seminary leadership. During the 1830s, the sensational revivalist Jacob Knapp, who enjoyed wide success with his "sledgehammer" style of preaching in Rochester, Syracuse, and other cities, happily ignored procedural boundaries for the cause of evangelism. Officials at Knapp's alma mater, Hamilton Seminary, clashed regularly with this Baptist itinerant, eventually charging Knapp with financial irregularities. Conflicts did not simply run along lines between democratized evangelists and established educators, though. Baptist minister Elon Galusha, who worked as a missionary in Buffalo, held two master's degrees, served as a trustee of Columbian College, and helped promote Hamilton Seminary, collided with seminary leaders when he tried to bring an antislavery convention to a denominational meeting at Hamilton in 1841. Supported by Knapp and, according to Galusha, a majority of Baptist churches in the state, Galusha prevailed, holding the antislavery convention. But if the Baptists of New York could tolerate abolition, they could not abide Adventism. Fellow Baptist ministers forced Galusha out of his pastorate in Lockport, New York, in 1844 after he converted to the millenarian movement spawned by William Miller. Undeterred, Galusha set out as an Adventist missionary. In one session in March, he convinced eight hundred Rochester residents that Christ was going to return to earth the following October.[7]

The people of upstate New York took all of these issues seriously. They engaged questions of theology, salvation, slavery, women's rights, the structure of society, republican institutions, the future of humanity, and God's role in the events of history. And that is why Baptists in Rochester in that July of 1853 were perfectly capable of getting highly agitated over a speech about the education of ministers.

The ensuing debate laid bare existing tensions and competing impulses bound up in the Baptist missionary enterprise. In fact, Francis Wayland explicitly tied the concerns of the residents of Rochester with those of a seminomadic people living in the hills of Burma. None of those who commented on his speech afterward found this odd. Fully conscious of the previous decades of missionary work in western New York, Baptists saw evangelism as a task to be implemented among white Yankees and uncivilized Asians alike. To these evangelicals, missionaries extended the evangelistic activities that had given rise to their very own Baptist churches in upstate New York. Karen Christianity, then, functioned as a component of Baptist self-understanding.

A keen student of theology, moral philosophy, American society, and a host of other subjects, Wayland had spent several decades observing the Baptist enterprise in Burma. He had helped to shape the policy decisions of the Baptist missionary agency almost from its beginning. The acclaim he had received in 1823 for his address "The Moral Dignity of the Missionary Enterprise" propelled him from an unknown Baptist preacher in Boston to a leading spokesperson of American evangelicalism. Wayland not only played a key role in reorganizing the Baptist missionary agency in 1826 and 1845, but he also regularly served on the board of managers, acted as its corresponding secretary, and worked as editor for the mouthpiece of the movement, the *Baptist Missionary Magazine*. When the patriarch of Baptist missionaries, Adoniram Judson, died in 1853, Wayland wrote the official biography.[8]

By that time, Wayland had been working for several years to rein in the role that education played within the work of the American Baptist Missionary Union (ABMU). This was an odd stance, coming as it did from a college president, the author of the most widely used moral philosophy textbook in American colleges, and the most prominent intellectual among American Baptists. Wayland had first raised the education question while chairing a committee on expenditures during the 1848 ABMU annual meeting. The committee had been formed, in part, because the vigorous growth of Karen Christianity had compelled the ABMU to establish priorities for the use of its limited resources. Wayland asked whether the board should not consciously reemphasize the primacy of oral preaching, not just by missionaries but also by "native assistants." He took care to indicate that theological schools, though "invaluable," should "not be multiplied beyond necessity."[9]

At Rochester, he laid out a more fully developed position. The Karen in Burma, Baptists in Germany, and evangelicals in upstate New York, Wayland declared, all developed according to the same missionary principles. Placing democratized evangelism and primitive Christianity at the center of healthy church life, Wayland termed this form of evangelicalism the apostolic ministry. One of those odd birds who actually worried about the abuse of power wielded by those with his same interests, Wayland warned against developing a "ministerial caste" set apart by specialized education. In what must have been a hard sell to the founders of a theological seminary, the university president declared that even though the church needed contributions from highly educated individuals, seminary education ought to be viewed as only one possible way of educating ministers.[10]

Wayland emphasized the influence of democratized evangelicalism in Germany, Burma, and America. In Germany, Baptists had gathered 4,215 communicants into forty-two churches in little less than two decades "without the aid of a single classically educated laborer," from a society where "education had been more widely diffused" than anywhere else on earth. Success among the Karen people in Burma came from "rude" and unlettered men who worked with only a few books, some tracts, and the New Testament. The "Holy Spirit was poured out, and sinners were converted" when "one, or two, or ten, or twenty" ordinary hearers heard missionaries preaching Christ to them. When these converts "in the jungle" formed congregations, ministerial gifts had manifested themselves among ordinary Karen who then told their neighbors about Christ.[11]

So it had gone in America. The prosperity of Baptists in western New York grew from the efforts of earlier generations of "plain men, generally of ordinary education," who "preached repentance towards God, and faith in our Lord Jesus Christ." Wayland criticized ministers who sought "to build up a good society" while collecting around them "the rich and the well-conditioned." A preacher will enjoy the most success whose "habits of thought are not greatly elevated above those of his hearers." Wayland took a clear stand on the civilization-or-evangelism-first issue. "The Son of God has left us no directions for civilizing the heathen, and then Christianizing them," he declared. "We are not commanded to teach schools in order to undermine paganism, and then, on its ruins, to build up Christianity. If this is our duty, the command must be found in another gospel; it is not found in the gospel of Jesus Christ."[12]

Wayland gave a stirring speech, but it did not go unchallenged. This was Rochester, after all. As soon as he finished his sermon, Barnas Sears immediately rose and requested permission to respond. Sears had served regularly on the board of managers of the ABMU and had sparked American Baptist missionary efforts in Europe in 1833 by baptizing a young German man, Johann Oncken, who worked as the American Baptist point man in Europe. No academic slouch, Sears held credentials as a Baptist minister, etymologist, linguist, scholar of Prussian educational methods, former professor at Hamilton College, secretary of the Massachusetts Board of Education, and editor of a literary and religious quarterly.[13]

He responded as might be expected. Wayland's plan, Sears declared, would derail Baptist progress toward effective theological education. As Wayland had, Sears addressed Christianity in Germany, America, and Burma in the published version of his speech, *An Educated Ministry*. Sears mixed the old custodial instincts of the religious establishment with a characteristically Americanized interpretation of the history of Christianity. Grounding his narrative in New World concepts of progress and republicanism, Sears promoted a nineteenth-century version of the Puritan "errand into the wilderness" theme, arguing that evangelicalism in America had planted and cultivated the best elements of the historic Christian faith in a new land, free from the corrupting influences of European Christendom. Baptists could revitalize a European Christianity "still shackled with the remains of feudalism" with a Gospel liberated by an American republicanism that had now "reached a point of comparative maturity and stability."[14]

Sears saw "*true* progress," in the form of public education, increased literacy, and higher education. These would infuse an often crass and ignorant American evangelicalism with the intellectual riches of historic Christianity. The greatest lights of the church from the apostolic era to the present had been "men of talents and learning," Sears argued, listing Origen, Augustine, Luther, Calvin, Edwards, and Adoniram Judson. "Rhapsodical and ranting preaching may produce high excitement with an ignorant people," he declared, "but it will not elevate them, nor fit them for well-directed activity and influence." He held up, apparently as a self-evident truth, the "pitiable spectacle" of Baptists in the south and the west as proof of the conditions that churches could expect when they did not accept the "guidance of a well-informed and properly qualified ministry."[15]

Sears's speech wandered into Burma, too, although this territory proved to be far less familiar. "Thirty or forty years ago," he declared, "there was scarcely an individual in all Burmah that believed in the existence of an eternal God." But now, he ventured in a wildly inaccurate claim, "probably not less than two-thirds or three-fourths of all the people believe in one." Baptist missionaries had elevated the people "not so much by oral preaching, as by books and schools."[16]

It may seem curious that Sears placed Adoniram Judson in the same category as Origen, Augustine, and Jonathan Edwards, but it fit within the "civilization first" school of missionary thinking. For Americans captivated by the image of Baptist missionaries heroically spreading the Gospel in exotic Burma but unclear on the details of how the process actually worked, the claim that Judson's teaching had been primarily responsible for the growth of Christianity could seem quite compelling. Judson certainly influenced many missionaries who followed him, wrote tracts in Burmese that Karen Christians had used, and brought Ko Tha Byu to Christianity. But Judson worked primarily among the Burman people, comparatively few of whom converted to Christianity. He very capably translated the Bible into the Burman, not the Karen, language. He did not produce literature for the Karen or educate many of them. These points seemed to be lost on Sears. He unceremoniously lumped all of the people of Burma together as those living in "a heathen country," revealing that by neglecting to make any distinctions between the Burman and the Karen people, the etymologist failed to identify any cultural or linguistic dynamics that might have helped explain the emergence of Karen Christianity.[17]

Sears saw academia as the heavy artillery of the missionary enterprise. "An ignorant heathen population" must be given educational institutions, he wrote. "Heathen children may be taught to read, and then, a printed Bible, a Saint's Rest, a Pilgrim's Progress, may reach more persons than the oral discourses of a hundred preachers." Evangelistic progress in Asia could only come at the hands of scholars who can "reason, and expound the Christian religion, as well as exhort."[18]

Scholars can also plot strategy. Sears and Wayland had already taken measure of each other in earlier skirmishes. At the 1851 annual meeting of the ABMU, Sears chaired a committee that sought for Burma what he believed Baptist churches in America needed: individuals with the "highest qualifications," meaning ordained American ministers with a seminary education. Wayland responded by declaring that he did not want the "impression to go forth, that no man can preach the gospel here, or in a Karen jungle, without having received a complete education." The proposals of the committee might be "limiting the Holy Ghost," Wayland declared, since the history of Baptists in America showed that "the men who have first struck at the root of the tree have been those who have been honored with but little education."[19] Here, then, lay a key difference in their dispute. Each believed that a particular kind of human flaw inhibited the growth of Christianity. Displaying democratized sympathies, Wayland worried that controlling elites would quash the gifts of ordinary laity. Along with his fellow formalists, Sears worried that those who interpreted the Bible for themselves would produce theological distortions and errors.

The audience at Rochester might be forgiven if they held an oversimplified view of religious life in Burma. While Sears probably constructed his perceptions of Burma from reports made by missionaries such as Francis Mason, he ignored, overlooked, or misinterpreted evidence that "uncivilized" Karen evangelists, rather than seminary-educated missionaries, had converted the vast majority of the Karen Christians. His conception of education and enlightenment allowed very little room for the possibility that poorly educated missionaries, let alone a barely literate convert like Ko Tha Byu, might be principal actors in evangelism. Wayland, meanwhile, recognized that "rude" evangelists played a critical role in the development of Karen Christianity. However, he overestimated the amount of preaching done by missionaries, as compared with Karen evangelists. And he tended to describe successful evangelism as a rather simple matter of identifying the correct techniques for mobilizing populist evangelists. Wayland did not, for instance, explain why the apostolic ministry did not catch fire among the Buddhist Burman people.

The 1853 Wayland-Sears debate lasted for more than a year. Fellow Baptists, naturally, joined the fray, publishing a flurry of articles and letters debating the merits and dangers of an educated ministry. These debates about theological education in the 1850s came firmly attached to issues such as economic prosperity, respectability, democratization, political power, social reform, and cultural custodianship.[20] As such, they shaped missionary visions that simultaneously supported and opposed different aspects of American culture.

By championing the laity and "unlettered" evangelists, Wayland promoted the democratized characteristics of American culture. That same democratized framework led him to argue that ministerial gifts could manifest themselves among the "uncivilized" Karen in "the jungle." His primitivism, however, countered modern conceptions of progress that saw higher education, rather than apostolic religious movements, as the engine that pulled society into an increasingly brighter world. Like many Americans, Wayland tended to place faith in pragmatic techniques to promote movements in society, but he also ran against the grain of modern thought by repeatedly granting specific agency to the "power of the Holy Ghost."

On the other hand, Sears embraced a modern faith in the power of unencumbered rationality and higher education to bring about a just and virtuous society, but he expressed more traditional doubts about the extent to which ordinary individuals could contribute to that process. His praise for progress and republicanism was built from the materials of modern America, but his assumption that this brave new world would be led by theological luminaries had been losing traction in America for more than a century. Sears's references to "providence" would soon fall from favor in academic circles, but he tended to cast these providential references in very modern terms, as an immanent force that unfolded in long developmental and rationalized processes. And unlike Wayland, Sears avoided references to the agency of the Holy Spirit.

A vigorous but unquantifiable proportion of northern Baptists shared Wayland's vision, while an equally vigorous but unquantifiable proportion opposed it. This may explain why the ABMU board did not announce the departure of two of its representatives until two months after they had left for Asia. This deputation consisted of James Granger, a Baptist pastor and member of the board of managers, and Solomon Peck, the ABMU official who had publicly struggled to make sense of the portrayals of the Karen by Abbott and Mason in the 1840s. The board instructed the two men to investigate and address a number of issues, the foremost involving the role of education in missionary work.[21] Peck and Granger left in October 1852, before Wayland had presented the *Apostolic Ministry*. They arrived back in the United States in early 1854, right when the Wayland-Sears addresses appeared in print. Even as Wayland and Sears debated each other in Rochester, Baptists in America waited to hear news of a six-week series of missionary meetings at Moulmein that Peck and Granger had concluded.[22]

Moulmein symbolized the center of American Baptist missionary activity in Burma. Its missionary history went back a quarter of a century to Adoniram Judson. All of the sixteen missionaries living there in 1853 involved themselves with some sort of educational work, but only one worked in direct evangelism, a point made by those who believed that the mission had strayed from its apostolic role of evangelizing before civilizing. Since his public musing about the "native character" of the Karen evangelists, Peck had shifted toward Abbott's democratized camp. At Moulmein, he pointedly asked why only eleven of the 120 preachers in Burma had been ordained.[23] Most missionaries at Moulmein seemed to take this question seriously, issuing a report declaring that "*A long continued supervision*... would be attended with many serious evil results," incapacitating Asian Christians for a "state of independence and self-sustenation." Five more Asian pastors were ordained soon after the convention.[24]

The relationship between evangelism and education proved to be far more complicated, bogging down the convention for twelve full sessions. All agreed that their primary purpose centered on the preaching of the Gospel. But further discussion revealed differences about what was meant by preaching the Gospel. Did the translation of Scriptures, the distribution of tracts, and the establishment of schools count? With the help of several missionaries, Granger and Peck attempted to steer the convention toward a fuller acceptance of Wayland's position, while carving out what they considered to be an important but proper place for schools. The final report declared that schools should be established for the purpose of providing instruction for Christians, not as a means of evangelism. The convention disbanded the Moulmein boarding school and restructured the Karen normal school. Theological schools, meanwhile, would train only those called to the ministry and would be conducted completely in the vernacular, since the convention worried that English would "denationalize" pastors.[25]

The use of the term *denationalize* is instructive. Decades of missionary engagement had compelled Baptist leaders to give deep consideration to issues of culture. With the possible exception of African-American thinkers such as Hosea Eaton, Wayland may have understood the thorny problems of cultural difference better than anyone else in antebellum America. Building on evangelical thinking, Wayland promoted ideas of culture similar to those that entered mainstream American intellectual life more than a half-century later, when Boasian anthropology appeared. In a report for the 1854 ABMU meeting, Wayland argued that missionaries should not "attempt to transform the Oriental into the European character by any process of instruction" but should "strive to improve and perfect the forms of character now existing, instead of making them into our own." Wayland argued that "a foreign people may give the impulse and set the example, but the natives themselves must carry the work forward." Furthermore, teaching should take place in the vernacular, for "nothing could be more disastrous than to confine knowledge to a few and teach men to despise their native language." Wayland pointed out the limited knowledge held by Americans of "a nation so very dissimilar from ourselves." With humility rarely found in nineteenth-century thinking about cultural differences, he urged his fellow Baptists to carry out carefully "our ideas as being ourselves learners."[26]

More than just the Baptist experience in Burma informed Wayland's understanding of missionary engagement. Challenging Alexander Duff's missionary theory, his report noted that "it has been said that the pupils of the best schools in India, as a class, prove to be the most virulent opposers of the gospel." This observation most likely came from Rufus Anderson, the corresponding secretary of the American Board of Commissioners for Foreign Missions (ABCFM). In

Anderson, Wayland had found a fellow missionary theorist and agency official who shared his concerns about problems of paternalism. Anderson attempted to steer the ABCFM away from its "civilization first" policies, arguing that missionaries ought to plant churches and move on, allowing indigenous ministers to lead churches.[27] Wayland agreed. In a letter to Anderson, Wayland wrote that when missionaries planted churches and moved on to new work, they broke up "the tendency to make every station a little Christian city, with translators, periodicals, presses, schools, and every element of European civilization."[28]

These policies coalesced into the Three-Self Theory of missions, in which missionaries sought to establish churches that were self-governing, self-supporting, and self-propagating. The Three-Self model, which affected every major American evangelical missionary agency, emerged from missionary contact with new movements of world Christianity. At the same time that Anderson and Wayland worked through their policies, another missionary official across the Atlantic, Henry Venn, worked to establish very similar Three-Self policies within the evangelical Church Missionary Society of the Church of England. In earlier years, Wayland, Anderson, and Venn had each spoken in the terms of the "civilizing mission," but the evangelistic success of "uncivilized" Christians led them to adjust their thinking. Just as Karen Christianity had influenced Wayland, Hawaiian evangelists influenced Anderson by leading a wide movement of Christianity in Hawaii in the 1830s and '40s. The evangelical activities of African pastors such as Samuel Ajayi Crowther had influenced Venn.[29]

This was not an insignificant development. Well beyond the nineteenth century, the Three-Self model and the civilizing mission vied with each other for influence, sometimes conflicting with each other, sometimes overlapping, and sometimes merging together to form new variations. The civilizing mission has received the lion's share of attention from scholars, since it very often found expression in missionary links to imperialism. Yet the Three-Self theory, which has received far less scholarly attention, persists to the present day, appearing in Christian bodies on every continent in some form or another, primarily because it meshes so well with the dynamics of evangelicalism. It informed the thinking of African Independent Churches. L. N. Mzimba, whose father founded the African Presbyterian Church in 1898, argued that black Africans desire to "plant a self-supporting, self-governing and self-propagating African Church." The theory became so deeply embedded within Chinese Christianity that the Communist government in the late twentieth century even appropriated the Three-Self terminology when it named its system designed to regulate Christian bodies detached from Western influences.[30]

Of course, American Baptists in 1854 could not foresee this. Focused on the issues of the moment, they were not about to accept the Three-Self Theory or the report of the Moulmein convention without a good debate. Before the 1854 ABMU meetings in America began, several dissenting missionaries in Asia had written letters to friends in America, who published their complaints in Baptist newspapers. These allies arrived at the ABMU meeting determined to challenge the report of the Moulmein convention. They put the recently returned deputation on the defensive by arguing that Granger and Peck had an "assumption of power" and "an arbitrary tone of action." Baptist minister William Hague argued that the actions of the deputation were "anti-Baptistical, and destructive of enlightened individuality."[31] Despite these arguments, most ABMU members supported both the deputation and Wayland. The ABMU passed a resolution affirming oral preaching as the top priority of missionary work. It then hedged its bets by vaguely adding that Christian schools were still necessary for the development of Christian life and the "elevation and progress of society."[32]

Resolutions do not silence loose cannons, though. Justus Vinton, a missionary in Burma who refused to attend the Moulmein convention, complained to supporters in the United States that board officials violated missionary freedom. Turning Baptist polity back on the heads of the deputation, Vinton argued that the ABMU board, not individual missionaries, posed the true threat to the independence of the Karen church. Vinton declared that his own practices that now violated board policies actually developed independent Karen churches.[33] The board of managers responded by deliberating all day and into the evening for seven days in March 1855, before upholding the actions of the deputation. But in February 1856, eighteen missionaries from Burma sent a letter to the ABMU complaining that the executive committee treated them in a hierarchical manner as employees, rather than on the proper "fraternal" basis as equals. Nine months later, Vinton resigned from the ABMU, the first of five who resigned by 1858. After the agency had reworked its policy to grant more independence and initiative to missionaries, three of these missionaries returned to the ABMU. The missionary mini-rebellion had been stemmed, but not before claiming Peck as a casualty. Having lost the confidence of the missionaries in Burma, Peck stepped down from his position as corresponding secretary.[34]

The dispute with the board diverted the issue from indigenous autonomy to missionary autonomy. For decades, individual missionaries in Burma had made countless decisions without much guidance from the board, a system that reinforced the conviction that their own personal judgment was the best standard for promoting evangelicalism. Like good American Baptists, these missionaries felt it was their right to minister free from the dictates of government, established church officials, or leading society members. They did not necessarily raise questions about whether Karen evangelists had the right to minister free from the dictates of the missionaries. This concern moved the board beyond its longstanding practice of simply giving the missionaries general guidelines and inspirational sermons. Thus, board policies designed to encourage independent indigenous movements provoked several offended missionaries to claim their independence from board members in America. The question became one of who was to be free from whom? And in what way was one to be at liberty?

The internal squabbles of the ABMU left a number of issues unresolved. Wayland's democratized-ministry vision did not effectively address how missionaries were to respond to requests for education or how Asian Christians were to attain financial self-sufficiency. The civilized-ministry vision did not contain a clear standard for determining how or when indigenous Christians ought to exercise religious authority. Both models represented different versions of the native-ministry ideal, one emphasizing the evangelistic capabilities of indigenous leaders and the other emphasizing their educational capabilities. The native-ministry model that emerged in the 1860s combined elements of *The Apostolic Ministry* and *An Educated Ministry*, while fully conforming to neither one. Baptist missionaries designed this synthesis to fit Baptist work in Burma. The American Civil War turned it in a wholly unexpected direction.

The people of South Carolina hardly expected to play a key role in the evangelical missionary enterprise when they entered the American Civil War, but then, few people foresaw the breadth and depth of the changes to come. War and emancipation unexpectedly created a situation that gave southern blacks religious freedom and northern missionaries a new field in which to implement their policies of the native ministry. The first change along these lines occurred after the Union navy attacked the Sea Islands of South Carolina in November 1861. Virtually all of the white landowners fled approaching Union troops, attempting to persuade the slaves, often by force, to flee with them. The vast majority of the ten thousand blacks of the islands stubbornly refused to go, for they knew that regardless of what awaited them with the arrival of Union troops, they would at least be out from under the bondage of the white masters. Over and over again, black Christians on the Sea Islands explained how they believed that God used the Union military as tools to help them achieve their liberties. "When I see the ships come to Hilton Head," one former slave explained to a white northerner, "I go into my little cabin, and fall down before the Lord, and pray all night.... Master was angry, but I must pray for the coming of the Lord, and his people."[35]

In these early months of the Civil War, well before the creation of the Emancipation Proclamation, Sea Island blacks took advantage of the absence of the white slave owners to stake out a free life for themselves. During several weeks of uncertain status, they tore down visible links to the slave system, destroying cotton gins and sacking plantation houses. A number of former slaves joined white Union soldiers in a newly formed black regiment, sensing that a Union victory would ultimately overthrow the slave system. Eager to construct their communities on new terms, the Sea Island blacks occupied abandoned land to plant potatoes and corn for their own subsistence, resisting any suggestion that they plant the "slave crop," cotton.[36]

The same independent spirit held true in religion. Many Sea Island blacks saw the absence of whites as an opportunity to enjoy the full fruits of the Christian faith, free from the limitations and controls that slavery had placed on their religious lives. Blacks did not attack the churches as they did the cotton gins, for they did not see Christianity as a slave institution or simply as a "white man's" religion.[37] Black evangelists preached freely, without worrying about retribution if their messages proclaimed themes of liberation. African Americans formed independent congregations, free from the controlling hand of white leaders who led antebellum churches. All across the south, freed people seized the opportunity to direct their own religious lives, fueling a boom in the growth of independent black Baptist and Methodist churches.

In one sense, it was true, as freed people sometimes explained, that they just wanted to be "let alone."[38] But the freed people also clamored for literacy and education, a prospect that presented challenges for their simultaneous goal of independent living. How could southern blacks learn to read and get an education when they had precious little income, books, teachers, or schools among them? In the end, African Americans would use the meager resources they controlled to establish educational systems. But they also welcomed the support and cooperation from those in power who were willing to protect their new freedoms and help provide the opportunities they sought.

This is where white northern missionaries came in. Right on the heels of the Union troops, missionaries and reformers from a rabble of different religious and philanthropic organizations also arrived. The Sea Island blacks flocked in droves to the schools that they set up. Black Christians saw the teachers as tools of God to ensure their freedoms and strengthen their religious life. One missionary noted that in their prayers, black Christians regularly thanked God for "this liberty, this opportunity, these kind teachers."[39]

But the freed people did not naively put full trust in all white northerners. Slavery had familiarized them with authority figures who spoke of Christian ideals but acted contrary to them. Evangelical and Episcopalian slave owners still broke up slave families, used violent means to control slave labor, and restricted slave religious life. The soldiers from the same Union regiments that liberated the Sea Island blacks in 1861 abused the former slaves in several ways, stealing their food, killing their livestock, and raping some of their women.[40] It was a painful type of inconsistency that slaves had grown used to. That is why a black Christian on the Sea Islands could say of a former master, "Oh, I pray, I pray he will be saved!" The former slave didn't "wish him any evil," but he still prayed that "he never come back no more, for he abuse we; never have dominion over we, no more, no more!" As in many other areas in the years to come, freed people made countless calculations about where to defend their autonomy and where to seek ties with whites. Sea Island blacks, for instance, were suspicious of those missionaries who held the position of superintendent but eagerly welcomed those who came as teachers.[41]

The northern Baptists were quick to send missionaries to the Sea Islands. The first to arrive was Solomon Peck. Eight years after his deputation tour to Burma and six years after relinquishing his duties with the ABMU, Peck began a new career in South Carolina, working for the domestic wing of the northern Baptist missionary enterprise, the American Baptist Home Missionary Society (ABHMS). Peck performed the same tasks among the freed people that Elisha Abbott had among the Karen. He preached, examined candidates for church membership, baptized those candidates, held communion, and helped train a fellow minister who had been appointed by the ABHMS as an assistant. Although the documents do not say one way or another, it is quite likely that the preacher who assisted him, Reverend Andrew Wilkins, was African-American.[42]

Peck and Wilkins were two of several dozen missionaries from New England, New York, Pennsylvania, and Ohio who descended on the Sea Islands in 1862. A motley mix of evangelists, reformers, businessmen, lawyers, ministers, abolitionists, and teachers from a range of religious backgrounds, they all had their own ideas of what the freed people needed. The biggest differences emerged between the evangelical missionary agencies and those represented by the American Freedman's Union Commission (AFUC), which was made up of reformers from Unitarian, Universalist, Garrisonian, and freethinker backgrounds. The evangelicals, who tended to emphasize conversion, religious instruction, and schools, brought with them a religious vision that had implications for civil society. The AFUC reformers, who tended to concern themselves with free-labor cotton production, moral instruction, and schools, brought with them a vision for civil society that had religious implications.[43]

Although these groups cooperated widely with one another, they also annoyed one another with their differences. The lack of piety in the AFUC camp bothered the evangelicals. The Methodist missionary Austa French publicly castigated a fellow reformer who failed to kneel during evening devotions, declaring that she hoped the offender "would *always* do it, and set such an example to the colored people." AFUC reformers, in turn, found evangelical religion too sectarian, too emotional, too impractical, and, too often, downright embarrassing. Years later, a few of them recalled the "contempt and ridicule" they received from "pro-slavery officers" when, upon the first arrival of the party at the Sea Islands, French had rushed up to a black woman and thrown her arms around her, sobbing, "Oh my sister!" The evangelicals, another reformer explained, appealed "too much to the Religious sentiment of the people" and did not work "sufficiently to strengthen them in principle and purpose."[44]

Evangelical missionaries also brought a different model with them for engaging the freed people. Instinctively and often explicitly, evangelical missionaries turned to the native-ministry framework from the foreign-missionary enterprise. Northern Baptists followed Peck's efforts to train black ministers, as did fellow evangelicals from Methodist, Congregationalist, and Presbyterian missionary agencies.

And yet emancipation turned the native-ministry model in a distinctive direction. White evangelical agencies discovered that they would not be doing as much of the evangelistic and ministerial work as they had expected. The earliest statements by the ABHMS of their work among the freed people stated that Baptist missionaries were to win the freed people to Christ, to gather them into churches, to teach them to read the Bible, and to train black ministers, a formula right out of Moulmein, Burma. Consistent with Wayland's vision for Burma, Peck seems to have seen himself primarily as a preaching missionary.[45] But white northern Baptists quickly discovered that while black evangelicals shared their basic religious commitments, they didn't really want whites as pastors.[46] The demise of slavery brought a new kind of religious disestablishment to the south, where whites no longer had the power to exercise religious authority over blacks. This, combined with Baptist polity and the instinct to adapt movements to the demands of an evangelical audience, convinced the ABHMS to adjust its missionary movement to the concerns of black evangelicals.

Black Christians, who were quite eager to evangelize fellow African Americans without white assistance, turned to whites for educational resources for their children, their teachers, and their preachers. Despite the missionary policies he implemented in Burma, Peck soon found himself, like the other missionaries in South Carolina, establishing a school for freed people. He eventually employed four black teachers and his daughter in the education of children and adults.[47] "I have a hungering and thirsting after education," said one black pastor, "and this school is the only thing that satisfies that desire." When the ABHMS invited a delegation from a black Baptist convention from Tennessee to speak at its annual meeting in 1868, a black pastor named R. L. Perry emphasized the point that "we want our people so trained as to call no man 'Massa.'" But Perry also asked for help, detailing the meager funds they had to work with. "We want to be recognized and aided, for we are trying to help ourselves," he reported. "Do all that you can for us."[48]

Baptist missionaries didn't need much prodding. They filled their home-missionary publications with the cause of educating preachers and teachers as their primary work among southern blacks.[49] The 1865 and 1866 annual meetings of the ABHMS resolved to "give especial attention to the religious education of colored preachers" by holding classes at central points. In 1867, the agency decided that they would establish institutions for this purpose.[50]

As the American Civil War and Reconstruction unfolded, northern white Baptists began to see their work in the south as something quite similar to what they had been doing in Burma. A racially distinct but largely illiterate people, led by enthusiastic and effective evangelists, had asked for education. As the ABHMS leaders explicitly pointed out, this was the native ministry in the United States. James Simmons, the corresponding secretary of the ABHMS, used the term *native ministry* to describe black pastors in the south, urging supporters in 1868 that "we must have a native ministry trained up as fast as possible."[51] In 1867, the *Baptist Missionary Magazine* published a letter from a missionary in Burma who, in what was now a time-honored tradition, exalted Karen Christianity as the guiding light of the Baptist missionary cause. This time, however, he did this to defend home missionaries who had been criticized for trying to teach theology to African-American pastors who had limited reading and spelling skills. "Every Burman missionary in Burmah is giving instruction in theology to native preachers who cannot write and spell correctly," he explained. Bridging the racial divide also, he went on to point out that few of the white "pioneer Baptist ministers" in New York and Pennsylvania could have "written out and spelled correctly a report of their labors," yet they converted souls, planted churches, and prepared the way to establish Baptist seminaries.[52]

Missionary comparisons between Burma and the American south continued into the 1880s, usually employing the terminology of the native ministry.[53] African-American leaders did not miss the conceptual link between black education and foreign missions, either. Joseph E. Jones, a black Baptist professor at the Richmond Institute, urged delegates at the 1880 ABHMS meeting to continue to educate and Christianize African Americans "as you do the Indian, the Burmese, the Chinese, and the other races of the world." Jones, however, pointedly included an admonition with his plea: "Do not check and modify their efforts to rise higher in the scale of being by telling them they cannot become the equals of white men."[54]

In May 1867, the ABMU and the ABHMS, the foreign- and home-mission agencies of the northern Baptists, held their annual meetings back-to-back at the First Baptist Church in Chicago. A fitting meeting location, Chicago symbolized the new centralized urban centers of Gilded Age America, led by a rising middle class of professional bureaucrats, academics, and business leaders. Adopting the nation-building characteristics that had previously been claimed by ministers, the industrial elites of the Gilded Age saw their regulation and control of an increasingly complex industrial society as a necessary condition for progress and advanced civilization.[55]

Affirming these cultural trends, many Baptist missionary leaders shifted the terms of the native ministry away from Wayland's democratized ideal, with its antiformalist impulses, to the formalist institution building of the civilizing mission. Since most of the men who established policy served on both the ABHMS and the ABMU, this vision took hold in both the home- and foreign-missionary agencies.[56] Baptist missionaries were to train leaders to provide the proper foundation for their civilizations, whether in Burma, the American south, or elsewhere.

If Christianity were to remain "pure and permanent among an unlettered and ignorant people," declared William Hague, the outspoken critic of the 1853 deputation to Burma, "then schools must follow close upon the heels of the church, and education in the wake of faith."⁵⁷ With Wayland most likely in mind, the executive committee of the ABMU declared that fifteen years previously, some had doubted "the wisdom of expending so much labor and money" on education. All missionaries in Asia now supported such a policy, "and some of them even go so far as to tell us that such schools are indispensable to success."⁵⁸

So it ran in the ABHMS meeting. A home missionary told his audience at Chicago that all across the south, black Baptists had separated from white churches and "desire to have pastors of their own race." But, he continued, sounding like Francis Mason in Burma in the 1840s, "these pastors are not competent to render efficient service without training. Who shall give them this training? Northern Baptists only are prepared to undertake it."⁵⁹ Another missionary emphasized the importance of the "education of colored ministers" by noting that blacks were "henceforth to take part with us in the race of civilization. They are hereafter to stand side by side with us."⁶⁰

If the need to provide freed people with higher education encouraged a formalist evangelical missionary vision, the increased influence of a civilizing role for missionary women sealed the deal. During the 1860s, women within the major evangelical denominations began to argue for an increased and distinctive role in the missionary movement, one that went beyond a secondary role as an assistant to male missionaries. Many turned to female institution building to accomplish their goals. In 1868, Congregational women established a foreign-missionary agency for women, with ties to the ABCFM. Women in the other major evangelical agencies quickly followed suit, including Baptist women, who established the Woman's Baptist Foreign Missionary Society in 1871.⁶¹

The primary justification for these missionary institutions lay in a missionary theory known as Woman's Work for Woman. These women argued that patterns of gender segregation in many Asian cultures gave male missionaries no effective way to make contact with Asian women. Female missionaries, though, could transform Indian society by bringing Christian womanhood to the home, an institution that many saw as the foundation of civilization. "When the wife and mother is converted, the influence extends to the whole household," explained the Baptist editor of *The Helping Hand*, adding "in most of the heathen countries, none but women can reach women." Victorian conceptions of the school as a site suited for the virtuous, nurturing gifts of women further reinforced the importance of education in missionary work. In its most forceful forms, the Woman's Work for Woman concept neatly wove conversion, domesticity and civilization into a seamless whole. The opening issue of the Methodist periodical, *Heathen Woman's Friend*, laid the groundwork for the next four decades with the declaration that "to Christianize the women, would be to capture their stronghold, and insure a better civilization."⁶²

Baptist men who overlooked the role of women in the missionary movement were doomed to swim against a powerful current in American culture. In 1853,

Wayland had ordinary men in mind when he spoke of an apostolic movement in America and Burma. On the one hand, this reflected a patriarchal element in American culture, in which men were seen as the primary leaders and authorities of religious life. On the other hand, Wayland's democratized support for the gifts of the laity unintentionally pointed to forces that were changing the roles of women in America. Women had formed the backbone of evangelical church life since the beginning of the century, outnumbering men in revivals and church membership. By the 1830s, Yankee women had established prayer groups, missionary societies, charitable organizations, maternal associations, and Sabbath school organizations. In 1890, women accounted for 60 percent of all American missionaries.[63] Consistent with Wayland's observations about laity, if not his thinking about gender, the men in the Baptist hierarchy faced a rising tide of women who considered themselves "generally of ordinary education," dedicated to a life of prayer, "full of the Holy Ghost," and "responsible for making known to those that were around [them] the truth as it is in Jesus."[64]

Among Baptist missionary women, antiformalist and formalist impulses had battled for decades, but formalist impulses gained the upper hand during the Gilded Age. In the heady years of the 1830s, Karen Christianity helped to draw antiformalist impulses out of Sarah Boardman, Calista Vinton, Deborah Wade, and Eleanor Macomber, who disregarded existing gender roles to preach, itinerate, and supervise evangelists. Had Wayland seen fit to address the ministerial gifts of women, a good portion of the rising tide of female missionaries might have embraced his apostolic vision. But the men who debated missionary policies in the 1850s did not pay attention to the activities of women missionaries. By then, most northern Baptist women and men were busy adapting to middle-class Victorian culture, which linked women to civilization building.[65]

Thus, eighteen missionaries from Burma sent a report to the ABMU in 1867, proposing the establishment of a Burmese female boarding school. Even though the report admitted that the people of Burma did not make a request for this type of institution, it declared that the school "would exert a direct and powerful influence in favor of Christian civilization in Burmah." Gendered arguments also animated support for institution building among the freed people. Two months before the Chicago meeting, the *Macedonian and Home Mission Record* argued that it needed "intelligent Christian women" in the south who "shall exert a potent influence in the molding of the social character of colored Baptist churches, now in a formative state."[66]

The passion for institution building did not eliminate antiformalist impulses among northern Baptists. The ABMU maintained faith in the evangelistic capabilities of "uncivilized" nonwhites, ordaining 343 indigenous ministers by 1886, two and a half times more than the ABCFM, which boasted twice as many foreign missionaries.[67] Meanwhile, Adoniram Judson Gordon emerged as a vocal critic of missionary efforts to build Christian civilizations. Pastor of the Clarendon Street Baptist Church in Boston, revival compatriot of Dwight Moody, and a member of the executive board of the ABMU from the 1870s into the 1890s, Gordon questioned the way education functioned in the missionary movement.[68] Reasserting arguments that Wayland had used five decades earlier, Gordon criticized efforts to work "from above downward" to catch "high-caste fish by highly cultured orators," instead of the "primitive order" of the Gospel, which reached "the lowly and illiterate" first. "Human wisdom says, 'Educate men that they may regenerate society,'" Gordon argued in 1893. "Divine wisdom says, 'Regenerate men that they may educate society.'" Several months after Gordon's death in 1895, an article in the *Baptist Missionary Magazine* argued that successful missions were not conducted by "the imposition of civilization—even Christian civilization—upon any people" but rather implanted "seeds of gospel truth," which, through "supernatural development," produced a type of Christianity "strictly national and natural to their environment" that "may not, and ought not to, conform exactly to that common in our Western nations."[69]

A few female missionaries, such as Murilla Ingalls, followed the antiformalist impulses set by Deborah Wade and Eleanor Macomber, rather than the formalist patterns of the Women's Work for Women ideology. Close observers of her published missionary accounts in the 1870s and '80s would note that Ingalls itinerated among Burman villages, preached, led worship, examined candidates for baptism, joined Burman ministers in voting on church members, supervised both male preachers and female evangelists, and instructed male Burman ministers on preaching styles.[70] Gordon upheld Ingalls to support his argument for women preachers, suggesting that "the spiritual intuition of the Church" has been "far in advance of its exegesis."[71]

Wayland's concern for autonomy also persisted, although northern Baptists now promoted this through the project of institution building.[72] At the urging of the ABMU leaders, almost all of the Baptist missionaries in Burma and seventy-five Asian leaders met in Rangoon in October 1865 to form the Burmah Baptist Missionary Convention, an institution designed to transfer much of the organizational authority to churches in Burma. Instructing the missionaries to make Asian leaders "a prominent part, we might say the *most prominent* part," in the convention, the executive committee advised the missionaries to "let them carry their measures sometimes, even against your judgment; better so, than to be always in subordination." This advice stemmed less from an acknowledgment of the fallibility of missionary judgment than from the ideal of autonomy, since it assumed that errors would come primarily from Asian Christians. "Let them have an opportunity to fall," the instructions continued, "that they may rise and stand the stronger, and *stand on their own feet.*"[73]

Back in the United States, the ABHMS elected blacks to its executive board, hired black professors to teach at its seminaries, and elected blacks to the board of trustees of the seminaries. ABHMS officials instructed the principal of the

Richmond Institute to aim for black autonomy. "The time will soon come when that School must be put upon a permanent basis and properly endowed, when we shall want to work into the Board much of the colored element," James Simmons explained. "Train them for it as fast as you can." Another white missionary in 1873 wrote that these schools "are theirs in the sense they *never can be ours*; theirs to cherish, theirs ultimately to own and manage, either with or without their Northern brethren; and theirs from which to derive untold benefits."[74]

Although cast primarily as the means by which God built evangelicalism, the native-ministry model also functioned as the means by which northern missionaries made sense of racial, ethnic, and cultural differences. In effect, new movements of world Christianity had provided northern Baptists with tools to form a distinctive racial framework. The native-ministry model sorted humanity into discrete racial or ethnic categories with clear labels but vaguely defined characteristics. It assumed that those vaguely defined characteristics gave evangelists from those groups, whether they were Karen or African-American, bonds of sympathy and identity with the people of their own race, which aided evangelism. The leaders of these racial or ethnic groups were capable of equal achievements in intellectual and moral attainments and could elevate the civilization of their race if they were infused with evangelical piety and a proper education. The *Macedonian and Record* exemplified the thinking in 1872. "Rev. Caldwell's report on 'Education among the Karens,' presented at Chicago, was admirably put, and applies equally to the freedmen," it declared. "Piety is power, but educated piety is a vastly greater power. This statement applies alike to red Karens, pale Americans and bronzed freedmen."[75]

The native-ministry model held important implications for the role that race played in issues of power and autonomy. Like most people in the modern world, American Baptist missionaries of the 1860s and '70s defined autonomy in racial, ethnic, and national terms. Northern white Baptists saw themselves linked to Asian Christians and black Baptists in a universal church, but the racial categories of the native-ministry model created an institutional dividing line between "theirs" and "ours." This formed the basis for autonomy.

Theoretically, autonomy under these terms seemed straightforward enough. Reality was more complicated. Evangelistic and congregational autonomy proved to be a far simpler issue than educational autonomy. From the vantage point of Karen or African-American Christians, academic autonomy could mean losing access to scarce resources. This dilemma proved to be particularly vexing for southern blacks, who deeply desired institutional autonomy. They fiercely protected their opportunities to direct their own churches independently, and many would have liked to have done the same with their schools, seminaries, and colleges. To that end, black Baptists formed the Consolidated American Baptist Missionary Convention (CABMC) in 1867 as an entirely black evangelistic and educational agency. Compared with churches, though, educational institutions are very expensive beasts. The 4 million southern blacks who just had emerged from slavery had extremely little capital at their disposal. Since the CABMC simply did not have the financial resources to build educational institutions on par with white schools, its leaders proposed that the ABHMS grant some of its southern missionary funds to the CABMC. ABHMS officials rejected this idea on several grounds. One argument, which was probably correct, predicted that northern whites would not give money to a black agency in which whites had no voice. ABHMS officials also found it harder actually to give up power when they could not set the terms for autonomy. The racialized divisions between "theirs" and "ours" cut deeply.[76]

It is more difficult to determine what the Karen Christians of the 1860s and '70s thought, but the missionary proposals for autonomy did not seem to interest them. Or, to be more precise, they seemed to be quite interested in autonomy but did not define it by racial and nationalistic categories. A group of Karen pastors from Bassein wrote a letter to the ABMU board in 1866, asking if the sons of the deceased Elisha Abbott might come to work among them. Explaining that they were "still weak, and there is still much poverty among us," the pastors lamented a decline in evangelism, conversions, piety, and interest in education among their villages. The Karen pastors were apparently unhappy with John Beecher, who had been in charge of their school during the previous five years. Beecher, who seemed to be more gifted with a spirit of personal autonomy than with a spirit of collegiality, had engaged in bitter disputes with Abbott in the early 1850s. A few years later, the ABMU had temporarily discharged him for refusing to follow agency policies. He clashed with older Karen evangelists in the mid-1860s. Beecher's perspective of his conflict with the Karen pastors stemmed from his judgment that the older evangelists were "incorrigibly illiterate, superstitious, and seriously obstructive" and could not be persuaded to step down from their positions to "allow some of the many well-educated young preachers to take their places."[77]

When Beecher left Bassein in 1866, the Karen pastors did not jump at the chance for racial autonomy, free from missionary oversight. In fact, the Karen ministers requested that a missionary work more extensively with them, traveling out into the villages to assist Karen pastors. They did not want a missionary to root himself in Bassein, as Beecher had done for five years. These Karen Christians, who had apparently rejected Beecher's attempt to install his choice of Karen pastors over them, displayed their own type of autonomy. Like good Baptists, they set their own terms for what counted as a good leader. In their minds, a cooperative missionary living among the Karen pastors was better than independent Karen pastors working with no missionary around at all.

To these Karen, kinship apparently trumped national or racial identities. The Karen evangelists figured that the sons of their beloved teacher would restore the previous "happy and steadfast" days. Their hopes were not fully realized, however. Abbott's sons, who were pursuing careers in law and medicine, declined the invitation. Instead, the board sent out Joseph Binney, who, after working to establish a seminary for African Americans in Virginia for a time, returned to reinvigorate the seminary he had founded in Burma in the 1840s. Once again, the attempt to implement autonomy turned out to be a complicated business.[78]

Karen Christians defined autonomy in different ways from white missionaries and African Americans because they worked from a different cultural context. Unlike African Americans, who had a long history with white control and oppression, the Karen had not experienced whites as people who dominated their political, economic, and religious lives. The Karen were much more cognizant of their long history with Burman and Siamese oppression, which is why many of them, Christian and non-Christian alike, sided with the British in their wars in Burma.[79]

Financial autonomy also had more appeal among prosperous missionaries than among economically poor Christians. Baptist missionaries, who sometimes spoke as if "self-support" were one of the New Testament fruits of the spirit, persistently pushed to make Karen or African-American educational institutions financially autonomous.[80] But northern Baptist congregations, which were awash in the robust economy of the Gilded Age, contained lawyers, clerks, small-business owners, and livestock farmers, as well as stockbrokers, soap manufacturers, textile manufacturers, and oil tycoons. Karen Christians, by comparison, had to borrow rice to survive a bad growing season. Many African-American Christians were compelled to scratch the parched economic soil of sharecropping for funds. Conscious of their comparative poverty, Karen Christians recognized that policies of self-support threatened to sever a vital link to educational, religious, and economic resources that they could not get elsewhere. Even so, under the missionary terms of self-support, the poorer Christians eventually needed to foot the entire bill. Karen and African-American Christians living in poverty contributed significant amounts to education, but in the end, neither group could scrape enough money together to make these institutions self-supporting. They were probably on the right side of the widow's mite parable, though.[81]

The native-ministry ideal embodied similar tensions in academic administration. Missionary convictions that Karen and African-American Christians could match whites in academic achievement paradoxically uncovered additional obstacles for institutional autonomy. The problem lay in the broader shifts taking place in American higher education in the late nineteenth century. The very first resolutions passed by the Burmah Baptist Missionary Convention of 1865 praised the role that education played in enabling Asian Christians to "approach the point of independence and self-support." Independence from "the guidance of foreign missionaries," however, could not be achieved until the leaders received "an education which shall approach in breadth and thoroughness to that of their present foreign teachers." In 1873, ABMU leaders calculated that effective education would enable missionaries to withdraw from schools after another twenty years.[82]

American higher education, however, evolved from seminaries to liberal-arts colleges to universities in the last decades of the century. Mirroring that shift, missionaries added new forms of education to their curriculum. In doing so, academics moved the goalposts of autonomy back. In the 1850s, Francis Wayland had based Karen autonomy on basic evangelistic skills. Missionary leaders of the 1860s and '70s had added a thorough theological education. By the 1880s and '90s, Baptist leaders not only required all of these characteristics but added the professional emphasis of administrative and financial-management skills to their list of qualifications for Christian leadership. ABHMS officials eventually handed black colleges over to black leadership, but the process proved to be contested, conflicted, and painful.[83]

Finally, while egalitarian impulses animated the Gilded Age model of native ministry, it did not encourage missionaries, Baptist officials, or American supporters to consider earlier missionary issues of how Christianity might adapt itself to different cultures. In the 1830s, '40s, and '50s, missionaries explained that Asian evangelists succeeded, in part, because they understood the language, "habits and sentiments" of their own culture better than the missionaries. In the Gilded Age, ABMU and ABHMS officials assumed that Karen or African-American evangelistic successes stemmed from their ability to match standards set by white missionaries, not from any distinctive cultural or religious understanding. In fact, missionaries in the 1890s found it harder than missionaries in the 1840s to conceive of Karen Christianity as anything other than a Western religion. The subtitle of an 1891 history of Karen Christianity, *The Progress and Education of a People from a Degraded Heathenism to a Refined Christian Civilization*, explained little about the cultural distinctiveness of Karen Christianity. It did indicate that the Baptist author and his readers had fully embraced the civilizing mission that coursed through the American establishment.[84]

Similar thinking shaped missionary perceptions of African Americans. The ABHMS pointed out in 1869 that the most effective home missionary in the previous year had been a black preacher. The writer did not conclude, however, that this preacher understood African-American communities better than northern white missionaries but exclaimed that "the complexion of ministers does not seem to have much influence with Christ, either way!" At the same time, white missionaries bemoaned the ignorance, error, "fanaticism," and superstition they perceived among African-American Christians and emphatically insisted that an educated black ministry would both elevate blacks and purify their Christianity.[85] Although Baptists looked upon this native-ministry model as one that advanced equality, it tended to promote a subtle but powerful sense that white northern Baptists represented the standard by which others must be measured. As one Baptist bluntly explained, the "superior training and force of character" made missionaries "chief among equals."[86]

And yet, even with its implicit paternalism and tone-deaf cultural impulses, the native-ministry model inadvertently challenged the most powerful beliefs about race in Gilded Age America. With the exception of former abolitionists in the Garrisonian tradition, no group of white Americans in the late nineteenth century operated with a racial theory that so fully recognized the capabilities of nonwhite peoples as did the northern evangelical agencies shaped by the native ministry. To be sure, those who operated with the native-ministry theory represented a minority among white evangelicals in the late nineteenth century, most of whom internalized a form of American nationalism that carried deeply racist baggage.[87] But the native-ministry model still had its impact. Without the influence of movements of world Christianity, the creation of black colleges, seminaries, and universities in the late nineteenth century would have been limited to a very tiny number.[88]

The idea was not a part of their missionary plans in 1861, but each of the major northern evangelical agencies eventually helped African Americans establish black colleges and seminaries. Some of them, such as Morehouse, Spelman, and Fisk, emerged as prominent black liberal-arts colleges. By 1882, the ABHMS had established twelve colleges, seminaries, or institutes for blacks, a number that rose to twenty-four by 1892.[89] While some colleges for African Americans grew from the heroic efforts of financially strapped black denominations, virtually every other black liberal-arts college established in the late nineteenth century came from northern evangelical denominations deeply involved in the foreign-missionary movement.[90]

The distinctive influence of the native-ministry model can be seen by comparing evangelical missionary work among the freed people with that of other white northerners. The Unitarian, Garrisonian, and freethinker reformers of the AFUC, who were similar to the northern evangelical missionaries in many ways, took a different educational path, based on a civic ideal of education and free labor. A handful of AFUC teachers continued to work in primary schoolhouses for many years after the Civil War, but the organization itself was short-lived. After primary schools had been built for the freed people and a free-labor market system had been established, financial support for the organization had declined. Most of its reformers had returned to the north, and the AFUC disbanded in 1869 with the declaration that it had completed its work.[91]

The same held true of other reform-minded northern whites. Most Republicans had tied their conceptions of black citizenship and education to a free-labor ideology. When this ideology disintegrated during the Depression of 1873, the Republican Party dropped its commitment to black "uplift," abandoned concerns for racial justice, and moved on to the economic concerns of the Gilded Age. By the time Reconstruction officially came to a close in 1877, most northern whites had decided that the problems of race should be left for southern whites and blacks to work out among themselves, a decision that reinforced an existing system of white dominance.[92] A small core of former abolitionist from both the Garrisonian and evangelical camps continued to work with black activists after Reconstruction to protect black legal rights, but they lacked the political power to implement their goals.[93]

The evangelical zeal of the native-ministry model, meanwhile, kept northern Baptist, Methodist, Presbyterian, and Congregational agencies involved in black higher education well into the twentieth century. Financial giving for black education among the four major northern evangelical denominations actually increased after Reconstruction ended. The missions budget for black education within these white denominations doubled from 1870 to 1891 and quadrupled by 1906, a trajectory that mirrored evangelical interest in foreign missions. More significant is that while few white Americans in the 1880s and '90s were willing even to consider the possibility of nonwhite intellectual capabilities, northern evangelical missionaries worked with African Americans toward the goal of giving black ministers, teachers, and administrators an education that would match that of highly educated whites.[94]

Philanthropists such as Andrew Carnegie and John Rockefeller began funding black industrial education in the 1880s and '90s, but their programs saw African Americans as little more than a source of manual labor for an industrializing economy. By contrast, the top ABHMS official argued in 1889 that Baptist colleges for blacks sought the "development of great preachers, lawyers, physicians, philosophers, scientists and statesmen," a distinctly different view of black capabilities. As late as 1888, the annual expenditures for black education from the ABHMS alone far exceeded the annual income of the highly visible Slater Fund, which funded industrial education for blacks.[95]

The native-ministry model for foreign missions reappeared in the terminology of the Talented Tenth, a term coined by ABHMS official Henry Morehouse (for whom Morehouse College is named) and then picked up by W. E. B. DuBois. Morehouse declared in 1888 that the best way to uplift the masses lay in bringing Christian teachers and ministers into contact with high intellectual influences.[96] That proved to be only a short step away from his 1896 "Talented Tenth" speech. Morehouse argued that industrial education might be satisfactory for "the nine men of mediocrity," but the "tenth man ought to have the best opportunities for making the most of himself for humanity and God." This statement very nearly matches the 1848 Baptist declaration of educating Karen preachers, teachers, and scholars who could "give a literature to their nation" and be "useful" to their country.[97]

For blacks, much of the appeal of the Talented Tenth model lay in its implicit support of social equality. DuBois reformulated the terms of Morehouse's

"Talented Tenth" speech into a call for black pride, declaring that black leaders "must be made leaders of thought and missionaries of culture among their people."[98] Indeed, the white Baptist missionary official Thomas Jefferson Morgan argued several times that black institutions could do for black men and women what Brown, Rochester, Bucknell, and Vassar had done for whites in the north.[99]

The native-ministry model not only formed a lens through which northern Baptist missionaries and other evangelical agencies viewed different races, ethnicity, and nationalities, but it also provided the basis for their engagement with southern blacks. Merging formalist and antiformalist evangelical impulses, it advanced local authority, while seeking institutional solutions to issues of autonomy and civilization building. The native-ministry model maintained faith in the capabilities of different races, although it also limited itself to those who adopted the Christian faith and often turned to paternalism.

We are left with an unexpected question: where would African-American higher education in the late nineteenth century have been without Karen Christians from the hinterlands of Burma? American society had long extended faith in the capabilities of ordinary whites. The native-ministry model extended that faith across racial and cultural lines, despite powerful countertrends that dominated nineteenth-century America. The "wild" Karen people of the lost book tradition never expected to have that kind of impact on American society.

PART TWO

4

An Appalachian Revivalist in Queen Victoria's Colonies

The missionary engagement with Karen Christianity produced particular kinds of paradoxes of power, culture, and influence. Missionaries saw their evangelistic goals, if not their educational goals, coming to fruition more fully when Karen evangelists operated without their direct supervision. These poorly educated but democratized evangelists translated Christianity into Karen culture while simultaneously undermining missionary conceptions of civilization. By bringing their missionary influence to Burma, Baptists found themselves influenced by Karen Christianity, as they developed a native-ministry ideology that guided their vision to establish black colleges in the American south.

Missionary paradoxes appeared again in other regions of the world where American evangelical missionaries operated, but the specific issues and situations changed. In South Africa in 1866, a revival that started among Mfengu and Xhosa Christians played a key role in reconfiguring the religious landscape of South Africa. A new movement of world Christianity gained vitality, bringing changes to Xhosa religion while reinforcing aspects of its traditional religious culture. Thanks to the evangelistic cooperation between an Mfengu named Charles Pamla and a visiting evangelist from the United States named William Taylor, the revival convinced British missionaries that they should ordain black Africans as ministers, temporarily challenging the conceptions of race and civilization emerging in the colony. This ordination of black Africans laid the foundation for independent black Christian movements such as Ethiopianism that emerged at the end of the century when white Christians in South Africa further restricted black leadership opportunities.

The revival of 1866 also affected American evangelicalism. It redirected William Taylor from itinerant evangelism into the missionary movement, where Taylor would emerge as the most popular American Methodist missionary of the late nineteenth century. Although the South African revival held implications for conceptions of race and civilization, it did not lead Taylor to articulate a new racial ideology, as Karen Christianity did within the Baptist program in Burma.

Instead, African Christianity helped convince Taylor that he could apply his old-school Methodism to non-Anglo peoples. Although he would never again enjoy the degree of evangelistic success that he saw in South Africa, Taylor's worldwide efforts to build old-school Methodism after 1866 sparked significant antiformalist impulses within American evangelicalism, laying the foundation for a holiness-missionary network that would, among other things, give birth to Pentecostalism.

Charles Pamla had a passion to communicate a message, and he was good at it, too. The grandson of a chief in the Zulu region of South Africa, Pamla sold his home and his farm to work as an unpaid evangelist with British missionaries farther south among the Xhosa and Mfengu people in the eastern Cape region in the early 1860s.

It had been tough going for this British Methodist agency, the Wesleyan Missionary Society, even though they had established more than a dozen mission stations among the Xhosa in the previous generation. When one British missionary reported in 1865 that his circuit had "prospered spiritually during the year," he ventured that "there is reason to believe that ... one or two conversions have taken place among the heathen." This is what counted as evangelistic prosperity when, after forty years of work, converts only numbered in the hundreds.

Figure 4.1. Charles Pamla. Illustration in William Taylor, *Story of My Life* (New York: Hunt & Eaton, 1895).

But that changed in 1866. In a cooperative effort among Xhosa, Mfengu, British, and American evangelicals, Pamla helped spark a revival that swept a land torn by war, famine, colonial conquest, social disruption, and spiritual uncertainty. Nearly three thousand blacks and one thousand whites in the eastern Cape and Natal regions converted in the space of five months.[1]

The 1866 revival hit a responsive chord among many Xhosa who, like most Africans, firmly believed that the spiritual world permeated all areas of material life. The Xhosa, for example, not only depended on their cattle as a source of food, wealth, political power, and dowry payments for brides, but they also sacrificed them in order to communicate effectively with the spirit world. Particularly concerned about the causes of misfortune, the Xhosa looked to the world of spirits to identify its source. In traditional Xhosa belief, dead ancestors influenced the world by bringing blessings or maladies. An individual who fell sick might be receiving punishment for a transgression or might be the victim of a malevolent spiritual force sent by a foe. The same went for untimely deaths, which particularly troubled the Xhosa. In several Xhosa oral traditions, suffering, illness, and death had come to the world because the people chose to believe a messenger who told them they would die, instead of believing a different messenger who told them they would live. These messengers had been sent by a supreme being who, like nature, was seen as unpredictable and undependable. Collective misfortunes, such as drought or smallpox, were not thought to be random or coincidental acts of nature. The Xhosa believed that these maladies had a spiritual source, either as the malevolent intent of witches or as a sign of divine displeasure at the disobedience of the people.[2]

The Xhosa certainly knew about collective maladies. By 1860, they had fought more than a half-dozen wars with the British in an attempt to stave off the intrusions of white settlers on their land. With each war, the British managed to assert more political, economic, and social authority over the Xhosa. In 1846, British colonial officials essentially instigated the War of the Ax in order to nullify a treaty they had signed after the previous conflict. When the governor of the Cape Colony, Sir Henry Smith, visited Port Elizabeth shortly after the war ended, he invited a Xhosa chief to his hotel, where, in front of settlers, he ordered the chief to his knees, put his boots on the chief's neck, and declared, "This is to teach you that I am come hither to show [Xhosaland] that I am chief and master here."[3]

Smith followed these public humiliations by openly tearing up the earlier treaty and annexing a large portion of the Xhosa land, which he then gave out to white settlers and those Mfengu who had allied themselves with the British. Smith also banned witch-hunting, an action that had the unexpected effect of intensifying fear and suspicion among the Xhosa, who now felt that they had no means of punishing those who sent malevolent spirits. When a terrible drought hit in 1850, a Xhosa prophet proclaimed that the nation could be set in order only if cattle were sacrificed and the British defeated in battle. A particularly ugly and tragic war followed. Unable to gain mastery over the mobile Xhosa warriors, British troops burned and destroyed the crops of the drought-inflicted Xhosa. Smith urged settlers to rise to "destroy and exterminate these most barbarous and treacherous savages." Some settler volunteers went into battle with "extermination" written on their hats. British soldiers killed unresisting Xhosa women, children, and elderly. Meanwhile, the Xhosa burned captive British soldiers alive, the same punishment they inflicted on convicted witches. While both sides suffered in the end, the Xhosa felt the brunt of the tragedy. As many as sixteen thousand Xhosa and fourteen hundred whites died in the war. The Xhosa lost more land to the settlers.[4]

Then a lung disease that afflicted cattle entered the eastern Cape region in 1854. As thousands of cattle began to die, a ten-year-old Xhosa girl named Nongqawuse prophesied that an ancestor had appeared to her and told her that the people had sinned. Once evil was purged from the land, the ancestors would rise from the sea, and abundance would come to the land. But in order for the resurrection of the ancestors to take place, the Xhosa must kill off all of their remaining cattle. The Xhosa were divided on the validity of this religious message. Some eagerly believed Nongqawuse and killed their cattle, while others refused to believe and continued as before. Still others wavered back and forth, hedging their bets by killing off most of their cattle but keeping some in reserve. Believers in Nongqawuse's prophecy attempted to persuade other Xhosa to kill their cattle. For a brief time, they even asserted that this sacrifice should also be undertaken by the British, who, after all, had their own sins to purge.

The cattle killings brought massive suffering, especially for those who believed in Nongqawuse's prophecy. By early 1857, children and the elderly began to die from starvation. Soon hardier individuals also began to succumb. Entire families gathered in clusters to die together. Some of the prophecy believers stole food from one another or cattle from Xhosa unbelievers. Others sought out distant relatives who had food or migrated into the settler towns or handed their starving children over to overwhelmed missionaries. A few turned to even more desperate measures, abandoning or killing their children. The combination of famine and deliberate slaughter led to the loss of about four hundred thousand cattle, devastating the agricultural and social system of the Xhosa communities. An estimated forty thousand Xhosa died, and more than three times that number became refugees.[5]

In Grahamstown, a group consisting of missionaries, the Anglican bishop, and several white civilians formed a committee in early 1857 to provide relief to Xhosa dying of starvation. Colonial officials, however, did not believe that the cattle killings were the expression of a sincere religious movement. They saw them as a political and military plot created by the Xhosa chiefs to stir their people to go to war against the British. The new governor, Sir George Gray, forced the relief committee in Grahamstown to disband. Privately agreeing with his top aide that the missionaries displayed "indiscriminate benevolence," Gray also refused to grant funds to the overwhelmed mission stations that were attempting to aid those who were starving. Gray was convinced, however, that the Xhosa could become "useful servants, consumers of our goods, contributors to our revenue," if they were properly "civilized." Gray took advantage of the disruption by implementing policies designed to break the power of Xhosa chiefs and move hungry Xhosa refugees onto white settler lands to work as laborers. Many European settlers interpreted this colonial initiative as an act of goodwill. Perhaps more than one hundred fifty thousand Xhosa were displaced, and six hundred thousand acres were turned over to colonial settlement. By bringing so many of the Xhosa under the influence of "civilization," Gray gained a reputation among the British, if not the Xhosa, as a liberal governor and friend of the Africans.[6]

Like the Xhosa, the Mfengu had spent several decades negotiating their way through a bewildering range of changes and collective misfortunes. A new ethnic group that began to coalesce among Africans who had been dislocated by various upheavals after the war of 1835, the Mfengu were probably mostly Xhosa who had moved into British farms, towns, and mission stations for a variety of reasons. Some had been seized forcibly by the British as indentured servants, while others were looking for work after their own farms had been destroyed. Some, like Charles Pamla's family, had been non-Xhosa refugees displaced by intra-African wars in the Zulu lands to the north.[7] The British government gave some of the Mfengu land so that their communities would act as a buffer between white settlers and the Xhosa who lived beyond the colonial boundaries. Colonial officials also encouraged rivalries between the Xhosa and the Mfengu in an attempt to divert Xhosa animosity away from the British. This might explain why the Mfengu developed a reputation for being loyal to the British and eager to embrace British civilization. However, a sizable proportion of the Mfengu clearly had been brought into Cape society against their will. Very few Mfengu had converted to Christianity.[8]

Even though these Africans resisted conversion, Christianity still influenced Xhosa and Mfengu communities. Even before the arrival of whites, the Xhosa, like most African people, had adopted religious concepts and practices from neighboring peoples. For instance, traditional Xhosa religion had acquired a large number of religious terms and conceptions of a supreme being from the Khoisan people a century earlier. In the decades after 1800, the Xhosa adopted a belief in resurrection, if not a belief in the divinity of Christ, from the missionaries. In fact, the Xhosa had been quite willing to turn to both Khoisan and Christian religious leaders to see if they could gain access to a spiritual power that provided rain. Several of the early missionaries, who apparently believed that God would bring rain to the Xhosa if they expressed belief in Christ, gave accounts of rain appearing after they had prayed. The Xhosa did not, however, respond favorably to the missionary insistence that they stop killing witches, since the Xhosa believed that this would only promote sickness and death.[9]

The few Xhosa who had converted to Christianity before 1866 tended to be outcasts from Xhosan society—political refugees, the disabled, alleged witches, those fleeing violence, or women fleeing abusive husbands. Along with several other unconverted but favorably inclined Xhosa, these converts had left their traditional villages to live on mission stations. The cattle killings provoked greater numbers of Xhosa to migrate to the mission stations, but unlike previous non-Christian migrants, most of these Xhosa were not favorably disposed toward Christianity or willing to submit to missionary expectations that they abandon polygamy or female initiation rites.[10]

It is difficult to determine precisely why so many Xhosa and Mfengu converted in 1866 but not earlier. It is quite possible, as some historians have argued, that the devastation of the cattle killings led many Xhosa to doubt the efficacy of some of their traditional religious practices. Since traditional Xhosa religion did not provide a clear and consistent means for determining the spiritual causes behind maladies, many might have been searching for new ways to handle the difficulties they faced. Even so, this interpretation does not explain why a decade passed between the cattle killings and the revival, although a drought that hit in 1865 might have brought a spiritual crisis to many.[11]

We do know that the revival came immediately on the heels of Charles Pamla's sanctification experience. Converted to Christianity in 1853, Pamla had read Wesley's sermons and began praying for "entire sanctification" in early 1866, after a conference with missionaries and African evangelists. Methodists often described entire sanctification as a second spiritual experience, similar to conversion, which empowered a person by freeing him or her from the control of sin. In early May, Pamla felt "a small voice speaking through my soul, saying, 'it is done, receive the blessing.'" He felt ease from "different kinds of thoughts, ease from the world, and from all the cares of the flesh."[12]

Pamla shared his message with the Xhosa people around him at the mission station at Annshaw. A church member found sanctification, and two non-Christians converted. Then three more converted. At a Sunday service a few days later, Pamla "put a few strong words in," to make his message "plainer to the hearers." The Xhosa congregation began to shake and cry aloud, as Pamla reported that "it seemed as if every one of them were condemned by the power of the Holy Ghost." Inspired by this reaction, Pamla held a prayer meeting after the service, then a third religious service that night, and then another on Monday morning. By that time, several people had come in from surrounding areas. Twenty-six members, a "backslider," and a ten-year-old girl "found peace," and nine non-Christians converted. A couple of weeks later, Pamla and a Xhosa evangelist preached at another mission station, and seventy more hearers "found peace." One hundred twenty more converted at a series of meetings he held at another station a few days later. Then Pamla returned to Annshaw, where he met William Taylor for the first time. The two teamed up for a series of meetings. Over the next five days, three hundred Africans converted. In July, Pamla traveled another fifteen miles to preach to an Mfengu settlement, where eighty more converted. By that time, more than six hundred Xhosa and Mfengu had joined the Christian faith.[13]

In some respects, Pamla preached standard Methodist fare that pointed converts away from traditional Xhosa religion. Telling his hearers to "trust the atoning work of Christ," Pamla drew from Wesley's sermons on justification by faith. He spoke of a "great baptism of the Holy Ghost" and described converts as "new creatures in Christ Jesus." Yet Pamla's message also resonated with a Xhosa culture that had not become disenchanted under the secularizing forces of modernity. Traditional Xhosa believed that if they misbehaved, they might bring disorder and injustice to "the homestead," which could refer to either an individual residence or their entire society. Xhosa prophets preached that the people must leave their evil ways to "put the country to rights," a message very similar to Pamla's call for the sinner to "repent and give up his sins." These prophets reported that they received these messages from spirits or ancestors, a pattern similar to Pamla's report of the small voice speaking to him and his conviction to "do as the [Lord] pleases." The Xhosa conviction that cattle sacrifices would reconcile them to the spirit world and bring "a happy state of things to all" was not far removed from Pamla's message of Christ's sacrifice and the resulting "peace" that came from sanctification.[14]

In fact, Pamla's revivalism might have resonated more deeply with traditional Xhosa ways of thinking than with the more highly disenchanted mind-set of the British and Boer settlers who had pushed their way into South Africa. Most modern people tend to compartmentalize religion, politics, economics, society, and the natural world, conceiving of religious or spiritual matters as private, individual affairs that have little bearing on the workings of the wider public world.[15] Even the Wesleyan missionaries, who were more willing than their countrymen to see spiritual forces at work in the wider world, did not believe that distinct spiritual forces caused illnesses, cattle diseases, or untimely deaths, although they did believe that the Holy Spirit brought conversion and just might, under very unusual circumstances, have something to do with rain.

The revival also challenged conceptions of race and civilization held by the British missionaries. None of the Wesleyan missionaries in 1865 would have dreamed that in a space of several months, an Mfengu evangelist would be instrumental in producing more converts than scores of British missionaries had managed in the half-century before. They also would have found it hard to believe that Charles Pamla was better equipped than they were for the task. After all, the missionaries were better schooled in theology, had more years of Christian experience, and embodied the qualities of a nation known for its advanced civilization. Pamla would have been seen as "semicivilized," at best.

In reality, Pamla was better equipped to lead an African revival than they were. He had a powerful speaking voice, sang effectively, and proved to be a perceptive observer of social dynamics. More significantly, Pamla held an expertise in the vernacular languages that the British missionaries simply could not match. As an Mfengu from Zulu lands who had worked with British missionaries among traditional Xhosa believers living under the Christian chief Kama, he knew firsthand the cultural complexities that his fellow Africans had to negotiate. The demographics of his audience reflected his variegated cultural landscape. Those who responded positively to his preaching were Mfengu and Xhosa, Christian and non-Christian. They lived on mission stations, in traditional communities, and in British towns. In other words, Pamla understood the African perspective of a world in which traditional and modern forces overlapped and intermingled.[16]

Not unlike the Karen evangelists in Burma, Pamla and his fellow black African evangelists impressed the British missionaries. By the time the revival wound down, a number of Wesleyan missionaries had become convinced that they needed to take the highly unusual step of ordaining black African evangelists whom they categorized as semicivilized. They might not have done it, however, without the contributions of a democratized, circuit-riding Methodist preacher from Appalachia.

Like Pamla, William Taylor had a passion to communicate a message, and he was good at it, too. Six feet tall, sporting a long, scraggly beard that draped down over a barrel chest, the forty-four-year-old American evangelist portrayed himself, in both style and substance, as a "Methodist preacher of the old school." Adept at charming his hosts, delivering folksy sermons, deflecting opposition, spinning humorous anecdotes, and promoting his own ministerial exploits, Taylor gained some fame after publishing two books (one that included "Embracing Incidents, Triumphant Death Scenes, etc." in the title) describing his preaching adventures on the streets of San Francisco during the California gold rush.[17]

In early 1866, Taylor had arrived in South Africa to launch an evangelistic crusade among the British and Boer settlers. He then stumbled into an evangelistic partnership with Pamla. The Mfengu evangelist and the California street preacher collaborated on an unlikely but successful revivalistic tour that increased Taylor's fame among Methodists worldwide (thanks to another book he published describing his "Christian Adventures in South Africa"). The revival also diverted his evangelistic energies into a foreign missionary career that would take him all over the world. More significantly, it convinced William Taylor that Methodism needed to rework how it engaged people around the world, a conviction that would eventually mobilize the missionary wing of the holiness movement.

Taylor did not come from the same mold as the respectable middle-class missionaries whom the British usually sent off to the distant realms of their empire. Converted at a camp meeting in the hills of western Virginia at the age of nineteen, licensed as a local preacher shortly thereafter, and admitted as a full minister at age twenty-one, Taylor had achieved ordination in 1843 without the aid of a college or seminary education. A member of the Methodist Episcopal Church (North), or MEC, he quickly earned a reputation in Virginia as a lively evangelist. In late 1848, while serving churches in Washington, D.C., Taylor had been asked by his bishop to move to California to establish Methodism among the emerging gold-rush population. After gamely telling the bishop that he supposed the Great Commission even included California, Taylor moved west with the initial wave of forty-niners. Fittingly, Taylor established a church in San Francisco that would not contain his restless ministerial energies. He seemed to take greater satisfaction in preaching in the streets to makeshift crowds of prospectors, sailors, gamblers, storekeepers, and whoever else might pass by, an arrangement that inevitably resulted in verbal contests and an occasional physical tussle with hecklers. After seven years, Taylor's ministry in California came to an end, when a fire destroyed a "bethel," or mission, that he had built for sailors.[18]

Casting about for direction, Taylor felt "an intimation from the Lord" that he should work as an itinerant evangelist and write a book describing his exploits in California, using the proceeds to help support himself and pay off the debts of his California ministry. After receiving permission to leave his appointment, Taylor returned east to work as an author and roving evangelist. Taylor's new evangelistic impulse, aided perhaps by the publicity and income generated by thirty thousand sales of his book, turned his ministry into a decade-long Methodist circuit-riding tour of the English-speaking world. He held revivals in churches and preached at camp meetings in cities and rural areas of New England, the mid-Atlantic states, Virginia, the midwest, Canada, Liverpool, Beirut, Australia, and New Zealand. In 1866, he accepted an invitation from a British Wesleyan missionary to visit South Africa.[19]

Taylor promoted a brand of Methodism that excelled in building movements within rapidly changing communities. Early American Methodism had encouraged both preachers and laity to use their imaginations to extend the movement throughout the young, expanding nation. Pragmatic, entrepreneurial, and highly mobile, these itinerant Methodist preachers had penetrated every corner of the American countryside in the early nineteenth century in their zeal to gather in converts, often arriving simultaneously with the whites who had migrated to frontier areas. Even though many Methodist ministers by the 1840s had "settled" into appointments that involved the care of just one or two established churches, Taylor served a circuit in western Virginia that required traveling over rugged, mountainous trails to poor, isolated settlements.[20]

Drawing on the antiformalist impulses of the early Methodist itinerants, Taylor sought converts in every situation in which he found himself and expanded the conception of sacred space to any place an audience could be gathered. He preached in fields, home drawing rooms, city markets, bars, jails, camp meetings, steamboat decks, and the California Senate chamber. He had preached from the tops of whiskey barrels in front of San Francisco gambling houses and seventeen hundred feet below the surface in a Cornish mine. He seems to have struck up a friendly conversation with every stranger he ever met, with the hope of turning the dialogue to spiritual matters. Eager to mobilize his audiences into an evangelistic force, Taylor began his revivals with exercises designed to identify "helpers," formed class meetings in each of his appointed churches, led family worship in homes he visited, and always elicited testimonies from converted women and men in prayer meetings.[21]

Taylor's antiformalist evangelicalism simultaneously affirmed and critiqued American culture. Holding a democratized confidence in ordinary humans, these evangelicals reinforced a pragmatic impulse that placed great faith in the human ability to produce desired results through the implementation of proper techniques, a characteristic that runs deep in American culture. In the evangelical context, this encouraged the belief that preachers with the right methodology could manufacture a revival. Most famously, Charles Finney declared that revivalists using "scientific methods" could produce results even more certainly than farmers who used the right methods to raise crops of wheat.[22]

Even with this faith in human capability, though, Taylor paradoxically believed that divine agency, rather than human effort or natural processes, ultimately controlled the events of the world, a conviction that ran counter to disenchanted features of modern belief. Antiformalist evangelicals were convinced that this divine agency could often be seen in direct, tangible, and supernatural ways. Reports of revivals deeply stirred evangelicals, who believed that they could see a transcendent and active God breaking through the ordinary material workings of the world to produce spiritual transformations. In the evangelical mind, the emergence of revivals, the growth of churches, the commencement of new missionary initiatives, and even anecdotes of individual conversions intensified a countermodern conviction that something more than human agency and material forces lay behind the workings of the world.

It was an evangelical style that could unsettle other Christians. In late April 1866, Taylor unleashed his peripatetic ministry upon the white settlers in South Africa. Apparently, they had never seen anything quite like an enthusiastic American revivalist in action. Immediately upon arriving in Port Elizabeth, Taylor presented a plan for a series of revivals to a British Methodist minister named John Richards. Obviously less enthused than the circuit-riding American about evangelistic prospects, Richards immediately lamented the poor timing of

Taylor's proposed crusade. He noted that the Catholics were holding a number of "imposing ceremonies" throughout the week to commemorate the opening of a new church, while a new independent minister was to meet the public at a tea the next day after preaching his first sermon.[23]

Catholic commemorations and English tea parties were not the sort of religious competition that worried the California street preacher. Taylor persuaded Richards to visit local stores and ask the shopkeepers to publicize his revivals. At first, Taylor waited outside while Richards went into the shops to announce his arrival. But in Taylor's estimation, Richards was not "raising the breeze fast enough." Taylor soon jumped in to insert ear-catching descriptions of his own revivalistic pedigree, mentioning Australia and California, noting the coming "work of God," and inserting an injunction to "bring your friends and have them saved by the mighty Jesus." Another Methodist preacher laughed when Taylor told him that the revival services would last until ten p.m., informing Taylor that the parishioners would not endure beyond eight o'clock. That night, Taylor dismissed the congregation at eight but invited people to stay for a prayer meeting. Most of the people stayed, and thirteen seekers "came forward," although Taylor felt that more would have made commitments if Richards had not ended the meeting at nine-fifteen. Taylor was encouraged to find that "we had some good workers, who came up promptly" to assist those seeking conversion "and wrought effectively." Over the next two weeks, Taylor averaged ten to twenty seekers each of the sixteen times that he preached. He also sought out those who "would not otherwise have heard" the Gospel by preaching on the courthouse steps to a crowd of about six hundred. There he improvised sermon illustrations based on a passing funeral procession and a bloodied criminal being hauled along by the police.[24]

From Port Elizabeth, Taylor moved on to the Boer town of Uitenhage, where he preached a half-dozen times to growing audiences in the Methodist and Dutch Reformed churches. Surveying a "very genteel-looking audience" at his first service, Taylor ventured that "we had some good stuff to work upon." When the congregation did not initially respond with much enthusiasm, Taylor worked at the next meeting to get the laity engaged. He explained that "a prayer-meeting should have more of the social element in it," meaning that the faithful should pray with others, tell their unconverted friends "what Jesus hath done for you," and, "as the Spirit may lead you," make efforts to "bring souls to Christ." Taylor then proceeded to sing a hymn and invited seekers to come forward "according to the method I had just defined." This altar call produced several dozen seekers who came forward to find peace and one stalwart who came forward to wield Calvinist theology against what he apparently believed to be emotional manipulation by an American charlatan. The young Boer angrily spoke out against the "blasphemous proceedings in this town," questioning Taylor's authority for leading such "outrageous proceedings." Taylor did not seem to be fazed by this conflict. According to his account, Taylor invited the religious adversary to sit in front and watch to see that this really was "a work of God." The man stormed out.[25]

All of Taylor's evangelistic fruit, so far, had been gathered among whites. In his initial contacts with black Africans, Taylor's Methodist enthusiasm wavered, perhaps the only time in his life that the circuit rider admitted any evangelistic insecurity. The California preacher had found it awkward and "very slow business" to preach through an interpreter. Concerned about the language differences, Taylor had little hope of "doing much good" with the Xhosa. He then traveled to the Wesleyan mission station at Annshaw for one night. Taylor, who had written that he really was called to "the English work," agreed to preach to the Africans as a favor to Robert Lamplough, the Wesleyan missionary at Annshaw. Lamplough selected Charles Pamla to be Taylor's interpreter.[26]

Ever intent on figuring out how to communicate his message effectively, Taylor pulled Pamla aside before the services and preached his sermon to him. The two then discussed the words and meanings of Taylor's sermon. In the midst of the conversation, Taylor instructed Pamla to speak naturally when he interpreted. Pamla cautioned Taylor that he must then "speak loudly sometimes," a warning that probably reflected his experiences with the more reserved British missionaries. "O, yes, as loudly as you like at the right time," Taylor replied, interpreting Pamla's comment to mean that the African simply wanted to use a range of rhetorical styles.[27]

It is likely, though, that Pamla understood this issue to be about more than just effective preaching techniques. Traditional Xhosa believed that when religious leaders spoke or sang in invocational settings, their very words carried power to engage the spiritual world. Pamla probably believed that Taylor had given him liberty to invoke whatever spiritual powers he could to unleash a supernatural engagement with the Holy Spirit. Although these cultural complexities were probably lost on Taylor, his democratized instincts led him to encourage Pamla's religious enthusiasm.[28]

Pamla proved to be more than equal to the task. The packed church that night consisted of Mfengu and Xhosa chiefs, Xhosa from the mission station dressed in Western clothes, Xhosa from outlying areas with their bodies decorated in traditional red ochre, and missionaries with their families. Pamla effectively interpreted Taylor's one-hour sermon. Taylor closed the service by singing "Why Will Ye Die?" a hymn that, possibly unbeknownst to Taylor, struck at the heart of traditional Xhosa anxiety about death. After each individual line sung by Taylor, Pamla sang and translated the lines into the Xhosa language on the spot. The audience remained silent during the whole service. Then Taylor asked for those who decided to "accept Christ as their Saviour" to come forward. More than two hundred filled the front, with "audible prayers, sighs, groans, and floods of tears."[29]

The sight of a couple of hundred Xhosa restlessly milling about at the front of the church seeking peace simultaneously pleased and unsettled Robert Lamplough. Reflecting a concern held by many British missionaries, Lamplough worried about what he defined as the emotionalism of such situations. The young British missionary suggested that Taylor dismiss the people and let the Africans go off alone to pray by the river, a practice that the Wesleyan missionaries had encouraged in the past. "The old missionaries have told me that it will not do to let them give way to their feelings," the British minister cautioned, "lest they run into wild extravagance." In the previous decades, Xhosa converts on the mission stations would sometimes unexpectedly break into dancing, loud weeping, or uncontrollable laughter during worship services. While expressive behavior was completely in keeping with traditional Xhosa religious practices, British missionaries saw this "wild extravagance" as a problem.[30]

The Annshaw revival opened up some cultural baggage that missionaries had brought with them to South Africa. That baggage arrived in the form of an intellectual and religious conflict that modern societies had been wrestling with since the seventeenth century. Many people from modern nineteenth-century societies contrasted emotions unfavorably with reason, since they were thought to compete for influence over the individual. Those influenced by Enlightenment thinker David Hume saw religious enthusiasm as an enemy of reason, leading to any number of evils, including social disorder, political radicalism, theological heresy, emotional derangement, and psychological delusion. Antiformalist evangelicals, meanwhile, saw enthusiastic religious expressions as a sign that the Holy Spirit was at work. They were quite willing to break social conventions if "enthusiasm" aided these religious movements. Some revivalists such as Jonathan Edwards and John Wesley took a middle ground, carefully distancing themselves from what they saw as the excesses of religious enthusiasm while arguing that fervent revivals were the means by which a loving God redeemed humanity.[31]

This long-standing issue of modernity reappeared at Annshaw, wearing new cultural clothing. Highly educated Westerners often perceived "primitive," "savage," or "barbarian" peoples to be at the mercy of nature, deeply enslaved by emotions and incapable of mastering the rational processes displayed by those from advanced civilizations. "The true savage is neither free nor noble," wrote British anthropologist John Lubbock in 1865. "He is a slave to his own wants, his own passions."[32] In the minds of Victorian missionaries, then, the "wild extravagance" of Xhosa religious expression could signify the irrational or superstitious characteristics of a people in need of civilization. More ominously, many British worried that the religious enthusiasm of black Africans could spark socially dangerous or potentially violent movements against colonists.[33]

Charles Pamla did not see the enthusiasm of the Xhosa as a problem. Just a couple of weeks earlier, this Mfengu evangelist had led a service at Kieskammahoek, where a congregation of African evangelists, church members, and traditional Xhosa shook and cried aloud. At the Annshaw service, Pamla and William Kama, a son of the Christian chief Kama, encouraged those who came forward in this expressive state, separating those who expressed a conversion experience from those who were still seeking peace.[34]

Taylor did not worry, either. Clearly cast on the antiformalist side in the old Protestant debate, Taylor had grown up amid an expressive, raucous revivalism in the hills of Virginia, where he regularly encountered "shouting" women, sobbing men, and prostrate seekers among his white and black audiences. In fact, these experiences had inspired him. As a young preacher on his first circuit, he had felt intimidated by the more respectable congregants, only to gain confidence when some "old sisters" began shouting "Glory to God!" during his sermon.[35] At Annshaw, Taylor reassured Lamplough that he was not simply witnessing "a rush of blind emotional excitement," for the inquirers were "now intelligently coming to Jesus." Taylor urged the missionary to let the revival play itself out, rather than trying to control it. "This is unquestionably the work of God," he explained. "We will just keep our hands 'off the Ark of God,' and let the Holy Ghost attend to His own business, in His own way."[36]

As John Wesley might have done, Lamplough briefly thought it over. Encouraged to see revivals unfold, he agreed to follow Taylor's advice. The fervent worship service continued until the unfashionable hour of midnight, when Taylor dismissed the people. The crowd came back for a sunrise prayer service the next morning, and then Taylor held an additional four-hour service at midday. Taylor left Annshaw that afternoon, but Pamla and William Kama continued to lead services over the next few days on both the mission station and out in the Xhosa *kraals*, where 165 more converted. An excited Lamplough wrote to his Victorian supporters that nobody had ever seen such a work "among the natives of Kama's tribe before, and I question whether there has ever been such a work for power and rapidity in this country before." He wished that he could follow Pamla and William Kama out to the *kraals* but had his hands full simply organizing the new converts on the mission station into Methodist class meetings.[37]

After the Annshaw services, Taylor and Pamla went their separate ways for several weeks, each holding revivals among different audiences. One month later, Taylor met up with Pamla, and the two set out on a four-month, six-hundred-mile revival tour. They preached at Wesleyan missionary stations, the Great Place of Chief Damasi, a Boer military camp, and the towns of Pietermaritzburg and Durban. Staying between three to ten days at each site and holding daily or twice-daily services, the pair preached to Xhosa, Mfengu, English, Boer, Mpondo, Thembu, Zulu, and Indian audiences. When Taylor preached, Pamla interpreted right beside him and not below the pulpit, as had been the practice in South Africa. Sometimes Pamla went off and preached to black audiences on his own, whereupon Taylor discovered how much he had come to depend on his African partner. On at least six different occasions in the eastern Cape region, they preached to mixed-race audiences in which blacks and whites came forward together to find peace. But in the Natal region, they encountered what Taylor called a "foolish 'caste' and 'colour' prejudice," and the two were compelled to conduct separate services.[38] A few places did not show much enthusiasm for the revival. Just about everywhere else, however, the people responded by the scores. By the time Pamla and Taylor had ended their tour, the British Wesleyan missionaries officially had recorded more than four thousand people as converts, about three-fourths of whom were black.[39]

At one point in his tour in the Natal, Taylor took note of a conversation between Pamla and an unnamed but "very intelligent and influential" British settler. The British man warned Pamla to stay away from the preaching of John Colenso, a famous Anglican bishop who had been creating a stir in South Africa with his unorthodox theology. The colonist worried aloud that the "learned, shrewd, and dangerous" bishop might shake Pamla's faith. "Shake my faith in what?" Pamla asked. "He might shake your faith in the truth of the Bible, and in the Divinity of Jesus Christ," the man responded. Thinking that this could not be done, Pamla insisted that the colonist give him the strongest argument that Colenso offered against the truth of the Bible. After some hesitation and a warning that "it might do you damage," the British settler finally relented. He explained to Pamla that Colenso showed by "arithmetical calculation" that according to the measurements given in the Bible, Noah's ark could not possibly have contained a pair of every kind of animal.[40]

"Indeed," retorted Pamla, "and that's it?" Unperturbed, Pamla replied that whatever modern "ignorance of ancient measurements" might be, if God had commanded him to build an ark and gave him the pattern, enough timber, workers, and "120 years to fulfill my contract," he would have made it big enough. "And I have no doubt that old Noah was as sharp as any Kaffir in Africa," he added. Taylor wrote triumphantly that Pamla had "at a glance grasped the fundamental points in the story," since one could not assume, as Colenso did, that a cubit should be twenty-one inches. Measurement terms in different parts of Mesopotamia could be of different lengths, Taylor explained to his readers, just as the sizes of acres differ in England, Ireland, and Scotland. Not only had the man failed to ruffle Pamla's faith, but Taylor proudly noted that "the Zulu took the bishop on his own ground."[41]

The anecdote reveals the existence of complex cultural tensions at work. Three evangelicals from three different cultures found themselves discussing questions that probed at a matter they cared deeply about: the foundation of their religious faith. Even though they used a common language and shared evangelical commitments, they viewed religious issues through their own specific cultural lenses, producing different conceptions of what was at stake.

The British colonist displayed the markings of an educated Victorian Protestant struggling to reconcile his faith with new epistemological claims. During the last two-thirds of the nineteenth century, scholars influenced by higher criticism, Darwinism, anthropology, and comparative religion challenged many of the authoritative claims of the Bible. A particularly heated debate had coursed through the intellectual and theological world of Great Britain after the publication of Darwin's *On the Origin of Species*. Many Christians felt deeply this challenge to evangelical biblicism and worried that it would undermine traditional Christianity. Others, such as Colenso, sought to reconcile religious faith with these new intellectual claims in ways that challenged several features of traditional Christianity, including biblical authority.[42]

In South Africa, however, epistemological claims were not the only issues at stake. The discussion between Pamla and the colonist also took place within a particular racial context. The colonist revealed a common nineteenth-century tendency within Western culture to categorize racial groups along some sort of position on a perceived scale of civilization. Despite his clear perception of Pamla as both literate and a Christian, the evangelical colonist worried that a semicivilized Mfengu did not possess the rational abilities to resist this challenge to the religious faith. Africans such as Pamla would have to advance farther down the road of civilization to handle effectively what the settler believed to be the weighty intellectual issues of the faith.[43]

Pamla, however, saw the exchange in different terms. His retort, "Indeed, and that's it?" very likely embodied two issues closer to his experience as an Mfengu Christian. First, modern debates about the scientific basis for biblical narratives simply would not have struck as live issues in his intellectual and theological world. Pamla lived among a people who had been inflicted with drought, cattle killings, wars, and the disintegration of traditional communities. Coming from an African tradition that believed that causal forces in society grew from supernatural and divine sources, Pamla would want to know the proper response to the Holy Spirit's activity amid these difficulties. It is highly unlikely that Pamla would have seen a debate over measurements in a biblical story as either very relevant or much of a challenge to a worldview based on spiritual causality. Second, Pamla's quip comparing the intelligence of Noah with any "Kaffir" (a term with derogatory connotations) pointed to racial tensions that existed between blacks and whites in South Africa. Pamla's response hinted at possible irritation or contempt for the patronizing actions of numerous Europeans such as the evangelical colonist who, at best, treated Africans as childlike in their spiritual and intellectual maturity or, even more perniciously, savage in their character.[44]

Taylor perceived the exchange through a third lens, which he presented to his readers. In its level of hermeneutical sophistication, his explanation provides what one might expect from a Methodist revivalist who held no formal seminary training and was not deeply ensconced in the academic debates of the Victorian era. Taylor offered a simplistic and easily understood argument against the complex ideas of historical and biblical criticism emerging at the time. Yet the most important questions of Taylor's faith involved the best means to spark revivals in the varied circumstances he encountered. Written for ordinary Methodist readers in America, rather than highly educated Victorians debating claims in the fields of biology, anthropology, and history, Taylor's anecdote quickly and almost perfunctorily disposed of the intellectual and theological issues embedded in Colenso's argument. In fact, in all of his writings through the end of the century, Taylor rarely indicated that the intellectual conflicts between religion and the claims of modern science bothered him very much.

Although he was aware of racial differences, Taylor did not see the complexity of the racial dynamics in South Africa. He did not highlight the racial dimensions of Pamla's conversation with the colonist. Yet Taylor's antiformalist instincts inadvertently short-circuited these racial issues anyway. In comparison with formalist evangelicals, Taylor placed less significance on theological education, worried less about the progress of civilization, and found more to admire in the enthusiastic spirit of the African revival. As a result, he championed the intellectual and religious capabilities of an evangelist who clearly belonged to a marginalized segment of South African society. He inadvertently challenged racist conceptions of African irrationality by writing that "the Zulu took the bishop on his own ground." In Taylor's missionary vision, the sanctified state of an Mfengu like Pamla would do more for the cause of the Christian faith than debates among Anglo intellectuals. To Taylor, the proof lay in actions on the ground. He wrote that during the five weeks when Colenso "caused such a lively stir among the newspaper reporters, correspondents and sensationalists of the church breaking order," the Anglican bishop had only *"baptized two babies."* Meanwhile, he exulted, "my Zulu and his black legion, and I, with my pale face," had converted in the same space of time "over 320 whites, and over 700 natives," a body that stood "in refutation of the skepticism and infidelity of the times."[45]

In the end, Pamla and Taylor had little impact on the "skepticism and infidelity" coursing through the academic world. However, they clearly affected missionary perceptions of the "uncivilized" Xhosa Christians. The 1866 revival emerged just at the time when Wesleyan missionaries had joined the transatlantic evangelical missionary debate over the native-ministry ideal. Methodist officials in London had been urging missionaries in South Africa to consider ordaining black evangelists, although missionaries were divided on the wisdom of this move. In 1856, Tiyo Soga, a Xhosa convert to Presbyterianism, had become the only black in South Africa to be granted full ordination by a British denomination. This ordination, however, had come only after Soga had outperformed whites at the seminary of the Free Church of Scotland in Edinburgh. While demonstrating that some Africans, at least, could master Presbyterian theology on its own ground, Soga's ordination also inadvertently reinforced a conviction that in order to qualify for ordination, black Africans would have to exceed the academic standards achieved by the vast majority of white ministers.[46]

Furthermore, missionaries in South Africa held deeper anxieties about granting authority to indigenous evangelists than missionaries in other lands. Conceiving of Great Britain as a Christian nation, many British supported colonialism for bringing the blessings of civilization to primitive societies, where lawlessness and superstition were thought to reign. Many missionaries, then, were convinced that blacks must be highly civilized before they could be ordained. The missionary practice of building mission stations to bring Africans under the institutions of Christianity further reinforced the conceptual division between the civilized and the primitive. Xhosa or Mfengu individuals who could be coaxed onto stations would be required to attend worship services, engage in "honest industry," attend school, and wear Western clothes, which would promote "the thoughts and feelings of civilized life."[47] Needless to say, the system tended to reinforce missionary paternalism. As the superintendent of the Wesleyan missions explained in 1850, the British "must think and act" for the Xhosa "in matters concerning their welfare when too ignorant to come to the right conclusions themselves."[48]

British missionaries in South Africa operated from positions of political, economic and military power similar to American missionaries working among Native Americans. As a result, they not only internalized the conceit that they could construct institutions of civilization to control African religious, intellectual, political and social life, but found it difficult to see how Christianity might function in alternative ways. Meanwhile, American Baptists in Burma, the ABCFM in Hawaii and the British CMS missionaries in West Africa operated in areas where, up to the 1860s at least, colonialism had not yet gained strength or even arrived. Identifying less strongly with a colonial "Christian civilization" and enjoying fewer tools of political, economic, and social power at their disposal, these missionaries were more likely to grant more freedom to indigenous Christianity.

Many of the Wesleyan missionaries in South Africa, then, worried that Africans were insufficiently "advanced" to handle the duties of a minister. Despite a fair amount of hesitation, resistance and skepticism, the Wesleyans tentatively ventured out on an experiment in 1865, putting Pamla and the three others from Annshaw on a trial period as "Native Assistant Missionaries." Under this plan, the missionaries would consider ordination after four years, but only if the evangelists passed a set of exams and effectively preached an annual sermon that the missionaries would grade.[49]

Then the 1866 revival broke on the scene. It surprised the Wesleyan missionaries, challenged their conceptions of black capabilities, and destabilized their missionary vision of a long, patient, "civilizing" process in which no more than one or two people converted at any given time. "I know not how to record it," reported a veteran missionary at the Healdtown mission station. "I have never witnessed anything which so reminded me of the scenes of Pentecost." Another Wesleyan pastor highlighted the surprising nature of the revival by asking his British supporters to picture the "unwonted spectacle of two native villages in the very heart of heathendom" where more than half the population had converted. "Perhaps you would scarcely find a parallel even in England," he quipped suggestively. Like Lamplough, formalist evangelical missionaries wrote of their initial anxiety over the "chaos" and "confusion" of the Taylor-Pamla prayer meetings, before reassuring their staid readers back in British civilization that they had managed to "get them into working order."[50]

Pamla's preaching abilities also astonished the British missionaries. One group commented that they "had never heard such a display of Kaffir oratory in all their lives." Describing the revival to supporters in Great Britain, Lamplough wrote that Pamla and his fellow Xhosa evangelist had done most of the work, "whilst I have not been used at all, so far as I can see." Not unlike Elisha Abbott in Burma, Lamplough used the revival to press the case for the native-ministry initiative. "One thing that God is showing us in this revival," Lamplough informed supporters in Britain, "is the necessity of laying hold of, and making effective, our native men, and employing them much more largely than we have hitherto done." Picking up a common theme of the native-ministry ideal, he argued that "we do not want more English Missionaries; give us these natives, and the work can be done,—yea, and done well."[51] Four years later, the Wesleyans ordained Pamla and three other Xhosa evangelists, before ordaining dozens more blacks in South Africa in the 1870s and '80s. Wesleyan actions helped to pave the way for the Free Church of Scotland, the London Missionary Society, and the Church of England also to begin ordaining South African blacks.[52]

In contrast with the British missionaries, Taylor pointedly informed his readers that there was nothing amazing or remarkable about either the revivals or Pamla's evangelistic success. Democratized evangelicalism had prepared him for this reaction. Well before he arrived in South Africa, Taylor had operated with an old-school Methodist belief that the church ought to be in a constant state of revival. As he saw it, the Holy Spirit often led ordinary people to evangelistic successes that highly educated church leaders did not achieve. Ten years earlier in San Francisco, Taylor had argued that sailors, hardly the most refined, respectable, or educated representatives of American civilization, could be organized into a great evangelistic force to bring Christianity to the world through the shipping networks. While touring Ohio, Indiana, and Illinois in 1859, Taylor had met Peter Cartwright and several other former circuit riders who had established Methodism in earlier decades by promoting unrefined, poorly educated settlers into leadership positions as class leaders, exhorters, local preachers, and circuit riders. Taylor consciously studied these old preachers and modeled himself after them in his writings. In South Africa, he extended these principles of democratized evangelicalism beyond existing racial conventions. Pamla's preaching proved to the British missionaries that God intended to use black Africans to evangelize Africa, "a thing that none of them believed before, or could doubt afterwards," he declared overoptimistically.[53]

Taylor's evangelistic style tended to blur distinctions between "civilized" and "uncivilized." He had earnestly preached salvation to Americans, British, and Australians, all of whom had grown up in what they considered to be a Christian nation, with Christian education and Christian laws. In Taylor's conversionistic theology, these "nominal Christians," who had a knowledge of Christianity but no conversion experience, still had not achieved salvation. So it went in South Africa, where distinctions between Christian and non-Christian did not always conform to simple categories of white and black, civilized and uncivilized, British and Xhosa. At Kamastone, the white Appalachian preacher and the black Mfengu evangelist reaped conversions from an audience that included a Xhosa woman "well-dressed in English costume," a group of "white colonial farmers," and a "heathen doctor...decorated with strings of beads shells and all sorts of trinkets and charms." The converts from Taylor and Pamla's revivals included mission-station Mfengu, British merchants, traditional Xhosa, a former skeptic of "personal religion," town-dwelling Zulus, and twenty-three sons and daughters of missionaries. Inspired by the scope of this revival, one Wesleyan missionary asked, "Why should not Colenso himself be converted?"[54]

In Taylor's antiformalist understanding, the power of Christianity emerged less in education and the civilizing process than in movements built on spiritual experiences of conviction and crisis led by the Holy Spirit. All of the knowledge essential for salvation, he wrote, could be acquired "through the quickening power of the Holy Spirit" in a single sermon, or even "the prophetic witnessing of a few laymen." He built movements rather than institutions, enlisting the support of Xhosa evangelists, local Methodist preachers, pious women, and any other converts in his audiences. He championed Pamla's indigenous theological reasoning over the modernistic assertions of Colenso; instinctively found virtue in Pamla's vernacular oratory; accepted the expressive religiosity of the Xhosa, Mfengu, and Zulu converts at face value; and urged missionaries to keep their hands off African spiritual expressiveness.[55]

This did not mean that Xhosa Christianity conformed precisely to Taylor's conception of old-school Methodism or that Taylor clearly understood the terms by which African Christianity actually unfolded. The roving evangelist did not stick around in South Africa long enough to wrestle deeply with all of these conceptual issues. Nor did he have much of an eye for social or political analysis. The structure of society, the nature of institutions, and the influence of education, all of which occupied so much American and British thought in the nineteenth century, did not deeply shape his thinking about South Africa and did not receive much examination. In Taylor's view, good and ill in society resulted largely from the effects of whether or not individuals converted to Christianity. In very rare instances, the term *civilization* appeared in his writing as a descriptive device, but he did not employ it as a major explanatory tool or bother to critique it.[56]

When his focus did drift from movement building to the role of institutions, Taylor reverted, without much analysis, to reigning patterns of Anglo thought. Just as he accepted the religious expressions of the Xhosa Christians at face value, he accepted without question the British explanation that the Xhosa cattle killings of 1856 were a plot by the chiefs to stir their people against the colonists. He did not analyze colonialism in South Africa and accepted without question the British portrayal of Sir George Gray as a wise governor. Taylor's portrayal of Xhosa culture followed a similar pattern. His collections of stories and anecdotes described different features of Xhosa culture, some of which he approved of, some of which he described with little evaluation, and some of which he believed to be harmful, such as polygamy and "witchcraft." Yet rather than describing these features as components of a systematic social or cultural structure, Taylor framed them in terms of individual choice and spirituality. In Taylor's mind, polygamy and "witchcraft" in Africa, like alcoholism in America, could be eliminated simply through individual responses to conversion and sanctification.[57]

The one notable exception to this disregard for social structures stemmed, naturally, from a situation in which Taylor believed that evangelism had been impeded. In a brief discourse that appeared in two British religious periodicals, a local South African newspaper, and his own book, Taylor questioned the practice of establishing mission stations. Mission stations, Taylor explained, had served a useful function by providing a sanctuary for black Africans facing the possibility of persecution, torture, or murder from their fellow people, either for converting to Christianity or because they had been accused of witchcraft. But mission stations created a "new state," which required missionaries to handle civil matters that not only extended beyond the proper role of a missionary but also stole valuable time from their evangelistic tasks. Naturally enough, the California street preacher suggested that missionaries turn to "aggressive" revival methods, rather than focusing on trying to nurture a few converts along in an insulated compound.[58]

In disregarding the civilizing mission, Taylor argued for a missionary model similar to Francis Wayland and Rufus Anderson's native-ministry ideal, with the critical difference that indigenous evangelists, rather than white missionaries, conducted the pioneering evangelistic work. While acknowledging the accomplishments of Tiyo Soga, Taylor argued that missionaries should not let "the car of salvation stand still" while "we are waiting for the schools to turn out such agents as he." Since nearly every Xhosa "you meet is an orator," Taylor suggested that missionaries send out a team of "the best native preachers" into the midst of the most populated Xhosa areas, where they could plant themselves, gain the attention of the people, and "dispute with them daily" until somewhere between one thousand and three thousand people converted. After organizing the people into a church under an effective local pastor, the traveling preachers could then "strike their tents" and move off into another highly populated area, while the local people would support the new church. Although he did not identify it as such, Taylor's proposal would transplant the Methodist circuit-riding system of early-nineteenth-century America to Xhosa evangelists in South Africa.[59]

Even though he did not give a lot of thought to the social, economic, and political structures of the Xhosa people, Taylor did display a relatively thoughtful analysis of the religious and moral aspects of African cultures. About halfway through his revival tour, he began to "feel keenly my inability to penetrate...heathenish darkness, and grapple successfully with their prejudices and superstitions." To remedy this, Taylor read several books about the Xhosa, spent a great deal of time talking to Pamla about African cultures, and listened to observations by missionaries he met. Pamla facilitated discussions between Taylor and several Africans, gathering the elders from many of their revival stops to question them about "the customs and faith of their heathen fathers."[60]

Like other missionaries, Taylor had arrived in South Africa with perceptions of "heathenish darkness" and African "prejudices and superstitions" in tow. But rather than directing his cultural analysis down the road of the civilizing mission, Taylor took an antiformalist evangelical path that disregarded Anglo conventions about the irrational nature of "uncivilized" Africans. Like Methodist evangelists in the early republic who believed that the Gospel could be easily grasped by ordinary people, Taylor argued that nothing about African culture prevented the Xhosa from making an intelligent response to the message presented under the Holy Spirit.

Employing what he learned from his discussions with Pamla and the Xhosa elders, Taylor developed a sermon that he commonly preached as an evangelistic message to Xhosa, Mfengu, Thembu, Mpondo, and Zulu audiences. Using Paul's model of appealing to the Athenian temple to the "unknown God" when preaching to the Greeks, Taylor began this sermon on the common ground that both he and the Africans agreed that they had all been created by God. Unlike many missionaries, Taylor assumed that God had been present in Africa before the missionaries arrived; he explained to both his African audience and his American readers that the Africans called God "Dala," "Tixo," or "Inkosi." As Lamin Sanneh has pointed out, the use of African names for God held significant theological and cultural implications. Taylor did not develop further or fully recognize the implications of this key part of his sermon, but it anticipated a standard practice that the vast majority of African Christians in the century to follow would insist on.[61]

Asking the Africans to "come then and let us reason together about this Great God," he proceeded to explain that they could all agree that God gave them a mind and a body that housed their spirits, pointing out that the Africans said that a person's spirit went somewhere upon burial. Taylor declared that the spirits that God had given them had the power to abuse the laws of what was right, as first undertaken by Adam and Eve and then repeated by the generations that followed. "A great many of the things we have told you to-day *you* know to be true," he said. According to Taylor, the ancestors of the Africans knew God but did not obey his laws. Over the years, many of the laws had become forgotten, and the African people came to fear God without knowing him. After explaining the doctrines of the atonement and the coming of the Holy Spirit, Taylor concluded his sermon by reverting back to common ground, presenting conversion testimonies given by British missionaries, Charles Pamla, African converts, and himself.[62]

His sermon not only validated the spiritual components of the traditional African cultures but also depicted spiritual powers and divine activity in ways that proved to be closer to his Xhosa audiences than to many nineteenth-century missionaries or twentieth century scholars. Like the Africans who exclaimed that "Satan is overcome!" at the moment of their conversion, Taylor wrote of Satan as a real person or power who influenced human decisions. In line with his Xhosa audience, Taylor spoke of the spirits of their dead ancestors as real beings that searched for a home. As an aside to his readers, Taylor noted that "the eyes of our heathen auditors sparkle under the light of a new association of admitted facts, and nod assent."[63]

Andrew Walls has pointed out that in comparison to the modern Western culture from which the missionaries came, traditional African cultures had far more in common with the culture of the ancient Jews and the early church.[64] Taylor's primitivist biblicism ended up highlighting those commonalities with the ancient past, a connection that countered the Western tendency to exalt the progress of modern societies. Taylor approvingly linked the African practice of circumcision to Abraham and tied the Xhosa cattle sacrifices to ancient Jewish ceremonial sacrifices. He told both his Xhosa and American audiences that the African tribal laws against murder, stealing, adultery, lying, and disobedience of parents persisted as remnants of the original biblical commandments. These practices, Taylor preached, indicated that the African ancestors knew God and his teachings to Moses. Xhosa, Mfengu, and Zulu individuals who converted under this sermon almost certainly saw commonalities between the religious world they had grown up in and the Old Testament characteristics that Taylor described. Taylor's validation of sacrifices, ancestors, spirits, ancient laws, and the judgment of a creator God resonated more deeply with his African audiences than he probably even realized.[65]

Yet the 1866 revival also brought changes to African religious life. Similarly to Karen Christianity, this new movement of world Christianity added the person of Jesus Christ to traditional religion, an addition with significant theological, intellectual, and cultural implications. Divisions between Christians and non-Christians widened in Xhosa, Zulu, and Mfengu life, although those divisions did not run along simple dichotomies between "Western" and "African" cultures. In its social dimension, the evangelical call by Pamla and Taylor to join a new Christian community resonated with many displaced Xhosa, Mfengu, and Zulu people who still sought religious direction to their lives as they adjusted to a modern society characterized by unstable, shifting relationships amid a cacophony of competing claims for religious, intellectual, and social loyalties. In the next few decades, Xhosa and Mfengu Methodists forged communities with powerful loyalties to their denominations. Along with Xhosa Presbyterians and other African Christians, they produced a new form of African leadership, blending African and European cultures in different ways.[66]

After 1866, the center of gravity for Methodism among black South Africans shifted from mission stations under the authority of British missionaries to local congregations organized and led by black Christians. Black evangelists took it upon themselves to establish Christian congregations, with or without ordination from the hesitating Wesleyan missionaries. Some black missionaries worked without pay for the Methodists, unsupervised for many years at a stretch. In the Natal alone, more than one thousand Methodist local preachers were at work by the 1890s. As in Burma, missionaries discovered vibrant Christian communities already established in areas they had never visited.[67]

Colonialism, of course, ensured that racial issues loomed over every new social development. Implicitly, if not explicitly, the 1866 revival had promoted conceptions of racial equality. Pamla and Taylor preached side-by-side, testified together to their similar preconversion states of being "poor sinners," and elicited conversions from whites and blacks together in evangelistic meetings. But Taylor, with his overriding passion for conversions, did not push these implications of racial equality any further. He occasionally disapproved of white discrimination against black Africans, defended the character of blacks in the face of ill treatment by whites, and recognized that racist attitudes could harm his goal of spreading Christianity. But because he viewed societies as aggregates of individuals rather than frameworks with their own distinct social structures, Taylor implied that individual converts and black evangelists would effectively address whatever problems race and culture might throw at South African society and left it at that.

Here we see the strength and the weakness of antiformalist evangelicalism. By disregarding the civilizing mission with its assumptions about the irrational and primitive character of black Africans, Taylor's democratized Methodism could engage black Africans from a more egalitarian position. But because it privileged individual choice and individual capabilities, Taylor's antiformalist evangelicalism did not give him the tools to perceive very clearly how the structures of British imperialism combined with racialized discourse to embed injustices in South African social, political, economic, and religious structures. Nor did the 1866 revival arrest the onslaught of racism and colonialism that increasingly besieged South Africa. The ordination of black evangelists marked a brief cultural moment in nineteenth-century South Africa when British Wesleyans and other Protestant missionaries validated the capabilities of black ministers. But in the long run, the powerful forces of race segregated religious life in ways that overwhelmed these impulses among whites.[68]

Taylor, meanwhile, discovered a new dimension to his itinerant calling. He reoriented his restless energies into what would become the leading edge of a rising tide of antiformalist evangelical missionaries flowing out of the United States. Until 1866, he had preached primarily to white, English-speaking audiences in North America, Great Britain, Australia, and South Africa. Now he believed that he had found a way to negotiate the cultural differences of the non-English-speaking world. The positive response of the Mfengu, Xhosa, and Zulu audiences and the effectiveness of Pamla's preaching convinced Taylor that his old-school Methodism could readily engage any people on earth.

The 1866 South African revival, then, represented something new for American evangelicalism. While early American Methodism had established itself primarily among communities with fairly homogeneous racial and cultural characteristics, the 1866 revival crossed formidable barriers of race, civilization, and culture. The South African revivals solidified Taylor's belief that the Gospel will adapt itself to "every variety and condition of human kind," a point that he would argue numerous times in the years to come.[69] Employing the biblical imagery of Elijah handing his mantle over to Elisha, Taylor wrote that Pamla would be God's instrument to take the Gospel into the interior of Africa. Significantly, Taylor did not see Elijah's mantle falling on Lamplough or the other British missionaries. The roving evangelist, on the other hand, was ready to move on and try his hand elsewhere. "The heathen world seemed suddenly opened to my personal enterprise, as an ambassador for Christ," Taylor had decided. He had set the bar high for himself.[70]

5

The Circuit-Riding Missionary and Gilded Age Methodism

South Africa launched William Taylor onto a global stage. Between 1870 and 1896, Taylor lived as a roving missionary, preaching in the Caribbean, Australia, Ceylon, India, the west coast of South America, Brazil, Liberia, Angola, and the Congo basin, not to mention numerous locales in Great Britain and across the United States. Taylor's popularity grew to the point where he became the most famous, the most controversial, and arguably the most influential single missionary in the largest Protestant denomination in America, the Methodist Episcopal Church (MEC). In a paradoxical but typically evangelical fashion, Taylor's fame and influence as a missionary of the MEC grew from a critique of that same denomination.

The critique grew from Taylor's old-school Methodist view of how missionary work ought to be done. This vision held important implications for cultural engagement. Taylor's old-school Methodism embodied American characteristics of individual autonomy, democratization, religious disestablishment, and pragmatic attitudes toward media, transportation, and technology. But Taylor's old-school Methodism also ran against powerful trends in Gilded Age American culture in that it resisted bureaucratic centralization, harked back to primitivist theological authorities, and pointed to a more supernaturalistic view of how the Holy Spirit moved.

Taylor's attempt to influence religious life in South Africa affected his missionary vision in one more paradoxical respect. Charles Pamla and other black Africans helped convince Taylor that ordinary, "uncivilized" individuals were perfectly capable of building Methodism from the ground up. This conviction created tensions with many in the Methodist establishment who embraced the progress of civilization. Taylor's faith in "uncivilized" individuals pulled his missionary program toward positions where he began to downplay Western conceptions of race, ethnicity, gender, and nationality.

Taylor's missionary program resonated deeply with a segment of American evangelicalism known as the holiness movement. Increasingly dissatisfied with the disenchantment, systemization, bureaucratization, and centralized control that characterized much of late-nineteenth-century American culture and religion, the holiness movement would, among other things, lay the foundations for another new force in world Christianity, Pentecostalism. Although the most dramatic developments took place after Taylor's career had ended, his uneasy relationship with the MEC establishment and antiformalist pattern of missionary engagement produced missionary dynamics of culture, power, and influence that would characterize new Pentecostal movements.

On leaving South Africa, Taylor sailed to Europe and the West Indies for a series of preaching engagements. In the midst of this tour, he received a letter from James Thoburn, an American Methodist missionary in India. Copies of Taylor's book *Christian Adventures in South Africa* had made their way through the Methodist missionary network, landing in India, where they had inspired Thoburn to invite the California preacher to bring his evangelistic program to Lucknow. Unable to resist either this invitation or the "variety of providential indications" now laid before him, Taylor reset his erratic evangelistic navigational system for India, sailing by way of England, Ceylon, and Australia before finally arriving in Bombay in November 1870.[1]

Over the next four years, Taylor logged three thousand miles back and forth across the Subcontinent, preaching in Calcutta, Kanpur, Bombay, Bangalore, Madras, and many places in between. John Wesley and Francis Asbury would have been proud. In old-school Methodist fashion, Taylor founded scores of fellowship bands, prayer meetings, and churches, an evangelistic harvest that exceeded that of most missionaries in India. He mobilized hundreds of converts, class leaders, local preachers, and missionaries. Nearly single-handedly, he established an entirely new conference of the Methodist Episcopal Church. In the process, the California preacher shook up the Methodist missionary establishment, attracted the attention of the nascent holiness movement, and gained notoriety in evangelical missionary circles as a maverick with a quirky plan for extending the Gospel in India.[2]

Although many Christians in India proved to be quite supportive of Taylor, his old school Methodism and aggressive revivalism clashed with missionaries in almost every city he visited. He was an antiformalist evangelical fish swimming in a formalist evangelical pond. After preaching for several weeks with the American Methodist missionaries in Lucknow, Taylor received an invitation from a British friend to come to Kanpur to preach. But Kanpur lay outside the Methodist Conference boundaries, and the American agency had no money to employ any converts Taylor might make. To his surprise, some of the Methodist missionaries objected to this invitation, expressing concern about the overextension of missionary resources. The roving evangelist bristled at the suggestion that his ministry should be contained within prescribed geographic or spatial boundaries. He appealed to John Wesley's statement, "The world is my parish," perhaps unaware that his Methodist hosts might not interpret that maxim literally. The missionary objection about employment of converts genuinely baffled Taylor. "I never heard of the like before," he declared, without further elaboration.[3]

But then, Taylor did not have a very deep understanding of the cultural complexities he faced. Because traditional Indian cultures linked kinship and religious adherence in deep and complex ways, Muslim and Hindu converts to Christianity were often disowned by their families and local communities. To help provide for converts who had suddenly lost traditional economic ties, many agencies hired them to work on their mission stations. The basic cultural contours of this relationship between kinship and religion was lost on Taylor, who had internalized the modern assumption that autonomous individuals simply chose what to believe, free from external influences. At any rate, the Methodist missionaries finally consented to Taylor's wish after he agreed that the Methodist Missionary Society would not be held responsible for any of his actions while he was out from under its jurisdiction. Quite likely, these missionaries believed that they had enough on their plate without the prospect of cleaning up whatever mess an itinerant evangelist might leave behind. Taylor, meanwhile, saw their objections as growing from the flaws of a system that inhibited the movement of the Holy Spirit.[4]

This marked the beginning of a tumultuous relationship with the Methodist missionary establishment. Taylor began by critiquing his fellow Methodist missionaries. He wrote that James Waugh, though "earnest and loving," needed a full baptism of the Holy Spirit. He described James Thoburn as "frightened" or "paralyzed" in his faith, hesitating to meet those who responded to Taylor's invitations with "decisive advance action." Despite this public criticism of Thoburn, the two became solid supporters of each other, with Thoburn acting as Taylor's most influential advocate in India. Initially, however, Taylor wondered how the Gospel was supposed to advance while under the care of such a "doubting, hesitating church."[5]

While Taylor took measure of his fellow missionaries, they took measure of him. If American Methodists, with their revivalist tradition, hesitated to embrace Taylor's enthusiasm, antirevivalist missionaries from Calvinist and Anglican denominations could hardly be expected to jump excitedly to his side. In Bombay, where the Methodists did not have any missionaries at work, Taylor quickly decided that those earnestly working for God were "too few and too feeble." At a chapel organized by the American Board of Commissioners for Foreign Missions, Taylor preached "very cautiously" for a week or two, in order to allay prejudices and secure "their concurrence and intelligent co-operation." His caution did not produce the intended result. After one of the services, he found himself debating a Calvinist member of the congregation over the old theological issue of the role of human agency in revivals.[6]

Later, in what must have been an act of self-restraint, Taylor preached nightly for two weeks in a Scottish church without inviting the audience to accept salvation. When he finally made his evangelistic pitch, Taylor reported that the missionaries seemed surprised at the "novelty" of it and informed him afterward that he probably should not do such a thing. The chaplain of the local European jail tried to ban him from preaching to the prisoners, and the local Anglican minister denied him a pulpit, explaining that he did not recognize Taylor's ordination. When Taylor applied for a permit to use the town hall for a service, as other missionary agencies had done, two ministers opposed his application, and he was rejected.[7]

Part of the conflict with the other missionaries in Bombay stemmed from Taylor's democratized impulses to rally the laity for active evangelistic tasks. Even though some of the Calvinist missionaries demonstrated, in his judgment, a modicum of earnestness, Taylor decided that their system suffered from an absence of lay activity and enthusiasm. "Officers, but no army," he quipped. At a mission run by the Free Church of Scotland, a dozen girls "came forward" at Taylor's invitation. The Scottish missionaries did not think that Taylor should let the girls publicly testify about their experience right away, since, in good Calvinist fashion, they needed to be examined to determine the soundness of their faith. Taylor was appalled. To show "suspicion and doubt in our conduct towards them, is to give help to Satan in his first assault," he fumed. When he failed to persuade the Scottish missionaries to accept this analysis, he blamed their intransigence on the "dark shadow of their education" and Calvinist theology. "These are dear good people," he decided, "and I love them [but] they are unwittingly victims of their creed."[8] The tepid reaction by the Calvinist missionaries in India only intensified Taylor's conviction that the missionary establishment hindered revivalism. He decided that he would have to build a Methodist system himself, without the cooperation of existing agencies.

He got his program in Bombay up and running in a hurry. The city had no Methodist presence when he arrived in October 1871, but with the help of local evangelicals from other denominations, he launched a series of revival services. In old-school Methodist fashion, Taylor elicited conversions, organized the new flock into fellowship bands, appointed "prayer leaders" to head the new bodies, and scheduled a quarterly conference meeting. Five months later, Taylor claimed 130 new converts who met weekly in nine classes, with more souls "added daily." The MEC could not help but welcome these small bodies of believers on equal footing with the churches in America. At least, that is how Taylor saw it. He sent a petition to the 1872 General Conference of the MEC, proposing that these incipient churches receive a charter as a new annual conference, as had been done with new churches in California. "Why should we not organize a conference in Bombay, just as we would in any of our Western States or Territories?" he asked in a letter published in the *Christian Advocate*, the flagship newspaper of the MEC. As simply as that, Methodism had been established in Bombay.[9]

Or so Taylor thought. MEC leaders weren't so sure. For one thing, it seems that they did not even know that any Methodists existed in Bombay until they read Taylor's petition for a new conference. The California street preacher had struck out for that city without direction, approval, or even communication with the Missionary Society.[10] Furthermore, Taylor had asked for two missionaries to be sent to lead these new churches but stressed that they should not be paid salaries and should not be placed under the authority of the Missionary Society. These procedural irregularities did not sit well. Finally, Taylor's proposal for a new conference in India arrived at a time of uncertain status for conferences residing outside the boundaries of the United States, feeding a debate that had been under way for two years.[11] In the end, Taylor's petition never made it out of committee at the 1872 General Conference. He interpreted this response as a personal insult.[12]

Naturally, he plowed forward anyway. Writing in the *Christian Advocate*, Taylor informed readers that God had led him to organize converts in India "into an old-fashioned Methodist Church." To Taylor, this meant that his Bombay churches, unlike the North India Conference, should neither fall under the jurisdiction of the Missionary Society nor receive funds from it. Ministers would "forego their rights as regards salary" along with their ministerial social standing and live "as near the level of the natives as health and efficiency will allow." His missionaries would have to trust that God would provide funds through supportive Christians living in India.[13]

Taylor built his own explanations for his notable but not quite electrifying work in India on a democratized critique of the missionary system, a critique that would drive his missionary efforts through the rest of his life. In true democratized fashion, Taylor concluded that he was held back by constraining features of institutional power, a characteristically Protestant, characteristically modern, and characteristically American reaction. The longer he stayed in the Subcontinent, the more Taylor argued that the Gospel needed to break free from the institutions, theologies, practices, and economic systems of the missionary establishment. It was a formula that would thrill, befuddle, and genuinely annoy different segments of American Methodism.

Even though it identified valid problems in the Methodist missionary system, Taylor's critique also contained flaws, which would show up later in his career. Taylor raised expectations for future evangelistic triumphs by boldly trumpeting his previous successes in California and South Africa, implying that he could easily replicate these revivals anywhere in the world. His book *Christian Adventures in South Africa*, with its underlying message that he had found solutions where other missionaries had failed, put his reputation on the line. Although his critique of the missionary system no doubt grew from sincere convictions and reasonable questions, Taylor seems also to have been contending with his own ego.

He also did not identify all of the key factors that produced the 1866 revival. For instance, Taylor did not further develop the cultural insights that he had started to form in South Africa. Although he maintained a strong faith in the role of the laity, he did not recognize the crucial linguistic and cultural expertise held by evangelists such as Charles Pamla. As he pursued conversions rather than theology, Taylor's passion for quick results might have prevented him from engaging in the careful reflection that could have aided his cause. Of course, he was an evangelist rather than an intellectual. His gifts lay less in incisive social analysis than in stirring up movements—and stirring the pot.

As more reports of "California Taylor's" activities in Bombay appeared in the Methodist newspapers, MEC officials had to decide how they were going to handle this maverick evangelist. While supportive of church growth, denominational leaders worried that independent evangelists working outside denominational structures could create any number of problems, both in India and in the United States. In language that reflected the influence of an industrializing economy on the mission of the church, the General Missionary Committee declared that "efficient" and "economical" action dictated reinforcing and strengthening established centers. Danger lay in "doubtful or uncertain experimenting," "too much extension," and "the unwise multiplication of missionary posts."[14] But official declarations such as this did not slow down religious enthusiasts. Taylor continued to go his own way, conflicts with the Methodist establishment continued to arise, and his fame—or notoriety—continued to grow.

Taylor referred to "old-school Methodism" to highlight his conviction that the denomination had strayed from its movement-building roots. In one sense, he was correct. In the late eighteenth and early nineteenth centuries, the Methodist "connectional" system deployed itinerant ministers to all corners of the American nation, where they established churches, distributed resources, and mobilized ordinary laity for evangelism. Democratized Methodism appealed to poor and marginal members of society, drawing in rough-hewn frontier farmers, unlettered artisans, and petty merchants. Unprecedented in its capacity to open leadership roles to segments of society that previously had little religious authority, Methodism granted women active roles in shaping the movement and made significant headway among African Americans by promoting black ministers. Class meetings, love feasts, quarterly meetings, and camp meetings propelled these poorly educated laity into leadership roles as class leaders, lay stewards, exhorters, and local preachers. The system exemplified antiformalist evangelicalism. It encouraged democratized leadership, validated ecstatic religious experiences of ordinary people, determinedly sought out individual conversions, and willingly ignored social conventions for the sake of evangelism.[15]

But there was more to early American Methodism. The very connectedness of the Methodist system simultaneously embedded institution building and bureaucratic systemization into the movement from the start. At the grassroots level, local leaders from a given circuit not only gathered at quarterly meetings for preaching, singing, love feasts, and religious fellowship but also examined and licensed preachers, handled the more serious disciplinary cases, recommended candidates for itinerancy, and collected contributions. Presiding elders not only preached but also functioned as middle managers, acting as liaisons between local evangelists and the bishops, supervising preachers in districts, managing camp meetings, and collecting money from book sales. As Methodism grew, it organized its churches into regional networks called conferences, which eventually emerged as the organizational heart of the MEC. Ministers gathered annually at specific regional conferences, where superintendents or bishops appointed them to existing churches or sent them out to new circuits, further propelling the evangelistic reach of the denomination.[16]

This dynamic combination of institution building and movement building made Methodism particularly well suited for an expanding, entrepreneurial, industrializing America. Its roots may have grown among marginal members of society, but more than any other denomination, Methodism captured the restless, competitive, sprawling energy of the emerging middle class. With fewer than one thousand members in 1770, Methodism grew phenomenally, to more than two hundred fifty thousand in 1820 and more than 1 million in 1850. Despite the fact that Methodism had splintered into several denominations, Taylor's branch, the MEC, boasted the largest membership of any Protestant denomination in the United States in 1876, at 1.6 million.[17]

Evangelical growth transformed Methodism. As Nathan Hatch states, it went "from Francis Asbury's 'boiling hot religion' to the Gothic-cathedral Methodism of William McKinley."[18] Many Methodists in northern cities built impressive edifices, complete with pipe organs, cushioned pews, stained-glass windows, paid choirs, and ushers dressed in coats with "tails." Methodists included senators, governors, and Supreme Court justices by the 1850s, signaling their new influence in politics. Wealthy industrialists such as Daniel Drew donated large sums of money to Methodist causes, particularly colleges and seminaries. In the three decades before the Civil War, Methodists founded more than two hundred schools and colleges. Like the northern Baptists, northern Methodists pushed for an educated ministry, provoking anguished debates over identity.[19]

MEC officials constructed a massive denominational machine, patterned after the institutions of industrial capitalism. Gilded Age America produced a rising middle class of professional bureaucrats and business leaders who saw their regulatory leadership of society as a necessary condition of advanced civilization. Centralized urban centers, with their control over finance, marketing, communication networks, and higher education overwhelmed the personal, informal, and local structures of rural and small-town life. Effectively adapting their institutions to these trends, Methodist churches across the nation created boards of trustees, led by professionals who managed local church affairs according to what they considered to be sound business methods. The MEC began to look a lot like a corporation.[20]

This systemization transformed missionary work. American Methodists had created a Missionary Society in 1819, primarily to coordinate funds from all of the annual conferences for special missionary efforts. By the 1850s, the Missionary Society had organized a board, established a missionary periodical, and placed its jurisdiction under the General Conference, the quadrennial legislative body that oversaw all of the annual conferences of the denomination. In 1872, the General Conference voted to centralize all benevolent societies of the MEC under the control of governing boards, effectively shifting missionary activity from local annual conferences to a national organization.

Gilded Age Methodist officials believed that these pragmatic acts of economic efficiency strengthened an institutional system by which the Methodist church would carry out its mission. Alpha Kynett ran the Board of Church Extension on modern banking principles, establishing a permanent loan fund, selling life annuities, investing annuities, and creating an apportionment system that required minimum contributions from every Methodist church. Kynett, in fact, explicitly linked the centralizing principles of these modernizing activities to the civilizing mission, proclaiming that "the supreme legislative body of the Church" would now lead "all its great interests for the diffusion of Christian civilization," including a "controlling power" in all missionary operations.[21]

Kynett could not, however, exercise a controlling power over William Taylor. While Methodist officials busily retooled the denominational machinery to face a bright postmillennial future of bureaucratic efficiency, Taylor pushed a primitivist "Pauline" plan of self-supporting missions. Modeled on what he believed to be the principles of the ancient church of the New Testament, Taylor's plan envisioned populist evangelists making unexpected "Spirit-led" decisions, while trusting God to provide financial support along the way. Holding off the Methodist missionary institutions with one arm, Taylor embraced the Methodist media with the other. He kept Methodist newspapers apprised of his "Pauline" activities in Bombay, trawling for popular, if not financial, support. By December 1872, three missionaries had arrived in Bombay in response to Taylor's call. Two of them came with the approval of the Missionary Society, which had agreed that Methodists should not hesitate to enter a "door so suddenly and strangely opened." The third missionary, William E. Robbins, had read of Taylor's appeal and departed for India at his own expense, without "falling in with a Mission secretary, or bishop." Robbins represented a harbinger of things to come. Over the next half-century, this claim that missionaries should trust God rather than institutional systems became so common within the holiness movement that it practically became a point of theological pride.[22]

Antibureaucratic decision making seemed to be something of a point of theological pride for Taylor, too. Without consulting Methodist officials, he decided to set out for new evangelistic fields, crossing India to found more self-supporting fellowship bands in Calcutta and Madras, confident that the small bodies of converts in Bombay would grow and strengthen without his supervision. A portent of the future suddenly hit MEC officials in America: new Christians on the other side of the world scampering about without their systematic guidance. To stave off this development, the Missionary Society wrote to Taylor offering to send out a "man of years and experience" to act as superintendent of the new churches in Bombay. Taylor pointedly replied that experienced supervision already existed in the persons of himself and George Bowen, a former ABCFM missionary who had signed on with Taylor's Bombay program.[23]

Taylor managed to aggravate more than just Methodist bureaucrats. Slipping into democratized mode, he described the upper class of Europeans as "the most imperious of all Indian castes." He linked missionaries to caste hierarchies by declaring that they had accepted the "prevailing idea" that in order to elicit respect, missionaries had to live in a large house, employ a half-dozen servants, and maintain a lifestyle equal to that of a military officer. His comments were not universally applauded. John Gracey, a former Methodist missionary in North India, fired back that "the Church asks for heroes, not ascetics." Gracey characterized Taylor's methods as "crude and misleading" and advised him instead to make a "prudent husbandry of his resources, or their waste in a less damaging direction."[24]

Despite these rhetorical spats, many Methodist officials supported the old-school revivalist, developing an uneasy but workable relationship with Taylor. While on a global tour of Methodist mission stations in 1873, Bishop William Harris stopped in Calcutta to make a personal evaluation of Taylor's efforts. An inspection of the churches and an interview with Taylor mollified his concerns. The bishop approved Taylor's superintendency of his new churches and sanctioned Taylor's "Pauline" principles. Back in the United States, Daniel Curry, the editor of the *Christian Advocate,* summed up the stance of most Methodist leaders, deciding that while Taylor's plan might not prove to be "practicable," it at least ought to be given a chance.[25]

Taylor's democratized Christianity challenged more than just Methodist bureaucratization. Undoubtedly, issues of finance and polity figured prominently in the minds of Gilded Age Methodists; both Taylor and established Methodists wrote as if the distinctiveness of his "self-supporting" plan resided in its economic features. Yet there was more afoot here than pragmatic questions of missionary finance. Taylor's old-school Methodist missionary revivalism ran against the tide of the Gilded Age discourse on race and civilization.

Most Gilded Age Americans believed that the United States represented the highest human achievement in democracy, intellectual advances, and moral progress. Advances in technology, industrial growth, and bureaucratic systemization reinforced these convictions. However, these views of the American nation also became intricately linked to beliefs in white superiority. The progress of civilization, it seemed to many, came through the work of whites, who needed to restrain harmful activities of other races. In the early 1870s, most segments of white American society abandoned the Reconstruction promises of racial equality embodied within the Thirteenth, Fourteenth, and Fifteenth Amendments. While the Democratic Party openly declared itself the party of the white man, the Republican Party, which had previously supported black rights, internalized new stereotypes of irresponsible and ignorant black politicians harming the American nation. In 1874, a former antislavery Republican published a widely popular book, *The Prostrate South*, which described African Americans as "ignorant, narrow-minded, vicious, worthless animals." Black politicians, the book explained, led a "rule of ignorance and corruption" of "barbarism overwhelming civilization."[26] Prominent northern periodicals, such as *The Nation*, *Scribner's*, *Harper's*, and the *Atlantic Monthly* all echoed these depictions of black politicians. *The Nation*, which had been founded as an antislavery periodical, favorably reviewed *The Prostrate South* and declared the intelligence of blacks to be "slightly above the level of animals."[27]

A majority of white southerners conceded the demise of the slave system, but they did not abandon ideas of white superiority on which that system had been built, a point that became apparent when Redeemers came to power in the 1870s. Wishing to avoid messy political and social issues, many white northerners, among whom ideas and practices of racial equality never sank very deep, reconciled with white southerners by accepting their model for white dominance in the south. Many white evangelicals who were enamored with an American republic based on power, prosperity, and stability not only approved of this civic arrangement with whites in control but often helped to promote it in their religious institutions.[28]

Racialized conceptions of civilization also made matters difficult for other nonwhite groups. A new round of military conquests in the American west reflected white perceptions of Native Americans as obstacles to railroad growth, westward expansion, and the progress of American civilization. The federal government formulated new policies that segregated Indians onto reservations, where, as the commissioner of Indian Affairs explained in 1872, their tendency to descend into the "lower and baser elements of civilization" could be arrested. Chinese immigrants, facing intense labor competition, were likened to both blacks and Native Americans. The federal exclusion of Chinese immigration in

1882 marked the beginning of a series of federal laws that would exclude immigrant groups on the basis of race. "We do not let the Indian stand in the way of civilization, so why let the Chinese barbarian?" asked New York governor and former presidential candidate Horatio Seymour in the *New York Times*.[29]

Scientific consensus of the era, despite laudable accomplishments in many other fields, also claimed superior capabilities for the white race. The application of Darwinian ideas to human development would emerge in complex, inconsistent, and changing ways, but more often than not, proponents used Darwinism to support ideas that white civilization had evolved to a higher plane than the rest of the world. Seymour's vice-presidential running mate in 1868, Frank Blair, fired opening salvos of a new strain of racist argument after reading *On the Origin of Species*. Blair rallied Democratic opposition to Reconstruction by decrying the rule of a "semi-barbarous race of blacks" in the south, who, in their desire for miscegenation, would reverse evolution and destroy "the accumulated improvement of the centuries."[30]

Darwinian anthropological models of the 1860s eliminated theories of polygenesis, at least, which had been used to describe nonwhites as separate and inferior species. But because the Darwinian source of human unity occurred millions instead of thousands of years earlier, most nineteenth-century proponents wrote of natural selection in ways that preserved some of the older racial ideas in new forms. Revising an older ethnological metaphor of a "tree" of humanity, these Darwinists spoke of a single cultural "ladder" to describe how natural selection enabled some people to reach higher levels, a model that reinforced distinct and deep-seated differences among human races. "The savage state," explained E. B. Tylor his influential book *Primitive Culture*, "in some measure represents an early condition of mankind, out of which the higher culture has gradually been developed or evolved." By the 1870s, sociocultural evolutionists were studying Fuegians, Aborigines, and Tasmanians in an attempt to discover how humanity had evolved from an ignorant, impulsive, and brutal state of savagery to the refined, moral, and scientifically minded British gentleman. Arguing that the human brain evolved differently among different races, Herbert Spencer declared that the impulsive and passionate "inferior races" might be good at observation and perception, but they could not "grasp the complex ideas readily grasped by European children."[31]

By contrast, evangelical missionaries who embraced the native-ministry model believed that nonwhites could master the complex ideas grasped by European intellectuals such as Herbert Spencer. That is why they taught theology and natural philosophy to the Karen, West Africans, and Hawaiians. A determined band of radical Republicans also believed in nonwhite capabilities, as did, of course, African Americans, Chinese immigrants, and Native Americans.[32]

But powerful forces in American culture continually pulled whites toward racist thinking. White evangelicals in the late nineteenth century who wished to actively engage the latest intellectual claims from anthropology and biology became quite susceptible to racist trends. Highly educated evangelicals who hoped to maintain their positions of power and high status in academic life "confidently proclaimed," in the words of George Marsden, "that they would follow the scientific consensus wherever it would lead."[33] In the realm of human development, that scientific consensus led many highly educated evangelicals right into academic theories of white superiority.

Take, for instance, Thomas J. Scott, an MEC missionary who founded the Bareilly Theological Seminary in North India. An article he wrote in 1869 for the *Methodist Quarterly Review* demonstrates how the reverence for scientific authority could push aside traditional Methodist theological conceptions of human nature. A graduate of Ohio Wesleyan University, Scott turned to current anthropological theories to describe race, Anglo civilization, and Methodism in India.[34] Missionaries, Scott explained, needed to consider the differences that had developed among the races, since "decided diversities are apparent in their intellectual, social, political, and moral capabilities." Taking his cues from anthropology rather than the native-ministry ideal, Scott questioned the effective potential of Christianity and civilization among the "wild and reluctant" Native Americans and the "degraded savage tribes" of Africa, since "races and peoples have a hereditary character, just as individual men." India offered hope to missionaries, though, because its Aryan people shared the same race as the ruling Caucasians. The presence of the British government, which he described as an "untold blessing and mercy on the land," had provided law, order, "improvement in art, and enlightenment in science." Victoria's government provided "enlightened instruction" by funding education, while the English language itself exerted powerful influence in the "aid of Christianity and civilization."[35]

Scott's grouping of Indians and Caucasians together under the category of "Aryan" revealed the influence of anthropologist Henry Sumner Maine. Although Maine wrote from a pre-Darwinian framework, he explained cultural differences and human capabilities in terms of the long historical development of societies. Maine argued that barbarian societies had codified the irrational and superstitious forces of their religion into their customs and laws, preventing them from progressing in material civilization. India and Europe, in this scheme, shared common Aryan roots. India had merely preserved the older institutions, while western Europe had escaped stagnation, allowing a utilitarian legal system to develop, which promoted civilization.[36]

Here, then, lay a real problem for Protestant missionaries. How was one to reconcile the native-ministry assertions of non-Caucasian capabilities with powerful scientific claims of nonwhite inferiority? The typical solution explained that nonwhite capabilities would emerge in a very distant future. As racist ideas gained greater academic authority in the hard sciences and the social sciences, highly educated Protestants extended the time in which it took nonwhites to become "civilized," from years to decades to generations to centuries.[37]

William Taylor, however, believed that nonwhites could assume Methodist leadership instantaneously upon conversion. This way of thinking about conversion worked against the tendency to make racial and national identities the essential markers of identity. Although he did not make it a very prominent part of his plan, Taylor attempted to build a system of color-blind revivalism in India. During an era that increasingly employed racial categories to segregate, Taylor organized Christians from different races, nationalities, and cultures together in revivals, prayer meetings, and churches. He placed British, Eurasian, and Indian converts together in fellowship bands and expected them to evangelize Hindus, Muslims, and nominally Christian Europeans.[38]

Following the pattern of Methodists in early America, Taylor expected class leaders, exhorters, and local preachers to emerge from these mixed-race gatherings. He explicitly refused to present conference membership reports with separate categories for "black, white, or mixed." He wrote, "I have confidence in God and in His glorious Gospel; and I have confidence in man—no matter what his nationality, colour, or condition." Because the pastors' "subsistence allowance" would put them on the same economic level as the ordinary people, Taylor predicted that his missions would eliminate the "white preacher caste" that distanced the missionaries from the ordinary people. He also expected Methodists in the United States to grant his multiracial conference an equal measure of status and respect. By 1875, Taylor's multiracial but English-speaking fellowship bands had evolved into churches in seven different cities in India. They formed the basis for the South India Conference, which the 1876 General Conference finally recognized.[39]

In February 1875, Taylor received an invitation to assist Dwight Moody for four months in his London campaign. Taylor later wrote that even though he had "not for a moment" entertained the thought of leaving India, he decided the day after he received the invitation that God wanted him to travel to London and then on to California to visit his family. After his campaign in London, he traveled through the United States for two years, preaching, recruiting missionaries for his work in India, and publishing another book, *Four Years' Campaign in India*. As late as August 1877, Taylor told a crowd at a camp meeting in Minnesota that he had bid farewell to his family and was making his way back to India.[40] Instead, he ended up in Chile.

By now, nobody should have been surprised by this change in plans. A ministerial friend had convinced Taylor that Chile and Peru offered great opportunities for evangelism in the English-speaking but nonevangelical Protestant churches in the port cities. Taylor reaffirmed an unstated but entirely characteristic principle of his self-supporting mission plan: it gave him the liberty to pick up and leave for new religious destinations at a moment's notice. He never returned to India, despite his stated intentions.[41]

Just when the MEC had worked out a fragile system for accepting Methodism in South India, Taylor gave them more bureaucratic headaches in Chile and Peru. He began recruiting missionaries for South America and published two more books to gain popular and financial support for his "self-supporting" mission. Again, he declared that organized denominational systems would be established only after spiritually awakened individuals had formed local bands of believers. His strongest supporters agreed. Praising the "apostolic pattern" of Taylor's method, a writer in the *Christian Advocate* argued that the "Church and its missionaries must learn that the world can never be converted by *ecclesiastical machinery*."[42]

Ecclesiastical machinery had it purposes, though. Taylor still needed Methodist bishops to sanction his efforts as true Methodism, particularly the ordination of ministers. In an attempt to rend asunder what Kynett's denominational centralization had joined together, Taylor argued that the Missionary Society held jurisdiction only over those geographic areas where it gave financial support to missionaries. In Taylor's interpretation of the handbook of Methodist polity, the *Discipline*, the Board of Bishops would simply ordain the preachers he recruited and allow them to keep membership in a conference in America. The bishops denied his request. Taylor forged ahead on his own anyway.[43]

By the end of 1879, Taylor had recruited and sent nineteen missionaries to Chile and Peru. With more recruits in the pipeline, Taylor asked the bishops to ordain the ministerial candidates who had not yet departed. Replying that they had no power either to create a mission or to appoint men to one that did not exist, the bishops ruled that these men could not be elected to orders or placed under episcopal authority unless Taylor's mission was in "a region within the control of the Missionary Society." Taylor "appointed" the candidates to his new mission field anyway, forcing the hand of the denomination. At the request of the bishops, the General Missionary Committee then extended the jurisdiction of the Missionary Society to include all of Central and South America and appropriated five hundred dollars for the general support of Taylor's missionaries. The bishops then wrote to Taylor offering to ordain the candidates, since they were now under "control of the Society."[44]

This Taylor would not accept. The democratized missionary protested that accepting funds from the Missionary Society and recognizing its jurisdiction not only would limit his freedom but would also, of course, bring his mission under authority of the Missionary Society. He pointed to the South India Conference as a precedent for his system. The Society responded by withdrawing both its money and its claim of jurisdiction, leaving Taylor's missionaries still without any kind of official status within the denomination. Realizing that Taylor's missions would forge ahead with or without their blessing, the bishops finally agreed to ordain Taylor's ministerial candidates, sending a bishop to South America in 1881 to accomplish this task. The exact status of Taylor's self-supporting mission in South America remained up in the air, however. In order to rally popular support for his cause and defend his self-supporting system against growing criticisms, Taylor published yet another book, *Ten Years of Self-Supporting Missions in India*. He made his stand clear by publishing his correspondence with the bishops on the ordination issue, while throwing in sarcastic barbs directed toward the Missionary Society, defensive references to the success of his missions, and claims that God led him in all of his decisions.[45]

These clashes were not simply about ordination and finance. They involved differing conceptions of race, civilization, and the meaning of the term *missionary*. To many, Taylor's color-blind revivalism simply did not qualify as missionary work. Charles Fowler, the editor of the *Christian Advocate*, assured his readers that Taylor "worked in harmony" with "the missionaries," but his prime purpose lay in bearing the gospel to Anglo-Saxons scattered around the world. As a result, Taylor's work was special, auxiliary, preparatory, and "entirely distinct in its character" from the work of the Missionary Society.[46] The General Missionary Committee claimed in 1881 that the South India ministry "does no work among the heathen" and spoke of the "unfitness" of many of Taylor's appointments. After declaring that Taylor siphoned off contributions that would go to the Missionary Society, one bishop wrote that Taylor gave the wrong impression of his work. "He was not carrying the Gospel to the heathen at all," the bishop explained, "but to the English-speaking inhabitants. This our people should distinctly understand."[47]

These comments demonstrated how a racialized, nationalized, and rather new meaning of the term *missionary* had come to dominate the Gilded Age. To these Methodists, "real" missionary work meant crossing a distinct divide to evangelize and educate those with different racial, national, or ethnic characteristics. It had not always been this way. In early American Methodism, Francis Asbury not only considered himself and his circuit-riding preachers to be missionaries but also expected each lay member to evangelize his or her neighbors. The "whole system is a missionary system," Nathan Bangs wrote in 1820, explaining that in his denomination, *Methodist* and *missionary* were practically synonymous. The expansive "missionary system" of early Methodism targeted native-born whites, blacks, German immigrants, and Native Americans for conversion and then mobilized them all as evangelists.[48]

Over time, denominational bureaucratization helped establish "missionary" work as systematic efforts built on distinct categories of race, nationality, and ethnicity. The MEC saw no contradictions in 1864 in giving a new division the oxymoronic title of "Domestic Foreign Missions." The agency operated in the United States, sending whites to Native Americans, blacks, Hispanics, and immigrants. American whites, clearly, were no longer the targets of missionary work. This definition of *missionary* clearly annoyed Taylor and his supporters. After James Thoburn took up the position of superintendent of Taylor's churches in South India, he reported that many of his friends told him, "you are doing a good work, no doubt; but I cannot help regretting that you ever gave up *missionary* work."[49]

The color-blind dimensions of Taylor's missionary revivalism also faced complicated cultural obstacles on the ground in India. Hindus or Muslims who converted to Christianity in British India took on formidable social, political, and cultural challenges. On a social level, converts who returned to their families and friends often faced rejection, intense pressure to renounce their new religious commitment, and the possibility of physical harm, all of which had led missionaries to establish the missionary compound system. Furthermore, the British legal system in India judged Hindus according to Hindu law and Muslims according to Islamic law but judged Indian Christians according to European law. British law, in effect, imputed a European identity on Indian Christians even if, as was true of most of these converts, they still considered themselves to be fundamentally Indian and had not adopted the kinship, social, or cultural patterns of Europeans. This left Indian Christians in a marginalized position, fully accepted by neither Indian nor European communities. Formalist missionaries worked, unsuccessfully, to persuade the British government to protect the rights of Indian Christians and to regard Indian Christians as Indian.[50]

Unlike many formalist evangelicals, Taylor ignored these intricate legal niceties. His old-school Methodism handled matters individualistically. Taylor knew people in western Virginia whose conversion to Methodism provoked beatings, familial rejection, and destruction of their houses. He himself had faced verbal abuse and occasional physical violence while preaching on the streets of San Francisco. The idea that Indian converts would face persecution, then, did not seem out of the ordinary to Taylor, who had come to expect audiences occasionally to react violently to evangelistic activities. The California street preacher believed that God would enable converts to bear these trials without striking back violently. In what sounds callous to some, Taylor wrote that death should be accepted as a possibility for converts but one that granted the heavenly reward of a "martyr's crown."[51]

Taylor could not see why the cultural differences of South India or Chile should prevent Methodism from expanding in the same enthusiastic, popular manner as it had in the United States. In his view, the fact that these new churches resided outside the United States did not necessitate supervision of a bureaucratic missionary agency, just as new churches in Virginia or California did not need this kind of oversight. He found it hard, though, to continue to speak of his mission in color-blind terms. In defending the true "missionary" nature of his work, Taylor took pains to present evidence of South India's work among the "heathen." He began to make clearer racial distinctions, inserting statistics on the numbers of nonwhite converts in the South India Conference, something he had proudly refused to do several years earlier.[52]

By mid-century, MEC officials had abandoned one component of American culture—democratized Christianity—to help build another component of that same culture, the Protestant establishment. They did this by increasingly linking Methodism to university-educated leadership, ecumenical cooperation among leading Protestants, funding from prominent businessmen, ties to the American political establishment, civilizing roles for women, and rationalized control of society by professional bureaucrats. In missionary terms, the embrace of the Protestant establishment pulled them toward the civilizing mission, both in the United States and abroad.

Not all Methodists followed this trajectory. Taylor tapped into spheres of evangelicalism where itinerant evangelists held lively revivals in small midwestern towns, working-class urban women gathered in homes to lead prayer meetings, earnest laypeople explored practices of faith healing, and Methodist enthusiasts gathered at rural camp meetings to give testimonies, sing Gospel songs, and seek new experiences of grace. These evangelicals often ignored the workings of the denominational machinery and the formal mechanisms of civil society. One branch of these antiformalist evangelicals, found largely but not exclusively within the various Methodist bodies, coalesced in the 1860s and '70s into decentralized, shifting, and loosely connected groups collectively known as the Wesleyan holiness movement. Among its many features, the holiness movement produced enthusiastic revivalism, a deep yearning to experience the power of the Holy Spirit, conflicts with the Methodist establishment, and a host of potential missionaries eager to join Taylor's cause.

The holiness movement grew from particular theological ideas within Methodism. For more than a century, many Methodists had supported some form of John Wesley's doctrine of sanctification, which emphasized the need for spiritual experiences that produced holy living after conversion. During the 1840s to the 1860s, an "ordinary woman" named Phoebe Palmer developed Methodist conceptions of sanctification into a distinctive "holiness" theology. Holy living, in Palmer's reconfiguration, came through a second instantaneous religious experience much like conversion, a "second blessing," which produced spiritual power. She gave special urgency to the idea that the laity should extend this "baptism of the Holy Spirit" to others. Her holiness spirituality not only fueled evangelical zeal among the laity but also enabled many individuals who lacked traditional trappings of authority to bolster their own religious claims. Falling on the fertile soil of a denomination steeped in democratized traditions, Palmer's theology yielded vigorous strains of evangelicalism that would keep producing well into the twentieth century.[53]

Palmer spread the language of holiness to Methodists and non-Methodists alike through a series of weekday meetings, holiness periodicals, books, and speaking tours. She spoke at camp meetings and revivals, playing a critical role in the 1856–57 revivals that spread across many parts of the nation. By 1867, *The Way of Holiness*, which Palmer first published in 1843, had run through fifty-two editions. In 1865, she and her husband purchased the holiness periodical *Guide to Holiness*, which soon reached thirty-seven thousand subscribers. Methodist notables such as Nathan Bangs, Frances Willard, Catherine Booth, and William Taylor attended her meetings and claimed a second blessing of sanctification.[54]

Holiness theology played out in several different ways. It could be incorporated comfortably into a respectable Victorian lifestyle among Methodists reared in urban, middle-class churches along the eastern seaboard. Among these people, holiness might bring changes to individual piety but did not necessarily challenge assumptions about the structure of society. But holiness theology could also create a broadly popular religious movement among Methodists closer to the margins of American culture, particularly those in small midwestern towns and the rural south. Many Methodists who did not make the move to respectable, urban, middle-class Methodism found in the Wesleyan holiness movement something closer to the old revivalism that had spawned their denomination.[55]

This was a movement that could undermine the authority of denominational elites and their cultural vision. Although conversion and sanctification lay at its heart, the holiness movement generated by-products that stood at odds with several modernizing impulses of Gilded Age America. Holiness advocates often expressed a deep dissatisfaction with what establishment Protestants upheld as examples of the progress of civilization. An 1881 article in the *Advocate of Christian Holiness* complained that a church always managed to find substitutes for purity when it had lost its "primitive piety and supernatural power." The writer railed against Methodists who worshipped "Mental Culture," defined as preachers who read more about culture than Jesus. Others, the writer continued, idolized statistics, "church machinery and ritualism," or ecclesiastical systems. Reworking a democratized theme that dated back to the birth of American Methodism, holiness advocates complained that ministers and missionaries tried to convert people through science, civilization, "fine churches," or theological schools. "How many rich laymen and fashionable ladies, and profound preachers in Methodism are devoted to a mere Church system," asked a holiness preacher, instead of the "historic experience of old Methodism?"[56]

Like William Taylor in India, holiness evangelists in America claimed "divine prerogative" for penetrating areas where holiness did not exist. Even if established religious leaders objected, holiness individuals blazed forward with religious activities if they were convinced that the Holy Spirit led them. This formula produced a flurry of popular religious initiatives that bypassed the formal institutions of the MEC. Holiness proponents formed the National Camp Meeting Association in 1867 without official denominational approval. Holiness evangelists crossed the countryside without directives, guidance, or authority from Methodist officials. Unordained female itinerant evangelists led holiness revivals in small churches. Holiness editors established religious periodicals without denominational sanction. Independent Bible schools and missionary training institutes sprang up under the leadership of Methodist laity.[57]

The most significant holiness departure from Gilded Age culture might have been its rejection of a "disenchanted" world. By the 1870s and '80s, holiness advocates began describing their efforts in terms in which the Holy Spirit provided for them in unexpected and miraculous ways. These narratives implicitly challenged the naturalistic and materialistic assumptions of those who promoted systemization, rational planning, bureaucratization, and "sound business methods" in a rapidly industrializing society. Regularly invoking what Grant Wacker has called "The Lord Knows Tomorrow Test," holiness advocates described how God miraculously provided for them when, by the promptings of the Spirit, they had ventured out without planning, financial support, or a clear destination.[58]

Take, for instance, the account written by Oscar von Barchwitz Krauser. A German immigrant who had embraced holiness at a revival in Ohio, Krauser framed his missionary call in the language of supernatural guidance. One morning in May 1878, Krauser abruptly quit his job in Indianapolis to join a friend who also felt called to preach. That afternoon, Krauser boarded a train with forty cents in his pocket, no particular destination in mind, and a conviction that the Holy Spirit would arrange matters. Over the next few months, he and his friend traveled through Indiana and Ohio conducting holiness revivals. Krauser punctuated his narrative with descriptions of religious visions, critics who abruptly converted, and preaching ideas that came to him in a flash. On sixteen different occasions, he received unsolicited gifts of money, food, clothing, or lodging, usually from grateful participants in his revivals.[59]

He then received a letter from William Taylor in October. Taylor, who had met Krauser at an August camp meeting, let him know that the Lord wanted Krauser to go to South America on a "self-supporting" basis to preach to German immigrants in Chile. Krauser responded with an affirmative answer. After meeting Taylor a second time for an evening of singing, prayer, and discussion of South America, Krauser set off for New York, again without funds, implicitly trusting that the Holy Spirit would provide them. In New York, he unexpectedly received a letter with $333 in it from a person who had read that Taylor had recruited Krauser for work in South America. Six months after he had set out on itinerant preaching and one month after his first letter from Taylor, Krauser boarded a ship for South America to begin his career as a missionary. The machinery of the

MEC did not appear in Krauser's account, but the Holy Spirit played a starring role.[60]

MEC officials often worried about the independent nature of holiness advocates. Their attempts to bring accountability and control to the movement did not usually solve the problems. In 1881, the MEC bishops announced that sanctification "can best be maintained and enforced in connection with the established useages of the church."[61] The bishops' declaration only threw gas on the antiformalist fire. "When churches and officials begin to complain of irregular and unauthorized efforts, of intrusion, and the like," declared a writer in the *Advocate of Christian Holiness*, "then you may know that somebody is out of the old ruts, and waking up sleepy souls, and doing something to save men."[62]

William Taylor could hardly be anything other than a hero to holiness advocates. He had obtained the experience of sanctification at an 1845 camp meeting. He joined Phoebe Palmer in holiness meetings. He held special prayer meetings where he encouraged converted evangelicals to seek sanctification. And, of course, he pitched his critique of the Methodist establishment right into the holiness wheelhouse. The "combined official forces" of the denomination, he wrote, had allied with English Methodists at the 1882 London Ecumenical Conference "to stigmatize and crush one poor Methodist preacher because he dared to obey God and found a Conference in a heathen country, without permission from the Missionary Committee in New York." Making a common holiness claim that his decisions were led by the Holy Spirit, Taylor declared, "I believe in creating missions in foreign lands by the power of God, but do not believe in a fictitious creation of foreign missions in New York by the policy of men."[63] Holiness leaders, in turn, saw Taylor as proof of what holiness could do on the mission field. "One man," proclaimed the *Advocate of Christian Holiness*, "without money and without authority, save that which comes directly from the Lord of the vineyard, enters the field, opens twelve centres, and provides, on the spot, for the support of some fifteen."[64]

Taylor's program and recruiting system provided an ideal missionary outlet for restless holiness energies. Taylor happily donned the mantle of the holiness-missionary champion when he spoke or wrote to the holiness faithful, depicting himself as an ordinary but spirit-filled believer who simply provided the spark that lit the spreading flames of revival. One of his favorite phrases, to travel without "purse or scrip," made the Lord Knows Tomorrow Test a common feature of his work.[65] But Taylor was also careful not to limit himself to the holiness label. He knew how to talk in more broadly evangelical terms when addressing general audiences. He did not make holiness, per se, the foundation of his cause. Nor did he care to narrow his recruitment opportunities by explicitly labeling his self-supporting mission as a holiness organization.

As a result, Taylor's broad recruiting methods also drew in missionaries who did not draw from the holiness brand of spirituality. This made for some tricky situations. One band of nine Methodist missionaries, consisting mostly of female schoolteachers and young men who had recently graduated from Boston University School of Theology, arrived in New York in 1879 expecting to find funds waiting for them for first-class passages to Taylor's mission in Chile. The available funds failed to cover that expense, and Taylor was, typically, off in some other part of the country. So the group reluctantly decided that they had no choice but to travel with the "lowest class of emigrants" in steerage. Holiness enthusiasts habitually described such worrisome situations as joyous opportunities for evangelism, with opportunities to experience a miraculous and victorious provision from God. The Boston University graduates described their situation in terms of the misery and suffering that missionaries must endure for the Gospel. Lelia Waterhouse described how she could not bring herself to eat from the huge dish that "contained the mess from which we were supposed to dip" and ended up falling ill. Toward the end of their journey, they all managed to pay their way into first class, only to run into more difficulties in Chile, when Taylor's contact backed out on his promise to help them start a school. They did not describe this as a victorious development.[66]

A decidedly nonholiness perspective framed accounts given by several other Taylor recruits. Goodsil Arms, who identified himself as the "pastor of the important Methodist Church at Newport, Vermont," signed on with Taylor's mission in 1888. A graduate of Wesleyan University, Arms fit the Missionary Society mold of a respectable, educated, and highly qualified Methodist missionary. He quickly decided that the well-meaning Taylor recruited too many "misfits" and created a mission with "no uniformity, no general organization, no central authority." Over the next few decades, Arms helped move the mission away from Taylor's self-supporting basis to the regular operations of the denomination. In 1921, when Arms wrote a history of Taylor's mission in Chile, he did not mention the enthusiastic revivals that working-class holiness advocates in Chile had spearheaded. He did, however, praise the efforts of the Methodists in Chile to reach many of the "hearts and minds from the most influential families of the republic." Like many other Methodist missionaries who sought inroads in Latin America by establishing schools for the middle class, Arms viewed missionary work as an effort to uplift Latin American society to the standards of North America, which he considered "the forefront of the most advanced Christian civilization."[67]

South America did not hold Taylor's attention for very long. He found himself en route to Africa in 1884, representing, of all things, the denominational machinery of the MEC. It was a strange turn of events. For some time, a few Methodist officials had been looking for opportunities to steer his missions in a more orderly direction.

The opening came at the 1884 General Conference. Methodist polity outside the boundaries of the United States had become so irregular that Taylor had been elected as a lay delegate from the South India Conference, even though he was not a layperson and had not set foot in India for six years. He arrived at the General Conference with petitions designed to bolster the status of his free-wheeling self-supporting missions in South America and India. He left as bishop of Africa.[68]

The nominations for a bishop for Africa had come embedded in a complex collection of issues tied to American racial arrangements and the missionary polity of the MEC. For two decades, an abolitionist-inspired wing of Methodism had been working to elect a black bishop in the United States. Amid the political maneuvering, nonabolitionist delegates sometimes deflected these attempts by nominating an African American as a "missionary bishop" for Africa, a position with considerably less status and authority than a full-fledged "bishop" in the United States. These proposals, in turn, unleashed unresolved issues of bishop residency overseas, the authority of a "missionary bishop," and the status of overseas conferences. The political machinations continued at the 1884 General Conference. Over a two-week period, a range of nominations and proposals touching all of these issues had been debated and voted down.[69]

Then a delegate suddenly nominated Taylor as missionary bishop to Africa. Many Methodist observers saw this proposal as providential. But then, the various factions at the General Conference held different ideas about just what Providence was up to. To one of Taylor's holiness supporters, the proposition "fell on the Conference like a clap of thunder out of a clear sky." He described a God of direct, unexpected, and immediate activity at work:

> Without premeditation, without knowing whither they were moving, until they were at the very point of landing, this body of as strong men as Methodism ever gathered in council, when the proposition flashed like meridian sunlight out of Egyptian darkness, received it as the will of God, and heartily, determinedly gave it their approving votes. In a whispered canvass of our delegation and those about us I found one sentiment—"*It is of God, and we must not withstand him.*"[70]

Most modern observers probably would not identify a lack of reflection and ignorance about institutional direction to be praiseworthy characteristics of a denomination's legislative body. But as this holiness advocate understood the situation, a God of direct, unexpected, and immediate activity was at work in ways that ordinary humans could not always predict.

Other Methodist delegates believed in a Providence of more methodical and orderly mannerisms. Some supported Taylor's election as a way to distract attention from the issue of a black bishop, thereby defeating the issue for another four years. Others felt that his appointment just might wheel in his renegade impulses.

Still others, frustrated by an African mission that produced numerous missionary deaths and few conversions, were ready to take a stab with the enthusiastic missionary revivalist. In any event, a collection of conflicting interests ended up electing Taylor to the position of bishop, a rather messy process befitting the complicated political workings of the largest denomination in the American republic.[71]

Taylor accepted the nomination but only after receiving assurances that he would be able to operate free from the oversight of the Missionary Society. Thus, his election could be seen as a triumph of Taylor's ability to parlay popular support into a prominent office in the MEC. Or it could be seen as a successful co-optation of a loose cannon by the Methodist establishment. Either way, critical tensions still had not been resolved. On the day after Taylor's ordination at the General Conference, Bishop Edward Andrews extended an official invitation to Taylor to take a seat with the other bishops on the platform. Taylor declined. An issue of authority underlay this seemingly innocent and courteous invitation. Taylor explained to the body that he understood that he was only a bishop while in Africa, pointedly adding that if Andrews should visit Africa, Taylor would extend the same courtesy to him.[72]

Figure 5.1. William Taylor, combining bishopric authority with a personalized message. Photograph in William Taylor, *Story of My Life* (New York: Hunt & Eaton, 1895).

This power struggle reflected more than just a conflict over the relationship between Taylor's "Pauline" program and the Methodist Missionary Society. The very fact that the status of "missionary bishop" had been at issue before the 1884 conference demonstrated the ongoing struggle of the MEC to reconcile the consequences of evangelical growth with powerful cultural forces tied to race, civilization, and the nation-state. The position of "missionary bishop" had been created in 1858 for Francis Burns, an African-American missionary in Liberia. Were he not limited by the term *missionary bishop*, Burns would have enjoyed the same powers as white bishops. He would have been able to appoint white preachers, ordain white ministers, and preside over annual conferences in America. By implication, the Liberian conference also would have enjoyed equal standing with conferences in the United States. But Burns was black, so it was not to be. After Burns and his African-American successor had died, the position of missionary bishop lay dormant for more than a decade. Many Methodist leaders had refused to accept the position, describing it as a "second-class Bishop." By implication, African Christians remained second-class members of the MEC.[73]

To some, Taylor's ordination as a "missionary bishop in Africa" implied that he was to be bound by the same restrictions as Francis Burns. A year after Taylor's ordination, when an official declared that he was not a "regular and constitutional Bishop," a Taylor supporter retorted that Methodists needed to "believe the people of Africa as well worthy of the best gifts as the people of America." Quoting a speech from the 1868 General Conference, which had stated that missionary conferences must not be restricted in authority because they were "foreign" and "made up of black men," the writer asked, "Have we not now gone by the days when either or both of these arguments should be used against Africa?"[74] Taylor himself expected his self-supporting missions in Africa, like those in South India, to develop into independent conferences under the jurisdiction of the General Conference. This would have placed African Methodists on equal legislative footing with Methodists in the United States.[75] The simple prospect of Africans converting to Christianity, then, exposed the reality that Methodist polity had established inequities based on racial and national identities. American Methodists could ignore this reality as long as Methodism did not provoke the issue by presenting the MEC with large numbers of African converts who could challenge the system.

Taylor, meanwhile, faced his own particular challenges. He suddenly needed to prove that his self-supporting method would work in parts of Africa where other approaches had failed. But the terms of cultural engagement in Liberia and Central Africa were not like anything he had faced before. In both South Africa and the cities of India, Taylor had toured communities where Africans and Indians had been interacting with Europeans for decades and, in a few places, for centuries. In trying to convert "nominal" Anglo or Boer Christians alongside Xhosa or

Indian converts, Taylor's old-school Methodism had come equipped with an implicit critique of the existing colonial society, with its systems that claimed white superiority.

In the African interior, however, Taylor no longer enjoyed the luxury of an existing mission station or colonial society that he could simultaneously critique and use as a base. He could not revive a multiracial body of "nominal Christians" to move forth as his "entering wedge" in society. Taylor toured sections of West Africa, the Congo basin, and Angola, where contact between African peoples and Westerners had been minimal. Colonial forces were only beginning to exert themselves. He then attempted to set up a string of missionary stations that stretched one thousand miles inland from the coast of south-central Africa. Soon thereafter, Taylor worked to form similar lines of stations in the interior of Liberia and the Congo basin.[76]

This situation did not compel Taylor to dig deeply into linguistic and cultural issues, which had never been his strong point. Charles Pamla, with his knowledge and understanding of Xhosa and Mfengu cultures, had spearheaded the revivals in South Africa in 1866. He had also helped Taylor negotiate cultural hurdles. In his twelve years as missionary bishop in Africa, Taylor found no equivalent of Pamla. Nor did the roving bishop ever stay in one place long enough to learn any of the scores of African languages he encountered, a factor that greatly limited his ability to communicate effectively. Finally, in South Africa and India, Taylor had the freedom and financial resources to oppose the Missionary Society because he could rely on the political and economic support of prosperous individuals in the local community. The villages in the interior of Africa provided no such support.

Taylor's twelve-year venture as bishop of Africa was not an evangelistic success. The realities of the African interior brought to light how much the antiformalist evangelicalism of his old-school Methodism actually depended on established structures of modern societies. The bishop of Africa had not anticipated this. Like many individuals from modern societies, Taylor assumed that he could find a way to operate as an autonomous free agent, uninfluenced or unencumbered by the structures, institutions, and culture of his society. In Central Africa, Taylor discovered that he had to spend a great deal of time on institution building rather than movement building. The logistical demands of his self-supporting mission limited the amount of time that he or the missionaries he recruited could spend on evangelistic work. He supervised fellow missionaries, administered travel details, and attempted to establish an economic base for his missionaries, skills in which he did not excel and which his old-school Methodist impulses did little to improve. The cost of supplies proved to be higher than he had calculated, and Taylor sometimes failed to ensure that they reached their destination. A missionary recruit whom Taylor deemed of "superior ability and integrity" ended up spending his outlay funds in questionable business speculations, plunging himself and the mission into debt. After finding navigation service between his stations on the Congo River to be unreliable, Taylor raised funds to build a steamer, only to discover later that the parts were too heavy to haul to the appropriate spot. The boat was finally made operational five years after he had first ordered the parts, by which time alternative navigation systems on the Congo had improved considerably.[77]

Taylor also started drifting toward a stronger civilizing depiction of his work. Whether it stemmed from his new status as a bishop, a desire to stir up more support in the United States, frustration over a lack of dynamic evangelical movements on the ground, the challenge of engaging cultures with much less Western influence than he had ever experienced, or some combination thereof, Taylor began portraying himself less as an ordinary revivalist than as an evangelical explorer and institution builder in exotic lands. He enlisted the famous explorer Henry Stanley to write an introduction to his new book, *The Flaming Torch in Darkest Africa*, a work that was part history, part popular anthropology, and part evangelical appeal. Although he declared that "one day Africa may lead the world in learning and culture," Taylor began speaking in terms of bringing the benefits of civilization to a benighted land.[78]

The absence of modern economic infrastructures in Africa compounded his administrative puzzles. Taylor's "self-supporting" theory dictated that the missionaries should quickly support themselves financially. This almost always meant receiving funds from local donors. African realities forced him to concede that an initial outlay of funds would be required before "adequate indigenous resources" could be developed.[79] He tried to solve this problem by negotiating

Figure 5.2. William Taylor in explorer mode. Illustration in William Taylor, *Story of My Life* (New York: Hunt & Eaton, 1895).

with African chiefs for land on which missionaries could build houses, schools, and farms. The movement-building evangelist found himself building "industrial schools" and promoting coffee as a crop that missionaries could produce and sell in order to support themselves. Despite his claims for self-support, Taylor had to make repeated requests for funds. He also reported difficulties in negotiating with African chiefs who expected his missionaries to bring more financial resources with them. Some of the missionaries Taylor recruited, especially those influenced by the holiness movement, shared his willingness to cast themselves into Africa without material support and make do with whatever situation they encountered.[80] Others discovered that the system put them in desperate straits. Taylor faced a scandal of sorts when a destitute missionary named J. C. Waller returned to America and published reports about how he, his wife, and their two young children were left alone on a riverbank with few supplies, no shelter, and no idea of how to proceed.[81]

This could not help but stir critics in America. The *New York Times* described Taylor as a "dangerous crank" for leading forty men, women, and children into the interior of Angola to face "murderous savages." Suggesting that the American consuls in Africa throw obstacles in the way of the mission, the *Times* decided that it "would be quite proper to treat them as lunatics and to ship them home by the first vessel."[82] Perceiving the problem to be one of method rather than madness, several Baptist missionaries castigated Taylor for not putting forth "a missionary idea in any sense" but rather a "plan for Christian colonization." Similar to Taylor's critique of the compound system in South Africa years earlier, they argued that Taylor's missionaries spent so much time working to support themselves that they did very little evangelistic work.[83]

In the end, Methodists evaluated Taylor's program by the number of converts in his mission. This, of course, had been Taylor's standard. As long as revivals and reports of conversions appeared, he seemed to be effective enough that officials let him operate. When reports hinted at discouraged missionaries, financial difficulties, and struggling stations, Methodist officials concluded that Taylor's system did not work. Each of the three General Conferences from 1888 to 1896 brought Taylor's self-supporting missions under closer supervision of the agencies in the United States.[84] By 1896, the conference decided that Taylor needed to retire. When his successor, Joseph Hartzell, toured Taylor's string of "pioneer" Congo mission stations in 1897, he found only two still functioning. Of the fifty-eight missionaries Taylor had sent to the Congo, thirty-one had returned home, and twenty-two had died. Taylor confided to Hartzell his disappointment in the results of his self-supporting missions in Liberia. After Taylor retired, every independent mission he had established in Liberia, the Congo, and Angola reverted to the jurisdiction and authority of the Missionary Society, as had all of the independent missions he had established in South America.[85]

William Taylor, the most famous Methodist missionary of the late nineteenth century, quickly faded from view. The missionary program of the circuit-riding preacher, which had burst upon the MEC with such energy in the 1860 and '70s in the mixed-cultural settings of South Africa and India, ended with a fizzle among starker cultural contrasts in West and Central Africa in the 1890s. Like many Americans enamored by techniques and methodologies, Taylor had calculated that the self-supporting economic features of his system and the democratized opposition to bureaucratic machinery would reproduce the evangelistic successes of old-school Methodism. Holding its own love affair with methodologies and numerical results, the MEC establishment allowed the maverick bishop of Africa to operate outside the established missionary system for a time, in the hopes that his unorthodox system might bear fruit in a challenging field. When these methods failed to produce expected results, the MEC concluded that his self-supporting system did not work, and it moved on.

Both Taylor and the MEC establishment assumed that movements of Christianity were predictable enough that they could be produced by missionaries who discovered the correct revivalistic technique or institutional system. In thinking this way, both parties revealed American and modern attitudes, but they did not display an approach that always gave an accurate view of how religious movements actually emerged. Missionary engagement involved so much more than practical methodologies—the negotiation of language, race, religious authority, gender, human relationships, politics, and theology, to name just a few components of that complex framework we call "culture"—that it might be expecting too much to assume that any individual could master all of these issues with clarity. There was more at work on the ground in South Africa or India, for instance, than Taylor had perceived.

There was also more going on in his own global missionary enterprise than what he perceived. In the long run, Taylor's greatest influence resided not in the number of conversions he elicited overseas or the discovery of successful missionary techniques or the articulation of an effective missionary theory but in the unanticipated foundation he laid for the missionary wing of the holiness movement. That movement, a significant force in world Christianity in its own right, would cultivate the ground for another worldwide movement that nobody saw coming: Pentecostalism. Evangelicalism could fool even its own advocates.

PART THREE

6

The African-American Great Awakening

African-American Christianity is often understood according to important issues of freedom, racism, and civic arrangements. Religious faith, for instance, gave slaves hopes for freedom, black churches provided institutional resources for resisting racism, and African-American leaders carved out spaces for blacks to worship their own way. In other words, the story of African-American Christianity is often told according to the terms of the American nation.

But it is also a story about world Christianity. Replicating a centuries-old historical process in which the faith crossed cultural boundaries, Christianity swept over a people in the United States who held a historical consciousness grounded in Africa rather than European Christendom. This reality produced important consequences. Because the dynamics of race kept African ancestry before the eyes of both whites and blacks, African-American evangelicalism operated within a different historical framework from white Protestantism, which had been built on a Reformation conception of a people purifying a corrupt church within Christendom. White Protestants tended to see the "Christian civilization" of the United States as the latest and highest example of this Reformation, usually expressed in the terms of progress within Western culture. Most African-American evangelicals, however, saw themselves as heirs of a different lineage. They saw themselves carving out a religious sphere amid a cruel society that refused to recognize its own racial sins. And in a similar manner to Christianity in Asia, Africa, and Latin America, African-American evangelicalism did not simply conform to lines dictated by whites. Growing in a mixed and shifting cultural soil, African-American evangelicalism blended elements of African culture with cultural materials found in the United States.

This is also a missionary story. As such, African-American Christianity emerged from the paradoxical dynamics of power and culture within evangelicalism. From the 1740s to the beginning of the twentieth century, white evangelicals sought to extend Christianity among blacks, and the faith grew steadily among the African-American population. In that process, though, African-American Christianity emerged in ways that white American Christians did not anticipate and occasionally did not welcome. Black evangelicalism grew most vigorously in situations in which white Christians wittingly or unwittingly faced restrictions on their own power. In a manner similar to missionary engagement in Burma or South Africa, the overwhelming number of black conversions grew from the efforts of African-American evangelists, not from the hands of white missionaries. Black evangelicalism used components of American culture, such as democratization and religious freedom, to preserve elements of traditional African culture in their Christian practices. Finally, African-American Christianity implicitly challenged white Christianity to consider ways in which it had formed unholy alliances with racist dimensions of Western culture. As a result, the conversion of African Americans to Christianity confounded dominant conceptions of Christianity as an essentially Western, Anglo religion.

"This has been a year of revivals in Georgia," Henry McNeal Turner reported in November 1866. "I never expected to see such a sight this side of heaven, nor do I believe such a scene was ever witnessed before in America." Turner's black denomination, the African Methodist Episcopal Church (AME Church), had broken with the Methodist Episcopal Church (MEC) over racial issues more than half a century earlier. In 1866, the AME Church had appointed Turner superintendent of its missions in Georgia and pastor of a church in Macon. Unlike the MEC in the 1860s, which defined a "missionary" as someone who had to cross a racial or cultural boundary, the AME Church still held to the older Methodist conception that considered all of its evangelistic efforts as missionary efforts. With his typical energy, Turner had set right to work as a missionary to his fellow blacks, launching a series of prayer meetings and nightly revival meetings at the Macon church. After several days of prayer meetings, he held an invitation for salvation, and "scores came forward," much to his delight. "From that time till now convert has followed convert, till in every part of the city it looks like a jubilee," he wrote.[1]

The conversions extended to other churches in the region. Some churches reported as many as four hundred fifty individuals seeking salvation. "Persons who were thought to be immovable, have been brought into the church and powerfully converted, not under me, but under God," Turner declared. Time and time again, African Americans responded enthusiastically to this AME preacher as he traveled through Georgia ordaining new black preachers and planting independent black congregations. In Cuthburt, Georgia, Turner's revival services were so loud that a Freedman's Bureau official, perhaps unaccustomed to the enthusiastic dynamics of black religious life, sent a man to Turner with the message that "it was time to stop that noise!" Flashing a sense of indignation and firmness of purpose that would be repeated many times in his life, Turner told the messenger that "he was crazy, and that we were all free people." Turner continued with the meeting.[2]

One does not usually think of 1866 as a "year of revivals" for African Americans. This was, after all, the first full year after the end of the American

Civil War. With wartime destruction, the defeat of the Confederacy, the abolition of slavery, and the occupation of Union troops, the American south stumbled blinking into the stark sunlight of an uncertain new era. A host of unanswered questions hovered in the air. It was not at all certain how the social, political, economic, and religious relationships between whites and newly emancipated blacks would be structured. Many white southerners, still profoundly shaped by the culture of the Old South, hoped to maintain as much of the antebellum order as they could, even as they grudgingly accepted the demise of slavery. Radical Republicans in Washington, D.C., pushed a different vision for the southern social order, passing a civil rights bill in 1866 and ensuring the ratification of the Fourteenth Amendment. The freed people, for their part, did not wait for legislation from the federal government before they attempted to move out from under the authority of their former masters. Across the south, they embraced their newfound liberty by searching for new work, relocating separated family members, attending schools, looking for opportunities to grow their own crops, and joining political conventions. It was not a smooth process. Conflicting desires of blacks and whites sometimes erupted in unsettling violence. Major race riots broke out in 1866 in Memphis and New Orleans.[3]

Conflicts between independent-minded blacks and antebellum-minded whites also extended to the religious sphere. Turner described how a white man in Atlanta had given a group of blacks a plot of land the previous year on which to build a church. Now the man reclaimed the lot, saying "he never gave the lot for free negroes to worship on, but for slaves." Other whites turned to more drastic measures. In the middle of one night in June 1866, Turner reported, four whites near Auburn, Alabama, broke into the room of an AME pastor who had just arrived in the area. They beat and stabbed the minister nearly to death, telling him that "no d—d negro schools should be taught there, nor should any negro preacher remain there." During the beating, several black women rushed to a Freedman's Bureau agent for help. The northern white officer refused to leave his room, telling them that he could not do anything. "Such conduct is lauded by a certain class here," Turner wrote in the AME *Christian Recorder*. Along with Turner, readers must have wondered what sort of future lay in store for African Americans, Christianity, the south, and the nation. Independent black ministers and teachers, of course, could be seen as a threat to the racialized social order. "O God! where is our civilization?" Turner wrote in closing. "Is this Christendom, or is it hell? Pray for us."[4]

Sometimes, though, freed people and southern whites peacefully negotiated arrangements that accounted for new religious realities. In Griffin, Georgia, C. A. Fulwood, the white pastor of the local Methodist Episcopal Church, South (MECS), surprised Turner by mailing an invitation to him to come to Griffin. After Turner and Fulwood "negotiated on satisfactory terms," Fulwood granted Turner use of the Methodist church for the evening. "The news of a presiding

Elder of the black African Church...spread like lightning," wrote Turner, who was surprised at the throng that showed up that evening. After he preached for ninety minutes, he proposed to the congregation that they form an independent AME church. With the help of Fulwood and a local white judge, an AME church was duly established, consisting of the African Americans who had formerly attended Fulwood's MECS church, plus all of those from a Methodist Episcopal Church, North (MEC), which most likely had been established recently by a northern white missionary. "I have captured Griffin, Ga., and every one of the colored Methodists in it," Turner exulted, "...and left the [MEC] white preacher without a colored representation."[5]

Turner was obviously pleased that the new religious arrangement in Griffin included an independent black church. The thinking of Fulwood and the local judge is harder to determine. One or both of them might have sincerely believed that a black church would best serve the spiritual needs of Griffin's African-American Christians. Living in the shadow of the Civil War complicated matters, though. It seems likely that Fulwood had been losing black members to the new northern Methodist church in town. Fulwood and the judge might have calculated that they would be able to maintain more of their old influence over the freed people of Griffin if the black Christians belonged to an independent black church instead of a northern white denomination. Perhaps they feared that a northern minister would stir local blacks into acts of violence and disruption. Whatever the case, the Methodist maneuvering in Griffin mirrored a larger pattern of negotiation, contestation, and confrontation taking place among black and white Christians throughout the unsettled south in 1866.

Right in the midst of these upheavals and maneuverings, throngs of African Americans converted in services led by black preachers. Revival reports poured in from regions far beyond Turner's AME circuit in Georgia. "Some of my brethren say they have never witnessed before such an outpouring of the Spirit of God upon the Church," wrote a black pastor from Raleigh, North Carolina. In Texas, an AME minister reported that "the Holy Ghost came down with great power, and many souls were hopefully converted to Christ." The *Christian Recorder* reported news of additional revivals in Louisiana, Missouri, Tennessee, Georgia, South Carolina, North Carolina, Virginia, and Maryland. Men and women, the elderly and youth converted. Revivals took place in city churches, small towns, and "many plantations and secluded spots." Many commented on the unprecedented numbers of those who responded. "The revival is one such as I have never before experienced," wrote an AME pastor from Norfolk, Virginia, who received more than two hundred members and six hundred inquirers during a ten-week series of daily meetings. A black pastor in Annapolis, Maryland, reported that "the oldest inhabitants say there never was such a time," as the crowds were so big they were "obliged to put some of the mourners in the pulpit." At a black church in Lowell, Georgia, Turner found that "the idea of seeing a colored elder among them almost set the people crazy." The church was so full that scores of people could not get into the building.[6]

These black evangelical revivals marked the beginning of a widespread religious movement that might be termed the African-American Great Awakening.[7] From 1866 through the end of the century, revivalism swept the black communities of the south, fueling tremendous growth in independent black Baptist and Methodist churches. Black evangelicalism dated back to the 1740s and grew through the first half of the nineteenth century. The African-American Great Awakening, however, cemented evangelicalism as the central component of African-American religious life.[8]

Many historians have described how black Christians seized the opportunity afforded by emancipation to leave white-controlled denominations.[9] The evangelistic side of this expansion, though, has not received much attention. The postbellum growth of black Baptist and Methodist churches did not stem just from black Christians switching to new churches. African-American ministers noted that the revivals brought people into the church who had not been there before. Turner made a distinction between the 17,000 membership transfers to the AME churches in Georgia and the additional 14,300 new conversions that occurred between 1865 and 1871.[10] The two sets of numbers encapsulate two sides of the African-American Great Awakening: the movement of existing black Christians into independent black churches and the addition of new members to the Christian faith.

Statistics of nineteenth-century African-American religious adherence necessarily rely on estimates, but the evidence suggests that in many places, new converts might have represented as many as half of the members who joined postbellum black churches.[11] The number of black Baptists in the United States increased from about 400,000 in 1860, to about 800,000 in 1882, to 2.2 million in 1906. Black Methodists jumped from 190,000 in 1860, to more than 300,000 in 1876, to more than 1 million in 1906.[12] Some of this increase can be attributed to population growth and the institutionalization of unchurched slaves who had practiced Christianity in secret, but these factors cannot explain all of this growth. The highest estimates for African-American Christians in 1860 that include the "invisible institution" under slavery come to about 22 percent of the black population, an increase from 4 percent in 1800. By 1900, however, the percentage of African-American Christians had risen even more, to 42 percent.[13] Although these statistics cannot be nailed down with precision, the existence of widespread revivals, the reports of "immovable" blacks converting, and the massive growth of recorded black membership all point to large numbers of new converts in the decades following the Civil War.

This was no insignificant development. As Sylvia Frey and Betty Wood write, "the conversion of African Americans to Protestant Christianity was a, perhaps *the* defining moment in African American history."[14] Evangelicalism played the critical role in this process. Scholars have shown that evangelicalism gave American blacks the means to reconstitute a new identity from a collection of ethnic groups that had been torn from different African roots. Evangelical Christianity produced African-American leaders, provided blacks with an ideology of resistance to slavery and racism, shaped black domestic institutions, and acted as the primary conduit for African influences in America.[15]

While these developments began in the eighteenth century and took formative shape in the early nineteenth century, the African-American Great Awakening propelled African Americans into a critical stage in that process. Christian slaves could not avoid a white establishment that continually sought to bring black Christianity into line with the terms of the slave system. After emancipation, however, many southern African Americans would come to the faith in independent black churches that were led by black ministers who had the liberty to preach, expound the Scriptures, and conduct worship apart from the oversight of white Christians. The First Great Awakening, the Second Great Awakening, and antebellum slave religion laid the foundation for African-American Christianity. The African-American Great Awakening erected the framework and filled in the walls of the edifice.

That design, as with other evangelical endeavors, embraced certain features of American culture in order to resist other parts of that culture. On the one hand, the African-American Great Awakening thrived amid religious developments of Western culture: a disestablishment of religious elites, a range of religious options battling in a competitive atmosphere, energetic movement-building efforts by democratized leaders, the assertion of institutional autonomy, and the establishment of systematized denominational structures. Yet the African-American Great Awakening also wired black evangelicalism with resistors to key aspects of American culture. Emerging in the red-hot forge of Reconstruction and Jim Crow racial tensions, it preserved elements of African culture, held tightly to its supernaturalistic forms of religion, rejected reigning conceptions of Christian civilization, and hammered out a sense of peoplehood that contradicted nineteenth-century identities grounded in the nation-state. In each of these characteristics, the critical element of race shaped African-American evangelicalism in ways that distinguished it from dominant forms of white evangelicalism.

As early as the 1680s, white Protestants consciously attempted to spread the faith among blacks in the Americas. Those who stuck to their positions of political, social, and economic power, however, such as the Anglican Society for the Propagation of the Gospel in Foreign Parts, barely made any evangelistic headway. The first significant numbers of black conversions occurred during the First Great Awakening, which had begun to knock props out from under established structures of religious power. This process accelerated among democratized bodies during the early republic. As old hierarchies broke down and audiences no longer deferred to mediating elites, evangelical movements produced leaders from the ranks of their own poorly educated and marginal congregations. Many African Americans and whites were drawn to a common religious cause in this environment. In their antiformalist modes, Methodist and Baptist movements welcomed blacks as church members, speakers, and evangelists, a dynamic that encouraged black leadership and implied equality. Harry Hosier, a black Methodist minister, often accompanied Francis Asbury on his long-distance circuit-riding trips. Asbury regularly deferred preaching responsibilities to Hosier, who preached to black, white, and multiracial audiences.[16]

Evangelical success created new problems, though, particularly when it accompanied economic, political, and social gains for whites. Many upwardly mobile white Methodists and Baptists attempted, in the words of Nathan Hatch, to "take back with one hand what had been granted with the other."[17] Revivals brought many whites into the fold who did not want to accept black equality or allow blacks in positions of authority. As the slave system had expanded and hardened in the early nineteenth century, antislavery initiatives in southern Methodist and Baptist churches faded away. White Methodist and Baptist leaders in the south increasingly evoked biblical passages urging slaves to obey their masters. By the 1830s, a racialized religious establishment had recalcified itself in the south, limiting the free exercise of religion among evangelical blacks. A swath of new laws swept through southern states, reflecting a common desire to prevent black religious movements from unsettling the slave order of the Old South. Southern Methodist, Baptist, and Presbyterian denominations launched missions to the slaves that, though apparently motivated by a sincere concern for the faith of the slaves, simultaneously sought to ensure that blacks received religious instruction that supported the southern slave system.[18]

Taking solace in these missions to the slaves, many white evangelicals argued that slavery promoted Christianity among blacks. They were wrong. Slavery actually impeded the growth of evangelicalism among African Americans, which expanded despite the system of slavery, not because of it. The slave system and evangelicalism remained in conflict with each other in several fundamental dynamics. Many state governments passed laws making it illegal to teach slaves to read and write, a system that undermined evangelical biblicism. Some whites defied these laws, and many slaves taught one another to read, but the vast majority of slaves remained illiterate, unable to read the Bible for themselves. Many slave owners would not allow slaves to hold religious services during the week, and some prohibited all religious services among blacks. Some freed people reported that for years, they had wanted to be baptized but couldn't get their masters' permission. This was a system that impeded evangelistic zeal.[19]

As accounts from Christian slaves attest, slavery's racialized religious establishment obstructed the development of black preachers, a democratized feature that had always energized evangelical growth. Some southern states made it illegal to ordain black ministers, and most states made it illegal for slaves to hold religious meetings without white supervision. One slave reported that he had been whipped for allowing blacks to attend his worship services without documented approval. Another black preacher was threatened with five hundred lashes if he preached; he preached anyway and was executed after he resisted arrest. One freed person explained that some black slaves were good preachers, but under slavery, they "couldn't preach as they want to; [they] must preach as the master allowed." To be sure, southern white evangelical ministers often cooperated with black evangelicals in promoting the faith. Even then, though, the slave system placed blacks and whites in a system of unequal social relations that distorted white perceptions. Many white evangelicals sincerely cared about the spiritual welfare of enslaved people, but few understood the sort of struggles and trials that slaves faced, because slaves were not in a position to explain their situation clearly. "We couldn't tell, NO PREACHER, NEVER, how we suffer all these long years," one African American explained to a northern missionary during the Civil War. "He know'd nothing about we."[20]

Evangelical Christianity did grow under the slave system. Christian slaves enjoyed a limited amount of religious freedom. Black and white Christians worshipped together in many places and cooperated in promoting evangelical revivals. These situations did not reconcile deep religious, social, and cultural tensions, though. Where possible, black Christians carved out religious spaces for themselves where they did not have to follow the dictates of white leaders. As Eugene Genovese has written, "the whites of the Old South tried to shape the religious life of their slaves, and the slaves overtly, covertly and even intuitively fought to shape it themselves." So, even as slaves went to great lengths to shape their religious lives, they still worshipped under a de facto religious establishment.[21]

Then the slave system was struck down. The freed people suddenly had full liberty to form independent black religious bodies, learn to read the Bible, evangelize their neighbors, and promote religious leaders of their choosing. Eventually, when Reconstruction withered away, southern whites managed to reassert their power in the political, economic, educational, and social spheres. However, they held very few tools to direct African-American religious life. White evangelicals discovered that they could no longer promote the faith by wielding the religious oversight they had enjoyed for many decades. In that setting, black evangelicalism grew by leaps and bounds.

Yet it grew in a very particular way. With numerous religious and cultural options available to them, the freed people proved to be quite selective in the institutions they adopted, a selectivity that played itself out in both new conversions and church switching. Blacks left southern white Baptist, Methodist, Presbyterian, and Episcopal churches in droves, although a small number decided to remain in these denominations. The Roman Catholic church made some inroads among African Americans in the late nineteenth century, but this growth paled in comparison with independent black evangelical churches.²²

Northern missionaries and reformers also competed for black allegiance. The American Freedman's Union Commission brought liberal theological sensibilities derived from Unitarian, Universalist, Garrisonian, Hicksite Quaker, or freethinker backgrounds. Although they did not promote religious conversion, these AFUC reformers hoped that the freed people would adopt their cultural vision grounded in moral instruction, common schools, free-labor economics, and liberal theology. The freed people flocked to AFUC schools, exuding a passionate desire to learn to read. At the same time, however, they rejected the liberal theological vision that accompanied these programs.²³

Northern white evangelical missionary agencies presented another option. Congregationalists, northern Presbyterians, northern Methodists, and northern Baptists promoted a native-ministry model for training black preachers and teachers, not only during Reconstruction but on into the early twentieth century. Northern evangelical missionaries established seminaries and normal schools for African Americans, in addition to Sunday schools and common schools. African Americans made full use of these institutions. In fact, the vast majority of black teachers, preachers, businesspeople, and professionals with degrees in higher education by 1900 had been educated in institutions established by white evangelicals.²⁴ But African Americans would not simply accept at face value the religious visions that white evangelicals offered them, particularly since these initiatives did not guarantee that white evangelicals would share positions of authority equally with blacks. With a finely tuned sense of the pervasiveness and subtleties of racism, African-American leaders entered into an intricate and complicated dance with these northern missionaries, attempting to negotiate access to scarce educational resources while fiercely holding on to religious autonomy.²⁵

Another factor animated black religious decisions in the postbellum era. Most freed people desired education and religious autonomy, but they also yearned for spiritual fulfillment. Black evangelicalism apparently addressed those yearnings better than anything else. As the African-American Great Awakening swept black communities, black Baptist and Methodist evangelists led the way, in true democratized fashion. Most of them were barely literate. Even with new seminaries and colleges for blacks sprouting up in several places, the demand for African-American preachers far exceeded the comparatively minuscule supply that these institutions could provide. Given the choice between highly educated, civil-rights-minded, well-resourced white ministers and poorly educated but enthusiastic black evangelists just released from slavery, African Americans chose, decisively, the latter.

Henry McNeal Turner understood this dynamic as well as anybody. During the 1860s and '70s, he led the way for the AME Church in mobilizing black preachers, licensing hundreds of illiterate and poorly educated black ministers. He asked candidates simply, "Can you preach?" and sometimes resorted to "Can you sing and pray?" if they waffled on the first question. He later claimed that he gave each candidate a long examination, but the preaching candidate's desire to evangelize and willingness to undergo future training functioned as the most important qualifications. Turner licensed preachers on street corners and train trips, filling out the preaching certificate on whatever surface lay close at hand.[26] He recognized the visible appeal and power that a black evangelical leader could wield simply by appearing in front of an African-American congregation. Yet there was more to black evangelism than the physical presence of a black preacher. Turner also recognized significance in the ability of these ordinary black evangelists to stir audiences and articulate the particular spiritual issues of the freed people. And he recognized that these qualities were deeply tied to questions of African descent.

Religious freedom could not resolve all of the uncertainties and conflicts that lay at the heart of Reconstruction. The powerful force of race wove ancestral identity deep into the American cultural fabric. Political rights, education, economic opportunity, social relations, and religious life hinged on the question of what it meant to be descended from Africans rather than Europeans. Much of nineteenth-century American culture answered this question by insisting that blacks were not capable of full participation in society. This argument almost always posed a commonsensical appeal to the characteristics of civilization, particularly as it compared with "barbarian" Africa. The most visible counterevidence—that blacks were actually quite capable of embodying the finest qualities of civilization—appeared in the form of African-American ministers. All of the major Protestant denominations contained a collection of educated, devout, self-controlled, hardworking, and refined black ministers. They felt keenly the responsibilities of their position.[27]

No AME minister articulated this responsibility as fully as Daniel Alexander Payne, the most prominent bishop of the denomination. Born in 1811 to free parents in Charleston, South Carolina, Payne imbibed both their Methodist piety and a desire for education before he was orphaned at age ten. A vibrant spiritual conversion at age fifteen indelibly stamped this blend of evangelicalism and education on his mind. Years later, Payne recalled how he had "felt as if the hands of a man were pressing my two shoulders" during one of his prayers. He had "heard a voice speaking within [his] soul saying: 'I have set thee apart to educate thyself in order that thou mayest be an educator to thy people.'" Shortly thereafter, a slaveholder told him that "superior knowledge" was the only thing that separated master and slave. From that point on, Payne earnestly and tirelessly dedicated himself to the ideal of liberating his race through education and evangelical Christianity. He established a Christian school for blacks in Charleston, but the southern establishment did not look kindly on independent black evangelicalism. The state legislature forced the school to close, provoking Payne to leave South Carolina in 1835 to look for a teaching opportunity in the north.[28]

Payne's interactions with northern ministers, educators, and reformers reinforced his commitment to education and gave him hope that white and black Christians could work cooperatively for the benefit of the black race and American civilization. After a Lutheran pastor had convinced him that he could be of most use to African Americans as a minister, Payne studied at Gettysburg Seminary for two years and received ordination. He also met Lewis Tappan, who, in one conversation, converted Payne to the cause of abolition. Payne seriously considered work with the Anti-Slavery Society but decided that God had called him to be a minister.[29]

And so he entered the AME Church. For the rest of his career, Payne exerted tremendous influence on his denomination in the service of that great Yankee cause, Christian education. At the first annual conference he attended, he petitioned the body for more extensive academic requirements for the ministry. His efforts to raise the educational standards of AME ministers propelled Payne into the position of bishop in 1852. A decade later, faced with an opportunity that would pass if he did not move quickly, he unilaterally purchased Wilberforce University for the AME denomination, trusting that his fellow church people would raise the money to pay the debts of the purchase. Fellow AME minister B. W. Arnett aptly described Payne as "the apostle of an educated ministry," a conception not unlike that promoted by Barnas Sears among northern white Baptists.[30]

In the spirit of early Methodism, the AME Church had always seen itself as a missionary denomination, with a particular call to the black race. Payne attempted to work out that calling according to the terms of the civilizing mission. He believed that God would work through the AME Church not only to help abolish slavery but also to spread Christianity and provide southern blacks with the tools to build the proper institutions of civilization. Convinced that higher education would uplift and enlighten blacks who had suffered under "the errors which centuries of a debasing servitude fastened upon them," Payne mirrored highly educated Victorians in investing education with a powerful component of moral and spiritual authority. Christian education produced individuals "well-fitted for a Christian usefulness, a moral, a spiritual power, molding, coloring community, and preparing it for a nobler and higher state of existence."[31] For Payne, then, to be of African descent meant that one had all of the capabilities to achieve high civilization, even if some catching up needed to take place. Payne aimed to prove to whites that the black race was quite capable of mastering the expectations of civilization, but he also believed that the civilizing mission itself would bring great blessings to blacks.

Evangelical themes of sin, redemption, divine agency, and human responsibility permeated Payne's vision, which challenged reigning perceptions of blacks. Along with his fellow AME ministers, Payne vociferously denied that God had set the white race apart in any special way. "It is said that he is the God of the white man, and not of the black," he preached. "This is horrible blasphemy—a lie from the pit that is bottomless." In company with most black Christians, Payne believed that God orchestrated the events of the Civil War to abolish slavery and punish those whites who supported it. "His almighty arm," Payne proclaimed in 1862, "is already stretched out against slavery—against every man, every constitution, and every union that upholds it."[32] Payne not only campaigned for abolition but also challenged the Lincoln administration to accept the idea that blacks and whites could live together as equals.

In 1865, thirty years to the day since "the spirit of slavery" had forced him out of his school in Charleston, Payne stood in that city once again, moved to tears at the sight of Yankee abolitionists teaching African-American children. When the war ended, Payne had traveled south for a few weeks, bringing the trappings of Yankee civilization in tow. He had made his arrangements through the Congregationalist-dominated American Missionary Association, accompanying several white missionaries to Charleston and Savannah. Payne had preached several times and organized the first South Carolina Annual Conference of the AME Church. His deepest hopes, though, centered on the new school for black children that he visited under the escort of Union army officers and protection of black troops from the Union army. "It was there and then that I believed what I beheld was a prophecy of the future," he later wrote, "that New England ideas, sentiments, and principles will ultimately rule the entire South."[33]

And yet the freed people rebuffed this prophecy of the future. Payne found himself, along with northern white evangelicals, liberal reformers, and southern white evangelicals, watching helplessly as black evangelicals set off on a path that had not been laid out by the terms of the civilizing mission. This seems like a curious rejection, for Payne seemed to embody the finest ideals of Christianity, the black race, and the American nation. As the most famous bishop of the AME denomination, a champion of abolition, a spokesperson for the independent black church, an erudite theological leader, and an indefatigable promoter of education, Payne certainly promoted many aspects of the new society that freed people hoped to establish after the Civil War.[34]

What, then, was there in Payne's vision that did not sit well with southern blacks? The key lies in the type of evangelicalism that the black bishop promoted. Payne might be described as a formalist evangelical with deep suspicions of popular revivalism. Like several other elite black ministers, Payne regularly traveled

AME circuits, attempting, and usually failing, to eliminate certain enthusiastic religious practices among ordinary African-American Christians. The most famous example comes from a description that Payne gave of a ring shout at an AME "bush meeting" in 1878. He reported that "after the sermon they formed a ring, and with coats off sung, clapped their hands and stamped their feet in a most ridiculous and heathenish way." Expressing his unhappiness with the "strange delusions that many ignorant but well-meaning people labor under," Payne asked the black minister to order the congregation to stop their dancing and clapping and "sit down and sing in a rational manner." He then pulled the minister aside and explained that "it was a heathenish way to worship and disgraceful to themselves, the race, and the Christian name." Later that afternoon, the young AME minister approached Payne to defend the ring, arguing that "sinners won't get converted unless there is a ring." Payne replied that this singing would fail to convert anyone, because "nothing but the Spirit of God and the word of God can convert sinners." The young minister countered by declaring that "the Spirit of God works upon people in different ways." He explained that "at campmeeting there must be a ring here, a ring there, and a ring over yonder, or sinners will not get converted."[35]

This did not sit well with the AME bishop. The true Christian minister, Payne wrote, was "more anxious to make God's people intelligent and wise, than to excite their animal feelings and make them shout." According to Payne, "ignorant people" might have been swayed by a minister "whose tongue is full of fire," but "educated and intelligent persons" rightfully denounced this style of preaching as "flippant oratory and glittering rhetoric." At each of the churches he served, Payne attacked the "ignorant and deluded" singing and praying bands of Christians, who regularly worshipped late into the evening in the style of early Methodism. Payne described the popular religious music of AME churches as "transcripts of low thoughts, ignorance, and superstition" and campaigned to infuse the AME denomination with instrumental music, sacred concerts, and "scientifically trained" choirs.[36]

There was more at work here than issues of education and refinement. In his conversation with the AME preacher, Payne used the term *heathenish*, indicating that he recognized what twentieth-century scholars later demonstrated: the ring shout had some sort of tie to African culture. Over the years, elements of African culture had persisted in the United States in transformed configurations, blending with the materials of American society to produce African-American culture.[37]

Antiformalist evangelicalism, with its instinctive ability to adapt to different cultures, lay right at the center of this cultural mix. The ring shout, a rhythmic spiritual dance that can be traced to traditional African cultures, had appeared in Methodist prayer meetings and camp meetings at least as early as 1819. Slave spirituals evoked biblical themes through the use of African musical styles such as call and response, syncopation, hand clapping, foot tapping, repetition, improvisation, polyrhythms, and sliding from one note to another. African practices of spirit possession were transformed into the shouts, groans, and shrieks of blacks coming under the power of the Holy Spirit in camp-meeting revivalism. Traditional African religious practices that upheld roles for women as mediums or oracles found new expression in evangelical practices in which women testified publicly in camp meetings or even preached as itinerant revivalists. African beliefs about pervasive supernaturalism reconstituted themselves in African-American perceptions of the activities of Satan or God speaking though dreams. West and Central African rituals associated with symbolic death and instantaneous regeneration found renewed expression in the immediate conversionism of evangelicalism.[38] With its elements of African culture, then, the emergence of evangelical Christianity among African Americans represented a new variation of world Christianity.

Payne saw these "heathenish" practices as a problem. Internalizing the Enlightenment assertion that Western civilization had progressed beyond the "animal feelings" of barbarian societies, Payne and many of his fellow elite black ministers promoted a more pervasively modern conception of religion, typified by Payne's insistence that the congregation "sing in a rational manner."[39] Before the Enlightenment, many highly educated Christians had accepted supernatural activity, religious ecstasy, and visible manifestations of God's activities as realities. The Puritans, for instance, found no problem reconciling their perception of pervasive supernatural activity with erudite theological reflection. But Enlightenment advocates clamped down on religious enthusiasm as a threat to social order, defined accounts of supernatural activity as superstition, and claimed that special acts of God did not take place if they could not be empirically verified. Like many highly educated Americans in the nineteenth century, Payne became attracted to a more disenchanted faith, one that was seen as more civilized.[40]

Ordinary African-American Christians, however, believed that the Holy Spirit worked in ways that did not always conform to modern religious sensibilities. In this sense, Payne and the unnamed AME preacher reenacted a long-standing drama within American evangelicalism. Payne played the role of the famous minister Lyman Beecher, who, in his attempt to steer evangelicalism to a course that deferred to the authority of learned ministers, warned fellow evangelicals in 1814 to ignore popular Methodist evangelists such as "Crazy" Lorenzo Dow.[41]

Having learned his part well, Payne proved to be every bit as ineffective as the esteemed Beecher. The African-American Great Awakening grew through the enthusiastic efforts of ordinary blacks, not the "rational" direction of elite black ministers such as Payne. Forty years after emancipation, W. E. B. DuBois, the most insightful observer of African-American life, identified three defining characteristics of African-American worship, each of which would have met with Payne's disapproval. DuBois linked these elements to African culture, but they also represented a rejection of Enlightenment claims about the relationship between rationality and religious practice. DuBois famously described "The Preacher" who stirred the congregation into an enthusiastic response to Scripture, "The Music" that evoked both the joyful and the doleful realities of the African-American situation, and "The Frenzy," a variety of expressive responses grounded in the conviction that "without the visible manifestation of the God there could be no true communion with the Invisible."[42]

Payne's critique of the ring shout has been well noted by historians who wish to demonstrate that black elites drank deeply from the well of bourgeois chauvinism. As one historian writes, Payne was "swimming upstream in wrestling with the concrete issue of class divisions within the African-based community, expressed in terms of religion."[43] And yet this class-based explanation cannot quite carry the day. African-American Christians accepted other middle-class reforms proposed by elite black ministers, such as the use of new hymns and more regularity in service times. Freed people throughout the south enthusiastically welcomed the cornerstone of middle-class Yankee respectability, the common school.[44]

Tellingly, issues of class, civilization, or black identity did not emerge in the concerns of the young AME minister who debated Payne at the bush meeting. He did not protest by saying, "This is how common folk do things" or even "This is how we express our African ancestry." Instead, he said, "sinners will not get converted" without a ring. This minister had evangelical purposes in mind, not class purposes. Like countless others antiformalist evangelicals amid the African-American Great Awakening, the young AME preacher believed that he was part of a movement in which the Holy Spirit manifested itself in visible expressions such as the ring shout. His main concern was one of effective religious activity, expressed in class and cultural terms, not the other way around.[45]

These differences between Payne and the democratized blacks did not represent an unbridgeable rift. In fact, the cooperation between Payne and the freed people might be more striking than their conflicts. Dissenting evangelicals in disestablished settings had always found it easy to break free from established religious leaders to form independent denominations, a Protestant habit that was all the rage among freed people who had belonged to white antebellum churches.[46] But the freed people refused to break away from elite black leaders such as Payne, even as they disregarded his admonitions. In fact, they rushed to put themselves under the AME system. Antiformalists led the way in evangelizing fellow African Americans through enthusiastic preaching, expressive music, and ecstatic worship, while Payne and his fellow elite ministers provided the institutional structures, administrative expertise, and educational resources. In the end, the fundamental commitments to evangelicalism and the welfare of the black race outweighed these differences among African Americans in the AME Church.

Woven from African, European, and American cultural strands, the African-American Great Awakening carried the day after emancipation. The evangelical missionary impulse drove the dynamic growth of black Baptist and black Methodist churches in the south, with their popular black preachers, noisy services, exuberant music, supernaturalistic claims, evangelistic enthusiasm, independent institutions, distinct racial identities, and strong communal foundations. For most freed people, this represented the religious expression of what it meant to be an American of African descent.

This African-American variation of world Christianity compelled Henry McNeal Turner, as he first traveled through Georgia as a missionary, to revise his conceptions of black evangelicalism. The exuberant, noisy, enthusiastic promoters of the African-American Great Awakening challenged Turner's conception of black identity, evangelical faith, and its relationship to civilization. The evangelical paradox of influence appeared again: because Turner sought to influence southern freed people in his missionary work, they ended up influencing him. If it were not for his postbellum missionary experiences, Turner very well might have spent his life echoing Payne's disapproval of ordinary black religious life.

His life, to that point, seemed to trace a similar trajectory to Payne's. Born as a free black in South Carolina in 1834, Turner underwent an early religious experience that left him with a profound religious impression and an intense desire for education. At the age of twelve, Turner had a dream in which millions of people looked to him for instruction. Much later in life, Turner described this as a special call from God. After his conversion, Turner embarked on an intense program of self-education, a process in which he claimed that aid came from an angel that God sent to him while he slept. Licensed as an exhorter by the Methodist Episcopal Church, South, in 1851 and then as a preacher in 1853, Turner spent several years itinerating across the southern states, preaching and holding revivals among separate black congregations, biracial bodies, and an occasional all-white audience.[47]

Turner spoke affectionately of the white ministers who facilitated his own conversion, valued biracial worship when he found it, and occasionally teamed up with white revivalists, as he did with William Parks in a series of revivals in Athens, Georgia, in 1858. But he also seethed under the proslavery sermons that he had heard since childhood. Sometimes caustic, always blunt, and consistently strong-minded, Turner sparred with white groups who doubted his intelligence, and he drew inspiration from the strong sense of black identity that he discovered in separate black congregations where he had preached. Thus, when he discovered the AME Church in 1857, the separate character of what nineteenth-century evangelicals called African Methodism naturally appealed to him. The following year, he joined the AME denomination and traveled north to pastor AME churches in St. Louis and Baltimore, where his reputation as a powerful preacher grew. During the Civil War, Turner returned to the south to aid the freed people. As the first black person to be appointed as a chaplain in the army of the United States, Turner accompanied African-American regiments on their forays into the south, holding prayer meetings and conducting revivals along the way, both in his regiment and among the newly emancipated blacks they encountered.[48]

Like many elite black ministers, Turner worried about the morality, education, and habits of industry of the newly emancipated slaves. Or at least, he did at first. His initial encounters with freed people in North Carolina produced a sense of discouragement that bordered on disgust. "The foul curse of slavery has blighted the natural greatness of my race!" he cried. "It has transformed many into an inhuman appearance." To Turner, popular black worship seemed to be based mostly on emotionalism. "Let a person get a little animated, fall down and roll over awhile, kick a few shins, crawl under a dozen benches, spring upon his feet, knock some innocent person on the nose and set it bleeding, then squeal and kiss [or buss] around for awhile, and the work is all done," he wrote from North Carolina in early 1865. "If the individual had claimed justification under more quiet circumstances, its legitimacy would have been doubted," he complained. Turner perceived freed-people communities to be characterized by emotionalism, a limited knowledge of the world, a weak sense of industry, and poor levels of morality, raising questions in his mind about its level of civilization. "Nothing more than a partial state of civilization and moral attainment can be hoped for by the most sanguine," he lamented to the readers of the *Christian Recorder* in the summer of 1865.[49]

The discourse of civilization tempted Turner to cast the freed people in a paternalistic light and send him down the broad avenue of the civilizing mission. In the end, Turner did not take this road. The African-American Great Awakening diverted the AME missionary in a direction that defended the exuberant, ecstatic religious life of ordinary blacks.

One can see Turner striking down this new path in the years after the war ended. Just as Karen evangelists impressed Baptist missionaries with their determination, piety, and conviction under oppression, emancipated Christians impressed this AME minister, even if he did not find everything to his liking. In mid-1865, he expressed a wish that a black Methodist church he visited had more of the "milder and yet more powerful" message of Jesus than the "much cruder" message of "hell fire, brimstone, damnation, black smoke, hot lead, &c." And yet something in the spiritual vitality of the church affected Turner. "But, oh! what zeal and determination they manifest in their efforts to serve God!," he wrote. "I have to admire it as much as I admire the soldiers' prayer meeting in my regiment."[50]

Turner felt himself pulled by conflicting impulses. The courage of many of the "partially civilized" freed people impressed him, as they resisted efforts by whites who sought to reimpose former patterns of subjugation. He praised the blacks of Columbia, South Carolina, in early 1866 for being "brave, independent and fearless," with "none of this foolish crouching before white men." Then he added, without elaboration, "but, in other places I am disgusted."[51] At one point, he explained that "there are thousands" of freed people who "cherish old slavish habits and ideas, about which they need plain talk." He then quickly qualified this assessment. "But, some one may ask, why do you represent the freedmen as being more ignorant than any people I have heard of?..."No, that is not my intention; I claim for them superior ability." Latching on to themes of democratization, Turner declared that a poorly educated black slave from South Carolina spoke with more eloquence than any person he had ever heard, including Henry Ward Beecher and Charles Sumner. "The ablest historian, the greatest orator, and the most skillful architect and mechanic I have ever seen were all slaves in the South," he told *Christian Recorder* readers.[52]

Turner had many more opportunities to witness black zeal and determination in 1866, after Payne officially appointed him as a missionary to the fledgling AME movement in Georgia. Unlike Payne, who occasionally made short visits to the south in his role as bishop, Turner maintained an extensive missionary engagement with the freed people, worshipping daily with ordinary people, conducting revivals, licensing new ministers, and establishing new churches. He launched into old Methodist circuit-riding patterns, preaching nightly during the week and three times every Sunday in numerous locations around the state. He later claimed that in just one year in Georgia, he traveled more than fifteen thousand miles and preached more than five hundred times. Francis Asbury and Harry Hosier would have been proud.[53]

These regular missionary engagements pulled him further into the enthusiastic world of democratized black evangelicalism. Although he sometimes questioned the theological value of some African-American spirituals, he encouraged the lively "Zion" songs popular among camp meetings. By late 1866, when the revivals began to take off in earnest, he had discovered an effective assistant in an expressive evangelist named Joseph H. Jennings. "And by some hook and a crook I made [him] an assistant elder...and a hero he is," Turner reported. "I am not much for shouting, but I think a man is excusable for shouting when Jennings gets hold of him. I could almost excuse a horse."[54]

This was antiformalist evangelicalism at work, on both the freed people and the superintendent of missions. Turner became convinced of two key points about these southern people of African descent. First, even without education, newly emancipated blacks possessed qualities of courage and independent spirit that could be harnessed to battle racism, a battle that well-meaning northern whites did not always understand. Black leaders could not be "bribed by the deceptive flippancy of the oily-tongued slavocrats, who too often becloud the understanding of whites," Turner explained. Second, the enthusiastic "shouting" of African-American evangelicalism did not represent a "heathenish" form of African culture that needed to be eradicated but was a means by which the Holy Spirit moved in the African-American community. In the end, these two convictions explain why Turner, who remained a staunch supporter of education and "true" civilization, licensed many illiterate and poorly educated black ministers.[55]

Other evangelicals objected to this antiformalist turn. For a variety of reasons, leaders from the increasingly white Methodist Episcopal Church, South, protested against Turner's widespread licensing of poorly educated black ministers. Some whites in the MECS argued for higher educational qualifications for blacks in order to slow the growth of the AME Church, apparently worried that independent black denominations posed a threat to the social order they wished to maintain. Others supported the education of black ministers but wanted control or guidance over that process, probably believing that the black church needed the direction of more "civilized" whites.[56] Either way, southern whites could not keep blacks in white churches. They were powerless to set qualifications for black ministers. Southern whites could do little more than look on while this popular missionary movement built an enthusiastic, noisy, determined, and independent African-American church right in their midst.

Northern missionary groups did not get exactly what they envisioned, either. The theologically liberal AFUC burned brightly for a very short time before quickly dying out. The initial enthusiasm to establish common schools for blacks faded, except among a handful of dedicated teachers who continued to work in primary schoolhouses for many years. Nor did the AFUC find much in the African-American Great Awakening that resonated with its moral or religious sensibilities. AFUC reformers believed that white evangelical missionaries were sectarian, emotional, and embarrassing; they were even more unsettled by the religion of those of African descent, whose spirituality was far more expressive and supernaturalistic.[57]

Northern white evangelicals presented a mixed response to the African-American Great Awakening. Those with the deepest ties to abolitionism or the native-ministry ideal maintained faith in African-American capabilities, although they disapproved of the idea of poorly educated black ministers. The white evangelicals who worried about maintaining an orderly republic and seemed most bent on establishing a Christian nation, however, were unsettled by the African-American Great Awakening. In the 1870s, '80s, and '90s, those driven by the vision of forging the United States into a Christian nation wished to reconcile with white southerners. The problem was that white southerners usually insisted that northerners accept their terms of a southern order in which whites held positions of power. As a result, when white northern evangelicals and white southern evangelicals came together to promote causes such as revivalism or temperance, black evangelicals were often shoved to the side, an action that reinforced white hierarchies and racist assumptions of black incapability.[58]

Most blacks shared the native-ministry conviction that blacks were fully capable of high education. But tensions among formalist evangelicals and antiformalist revivalists would erupt from time to time, particularly over the question of black ordination. Turner discovered this very early on. Many of his fellow AME ministers, especially those from the north, expressed alarm at his ordinations, charging him with "recklessly licensing preachers by the cargo." Fearing that Turner's wholesale licensing of poorly educated pastors saddled the southern AME churches with dubious leadership, these AME pastors worried that the actions of uneducated pastors would tarnish their denominational accomplishments in the eyes of whites. When Turner presented seventeen freed-people candidates for ordination at the 1867 annual conference in Georgia, Wesley Gaines fretted publicly that the flood of new candidates threatened the standards that the AME Church had established for ministers. Gaines declared that Georgia "had enough of incompetent ordained ministers now, and he protested against so much liberality any longer."[59]

One year later, Turner accompanied fifty other men from the south to the quadrennial meeting of the AME Church's highest legislative body, the General Conference, and proposed that these freed people be accepted as full members. Because most of the southern ministers had not served long enough to qualify as voting members under AME polity and, by implication, did not possess the maturity or wisdom to vote on issues of denominational polity, northern delegates initially rejected Turner's proposal. After vigorous debate, including agitation from southerners about "taxation without representation," the body overcame its initial hesitation and voted to accept the southern ministers as full members. The debate over the nature of black leadership, however, would continue to rear its head in AME deliberations as the African-American Great Awakening continued through the rest of the nineteenth century.[60]

Turner felt soul saving to be of such importance that he also extended his antiformalist program to gender issues. He believed that many women had "as loud a call to the ministry as some of us." When the 1884 General Conference permitted female evangelists to be licensed to preach but barred women from becoming full ministers, Sarah Ann Hughes lost her church in North Carolina. Turner took it upon himself to ordain Hughes anyway. This touched off a controversy within the denomination that led Turner to back off his earlier stand. He then denied a new pastorate to Hughes. Still, he grumbled that "there are too many drunkards, gamblers, liars, thieves, lynchers, mobs, Sabbath breakers, blasphemers, adulterers, slanderers, and sinners in the land to stop and quibble over women preachers." By contrast, Payne promoted female activity in the church through roles linked to northern ideas of domesticity, promoting tasks for women, such as education. He fought against the ordination of itinerant female evangelists such as Jarena Lee, who bypassed denominational sanction in claiming that God had given her the authority to preach. And so, on the issue of female ordination, black evangelicalism simultaneously affirmed both democratization and middle-class domesticity, American cultural elements in conflict with each other.[61]

Female ordination was not the only area in which black evangelicalism displayed a conflicted relationship with American culture. Black Methodist and Baptist churches thrived amid the racialized religious disestablishment in the south, competitive religious arrangements, and opportunities for institutional autonomy. Yet the African-American Great Awakening simultaneously enabled ordinary black Christians to resist other characteristics of American culture. Black evangelicals differed from most white evangelicals in their understanding of the pervasive and subtle effects of racism, their resistance to religious disenchantment, their blending of African cultural elements into their religious practices, and the role of blacks in the American nation.

African-American evangelicalism developed an ambivalent relationship with the American nation-state. Turner's response to the beating of the AME preacher in Auburn, Alabama, questioning whether this society was Christendom or hell, would have seemed ludicrous to most white American Protestants in the nineteenth century. In fact, many black evangelicals would not have asked that question, either. Payne, for instance, trusted the American system, in part, because he experienced formative interactions with antislavery and abolitionist whites during much of his career. By marshaling ideas, sentiments, and principles against slavery, a coalition of black and white reformers could claim that they had successfully toppled the most oppressive system that had plagued American society. That same kind of work, Payne was convinced, could conquer the remaining vestiges of racism.

It was a stirring vision of black prospects in America. And Turner did not buy it. Unlike Payne's experience, Turner's formative interactions with whites exposed him to the pervasiveness of American racism, in both its sunny paternalistic guise and its virulent, violent eruptions. In the antebellum era, Turner had worked alongside white Methodist ministers in revival tours, but he had been denied full ordination by the Methodist Episcopal Church, South, despite his clear gifts as an evangelist. Turner's extensive contact with soldiers in Sherman's army and reformers from the north during the Civil War did not convince him that Yankee civilization provided the future hope for southern blacks, either. "I have been told, over and over, by colored people, that they were never treated more cruelly than they were by some of the white Yankees," he wrote in June 1865. While serving a brief stint with the Freedman's Bureau, Turner found that when benevolent white officials attempted to get a clear understanding of the former slaves, they rejected his advice, accepting instead the claims about blacks made by white southerners.[62]

Violence remained a constant threat in southern society. When Turner traveled to Opelika, Alabama, in 1866 to plant an AME church, a white group gathered to lynch him when he got off the train. Tipped off to the plot, he saved himself by posing as a different person and volunteering to help the mob find this Henry McNeal Turner fellow. Two years later, he spoke at a political rally in Columbus, Georgia, alongside George Ashburn, a prominent white Republican. Incensed by this promotion of a multiracial political order, a Ku Klux Klan mob murdered Ashburn half an hour later. They very well might have killed Turner if they had located him. That same year, Turner won an election to the Georgia House of Representatives, but the state legislature ignored the results and unseated him, along with twenty-three other black winners of the election. The United States Congress later ordered Georgia to restore Turner and the others to office. In 1870, he apparently won reelection to the legislature, but charges of voter fraud (which infected both political parties) provoked a recount, which was held illegally in the back room of a private home. White officials declared that Turner had lost the election. Because he continued to speak publicly against white racism, Turner received death threats from the KKK and had to hide "in houses at times, in the woods at other times, in a hollow log at another time." The *Columbus Weekly Sun* declared that "we should be neither seized with astonishment or regret" if Turner were lynched.[63]

These were not the sorts of experiences that encouraged one to think that the presence of a civilized black leader would convince whites that they really ought to grant African Americans respect and equality after all. Even during the most optimistic days of Reconstruction, as the freed people sang of the joys of emancipation, when blacks were elected to state legislatures, as independent black denominations grew, and while schools for black children were being established across the south, racial conflicts painfully dampened suggestions that American society would usher in the millennium for blacks. This reality explains another characteristic that often appeared in nineteenth-century African-American Christianity: the resistance to a type of civil religion that neatly equated Christianity with American nationalism. Given the racial violence, discrimination, and hardships heaped on them, many African Americans simply could not accept the idea that the American republic was specially ordained by God.

Obviously, racism looms as the prime culprit here, but it was a particular expression of racism, deeply linked to the modern concept of the nation-state. As Allen Dwight Callahan points out, since modernity grounded nationhood in blood and land, African Americans could not claim privileges to either. Modern nation-states tended to locate identity in an ancestry formed around a particular language or culture.⁶⁴ Given its ethnic diversity, the United States had a more complicated task than many European nation-states in this regard, but through the nineteenth century and for most of the twentieth, it tended to work out an arrangement that grounded American identity in a European ancestry, or what some historians call whiteness. This is where "blood" intersected with citizenship. Those of African ancestry were not granted full access to the American dream, while immigrant groups from Europe who could lay claim to the white race managed to gain access.

Assumptions linking land with national identity also limited blacks. White Americans consistently denied African Americans access to land, a resource at the heart of national identity, upward mobility, and the myth of the self-made man. This impulse ran so deep that even liberal and evangelical abolitionists from the north, who sincerely believed that they had the best interests of African Americans at heart, saw no inconsistency with rejecting the idea of granting freed people "forty acres and a mule," while simultaneously supporting an 1862 Homestead Act that gave western land to common white settlers and immigrants. Most northern liberal and evangelical reformers in the Reconstruction south insisted instead that African Americans work for wages on land owned by former slave owners, a program that denied them access to land ownership. The Fourteenth Amendment granted African Americans citizenship in theory, but actions on the ground concerning blood and land shaped national identity in ways that proved otherwise. Most African Americans felt this conflict deeply. As W. E. B. DuBois explained in a famous passage, the black person "ever feels his twoness,—an American, a Negro; two souls, two thoughts, two unreconciled strivings."⁶⁵

No wonder, then, that African-American evangelicals repeatedly found significance in the verse from Acts 17 that "God hath made one blood of all the nations." No wonder that African-American Christians mined Exodus not just for themes of liberation but also for its themes of landlessness and exile. Evangelical biblicism helped African Americans attempt to transcend modern conceptions of ancestry grounded in blood and land, challenging modernity to reconfigure its terms. That battle would last well beyond the end of the nineteenth century.⁶⁶

The failure of Reconstruction, the emergence of segregation, and the growing contagion of lynchings in the 1890s made it very difficult for many African Americans to buy into the idea that American civilization embodied the highest ideals of Christianity. Many former slaves might have been suspicious of the patriotic proclamations that labeled the United States as a Christian nation because they had heard a similar sort of civilizing concept extolled by the antebellum master class.

Turner certainly could not accept it. He described *Plessey v. Ferguson*, a "decision unknown in hell itself," as a sign of "the barbarous ages revived and surpassed." In 1902, he declared that the universities, newspapers, governmental system, transportation networks, communications system, churches, and pulpits gave the United States "all the forms and paraphernalia of civilization," but the "highest form of civilized institutions" had to be seen in light of the "barbarous and cruel" specter of the lynch mob. In a statement that would have seemed absurd both to white Americans and to members of the AME hierarchy, Turner declared that "no one can say, who has any respect for truth, that the United States is a civilized nation."[67] "The white people of this country have no true Christian civilization," he declared, as black lynchings in the United States reached a rate of three each week. "We are often confronted through the public press with reports of the most barbarous and cruel outrages that can be perpetrated upon human beings, known in the history of the world," he lamented. "No savage nation can exceed the atrocities which are often heralded through the country and accepted by many as an incidental consequence."[68] Without progressive millennialism driving his view of American civilization, Turner searched for another way to reconcile evangelicalism, African ancestry, and true civilization. The foreign-missionary enterprise provided an opportunity for him to try to work out these tensions.

7

The AME Church and South Africa

Evangelicalism in South Africa simultaneously inspired and restricted Mangena Mokone. A Christian from the Pedi people, Mokone had a deep desire to preach and teach. He had begun evangelizing shortly after his conversion and baptism in Durban in 1872. He worked as an unpaid evangelist for British Methodist missionaries, earning money as a carpenter's apprentice by day and taking classes at night from the local Wesleyan school. As an evangelist, he stirred up both blacks and whites, though not in the same way. In a manner common to African Methodists, Mokone led a service one night that was loud enough to disturb neighboring whites. Upon investigation, the neighbors discovered an entire congregation of blacks on its knees in tears. In a manner common to colonial Europeans, the whites contacted the supervising Methodist missionary and demanded that he replace the "boy" who had frightened the "poor niggers, lying on their guts." Mokone was not replaced, but he continued to feel the sting of whites in South Africa who attempted to control and limit his ministry, even as the inner logic of evangelicalism propelled him outward.[1]

The Wesleyan missionaries accepted Mokone as a minister on trial in 1880, but they did not permit him to enroll in their training institute at Healdtown, as he deeply desired. Nevertheless, he persisted. Even without an advanced education, Mokone displayed an array of linguistic, cultural, and spiritual gifts. He spoke Sepedi, English, and Dutch, while picking up some Xhosa and German along the way. Appointed to work in the boomtown of Pretoria in 1882, Mokone effectively expanded the work of Methodism in the socially unstable and shifting regions of the Transvaal. He planted churches, opened several mission stations, taught classes, and helped the missionaries establish the first African teacher-training school in the Transvaal. He even constructed the fittings for the school buildings himself. Eventually, the British Methodists noticed his accomplishments and appointed him principal of the Kilnerton Institute in 1892.

Even then, the two white missionaries who taught at Kilnerton could not bring themselves to relinquish meaningful authority to Mokone. Unofficially appropriating several duties of the black principal for themselves, the missionaries carried out administrative tasks without consulting him. They unilaterally expelled black students, brought in a white government official to administer punishments, and compelled ill students to attend class. Mokone later asserted that the missionaries accused these ailing blacks of laziness, even as the students shivered under their blankets.[2]

If the Wesleyan missionaries thought that they were effectively managing this African Christian, they were mistaken. They worked within a system that limited what they could do to control Mokone and like-minded black Christians. Evangelicalism encouraged Mokone to preach and evangelize, regardless of the opposition he faced. Thus, when he concluded that significant opposition to his evangelical vision came from none other than the evangelical missionaries themselves, he was, in fact, appropriating evangelical tools that the missionaries had handed him. In late 1892, Mokone broke from the Methodist missionary system. He sent a letter of resignation to the Wesleyan authorities and launched an independent black denomination, the "Ethiopian" church, named for the allusions to Africa found in the Bible.[3] Planting the denomination with fifty-seven followers in a private hut on the edge of Pretoria, Mokone enlisted about a dozen pastors over the next three years, who brought with them about one thousand congregants. After five years, through evangelism and recruitment in various parts of South Africa, the Ethiopian church grew to nearly eleven thousand members. Evangelicalism had grown once again after breaking free from evangelical missionary control.[4]

Then Henry McNeal Turner entered the picture. Mokone discovered Turner through a family friend who had made her way to the United States. Turner and Mokone began corresponding and exploring cooperative work. Excited by the existence of an independent black American denomination with educational resources, members of the Ethiopian movement voted to affiliate with the AME Church. They sent a representative, James Dwane, to the United States to facilitate the process. Then the AME Church sent Turner to South Africa to solidify the institutional system. Much as he had done in the Reconstruction south in the United States, Turner encouraged and helped organize a vibrant evangelistic movement in South Africa, ordaining sixty ministers and establishing annual conferences. The church doubled in size during Turner's six-week tour.[5]

On the surface, this new relationship seemed pretty straightforward. Black South African Christians and African-American Christians appeared quite compatible. Like the AME Church in the United States, the Ethiopian movement was a body of independent black evangelicals, most of whom came to the faith through a Methodist system. Mokone had founded his movement by breaking away from the racism and prejudice he faced among white Methodists, mirroring the same forces that compelled Richard Allen to break away from white Methodists and establish the AME Church in Philadelphia in 1816. Like that of the AME Church, the growth of the Ethiopian movement had been spurred on by the enthusiastic evangelistic efforts of ordinary blacks, who also desired opportunity, education, and respect in a white-dominated society that refused to grant them. The similarities alone between the Ethiopian movement and the AME Church would seem to make for a smooth and untroubled marriage.

It was not so simple. As in some marriages, the first years of the AME Church in South Africa were agitated by perplexity, tensions, and unanticipated conflicts, even as the relationship matured and grew. The Ethiopian movement did not just challenge the racism of South African society. It also implicitly raised questions among AME leadership about whether Western civilization ought to function as a normative standard that Africans should emulate. In other words, black South Africans presented the AME Church with a similar puzzle to that which the "wild" Karen people of Burma had presented northern Baptists: how were AME missionaries to engage an energetic, thriving Christian people who did not meet the criteria of an advanced civilization?

AME leaders did not present a united front on this cultural issue. They were, after all, evangelicals. Some, like Turner, were confident that evangelism and leadership by ordinary blacks in South Africa, assisted by cooperative AME missionaries, would produce a thriving and well-grounded movement. Other AME leaders worried that uncivilized African pastors needed guidance, supervision, and direction from civilized black missionaries from the United States. These divergent visions reflected unresolved questions about the relationship between race and civilization. But there was more. AME leaders were divided in their approach to the Ethiopian movement because they were divided about their own legacy as a movement built, in part, from religious practices shaped by African culture. In other words, AME leaders reacted differently to this new movement of world Christianity in South Africa because they themselves were still not in agreement about what to make of a different movement of world Christianity: African-American evangelicalism.

Many AME ministers were convinced that the way to overcome racism lay in proving one's fitness for civilization by emulating powerful whites. Unsurprisingly, Turner did not fall into this camp. In the many roles that he took on in his life, which included state legislator, bishop of the AME Church, editor of a black newspaper, civil rights campaigner, hymn book compiler, advocate for black emigration to Africa, temperance campaigner, writer of black theology, and missionary to Africa, Turner explicitly sought to build pride in the black race.[6] In fact, he is known today primarily as a black nationalist. In recent decades, scholars have been quite interested in Turner's thinking for the ways in which it anticipated the ideas of later leaders such as Marcus Garvey and Malcolm X.[7]

Turner's black nationalism, however, differed from that of Garvey and Malcolm X in that it grew from an evangelical missionary dynamic.[8] In 1898, he famously linked his black nationalism to the ultimate Christian authority, proclaiming that

"God is a Negro." Even here, Turner's evangelistic work in the Reconstruction south played a critical role, for this speech embodied a missionary dynamic whereby Christianity had been translated into the culture of the recipients. Whites and "all the fool negroes of this country," Turner fumed, "believe that God is a white-skinned, blue-eyed, straight haired, projecting nosed, compressed lipped and finely robed WHITE gentleman, sitting upon a throne somewhere in the heavens." Blacks, however, needed to see God as black. Turner pointed out that all humans believed that "the God who made them and shaped their destinies was symbolized in themselves." His theology sounded much like that of Andrew Walls, who argued a century later that "the divine Son did not become humanity in general, but a specific man in a specific place and culture; he is, as it were, made flesh again in other places and cultures as he is received there by faith."[9]

But Turner's black nationalism did not argue for black supremacy or black religious exclusivity. It stood for the relative and contingent nature of racial identities. If God were any color, Turner wrote, "we prefer to believe that it is nearer symbolized in the blue sky above us." The problem, in Turner's eyes, was that African Americans in 1898 were taught to associate whiteness with God, purity, and goodness, while associating blackness with the devil, sin, and evil, a situation that produced a "contemptuous and degrading" self-identity. Therefore, Turner much preferred African Americans to believe that God was black.[10]

For decades, Turner had tied evangelism, justice for the black race, Africa, and the evangelical missionary enterprise all together. Take, for instance, African-American emigration to Africa. In April 1878, as Reconstruction disintegrated around them, more than two hundred African Americans sailed from Charleston, South Carolina, aboard the *Azor*, a ship chartered by the newly formed Liberian Exodus Joint Stock Company. Disillusioned by their treatment in the United States, these emigrants intended to settle in Liberia, where they could build a new society for blacks. The *Azor* expedition sparked a heated debate within the AME Church about the fate of the black race, a debate that would continue to wax and wane through the end of the century. Turner stood right in the middle of it all. He gave the pastoral blessing to the *Azor* upon its departure from Charleston. Aside from his hobby of diving into the center of any controversy in sight, Turner supported emigration because of his distinctive mix of evangelism, black pride, and anger with the racial sins of American culture.[11]

Turner had not always supported the cause of emigration. Before the Civil War and his missionary work in the postemancipation south, he had opposed black emigration (or colonization, as it had been called). He viewed the scheme, as did most African-American leaders, "as one of the tricks of slavery, to rid the country of free negroes." By 1866, he had changed his mind. Turner was still deeply committed to battling racism in the United States, but he did not accept the widely held faith that the American nation-state would ultimately deliver justice and freedom to blacks. In Turner's eyes, most African Americans had misdirected their hopes by believing that the American republic would save them.[12]

Real hope, in Turner's eyes, lay in the missionary movement. In one report in 1866, he linked the missionary progress in his "field of labor" in Georgia with a similar vision for Africa. He excitedly described both a revival containing "over 500 persons praising God at once" and a state political convention of black men, which he felt ought to disprove notions that blacks could not govern themselves. Then he brought up God's purpose for Africa, whose people were "susceptible of the highest degree of moral intelligence and intellectuality." For Turner, who believed that freedom came from both an inward spiritual liberation from sin and an outward social liberation from oppression, conversion and black pride represented two sides of the same coin.[13]

Turner was not the first African American to make an evangelistic link between African Americans and Africans. The first coordinated engagement with Africa by African Americans came from evangelicals who, believing that God had granted them salvation and purpose through the Christian faith, felt a particularly deep desire to spread the Gospel to all people of African descent. As early as 1782, former slaves who had emigrated from Georgia and South Carolina evangelized blacks around their new homes in Nova Scotia, Jamaica, the Bahamas, and Sierra Leone. By the 1820s, free blacks in Baptist and Methodist denominations began to organize official foreign-missionary agencies, sending black missionaries to Sierra Leone and Liberia. By the end of the antebellum period, African Americans had left the United States as missionaries under several different denominations.[14] The AME Church unofficially supported African-American missionaries in Haiti and West Africa before the Civil War and officially sent missionaries to British Guinea, Haiti, Liberia, and Sierra Leone in the 1870s and '80s.[15] "What we do for the world at large," one pastor explained, "we do for ourselves individually." Domestic and foreign missions were "only two in name" but "one in fact."[16]

Turner carried on this tradition. African Americans, he believed, could only understand God's purposes for their race if they focused on Africa. In a letter to William Coppinger of the American Colonization Society, Turner declared his support for African emigration by explaining that "I am taking the ground that we will never get justice here, that God is, and will, [continue to] withhold political rights from us, for the purpose of turning our attention to our fatherland; that we are all destined to be missionaries to the millions of Africa."[17] When a contingent of blacks from the town of Greensboro, Georgia, had left for Liberia in 1866, Turner tried to assuage fears among the AME leadership that the emigrants were unwitting tools of a racist plot to rid the nations of blacks. These African Americans were not "driven, forced or expatriated," he told readers of the *Christian Recorder*. "Besides," he added, in an evangelical point he had made several times before, "the millions of Africa must be Christianized by some race of people, and I see none among all the inhabitants of the earth who are to do it, except the colored people of America."[18] He held that conviction to the end of his life.

And so, Turner blessed the *Azor* in 1878. It was not a wildly popular position within the AME hierarchy. Most of the leaders of the AME establishment, who were somewhat more removed from the day-to-day injustices facing ordinary blacks in the south, found it easier to combine evangelical faith with a faith in the American system. In the wake of the *Azor* expedition to Liberia, an association of AME ministers in Philadelphia criticized the idea of emigration by declaring that the United States promised prosperity and offered "more liberty and equality" than ever before. If African Americans could endure slavery, they could "contend with the remaining prejudices." The ministers invoked the landing of Africans at Jamestown to stake their claim to be "as truly American as any on the Continent." Confident also in their ability to see the hand of Providence in world events, they argued that emigration to Africa blinded blacks from seeing that God intended to bring success to them in the United States. Most provocatively, though, these formalist black ministers opposed emigration because African Americans labored under "inexperienced capacity as citizens and leaders of a Christian civilization."[19]

Those were fighting words. Turner's evangelical missionary work after the Civil War had convinced him that a lack of civilization and experience in democracy did not disqualify one from citizenship and Christian leadership. After all, he knew former slaves who displayed qualities of courage, piety, and character that could put whites and elite black ministers to shame. And Turner was only too happy to aid in the shaming process. He called the Philadelphia ministers the most worthless members of the black race and accused them of misrepresenting the emigration movement in the south. "Your language," he shot back, "has been the language of slaveholders from time immemorial."[20]

Three months later, Daniel Alexander Payne weighed in with his considerable influence, publishing a series of eight articles opposing emigration. The venerable black bishop pointed out that whites had already begun to enter and conquer Africa. Payne argued that the civilization brought by the white man, even with "all its evils," was better than "barbarism, with its monstrous forms of vice and crime." Since "the superior civilization of the white man leads him wherever he can find wealth and riches," blacks simply could not hope to isolate themselves from whites by emigrating. God made the races for fraternity, Payne argued, so African Americans needed to live alongside the white man "till he feels your excellence and acknowledges your equality."[21]

Obviously, one cannot discuss black equality, citizenship, emigration, and racial capabilities without grounding them in the missionary enterprise. Or at least, this was how nineteenth-century African-American evangelicals saw the matter. Whenever the fate of the black race made its way into AME discussions, evangelism and missionary work also inevitably appeared, attached at the hip. In eight lengthy articles, Payne hauled out extensive but meticulously detailed evidence of missionary work already under way in Africa, complete with charts and statistics, in order to argue against black emigration. Amid the flood of information, the learned bishop explained that African Americans need not worry about the spiritual state of the Africans, because "the *matured* churches of England" had set themselves to the "Herculean task" of Africa's redemption. Payne praised the "great outlay of brain work" that English missionaries had undertaken in "the work of *Christian education* by the pulpit, the school house, and the press."[22] Payne certainly embraced the native-ministry faith in educated African Christians. He applauded the educational and linguistic advances made by "hundreds of native preachers and teachers" who received a "thorough training" from the English Christians. The white man, however, was the "civilizer and conqueror," in addition to being the "successful Missionary and Christian educator."[23]

The modern, developmental, progress-laden, and morally infused version of civilization had reared its head once again. In this debate, it was probably unavoidable. Because the prejudice they faced came grounded in concepts of civilization, black leaders had to wrestle with the idea. William Taylor, by comparison, could blissfully ignore the idea of civilization, because his identity as a white man in white-dominated societies enabled him to relegate many nineteenth-century cultural concepts to the hinterlands of his mental world. The educated black leaders of the AME Church could not afford such an intellectual luxury.

Payne's formalist evangelical vision of civilization inadvertently exposed the fault lines of several dilemmas faced by black leaders. First, nineteenth-century concepts of civilization placed African Americans in a bind. Most Americans thought of civilization as a social state that exhibited, among other things, education, advanced technology, economic prosperity, democracy, individual morality, and Christianity. Having recently emerged from slavery, most African Americans could not display all of these qualities of civilization. Largely ignorant of earlier African civilizations, most Americans perceived African societies to have accomplished little by way of civilization. This meant, to most Western observers, that there was little in the "uncivilized" situation of blacks in Africa or America that seemed of value. Thus, in his desire to promote education, prosperity, and equality for blacks, Payne upheld white civilization as the ideal to which blacks should aspire, praising the "superior civilization of the white man." This was risky racial ground to tread.

Second, since this conception assumed that Western civilization contained all that was necessary to produce human flourishing, it discouraged advocates from considering perspectives of the uncivilized. It did not encourage one to look for cultural qualities outside of civilization. "What is Africa?" asked one

AME antiemigrationist who obviously had never visited the place. "The home of savages, the citadel of idolatry, the castle of ignorance and the bulwarks of superstition." He described Africa as a "country without schools, without agricultural arts, mechanical industries, railroads, steamers, telegraph wires, scientific academies, theological universities, mints, manufactories, Christianity or a God!" This black man had no use for the continent of his ancestors. "A capital home for the negro, I must confess," he concluded sarcastically.[24]

Third, Payne's conception of civilization contained an Enlightenment faith in the power of empirical observation to solve human problems. Like many well-educated AME ministers, he optimistically believed whites would drop their racism toward blacks once they observed the "excellence" of civilized blacks.[25] In other words, the program of "uplifting" blacks through the civilizing mission would, among other things, trump America's racism. Whites, it was assumed, did not need transformation so much as visual evidence. Once they observed highly civilized African Americans in their midst, they simply would be convinced of the truth.[26]

In the public arena, however, racism throttled this strand of empiricism. Whites demonstrated even less inclination to grant respect to civilized blacks in the 1880s and '90s than they had in the 1860s. In fact, Payne found himself at the center of a controversy in which his excellence of character did nothing to halt white racism. While traveling by train in Florida in 1882, the seventy-one-year-old AME bishop, theologian, and founder of Wilberforce University was ordered by a white conductor to move to a less respectable smoking car. When Payne replied that he would not "dishonor my manhood by going into it," the train was stopped, and he was kicked off. The elderly bishop had to walk five miles to Jacksonville. The incident provoked a round of protest meetings by African Americans in several American cities, but the protests did little to improve white powers of observation. The tide had already turned against the partially adopted Reconstruction ideal of equal racial treatment. Practices of segregation increasingly hardened across the nation. Soon a demonic spirit of lynching would seep into society. One year after Payne's train incident, the Supreme Court struck down the Civil Rights Act of 1875, setting the legal stage for the infamous *Plessey v. Ferguson* decision in 1896.[27]

Still, many AME ministers continued to promote the civilizing mission, with its assumptions of "superior white civilization," perhaps because they could not see any viable alternatives. Payne supported the idea of sending a very limited number of black missionaries to Africa, as long as they were "mature," highly educated, and fully funded. In 1884, he proposed sending two missionaries to Central Africa. Tellingly, he dispersed the funds directly himself rather than through the Missionary Department, which he feared would expand too quickly.[28]

This did not exactly stoke the fires of evangelical zeal. In fact, the logic of the civilizing mission led the black evangelical bishop to argue explicitly *against* AME missionary activity. As Payne explained in his response to the 1878 debate over the *Azor*, African Americans were not "mature" enough to undertake a work "so grand, so important, and involving so many and such great responsibilities as a mission in Africa would necessitate." They might, he thought, be ready in "thirty-five or a hundred years hence."[29] Other AME ministers argued the same way. A contributor to the *AME Church Review*, who declared that the "Negro's model of civilization must be that of his white brother," wrote that "the indications to-day are that Africa is not to be redeemed" by African Americans. "To speak plainly," he intoned, "the American Negro, as a class, is not prepared, neither financially, mentally nor morally, to build up a civilization." The civilizing mission, then, actually functioned more as a brake than as a driving force behind the African-American missionary enterprise.[30]

Turner would not stand for this. Influenced by the impulses of the African-American Great Awakening, he simply could not accept the assumptions underlying Payne's civilizing mission. Not about to wait thirty-five or one hundred years to send African Americans to Africa, Turner launched into a flurry of missionary activity. He infused the AME foreign-missionary movement with a level of energy that formalist evangelical ministers and their program of uplift simply could not match.

In the battle over AME missionary policy, Payne had established leadership on his side, but Turner knew how to build movements. Positioning himself as a candidate for bishop in 1880, Turner included a renewed dedication to missions on his agenda for that year's General Conference. After winning a contentious election, in which his strongest opposition came from Payne, Turner immediately set about doing what he did best, which was to stir the pot. He accused B. T. Tanner, the editor of the *Christian Recorder*, of neglecting to publish information on foreign-missionary work, an omission that explained "the missionary apathy that prevails in our church."[31] He then wrote *An Appeal for Africa*, which urged the AME Church to establish a fund to train missionaries for Africa. The trustees of Wilberforce University passed a resolution to that effect and named Turner manager of the fund. In 1884, Turner led an unsuccessful campaign to create a bishopric to oversee the foreign-mission field. In 1888, he was elected chair of the Board of Missions, and later he organized a new agency, the Woman's Home and Foreign Missionary Society, establishing branches in eleven states.[32]

In 1893, Turner founded a newspaper called the *Voice of Missions*. Advertising itself as "the only Organ Published by any denomination of Color in interest of Foreign Missionary Fields and African work," Turner's paper published a constant stream of articles on missionary efforts in Africa, plus occasional items on missionaries in areas such as China.[33] The *Voice of Missions* positioned itself as a corrective to denominational neglect. "Think of the stupid and heartless indifference with which our General Conference in Philadelphia met all appeals for Africa," wrote a subscriber to an early issue. "Our church could furnish [Turner] with thousands of dollars and never miss it, if it would."[34]

Turner's allies grew from the antiformalist evangelical soil that animated the African-American Great Awakening. Alfred Ridgel, a strong Turner supporter, decried the lack of evangelical enthusiasm among elite AME ministers. "If an old sister happens to shout or say amen...in the presence of those 'point-of-order' fellows," he declared, "they get up and decry the whole thing, often reprimanding the preacher who had the audacity or grace to get happy and preach a Holy Ghost religion." Ridgel linked this formalist stance to a slavish devotion to white norms that bolstered racism. "Well, says one, 'the white folks don't shout, and we ought not to do it,'" he argued. "Perhaps if they shouted more and enjoyed heartfelt religion our poor people down south would have a little respite from lynching."[35] After Turner recruited him as a missionary to West Africa, Ridgel found that the most tepid responses to foreign missions came from the established AME churches in the north. While trying to raise money for his missionary trip to Liberia in 1892, Ridgel was surprised to find an absence of "evangelical fire" in northern churches. "Ridgel you are foolish," Bishop B. T. Tanner had told him. "I would not think of going to Africa. If I had my way I would abandon our African mission field at once. We have no business in Africa."[36]

That sort of response reinforced Turner's conviction that something was amiss within the AME hierarchy. As he struggled to understand why elite black evangelicals lacked faith in ordinary blacks and discouraged missionary work in Africa, Turner reasoned in the same way that many democratized evangelicals had before him: AME officials placed too much confidence in the effects of black education. Turner certainly did not oppose higher education for blacks. He served on the board of trustees of Morris Brown College in the south, urged ministers to increase their education, and spoke regularly at Wilberforce University.[37] But he held a conviction that American higher education often refused to recognize movements of the Holy Spirit. In 1887, Turner criticized a perceived tendency among denominational leaders to forget the old Methodist belief that only the "heart-cleansing efficacy of the Holy Spirit" could solve the immorality of humanity. He raised Payne's hackles by writing that the AME Church had "literally deified learning." In typically blunt terms, Turner declared that "moral education as held up and glorified in our Church by many leading lights is false, misleading, obstructive to vital Christianity, and is sapping the foundations of our Church." Payne responded with the traditional Yankee assertion that the Bible taught that ministers were to "teach and cultivate moral education from the pulpit, the family circle, and in the school house."[38]

As with the 1853 Wayland-Sears debate, the missionary movement helped shape the terms of this debate in 1887. The use of institutional power played a role here. Payne, who had been unsettled by certain dynamics of the

African-American Great Awakening, tended to see his role of bishop as one in which he was to uplift ordinary blacks to the qualities that elite black ministers possessed. The south had opted for "quantity and not for quality," he wrote, "forgetting the historic fact that twelve well qualified men were enough to turn the heathen Roman empire into a Christian one."[39]

Turner had a different definition of what it meant to be "well qualified." His missionary experience in the south had compelled him to spend years on the ground rubbing shoulders alongside poorly educated freed people. As a result, the African-American Great Awakening had stamped him with a conviction that the AME Church would be built on movements made up of ordinary Spirit-filled blacks. Institutions of higher education, established by civilized leaders, had a role to play, but it must not quench popular evangelical movements. He criticized elite black disregard for the gifts of uneducated preachers and the evangelical vitality they often generated. "Refined or unrefined, popular or unpopular, common or uncommon, precedented or unprecedented, dignified or undignified, old-timish or new-timish, high-toned or low toned," he exclaimed in antiformalist evangelical fashion, "anything to beat the devil."[40]

A good mark of a dedicated antiformalist evangelical is the inability to sit still. Turner had to go to Africa himself, as a missionary. Taking advantage of his bishopric privileges, Turner traveled to Sierra Leone and Liberia in 1891, the first of three episcopal missionary trips he took to Africa. For many years, he had suspected that the common depictions of Africa contained profound inaccuracies, a conviction reinforced by the black-nationalistic writings on Africa by Edward Blyden and Martin Delany.[41] His personal experiences in the United States, however, provided the groundwork for this suspicion, since he was long cognizant of the ways whites and educated blacks alike caricatured ordinary African Americans.[42]

Even before he set foot on the continent, he began testing popular notions about Africans. "I had heard so much since I left Liverpool about the laziness, stupidness and worthlessness of the native African, that I had almost become disheartened," he began. He then pointedly reported how "native Africans" efficiently unloaded his ship, understood its steam engines, and "beat the Portuguese at Madeira all hollow in managing affairs." Turner punctuated this account with an anecdote about how a "half nude African" who had gotten into an argument with the ship clerk over some mathematical calculations proved the man wrong. So it went in West Africa. Turner searched for more admirable qualities in Africans, quite explicitly pointing out how his observations countered common perceptions of "uncivilized" Africa. "Great heavens, how white people on the one hand and scullion Negroes upon the other, have misrepresented Africa!" he exclaimed while describing a Christian worship service in Sierra Leone. "Some who got up in that love-feast to talk were what they called heathens, right from the bush, with a mere cloth over them, and while I could not understand a word, you could see they were full of the Holy Ghost." With a few cosmetic changes, he just as well could have been speaking about the freed people in Georgia in 1868.[43]

Even so, this was not an easy intellectual path to blaze. Wishing to reform rather than reject the concept of civilization, Turner sometimes cast Africa in a favorable light by pointing out its similarities to American civilization. At other times, African cultures reigned supreme because of features that had little to do with the technological and scientific triumphs of Western civilization. Turner attributed particular spiritual skills to Africans, albeit skills that would be fulfilled only by Christian conversion. "While the white man deals with the visible sciences, the African here deals with the invisible sciences," he declared. "I believe the black man is acquainted with secret agents in the realm of nature that the white man has never dreamed of, and will offset any telegraph, telephone or phonograph ever invented by white men."[44] This was either a venture in intellectual courage or an exercise in rhetorical foolishness. Few Americans in the 1890s dared to question the cultural authority of advanced technology, especially when pitted against the spirituality of uncivilized Africans.[45]

Turner returned to the United States in 1891, strengthened by the conviction that his evidence undermined Africa's bad press in America. He reinvigorated his efforts for African-American engagement with Africa, in both emigration and missionary work. On the emigration side, he worked to set up shipping to Africa, preached emigration at the Columbian Exposition in Chicago, and summoned a national African-American convention to consider emigration as remedy for race problems. To bolster missionary enthusiasm, he organized the Woman's Home and Foreign Missionary Society to supplement (or perhaps compete with) the older Women's Parent Mite Missionary Society, a northern-dominated AME organization that promoted domesticity and the civilizing mission. Turner then returned to West Africa in 1893 with three missionaries from America and ordained several more deacons and elders to assist the nine whom he had ordained on his first trip.[46]

The *Voice of Missions* kept up a steady barrage of protests against the racism of American society, punctuated by praise for Africa as the hope for the black race. Turner and his supporters argued that African-American Christianity would produce better missionary work in Africa than white Christianity because it did not suffer from the same prejudice that infected white Christianity. "It appears to be impossible for a white man or woman, be they friend or foe," Turner wrote in the introduction to a book on Africa written by a fellow AME bishop, "to tell the exact truth when they are relating or discussing the merits or demerits of the colored race."[47]

This is not to say that Turner believed that whites were irrevocably trapped by their prejudice. The integrity of white evangelicals, in Turner's mind, could be assessed by their support for black evangelism. Turner initially admired Dwight Moody's revival work, but his view of the famous revivalist turned sour after Moody decided to exclude African-American preachers from his revivals, followed by an awkward meeting between Moody and Turner in 1890.[48] On the other hand, Turner and his followers continued to praise William Taylor and his missionary campaigns in Africa, despite a few intimations that Taylor might not have given African-American missionaries in Liberia complete respect. Turner seemed to be convinced of Taylor's zeal for black conversions, which Turner understood to demonstrate genuine concern for Africans.[49]

Turner continued to highlight positive aspects of Africa and bemoan its misrepresentation in the American press. In typically blunt Turnerian style, he thundered that Americans who hear the term "heathen African...are foolish and stupid enough to believe, that the word means, idiot, simpleton, numskull lack brain, dullard imbecility, incapacity, shallowness, loggerhead, and such individuals as the above terms indicate." The Chinese and the Africans, he pointed out, in a moment of cross-cultural insight that was rare for the era, regard Americans as heathen, "and they attribute to us, as we do to them, cruelty, savagery, brutality, inhumanity and general disorder." He did not spare his own denomination. While he himself used the term *heathen* for those Africans who had not converted to Christianity, Turner disparaged the condescending way highly educated AME members used the term, arguing that "millions of heathen Africans" could teach "millions of African Americans, who think they know so much, for 10 consecutive years in books, mechanism and art, and thousands could teach them about God." He argued that "heathenism does not necessarily nor does it historically involve the absence of what the world now calls culture," before producing an all-star list of heathens from classical antiquity that included Julius Caesar, Cicero, Plato, Aristotle, and Homer. "Some of our college graduates use the word barbarous Africa and African barbarians to imply every quality," he continued. "That is low and monstrous, while they advertise by it their own stupidity."[50]

This stance held implications for cross-cultural engagement. The *Voice of Missions* argued that the Christian redemption of Africa would take on distinctly African characteristics. Turner's coeditor published statements by Anglican missionaries and Andover theologians who declared that the greatest hindrance to the development of African churches stemmed from "deep-rooted tendency which there is in the Anglo-Saxon character to Anglicize everything." Turner's coeditor concluded that "Christianity in the European mould will never and ought never to make advances in Africa." AME missionary supporters sometimes heard African Christians themselves make this point. E. Mayfield Boyle, who traveled from his native Sierra Leone under AME missionary auspices to earn degrees at Wilberforce University, told his American audience that Sierra Leone did not want "black Englishmen" but "those who would prefer being

African in the true sense of the word, with zeal and earnestness to labor not for salary but Christ." Turner spoke in similar terms. "I have a very high reverence for many of the customs and traditions of these people," he said.[51] Upholding the benefits of civilization but criticizing conceptions of whiteness and elitism embedded in the reigning discourse of civilization, Turner simultaneously affirmed and critiqued American culture. By dethroning Western civilization as the standard by which all other cultures should be measured, while promoting the transforming effects of evangelical Christianity, Turner also simultaneously affirmed and critiqued African culture.

Most likely, it was Turner's enthusiastic missionary stance toward Africa that drew leaders of the Ethiopian movement to him. In 1894, a black South African named Charlotte Manye had been enrolled at Wilberforce University, having made her way from South Africa to Ohio. Manye wrote a letter to her sister Kate, a family friend of Mangena Mokone, extolling the virtues of African-American education and speaking of the independent nature of the AME denomination. Significantly, it was Turner rather than the other AME leaders who captured Manye's imagination. She apparently wrote her letter on Turner's letterhead and commented about him. Mokone then began a long-distance correspondence with Turner. Mokone's letters appeared in the *Voice of Missions*, and Turner sent a number of copies of his paper to South Africa. Thus began the relationship between the Ethiopian movement in South Africa and the AME Church.[52]

In 1896, after receiving approval from the AME General Conference, the Ethiopian church voted to affiliate themselves officially as the Fourteenth District of the AME Church. They sent James Mata Dwane, one of their leading ministers, on a tour of the United States to strengthen ties with the AME Church and to obtain whatever sort of aid he could to help build Christian educational institutions for blacks in South Africa. Upon his return to South Africa, Dwane appeared before fellow ministers in Lesseyton to report on his trip. When he announced that the AME Church in the United States had promised to build a college for blacks in South Africa, the conference broke into excited prayer and thanksgiving. This response sparked a revival that spilled out of the conference, across the eastern Cape, and into the Transkei region. Over the next several months, the young AME movement in South Africa brought in thousands of new members. One minister reported that he had baptized more than two dozen adults and children every day.[53]

By Western terms, this was an odd reaction. Even the most excitable American Baptists or Methodists were not known to break into a revival upon hearing an announcement of a new college. Energetic evangelism, however, was quite in keeping with how black South African Christians in the late nineteenth century worked out their faith. In fact, the relationship between education and aggressive evangelism demonstrates a critical but often overlooked reason for the

Ethiopian advocates to have broken from the white missionary system in the first place. Scholars usually emphasize limitations on social opportunity and education when explaining Mokone's desire to get out from under the racist strictures of the white Wesleyans. Unquestionably, these factors played a critical role in the conflict, as they do in most situations with powerful racial forces at work. In a pamphlet listing his grievances, for instance, Mokone described how the ordained black pastor "cannot exercise his rights as a minister" and had been compelled since 1886 to hold segregated district meetings under the authority of white administrators.[54]

But race worked in other ways, too. African leaders of the Ethiopian movement also grew dissatisfied with white missionaries' lack of shared piety, their inattention to developing personal relationships with black Africans, and the limitations missionaries placed on African evangelism. In the same pamphlet, Mokone explained that white missionaries "don't even know the members of their circuits" and "never go to visit the sick or pray for them." Black ministers, meanwhile, "holds class meetings, prayer meetings, visit the sick, prays for them, preach, bury and teach school." The missionaries mainly conducted baptisms and communion, while living in homes they built "one or two miles away" from the congregation. "This is not Christianity, not brotherly love, not friendship," Mokone lamented.[55]

It is quite likely that Mokone believed that the white missionaries had lost something that they once had. The black Christians who joined the Ethiopian movement were, among other things, products of a form of revivalism and evangelical piety that had been shaped by the 1866 revivals led by Charles Pamla and William Taylor. James Dwane, a Xhosa, had lived at the Annshaw station with Robert Lamplough in the 1860s. He had agonized for three years before his conversion. "When I prayed the Devil told me that my prayer was disagreeable and annoying everybody in heaven," he explained three decades later. But after a prayer meeting at Pamla's house, he reported that "a new creation was effected within me," and suddenly "there was great ease, great peace and great joy." Three days later, Dwane began to preach. "A strong love for preaching took hold of me," he explained. "I felt that woe is me if I do not preach the gospel." Shortly after Dwane's conversion, Taylor arrived to aid the revival that Pamla had started, and Methodism swept through the eastern Cape and Natal regions. Lamplough then granted Dwane a license to preach, and he was ordained in 1881. Passionate evangelism remained a central part of his work. "During the course of my ministry I have seen great revivals of the work of God among the heathens," he said in 1897.[56]

Black Methodists such as Dwane displayed a greater enthusiasm for evangelism than most Wesleyan missionaries, who exhibited a formalist impulse to try to keep movements under their control. Without consulting the missionaries, black Methodist preachers in South Africa had taken it upon themselves in 1875 to meet at Edendale in order to form evangelistic initiatives that were more aggressive than what the missionaries had been providing. The black evangelists called these movements *unzondelelo,* meaning to desire earnestly or follow after a thing, a term derived from the Xhosa translation of John 2:17, "the zeal of thine house hath eaten me up." Funded by contributions from black Methodists, the *unzondelelo* became so expansive that the British missionaries began to worry that these movements of uncivilized Christians might create problems.[57]

And what might civilized Methodist missionaries do instead to help bring in the Kingdom of God? Naturally, they formed a committee. Consisting of twelve members, three of whom would be British missionaries, the Committee of Management was designed to supervise, and possibly control, the *unzondelelo*. There are times, however, when even the awe-inspiring power of the modern committee meeting cannot prevail against evangelical zeal. Black evangelists continued to roam far and wide, without missionary supervision. In 1881, the Wesleyan Methodists sent a missionary up to Driefontein in the north Natal district to investigate reports of unsupervised evangelistic activity. They discovered an untrained and uneducated seventeen-year-old African preaching to audiences of more than two hundred. There was little the missionaries could do about that. Black Methodists, in fact, had become so pervasive that the Zulu coined a term for them, *nontelevu,* which meant "the people who go about talking too much." They were in good historical company. Eighty years earlier in the United States, enthusiastic circuit riders had developed similar reputations. "Nothing out today but crows and Methodist preachers," went an early American aphorism about bad weather.[58]

But antiformalist movements eventually must develop institutions in order to remain viable. If that were to be done within the Wesleyan Methodist church, it would require deeper cooperation with the missionaries. Having embraced the native-ministry ideal to raise up black African preachers and teachers, James Dwane traveled to England in 1894 to raise money for a Methodist college for black South Africans. When Dwane returned home, the white missionary officials compelled him to turn over all of the funds he had raised to the general fund of the denomination. That fund was controlled by white missionaries.[59]

For Dwane, this was only the most recent frustration with the missionary use of power. In 1879, Methodist officials in England had sent James Kilner to South Africa in an attempt to encourage the missionaries to allow more black Africans into leadership positions. Given this native-ministry directive from Great Britain, in addition to the interracial evangelical legacy of the 1866 revival and the obvious success of black evangelists in extending the Christian faith, one might expect missionaries in South Africa to expand leadership opportunities for blacks. Instead, a new generation of white Methodist leaders in South Africa in the 1880s increasingly squeezed "uncivilized" black Africans out of the church-leadership structure. Believing that they were keeping the church from being led astray, Wesleyan missionaries at the 1883 General Conference in South Africa voted to segregate black ministers into separate district conferences, effectively denying them any vote or voice on denominational matters in the colony. Extending their control even more, the Wesleyans appointed white chairmen and secretaries to lead segregated black district conferences. The ordination of black ministers trailed off noticeably in the 1880s, even as the denomination continued to grow.[60]

And so, Dwane resigned from the Wesleyan Methodist church in 1894 to join Mokone's Ethiopian church. Tellingly, some missionaries expressed surprise. They had been largely unaware that black evangelists even held grievances.[61] This obtuse reaction was not simply a product of unobservant personalities. The generation of British missionaries who moved into the establishment in the 1880s and '90s had been shaped by several cultural factors that increasingly distorted the ability of whites to understand the perspectives of black Christians. Powerful intellectual trends such as social Darwinism, backed by the cultural authority of science, described black races as uncivilized peoples who would need centuries of development to match the heights scaled by Anglo-Saxon peoples. White missionaries in almost all of the Protestant denominations in South Africa believed that black African ministers did not have the capabilities to lead any of the institutions of the church without white supervision. When African ministerial students at Lovedale Institute, a seminary created from earlier impulses of the native-ministry ideal, protested in 1884 against restrictions placed on them, they were handed a plateful of civilizing dogma. "Starting but yesterday in the race of nations," the Scottish principal responded, "do you soberly believe that in two generations of the very imperfect civilization you have enjoyed and partially accepted, you can have overtaken those other nations who began that race two thousand years ago?"[62]

This generation of Wesleyan missionaries also tended to be more deeply committed to the idea of Great Britain as a Christian nation, with a divine duty to spread Christian civilization by means of the British Empire. Many British missionaries saw themselves as something akin to colonial agents. They supported British political subjugation of black Africans, required black evangelists to cook and clean three hours a day for superintendents, and paid black ministers 10 to 20 percent of the amount they paid white ministers. Moreover, by adopting modern bureaucratic roles as administrators of denominational institutions, Wesleyan missionaries lost opportunities to understand Africans more deeply because they had removed themselves from daily pastoral interactions with blacks. Unlike earlier generations, they spent less time in day-to-day ministerial activities with blacks, as Mokone pointed out. Finally, Wesleyan officials in the 1880s further undermined the native-ministry ideal by placing ordained black ministers under the direction of white ministers in established mission stations.

These actions had the effect of removing successful black evangelists from more remote villages and communities where much of the church growth had taken place. When black African ministers brought candidates forward for baptism, they were often challenged by white missionaries, who questioned the uncivilized ministers' standards in their evaluations of the converts' Christian faith.[63]

Dwane, Mokone, and the other advocates of the Ethiopian movement became convinced that they did not actually need the Anglo-Saxon race to carry out their ministry effectively. However, it should be noted that, unlike those in the American south after the Civil War, most blacks in South Africa did not immediately abandon the white-dominated churches when presented with independent black options. Charles Pamla, for instance, still ministered as an ordained pastor within the Wesleyan Methodist church in 1897. For a variety of reasons, most black Christians in South Africa as late as 1911 still maintained their membership in denominations that had been established by whites, although many of them must have felt misgivings about the racism they faced. Over time, though, independent black denominations similar to the Ethiopian movement would claim the majority of black Christians in South Africa.[64]

When Christians in the Ethiopian movement discovered an independent black evangelical American denomination, complete with colleges, they could not help but get excited. Turner's paper, the *Voice of Missions*, created quite a stir. "When I saw in your paper, your freedom, I could not help shedding tears for my poor native country," wrote John Tule from Capetown. "Don't put those talents in safes, and use them not to purchase the freedom of your brother in South Africa," he urged, "or in the whole of Africa." Clearly, the Ethiopian leaders began placing great hopes in the AME Church. "Your favorable letter has been the cause of our revival and strengthening," Mokone wrote in a letter published in the *Voice of Missions*. "When I see how you love Africa and pray for it to be saved from destruction of heathenism and the death of same, causes me [sic] to retire into seclusion and silence to meditate on my country people." Those hopes for the AME Church also reflected, in part, an insecurity that some black Africans felt about themselves as a marginal, lowly, and uncivilized people. "We never dreamed that [black Americans] recognized us as their fellow country people originally," Jacobus Xaba explained, "they having succumbed in the privileges of education, Christianity and civilization."[65]

Like Mokone and Dwane, Turner believed that the best way for blacks to deal with racism within the church would be to establish independent black movements and institutions. Thrilled with the missionary possibilities that the merger presented for his denomination and the black race, Turner set out in 1898 for South Africa and his third foreign-missionary episcopal tour. His AME missionary work in the South in the 1860s and '70s had established a pattern for his work in South Africa. Greeted by enthusiastic crowds of black

Christians throughout the region, Turner reported that he was struck by the "independence" displayed by the African Christians and found "a common sense that almost dumbfounded us."[66] As he had done among the freedpeople, Turner sought to stimulate and give structure to grassroots black evangelism. During his two-month tour, he organized two conferences and ordained fifty black ministers, some after a minimal examination, overlooking once again AME educational qualifications and the technicalities of Methodist polity in his ordinations. He also created an office of vicar bishop, appointed James Dwane to the position, and arranged to bring Dwane to the United States to solidify the new structure.

Turner recognized something familiar in the racism of Anglo South African Christianity. Upon his return from South Africa, he explained that for several months, he had refrained from saying anything about his "European brothers," because he did not wish to "waste time in throwing stones at others who profess at least to be engaged in the same warfare." The time for rock tossing had now arrived. Turner castigated European Christians for trying to establish a system of "religious slavery" in South Africa. Black Africans had been "snubbed, cold shouldered, proscribed and religiously scullionized." White South African religious leaders called Dwane "a lad," referred to his hair as a "curly pow," and described the Ethiopian movement as completely lacking in spirituality. "No wonder an Africanite said, if that is Christianity, I will choose devilanity," Turner fumed. "If this is the civilization our European brethren are carrying into South Africa," he continued, "the A.M.E. Church goes none too soon."[67]

Like many earlier advocates of the native-ministry model, Turner and his supporters began to articulate a vision that would build on and reform, rather than eradicate, indigenous culture. Arguing that the new AME college at Queenstown would do for Africans what Wilberforce University did for African Americans, H. B. Parks, the AME secretary of missions, grounded the educational mission in indigenous culture. "The South African will be taught the arts of civilization by people of his own race," Parks explained approvingly, "men and women born in his own village possibly, and who have never lost touch with native methods of thought."[68] An AME pastor explained that the Gospel of Christ would "correct social and national evils and conserve all that is pure, sound and true in society." Another writer to the *Voice of Missions* in 1898 reasoned that as vicar bishop, Dwane's thorough acquaintance with the "wants and weaknesses, possibilities and capabilities" of his people would enable him to develop the "native strengths, resources, and work out its own destiny."[69]

These cultural insights, however, were soon overwhelmed by competing impulses within the AME Church. Several factors played into this development. First, African-American goals of resisting racism, promoting conversion, developing educational systems, and encouraging opportunities for blacks weighed more heavily on the minds of AME missionaries than theoretical questions about the relationship between Christianity and African cultures.[70] More significant is that AME leaders held conflicting visions for just how to handle racism, evangelism, education, and black opportunity. Turner's native-ministry ideal quickly came into conflict with a civilizing-mission impulse. Fellow AME bishop Wesley Gaines opposed Turner's widespread ordinations of black African ministers and his creation of the position of vicar bishop. Arguing for "ministerial purity," Gaines accused Turner of bringing Dwane, the "self-appointed and self-elected Vicar Bishop," to the United States without proper sanction from denominational law. Complaining that Turner had overstepped his authority, Gaines charged him with maladministration.[71]

There was much more to Gaines's opposition than principles of church law. Turner and Gaines re-created a skirmish that the two had fought in 1867, when Gaines had opposed Turner's proposal to ordain seventeen former slaves at the AME annual conference in Georgia. In 1897, one year before Turner traveled to South Africa, Gaines had published *The Negro and the White Man*, in which he essentially regurgitated dominant white stereotypes used to justify disenfranchisement and segregation. He argued that the newly emancipated slaves had been totally unprepared for freedom, misusing their citizenship because of their lack of education. Praising the schoolhouse as "the birth-place of a nation's power, progress and civilization," Gaines argued that African-American elites had learned an appreciation for art, collected large libraries, dipped into the culinary arts, learned to play "better" musical instruments, and lived in neat, modern homes with "carpets and pictures, books, furniture, [and] a well-supplied board." Higher education not only opened the door to upward mobility but, in Gaines's way of thinking, also was necessary for true morality. "Who but the cultivated and refined can properly estimate the value of purity?" he asked in regard to marital fidelity. His was a deeply modern vision of civilization: education, technological progress, and economic growth would produce morality and intelligent leadership.[72]

Gaines explicitly declared that the hope for the black race lay in emulating white, Anglo-Saxon culture. The African American "touches now the greatest race that has yet appeared on the earth, the race whose genius and valor have conquered upon every field and left every nation and people far to the rear in their splendid march to conquest and power." The African American "aspires to be like his white brother, to imitate his progress, and to emulate his thrift and prosperity," the black bishop wrote. "His ambition is to become a sharer in his civilization, and to participate in the glorious destiny of Anglo-Saxon achievement."[73] The bishop's admiration for "conquest and power" revealed another fundamental problem that would beset the AME missionary enterprise. Despite their battles with racism in America, many AME missionaries in South Africa operated, structurally and conceptually, from a position of power in which, as civilizers, they hoped to guide, direct, and control uncivilized African Christians.

This was not a worldview that placed much confidence in the leadership capabilities of Zulu and Xhosa clergy. "The native has but little sense of propriety and no culture," ran an AME pastor's analysis of his denomination's African missionary work in 1898. "He has not been trained to stand temptation, which is the primary lesson of Christianity." Missionaries in Africa, the writer continued, must overcome the twin obstacles posed by "heathenism" and "semi-civilization." Liberia would prove to be a particularly difficult field, he decided, since the "heathen is a child, while the semi-civilized man is a half-grown boy."[74]

Gaines's criticism ended up hindering new movements of Christianity in South Africa. Still smarting from the defection of thousands of blacks, British missionaries caught wind of Gaines's accusations and brought them to government officials in South Africa. Anxieties about threats to the white positions of power and authority in South Africa further fueled these reactions. "These men, without control have as I said caused trouble," a Wesleyan missionary wrote in describing the new Ethiopian movement in 1896, "and the government are beginning to see the Native churches without a European head, will set the country in a flame if they are not suppressed." Reverting to old polities of an established church, British government officials promptly withheld official recognition of the AME Church. Among other things, this act rendered marriages performed by AME ministers illegal and restricted areas where black evangelists could travel.[75]

Not that the leaders of Christian civilization could really control such a movement. Dwane, who decided that he had seen the likes of Wesley Gaines and the AME Church before, resorted to a typically Protestant way of responding to such use of power: he defected again. In late 1899, Dwane led a number of his followers out of the AME Church and into the Anglican Church, complaining that Gaines's letter undermined his authority and that the AME denomination had failed to deliver on its promises of financial support. The Ethiopian movement had enjoyed impressive growth just before its merger with the AME Church and even greater growth directly afterward, but Dwane's defection caused a slight drop in membership in 1898 to 1900, from twelve thousand to ten thousand.[76]

This was not what Mokone or Turner had envisioned. African Americans and Africans began to discover, as James Campbell has aptly put it, "simplifications and misapprehensions" about each other.[77] Extensive cross-cultural engagement could not help but bring conflicting cultural assumptions to the surface, even those based on very similar religious and racial situations. Adept at promoting evangelistic movements but hemmed in by the institutional restrictions imposed on them by British missionaries, the Ethiopian leaders thought that they saw in the AME Church the key to a flourishing Christian movement in South Africa. Here was an American denomination, it was thought, that could provide institutional stability, access to higher education, and financial resources without racist impositions. Ironically, by turning to the AME Church for institution building, Mokone and Dwane brought upon themselves a host of evangelical AME leaders such as Gaines whose conceptions of civilization led them to respond to Africans in ways very similar to those of the British Methodist missionaries.

Dwane's defection reinforced doubts and stereotypes in the minds of many African-American leaders about the capability and spiritual maturity of African pastors. Gaines, in fact, foreshadowed the kind of AME leader the South Africans would be receiving from the United States in the next decade. Despite Turner's efforts to promote bishops to South Africa who shared his vision, a parade of AME bishops followed Turner to South Africa between 1900 and 1908 who explicitly upheld white civilization as the norm to which African Methodists should aspire. Well educated but holding little experience in cross-cultural engagement or grassroots evangelism, these AME leaders attempted to prove that black Christians were fully capable of forging respectable, civilized denomination like those that whites had established. To this end, they strengthened their own power by attempting to rein in enthusiastic African pastors, limit the geographic scope of AME evangelism, and curtail the authority of African leaders.

Bishop Levi Coppin, for instance, arrived in 1901, convinced that the AME Church in South Africa lacked "wise and competent" leaders. Coppin slowed down the rate of ordinations, declaring that the church in South Africa had relied too much on unsupervised and poorly educated evangelists. When British missionaries complained to the Cape government that an AME preacher, Henry Reid Ngcayiya, engaged in proselytization by encouraging black Africans to leave the Wesleyan church for the AME Church, Coppin sided with the Wesleyan missionaries and government officials. He ordered Ngcayiya to sever his ties with a congregation that had broken with the Wesleyans. At the 1903 joint meeting of the Transvaal and Cape annual conferences, Coppin proposed that the Africans elect two instead of eight representatives to the upcoming General Conference in the United States, with American ministers filling the remaining spots. Several bishops who followed Coppin enacted similar policies.[78]

This did not sit well with the South African Christians African ministers refused to support these proposals, openly questioned the judgment of the African Americans, and pointed out that the AME leaders who doubted the capabilities of the Africans had themselves violated established AME polity in their decision making. They also sent a letter of protest to the 1904 General Conference in the United States in which they declared that the proposed system "places us under the same condition which forced us to leave the white churches, to be placed under the superintendency of men who are ignorant of the people, their customs, traditions and life in general." Repeating a grievance that the original Ethiopian movement had expressed against the white Wesleyans, the pastors noted that these African-American leaders "do not always seem to have the sympathy of the people."[79]

Given the nature of these institutional conflicts, it would not have been surprising had the AME Church in South Africa fizzled and fallen apart. And yet it says something about the nature of evangelicalism in South Africa that even with the conflicts, fragmentation, and numerous defections, the AME Church grew dramatically. Its membership between 1900 and 1910 quadrupled, from ten thousand to forty thousand, soon to become one of the larger black denominations in Africa.[80] In the midst of its troubled formative period, the efforts by formalist evangelical bishops to pull the reins in on the church were not enough to dampen the evangelistic efforts of ordinary members of the AME Church. Although few sources exist to describe the story, the movements of evangelism and worship among ordinary African Christians on the ground, not the leadership at the top, seem to have formed the backbone of the church. It was a sign of things to come. As one of several independent black denominations emerging in South Africa in the last two decades of the nineteenth century, Mokone's Ethiopian movement represented the vanguard of a wide range of highly diverse Christian bodies that scholars call African Independent Churches (AICs). Since they usually were inspired by or broke away from evangelical missionary bodies (much to the chagrin of the missionaries), it should not be surprising that evangelical dynamics infused these AICs. Numbering more than six thousand denominations by the end of the twentieth century, AICs demonstrated antiformalist impulses to challenge existing social conventions for the sake of a Christian movement. Some AICs, such as Mokone's Ethiopian movement, challenged racism in the missionary churches by reconstituting Christian identity around a pan African vision of the black race. Other AICs intentionally reconfigured indigenous African cultural forms in new Christian bodies by reinvigorating an old African quest for supernatural power and emphasizing the spiritual sources of physical healing.[81]

AICs grew from grassroots movements of ordinary Africans, taking the spiritual experiences of ordinary people at face value and encouraging laypeople to question ministerial authorities, characteristics that had shaped evangelicalism in the First and Second Great Awakenings. While antiformalist evangelicalism in America upset existing conventions by propelling African Americans, uneducated white men, and, occasionally, women into pastoral roles of evangelism, AICs launched "uncivilized" Africans into positions of independent religious leadership of movements highly adaptable to African culture, amid a colonial setting that persistently attempted to control the activities of unregulated Africans.[82] Ironically, missionaries in South Africa rarely recognized that their own efforts had helped to provoke movements that, among other things, challenged the racism of Western civilization.

The AME General Conference, meanwhile, decided in 1908 to elect a bishop for South Africa from a pool of candidates who were willing to commit to long-term work there. The new bishop, John Albert Johnson, who served in South Africa for eight years, granted more autonomy to the African pastors and stabilized relations between Africans and Americans. The Americans also began for the first time to raise a fairly significant amount of money to help solidify educational institutions in South Africa. At the same time, three dozen South Africans who had studied in AME colleges in the United States between 1894 and 1914 began returning home, bringing academic expertise to the leadership positions of the church. Once again, new movements of world Christianity had moved in ways that the missionaries had not anticipated.[83]

PART FOUR

8

Holiness Conversions

American Methodists walked along a watershed in the 1890s. On the one side ran rivers that flowed gently but steadily toward mainline Protestantism. These waters, which many middle-class Methodists had already begun to explore, followed the contours cut by the forces of Western civilization: progressive politics, scientific authority, rationalized planning, modernist theology, systematic bureaucracies, industrial capitalism, American nationalism, and a belief in progress. The Methodist routes merged with deeper tributaries cut by denominations such as the Episcopalians, the Congregationalists, and the Presbyterians to form the indomitable river of the American Protestant establishment, which would continue to wield significant cultural influence through the first half of the twentieth century.[1]

Waters on the other side rushed toward the holiness movement and Pentecostalism. Originating as small, barely recognizable streams, they grew quickly, rushing over rapids and not a few waterfalls to produce movements based on supernaturalism, primitivism, apocalyptic eschatology, pragmatic methodologies, modern media techniques, democratized authority, multiracial and mixed-gendered leadership, and fragmented religious bodies. The tributaries of these rivers not only flowed from American Methodism to holiness and Pentecostal bodies, such as the Nazarenes and the Assemblies of God, but they also eventually joined the wildly rushing torrents of African, Latin American, and Asian Pentecostalism. Since they did not usually follow the broad channels cut by the dominant forces of Western civilization, these rivers looked unpromising at first. By the late twentieth century, however, they had forged a complex series of interlocking waterways with worldwide reach.

The evangelical missionary enterprise played a critical role in the emergence of these worldwide movements. This role was not, however, one of simply transplanting American holiness overseas. In the 1880s and '90s, the American holiness movement, through its zealous pursuit of conversions, began ignoring key signposts of "civilization," disregarding dominant conventions of race, gender, class, national identity, rationalized planning, materialism, and millennial progress. This disregard for civilization infused the holiness movement with forms of cultural adaptability and democratized religion that allowed African, Asian, and Latin American converts to shape new movements of world Christianity according to the issues of concern that dominated their local situations. News of these new movements of world Christianity then flowed back through holiness missionary networks to influence the American holiness movement itself. This news intensified ecstatic revivalism and supernaturalism within the more radical wing of American holiness. By the time the Azusa Street revival emerged on the scene in 1906 (an event traditionally identified as the birth of Pentecostalism), the holiness missionary movement had already linked enthusiasts in a worldwide network of Pentecostalism. Nobody anticipated this turn of events.

Although she could not make out the lay of the land before her, Agnes McAllister stood on the top of this Methodist watershed when she arrived in Liberia as a missionary in 1889. Determined, independent, and innovative, McAllister was made of just the sort of material admired by William Taylor, the Methodist bishop who had recruited her. Like many American missionaries who were gaining reputations around the world for their hurried, pragmatic, and task-oriented ways, McAllister briskly set off for the headwaters of the civilizing mission.[2] A small movement of African Christianity, however, eventually pulled her back from this course, toward the Spirit-filled activities of the holiness movement. McAllister not only embodied conflicting impulses found within American Methodism, but she also demonstrated how engagement with new African converts could pull missionaries away from the patterns of mainstream America.

She first arrived at the Kru village of Garraway on a Friday night in February 1889. A crowd of villagers welcomed her, fellow missionary Clara Binkley, and Bishop William Taylor with a generous meal of chicken soup, vegetables, sea biscuits, and coffee. Anxious to get rested up for the tasks ahead, the small missionary contingent ate the meal and then told the villagers that they had better go home. On Saturday, McAllister and Binkley met with the village leaders, set their house in order, and bade farewell to Taylor, who, true to his frenetic ministry style, departed for more adventures in missionary mobilization. On Sunday, the two missionaries held Christian worship to tell the people about Jesus, leading four different services during the day. On Monday morning, in McAllister's words, "we promptly opened our school." In just one weekend, the missionary machinery had been assembled and set in motion.[3]

The machinery did not produce results in the quick and efficient manner for which it had been designed. Granted, several Kru villagers agreed to let McAllister teach their children over the next years. They expressed curiosity about the missionaries' sewing machine, organ, camera, and small cookstove. One boy in the school converted. But even after four years of bustling about in a flurry of missionary activity, McAllister's hopes for sweeping transformations had been frustrated.

The disappointments did not stem from a lack of effort. McAllister established regular worship services from the very beginning. They had to be conducted through a translator and came off, as she admitted, more like school than worship. Confident that one of her tasks lay in getting the Kru to wear more than their customary loincloths, McAllister managed to get a few of her students to dress "like the white men" but failed to change the habits of the larger community. When fighting broke out between Garraway and a neighboring village, McAllister tried to persuade the people that they needed to resolve their disputes through negotiation. Village leaders would not listen to her peacemaking attempts, and she soon found herself offering medical aid to the wounded. She watched individuals accused of witchcraft drink poisonous sasswood in trials by ordeal but could not convince the people that this formed an inadequate system of justice.[4]

Like many missionaries who trawled for souls in the wake of the Enlightenment, McAllister attempted to disprove Kru religious beliefs through empirical demonstrations. She and Binkley very deliberately investigated a cave feared by the people, where a powerful spirit was thought to dwell. Their two Kru guides tried to stop the missionaries, explaining to McAllister that except for the *deyabo*, or doctors, who periodically went in to offer sacrifices to the spirit, anyone who entered the cave would not live. The two missionaries returned triumphantly from the cave, explaining that "there was no devil in the cave" and that "the devil-doctor was deceiving them." The people of Garraway were surprised but did not budge in their convictions that spirits could harm them.[5]

Conceptually, McAllister's missionary program did not differ greatly from that of the Episcopalians who had established mission stations a half-century earlier, twenty miles to the southeast at Cape Palmas. Shaped by the civilizing mission, the Protestant Episcopal Church had established schools, conducted translation work, and founded churches. They created "mission towns," gave their students Western surnames, and dressed them in Western clothes. By the 1890s, the Episcopal church at Cape Palmas numbered about two thousand Kru (or Glebo, as this particular branch of the Kru is sometimes known).[6] Kru Christians still maintained components of indigenous identity after conversion, for they kept their Kru given names and maintained a Kru linguistic core to their Christian practices, thanks to the vernacular translation of the Bible. Still, the missionaries largely saw Christianization as a process whereby civilization replaced primitive African culture.[7]

Even though McAllister embarked on similar practices, structural differences in her situation reconfigured her terms of engagement. First of all, thanks to Taylor's "self-supporting" missionary program, McAllister enjoyed less economic and political power than the Episcopalian missionaries. They built mission towns that served, among other things, as models of Christian civilization. McAllister, meanwhile, had been plopped down in the Kru village of Garraway with few external resources. She had limited power to establish a mini-civilization, even if she brought intriguing samples of the latest technology with her. Since she spent almost her entire time interacting with the Garraway villagers, the title of her book, *A Lone Woman in Africa,* seems rather curious. But that title reflected the limited number of Western colleagues who could help her with her ministry and the minimal cultural resources from the West at her disposal. Neither Binkley nor the other female missionaries sent to assist her lasted more than six months at Garraway. She could not appeal to colonial officials to overrule sasswood trials or adjudicate battles between villages. Furthermore, as a woman, McAllister did not enjoy the cultural authority that men could draw on.[8]

Ultimately, McAllister's relative position of economic and political weakness compelled her to adapt to Kru village life. She learned the Kru language well enough to "understand them when they talked among themselves." With this linguistic accomplishment in hand, she could more carefully consider Kru beliefs, practices, and conceptions of the world. One evening, after four years of constant activity, McAllister listened for the first time to several Kru oral traditions. During a casual conversation with some of her students, they told her stories that "they say their fathers received from the first people." One day in the future, they said, after the seagulls drank the oceans dry, sandpipers counted the sand on the beach, and woodpeckers cut down the trees, the sky would come

Figure 8.1. A "lone woman" amid villagers at Garraway. Photograph in Agnes McAllister, *A Lone Woman in Africa: Six Years on the Kroo Coast* (New York: Hunt & Eaton, 1896).

down, and the world would be destroyed. This struck McAllister. Taken with the similarities between this belief and her own premillennial beliefs about the second coming of Christ, she asked about more Kru oral traditions.[9]

McAllister soon came to the conclusion that the Kru already had their own modified version of the second coming, the fall of humankind, Jonah and the whale, and the coming of God's son into the world. She later described this as a sort of epiphany, recounting that the Kru oral traditions "threw new light on all my work." Garraway suddenly "seemed like a new place, now to learn that they knew and believed all these traditions, so like the Scripture records." In McAllister's new way of thinking, the Kru weren't theological blank slates; they already had a hazy knowledge of biblical accounts. "I had been telling them all these things," she wrote, "thinking they knew nothing about them."[10]

What does one do with such an epiphany? Many missionaries would have seen this as a great opportunity for intellectual progress. Perhaps one could sit down with the village elders to discuss the common religious and cultural ground they held, while using the Bible to clean up theological errors. Or perhaps one could establish a seminary to teach the Kru how their oral traditions demonstrated that they trod the same road of civilization as the white man; they would eventually advance with the help of Christian education. Certainly, the missionary would publish these cultural and theological insights, with the idea that better understanding would better equip missionaries who went forth in the future.

McAllister held a revival. This response made sense to a certain kind of evangelical. Despite her civilizing impulses, she believed in a form of old-school Methodist revivalism that saw the Holy Spirit working in clearly discernible ways at critical moments. She saw her discovery of common theological commitments with her Kru neighbors as an indication that the Holy Spirit was about to move in the hearts of her audience. Because she herself had undergone a conversion experience, McAllister saw revivals as the means by which God transformed her and others, thereby promoting good in the world.

This evangelistic impulse held important cultural implications. In good missionary fashion, McAllister did write a book. She described the religious activities that followed her epiphany in the climactic chapter, which she titled "A Revival." That title might seem a bit curious, for evangelicals traditionally used the term *revival* to describe a movement within a Christian society, the "reviving" of a dead or nominal Christian community. Early American Methodists, however, argued that the church should be in a continuous state of revival, regardless of the setting. They had extended conversion and revivals beyond the communities of nominal white Christians to non-Christian African slaves and Native Americans.[11] McAllister, then, did not hesitate to apply the concept of revival to a people who did not reside within a "Christian nation." Her conception of conversion provided her with a bond of identification with the Kru that crossed deep cultural divisions.

She extended that cross-cultural identification to American readers by drawing them into a worldwide community of revivalism. Even after all of her musings about sasswood trials, African clothing, and "devil-doctors," McAllister's final chapter did not read like an academic analysis of "primitive" people. It read, instead, like a traditional Methodist testimony. "The conviction came forcibly to me that I ought to have a religious meeting with the children," she wrote. She called her students together, told them to put their books away, "explained to them what it was to be saved," and told them that "Jesus wanted to take all the devil out of them and come and live in their hearts himself." Setting up a penitent bench, she explained that they were going to turn their attention to the conversion experience. All the next day, she wrote, "we felt the presence of the Spirit."[12]

Something about this sense of "the Spirit" resonated with several of the Garraway villagers. One boy converted and told the other students about his experience. About a dozen students converted over the next few days, and news spread through the village. Adult men began showing up at a subsequent series of prayer meetings. Several of them converted as well. "They threw their arms around each other, danced round and round the house, and shook everybody's hand, not able to give expression to the joy they felt in being born again," McAllister wrote. She joined several converts who led revival meetings in her school, and then "we all went out and marched around to three towns...to convince the people of sin and of his power to save."[13]

McAllister wrote with the Methodist terminology that pervaded the holiness movement. Individuals under spiritual conviction "sang songs of Zion" and soon "got through" with "shouts of victory." The revival appeared to be moving by spiritual forces from above. "I could see the Spirit hovering over us, ready to descend in blessing upon us," she wrote. Children grew hoarse from shouting and singing. One youth fell to the ground "with the power of God," tore his shirt "all to pieces," began to roll around on the floor, then rolled out the door and onto the ground outside, where he continued rolling for about a half-hour. This rather strange behavior called for some sort of interpretation. Alluding to a Bible verse familiar to her American evangelical audience, McAllister justified this action by describing how he got up, "walking, and leaping, and praising God."[14] For readers who needed a bit more reassurance, McAllister wrote that "we had the old-time Methodist shouting," adding that she herself was not inclined toward such uninhibited spiritual fare. "I myself am not a shouter; but I said a loud 'amen' to it all."[15]

The revival did not just affect the Kru. It drew McAllister toward the holiness side of the Methodist watershed. Wandering away from a world in which God was thought to move through the rationalized processes of the civilizing mission, McAllister had ventured into the ecstatic world of holiness revivalism, where the Spirit was thought to move in unpredictable and startling ways. When she had explored the cave with Binkley to prove that the devil did not live there, McAllister exhibited a powerful characteristic of the "disenchanted" modern world. In the Garraway revival, however, she rejected this powerful perception of disenchantment. She earnestly encouraged the people to allow Christ to take the devil out of their hearts, preached that the sky was about to come down, and validated the ecstatic religious expressions of the Kru converts.

This, she realized, placed her in a tenuous cultural position with an American society mesmerized by electric dynamos, chemical engineers, and the progress of railroads. McAllister's evangelistic fires burned deep enough, though, that she did not mind challenging dominant cultural conventions. Oddly, perhaps, she believed that a revival in an obscure village in West Africa held implications for the lives of fellow Americans. The final chapter of her book served, among other things, as a call to action for readers to pursue conversions among fellow Americans. Voicing a common evangelical anxiety about being seen as strange, McAllister asked her readers, "How often have you thought you should speak to some person about his soul, yet, because it would seem out of place or you would seem peculiar, you have not done so?" Christians should deliver "the message given by the King ... though all the people think us peculiar or crazy."[16]

This could have been an apologetic from a Pentecostal. McAllister, however, did not venture far enough along the holiness waterways to arrive at Pentecostalism. Keeping closer to the watershed, she still mixed her Methodist revivalism with comments about the "privileges of civilization." But the Garraway revival revealed dynamics that, over the coming decades, would pull holiness missionaries farther in these unconventional directions. To many of their fellow Americans, Pentecostal "Holy Rollers" appeared peculiar or even "crazy."[17] In a disenchanted era of industrial capitalism, scientific management, Darwinian thought, and technological invention, it seemed increasingly bizarre to believe that one could see immediate, discernible supernatural activity at work, much less signs, wonders, miracles, and an apocalyptic end of time. Countless people in Africa, Asia, and Latin America, however, did not think that these ideas were so crazy.

McAllister's supernaturalism was not the only thing that put her out of step with most Americans in the 1890s. An additional characteristic marked the Garraway revival as rather uncommon: the leading preacher was a woman. To be sure, women provided the bulk of the work for most evangelical causes at home and abroad. McAllister, in fact, lived during an era when women outnumbered men in the missionary movement. But mainstream American culture tended to set fairly clear limitations on female leadership in religious settings. Women organized and spearheaded numerous religious activities, but they generally did not preach or lead worship, except in informal bodies made up entirely of women. McAllister, on the other hand, showed no hesitation about spearheading a revival. Granted, she initiated her revival among the children and youth of Garraway, a role that fit with dominant conceptions of domesticity. However, she quickly extended her revival to the adult males of the village, who joined her in marching around town.[18] Her old-school Methodism played a key role here. The same antiformalist impulses that pulled McAllister toward the radical-holiness side of the watershed also thrust her into the role of female evangelist and preacher.

This was not a new phenomenon within evangelicalism. Since the eighteenth century, tensions within American evangelicalism simultaneously challenged and reaffirmed existing gender arrangements. In the enthusiasm of the Great Awakening in the 1740s, radical evangelicals encouraged and defended women and girls who exhorted and prophesied publicly. Antirevivalists and moderate evangelicals, on the other hand, argued that this violated Scripture. In the 1750s and '60s, as evangelistic passions waned and attentions turned to questions of social order, many radical evangelicals groups shifted and began opposing female preaching. Intense revival fires from the 1790s to the 1820s again led numerous evangelical females to preach, but a backlash set in during the 1830s and '40s, as many evangelicals, in the words of Catherine Brekus, sought to "build their small, countercultural churches into successful denominations." Still, women formed the bulk of evangelical life in the nineteenth century, even apart from the small number of female preachers, so the potential for female leadership always lay just below the surface.[19] The evangelical missionary movement produced similar tensions. At one level, women influenced the foreign-missionary movement simply by outnumbering men. They traveled as single missionaries or as wives who divided their time in varying degrees between domestic roles and direct evangelistic work. Women in the United States supported both types of agencies through local auxiliaries, fund-raising, and public promotion. The missionary movement, in fact, proved to be a major arena for public activity by American women. By 1900, the number of American women participating in the foreign-missionary movement outnumbered American women in all other social-reform and women's-rights movements combined.[20]

Women also developed separate women's agencies within their denominations, such as the Women's Foreign Missionary Society (WFMS) of the Methodist Episcopal Church (MEC). From its inception in 1869, the WFMS and similar agencies promoted a missionary rationale, known as Woman's Work for Women, which was finely tuned to the sensibilities of the American Protestant establishment. The WFMS argued that since women were the foundation of society and the bonds of womanhood were universal, female missionaries ought to establish Christian womanhood through conversion and developing Christian homes. Often speaking in terms of uplift, enlightenment, and the progress of civilization, the WFMS periodical, the *Heathen Woman's Friend*, contrasted the glories of Christian civilization with the corruption and degradation seen in other societies.[21] This does not mean that WFMS missionaries believed Western civilization to be the only possible type of Christian civilization, for it incorporated conceptions already generated by missionary encounters. WFMS publicists argued that missionaries should not try to "Americanize" their converts, that it would be helpful to evaluate America from a non-Western perspective, and that missionaries needed to try to understand and sometimes even learn from other cultures.[22] Still, those who promoted the Woman's Work for Women philosophy more closely matched the dominant ethos of American culture by tying their thinking to concepts of progress, civilization, and domesticity.

The vision of securing a "better civilization" by building Christian homes did not stir the souls of all women, however. The WFMS also attracted holiness women who spoke of sudden outpourings of the Holy Spirit from above, validated individual claims to the sanctification experiences, and cast the events surrounding their missionary work in supernatural terms.[23] As these women (and men) saw the matter, true missionary work flowed from particular ways in which the Holy Spirit gave power to sanctified individuals for evangelistic tasks.

Phoebe Palmer's holiness theology, for example, animated several antiformalist impulses that had always been present in Methodism, not the least of which involved questions of gender. American Methodists had encouraged women to testify publicly to their own conversion experiences, in order to encourage more conversions from the audience. Palmer expanded on this practice by emphasizing the urgent need for women (and men) to testify publicly to their second blessing of sanctification. Like many other evangelical proponents of female preaching, Palmer not only served as a widely popular example of female preaching but also used both Scripture and conversions won by female evangelism to support her arguments, although she stopped short of advocating women's rights or ordination for women. For Palmer and other holiness enthusiasts, issues of political or ecclesiastical power for women were comparatively unimportant side issues. Conversion and sanctification were the ultimate goals.[24]

The democratized elements of the holiness movement held important implications for issues of culture, power, and influence. Because the holiness movement could disregard existing institutions by validating personal claims to the movement of the Holy Spirit, many charismatic leaders successfully led bands of followers off on their own idiosyncratic paths. In the 1880s, holiness leaders in Iowa, Missouri, Arizona, and California formed their own distinctive regional associations, periodicals, and Bible institutes, with their own distinctive doctrinal emphases. Holiness periodicals and official newspapers of the MEC battled one another over the meaning of sanctification, the use of ministerial appointments, the validity of faith healing, and the use of jewelry. Frustrated "come-outers" began to break away from the MEC to form new denominations, such as the Church of God (Anderson), the Pilgrim Holiness Church, the Church of the

Nazarene, and the Heavenly Recruit Church. In some areas, Methodist officials who openly opposed the independent behavior of holiness evangelists pushed or forced them out of the denomination. By 1923, more than two hundred different types of independent holiness groups had formed just under the rubric of the Church of God. The inability of Methodist leaders to control dissenters, of course, would hold implications for missionary engagement.[25]

These antiformalist impulses thrust women such as Lucy Drake Osborn into key roles in the holiness missionary movement. As an unmarried woman in the early 1870s, Lucy Drake had applied for missionary service with the MEC, but the board turned her down for health reasons. Like a good holiness enthusiast, she managed to find her way to India without institutional support anyway, most probably through holiness networks. Naturally, she ended up with William Taylor's program. She married fellow missionary William Osborn in 1879, and the couple established annual camp meetings in India. Ultimately, Lucy Drake Osborn did have to leave India for health reasons, but she still felt troubled by the "woes and agony" of millions in India who were "calling for the Gospel." The solution to this inner turmoil lay in building an independent school that sought to train "anyone giving satisfactory evidence they were called of God." In 1882, the Osborns founded the Union Missionary Training Institute in Brooklyn, with Lucy acting as the principal.[26]

The Union Missionary Training Institute might have been the first school for adults in America in which a female administrator supervised a mixed-gender faculty and student body. Most colleges or universities in the late nineteenth century were either all-male or all-female institutions. Men invariably headed up the few coeducational institutions in the United States. Lucy Osborn disregarded these conventions. As principal, she gave lectures on "Experimental and Practical Training Work" to the men and women. Traditional gender roles shaped some subjects, as women took lessons in cooking, dressmaking, and sewing, while men took courses in "building trades." But both women and men took classes in "soul-winning," theology, common school administration, and studies of "the people to whom they go." Some female graduates took on more traditional roles of common-school education, where they trained girls in "housekeeping, sewing and fancy work," but other women preached and planted churches.[27]

Oddly, perhaps, Osborn did not make much of the novel gender arrangements in her missionary institute. The school was billed in holiness periodicals simply as "Mrs. W. B. Osborn's Missionary Training Institute." Holiness advocates did not embark on a conscious campaign to address issues of women's rights or the status of women, as some other groups such as the Hicksite Quakers did. Instead, holiness spirituality created a deep urgency for evangelism, adding secondary justifications for their mixed-gender arrangements. A woman "under the power of the spirit" does "what inspiration affirms we shall do, that is, 'prophesy,'" declared an article in the *Advocate of Christian Holiness,* taking a typical antiformalist stance. "Do what you conscientiously believe to be duty, no matter who opposes it, or what mere ecclesiastical law forbids it."[28] Within holiness missionary circles, then, the passion for evangelism often shoved aside the Woman's Work for Women ideology that attempted to build Christian civilization through the transformation of the home. Holiness men cooperated, for the most part, by accepting the call of women in these evangelistic tasks. William Taylor, who never worried much about the proper foundations of civilization, enthusiastically recruited women for his missionary enterprise. In the first four years that Taylor began to recruit missionaries for India, thirteen Methodist women chose to work with his self-supporting mission. Meanwhile, nine women traveled to India under the WFMS, with its strong ideology of domesticity.[29]

While antiformalist evangelicalism often produced fragmentation, it simultaneously displayed impulses to draw people together from different backgrounds for the cause of evangelism. So it was with the holiness movement. Although she worked primarily through Methodist channels, Osborn's school drew in students and financial support from Presbyterian, Quaker, Baptist, and Congregationalist bodies. Not only did men and women mix together in the student body, but American students trained alongside students from other countries. Fewer than half of the forty-seven students in 1891 came from the United States or Canada. Twenty-one came from one of seven different countries in Europe, three students were Persian, and two were Chinese.[30]

The Union Missionary Training Institute also reinforced a sense that the Holy Spirit was at work in identifiably supernatural ways. Invoking the Lord Knows Tomorrow Test, Osborn opened the 1891 academic year hundreds of dollars short of needed expenses but then detailed specific instances when money arrived just in time. "My need was great," she wrote, "but the Lord knew, and He supplied." Graduates wrote similar accounts of divine activity. "I have no pledged support for my work from any human source," Helen Dawlly told readers in describing a school she established in India. "My expectation is from God, and it is He that has borne me up thus far, though sometimes through strange and winding paths." Annie Whitefield, who joined Taylor's mission in Liberia, described a serious illness in which she received a vision of herself standing on the banks of a river, where an angel held out a hand to her, beckoning her to heaven. A minister prayed "with power" to bring her back, however, "and God heard him."[31]

Osborn's missionary institute embodied a certain kind of cultural paradox. On the one hand, it opposed dominant features of American culture by granting women religious authority, resisting centralized institutional control, and embracing supernatural activity. Yet it drew on and reinforced other aspects of American culture in the process, including religious autonomy, the use of mass media to promote its cause, and the disregard of mediating elites. This, in turn, reinforced a paradox of power relations. For those who did not enjoy the advantages of respectable middle-class life, holiness spirituality and theology could reorganize a number of dominant categories of thought, smothering Victorian notions of domesticity, blunting racial edges, and overwhelming concepts of civilization. As it spread out to the periphery of American culture, the holiness movement selected charismatic leaders from the unlikeliest candidates.

Amanda Berry Smith seemed as unlikely a candidate as any. Born into slavery in Maryland in 1837, limited in educational background, and compelled to work as a domestic servant, Smith fell well short of the qualifications that most Americans believed one must have to be a leader of civilization. But then, holiness advocates often prided themselves on being peculiar. By the end of her life, Smith had achieved wide recognition within holiness circles as a powerful preacher, a notable foreign missionary, and a prominent leader of the movement.

Several years after her evangelical conversion at age eighteen, Amanda Berry married James Smith, who planned to be an itinerant preacher for the African Methodist Episcopal Church. Amanda Berry Smith envisioned herself ministering in the domestic pattern of several ministers' wives whom she knew, who led prayer meetings, prayed with the sick and dying, and kept beautiful houses. However, James Smith did not pursue preaching appointments with the AME conference. This deeply disappointed her. Living in New York City, James took on odd jobs, and Amanda cleaned houses, took in laundry, and frequented Methodist religious meetings, where she often spoke up during times of testimony.[32]

Amanda Smith then encountered sanctification. This experience, which she recounted numerous times in her career, blended with her African-American spirituality and powerfully shaped her subsequent ministry. In 1868, Smith visited a church in which John Inskip, one of the leading holiness preachers in America, gave a sermon on sanctification. Smith deeply desired the blessing, but it came attached to an intense internal struggle. She battled an impulse to flee the meeting because she had left her thirteen-year-old daughter to care for her baby son while she attended the service, a practice her husband disliked. Smith wrote that the voice of Satan kept telling her that great harm had befallen her baby while she sat listening to the sermon, even to the point where she distinctly heard the baby scream. But then a "sweet voice" told her that she had to "trust the Lord" and continue in the worship. With that conflict resolved, Smith found herself both enlightened and deeply moved by Inskip's sanctification sermon. She embraced the blessing.[33]

Then another internal conflict arose. Smith longed to shout out loud in praise for the blessing she had just received. As the only African American in the congregation, she worried that the white people would remove her from the building if she did shout. At the same time, she felt that her failure to shout out loud grieved the Holy Spirit, for she was failing to confess him. After another tortured bout of listening to Satan speak in one ear and another voice whisper in the other ear, Smith finally burst out with "glory to Jesus" on the final hymn. Like many a democratized preacher before him, Inskip immediately answered her with "Amen, Glory to God." Smith rejoiced in a "triumph for our King Emmanuel."[34]

Smith's testimony emphasized the increased courage she gained from sanctification. She left the service that night filled with joy, only to meet three black women from her regular AME church on the street outside. These "dignified" and "leading sisters," who "made you feel that wisdom dwelt with them," had always intimidated Smith. On this night, though, she "felt mighty." As she approached the women, she found herself swinging her right arm around the way boys sometimes did. "The Lord has sanctified my soul," she told them, leaving them speechless. "I suppose the people thought I was wild," she wrote, "and I was, for God had set me on fire!" She arrived home to find her children fine and her husband still away.[35]

When her husband, her pastor, and members of her church ridiculed her odd theology, Smith initially reacted by camouflaging her holiness language. This only depressed her. Gradually, holiness theology and spirituality gave her courage to confront opposition head-on. As she struggled with depression, Smith heard the Holy Spirit tell her to read the Bible, whereupon she turned to the passage "Perfect love casteth out fear." Emboldened, she immediately responded to a prompting from the Holy Spirit to testify to her sanctification experience at a black church that had strongly criticized holiness doctrine. When testimony time came, she negotiated her way through simultaneous shouts and testimonies until she held the undivided attention of the people. After speaking for a while, she reported, "I came to a point when it seemed a finger touched my tongue, and the power of God came upon me in such a wonderful manner." Smith wrote that the congregation responded positively. In her understanding of things, God had validated her lone venture into an unfriendly public arena.[36]

This set the pattern for Smith's preaching career. She understood seemingly ordinary details in her daily life, such as child care, to be intimately connected to a spiritual world where God and Satan waged battles. They were battles that were both cosmic in their significance and personal in their relation to her fears, desires, and needs. Whenever she faced a key decision or feared the actions of those with greater social power, Smith dipped deep into her well of holiness spirituality and theology. Claiming personal directions from God to speak, she steadily expanded her circle of speaking venues, particularly after her husband and her infant son died. During the year after her sanctification experience, she spoke mostly around New York City in black churches that allowed women to testify publicly.[37]

Then Smith heard a call to preach. The call did not come through a tightly reasoned analysis of the role of women in the ministry. She justified her authority to preach in the same way that black evangelical female evangelists did during the early days of Methodism.[38] She heard an audible voice saying, "Go preach," and saw and felt a vision of a cold, white cross laid on her forehead and chest. Convinced that her needs would be taken care of through divine means and emboldened to face all sorts of opposition, Smith set out on her evangelistic work. The Holy Spirit, she explained, called her to this uncommon role.[39]

It was the kind of decision that seemed all out of sorts in Gilded Age America. If Andrew Carnegie, the paragon of industrial capitalism, exemplified the spirit of the era, Smith exemplified the counterspirit. Obviously, her Gospel differed from Carnegie's "Gospel of Wealth," which claimed that "the problem of our age is the administration of wealth."[40] Less obviously, Smith remained unconcerned about the modern convictions produced by industrial capitalism, that one engaged the world by accomplishing tasks through careful planning, calculations of efficiency, rationalized financial practices, and powerful institutional structures. Instead, the black washwoman launched her preaching career by setting out on her own in 1870 for Salem, New Jersey. She had never visited the town before, knew nobody there, went without any known means of income, and ventured forth without the sanction of an ecclesiastical body. In retelling this story, though, Smith very pointedly declared that the Holy Spirit had instructed her to go there.[41]

Smith presented herself to the local minister in Salem. He indicated that, actually, he had not received a message from the Lord that they were to be blessed with Smith's preaching. Nor did he anticipate receiving any such word. However, the presiding minister of the quarterly meeting turned out to be Brother Holland, a former pastor of Smith's. Holiness readers of this account would understand that this was just one more indication that the Holy Spirit arranged matters that individuals could not predict. In fact, Smith probably knew that a quarterly meeting of regional AME members would be held in Salem, for she carried the name of a contact person with her. At any rate, Holland put in a good word for her with the local people and invited her to testify at the Sunday night service. Sitting on the platform with Holland that night, Smith felt quite frightened until he told her not to be afraid but to lean on the Lord. "After I had talked a little while the cold chills stopped, my heart began to beat naturally and all fear was gone," Smith wrote. "I seemed to lose sight of everybody and everything but my responsibility to God and my duty to the people." When several people converted after her testimony, the host pastor invited her to preach on the following Thursday. When she invited people to come to the altar, "a revival broke out." Smith preached on salvation and sanctification nightly for two weeks, sometimes staying at church until one or two in the morning, as blacks and whites from the surrounding area joined the services. The revival proved to Smith that "He indeed had chosen, and ordained and sent me."[42]

This was not the way establishment Protestants justified ministry efforts by women. Like that of other women in the holiness movement, Smith's evangelism differed from the domestic terms set by the Woman's Work for Women ideology, for she did not limit her preaching to women, and she did not attempt to transform the home. Nor did she attempt to claim ordination based on special gifts in the nature of women, as some did.[43] In fact, Smith devoted very little effort to the issue of female preaching. She understood keenly that many people did not support the idea of women preaching, an obstacle she faced throughout her life. But Smith's deep-seated identity as an individual consumed by the holiness experience and her intense desire to spread her religious experience to others mitigated her need to justify her ordination primarily in terms of gender. Instead, she found confirmation for her ministry in a long-standing feature of democratized Christianity: the positive response of her audience to her evangelistic appeals.[44]

Race, in fact, proved to be a greater obstacle than gender when Smith took her ministry to holiness meetings beyond the black churches. She sought out holiness worship services, weekday holiness meetings for women, and summer camp meetings where she was often the only black person in attendance. When faced with an unknown group of white worshippers, Smith carefully probed their reactions to her presence, trying to stay in the shadows until she was granted acceptance. Knowing that white worshippers might evict her, Smith almost always depended on invitations or commendations from white friends for these meetings. Even then, she received mixed reactions from white holiness advocates. Many people who heard her testify, sing, and preach welcomed her warmly and recommended her to others. Those who disapproved of her presence reacted in a variety of ways. On several occasions, Smith spoke of white people at camp meetings who were "cured" of their racial prejudice under the influence of the sanctification blessing. Others clearly did not think that sanctification ought to transform racial attitudes. One hostess in New York City felt so embarrassed by Smith's presence at her holiness meeting of middle-class women that she insisted that Smith leave. "Some people don't get enough of the blessing to take prejudice out of them," Smith wrote, "even after they are sanctified."[45]

Still, Smith began to attract the attention of white holiness leaders. She attended Phoebe Palmer's Tuesday meetings. John Inskip and other national holiness leaders invited her to speak at camp meetings and churches, while holiness friends paid for her travel and food.[46] By 1878, her reputation had grown to the point where even the most famous preacher in America, the nonholiness minister Henry Ward Beecher, described her ministry as a "great revolution." She spent two weeks leading services at one of his mission churches in Brooklyn.[47]

While Smith's gifts as a speaker explain much of her popularity, some of her notoriety stemmed from the spectacle of seeing such an unlikely individual in the pulpit. She understood that she was an oddity but wrote that a message from the Holy Spirit resolved this problem for her. Troubled at an early camp meeting by crowds who followed her around between services, Smith took advice from a friend, who pointed to a passage from Hebrews about Christians being a "gazing-stock," the same issue that evangelical women preachers faced seventy years earlier. After praying that God would help her to "throw off that mean feeling, and give me grace to be a gazing stock," the example hit Smith of people crowded around a window in New York, looking at a picture. "Did it injure its beauty?" she asked. "No, Lord," she responded, "I see it." During the rest of her career, Smith played up her identity as a "colored washwoman," as she often referred to herself. She became convinced that the novelty of her public preaching attracted listeners and represented a visual testimony to the possibilities of the power of the Spirit.[48]

Smith's ties to white holiness advocates propelled her onto the foreign-mission field, a move that sealed her popularity within the movement. Like William Taylor, Smith seemingly stumbled into the missionary movement by accident. Fittingly, she did not set out with a specific missionary objective carried out through the funding of an established missionary agency. Instead, she interpreted invitations from fellow travelers in the holiness network as signs that God directed her moves to unknown destinations through a series of surprising promptings.

In 1878, a female friend invited her to travel with her to England, a step that Smith at first considered absurd. Writing with wonder, Smith later exclaimed, "Amanda Smith, the colored washwoman, go to England!" But when the friend persisted, Smith asked for a clear message from God. The divine response, she wrote, was "so real and deep, that I could no more doubt that He wanted me to go to England, than I could doubt my own existence."[49] In England and Scotland, the "colored washwoman" created a stir by preaching at several different holiness gatherings over the next year. She also ran into an old holiness friend from America, who happened to be none other than Lucy Drake, soon to be Lucy Osborn. On her way to India herself, Drake told Smith several times that "the Lord has made it clear to me for you to go to India." Smith again thought that this was out of the question but prayed and received confirmation that the Holy Spirit wanted her in India. She joined Drake.[50]

It seemed absurd, but holiness advocates often saw absurdity as a virtue. "Amanda Smith is in India," the *Advocate of Christian Holiness* announced. "It seems a strange move, but the Lord does strange things sometimes, and would do more if He could find willing instruments." The *Bombay Guardian*, a holiness publication, hailed Smith's arrival in 1880 by reprinting a letter it had published in 1873 from a visitor to the Ocean Grove camp meeting. Claiming that Smith gave the greatest of all of the camp-meeting addresses, the letter had declared, "so wonderful is her simplicity, so great her instructive powers, so deep and rich her experience, that the learned heads, (and there were many of them there) would stand still (awed it would seem by her presence) and be taught." Now, in 1880, the editor of the *Bombay Guardian* wrote that he had a chance to observe Smith preach in person, marveling at the "spiritual power that accompanies her singing and speaking." After noting that she was "African in color," he upheld her as "a striking example of what grace can accomplish for those who have not enjoyed such educational advantages as others have."[51]

In India, Smith joined male evangelists in preaching publicly to male Hindus and Muslims. James Thoburn, the Methodist bishop for India, supporter of William Taylor, and longtime holiness missionary, became particularly impressed with the "rare degree of spiritual power" that Smith possessed. While admitting that the novelty of a former slave and "colored woman from America" in the pulpit would by itself attract an audience in Calcutta, Thoburn insisted that Smith's popularity grew primarily from her gifts as a preacher. "During the seventeen years that I have lived in Calcutta, I have known many famous strangers to visit the city, some of whom attracted large audiences," he wrote in an introduction to Smith's autobiography, "but I have never known anyone who could draw and hold so large an audience as Mrs. Smith."[52]

Thoburn also commended Smith's "clearness of vision," her "extraordinary power of discernment" and "buoyant hope." In doing so, he questioned whether understanding came only through education and theological training. "Profound scholars and religious teachers of philosophical bent seemed positively inferior to her in the task of discovering the practical value of men and systems which had attracted the attention of the world!" he exclaimed. Drawing on the old Methodist respect for the spiritual expressions of ordinary people, Thoburn wrote about how in America, he once supported a Methodist leader's appeal to young preachers to be willing to "learn from their own hearers" even though they might be "comparatively illiterate." Thoburn told the audience that he himself had "learned more that had been of actual value to me as a preacher of Christian truth from Amanda Smith than from any other one person I had ever met."[53]

Besides challenging categories of race, class, and gender, Smith implicitly questioned the modern tendency to view changes in society solely as products of human agency, apart from any divine agency. She reported that the Holy Spirit led her to pray for a new railroad to be built to a small missionary station that she visited in India in 1880. When the East Indian Railroad Company laid tracks near the place two years later, Smith did not feel particularly moved to marvel in the progress of civilization. She did imply, however, that God had brought about this nation-changing event by responding to the sanctified faith of one poorly educated black woman.[54]

Smith left India for Liberia in 1882. For the next eight years, the charismatic black female evangelist rubbed shoulders with a range of different people in that land. True to her restless itinerant style, Smith moved among Americo-Liberians in Monrovia, inland Methodist mission stations, Kru settlements such as Greenville and Krootown, the port area of Cape Palmas, Kru villages along the Cavalla River, and then back to Monrovia. She preached, observed Kru cultural practices, launched temperance campaigns, and promoted the holiness program wherever she went.

After eight years of ministry in Liberia, Smith could point to a moderate impact—a few individual conversions, several congregations inspired, the formation of a temperance society—but nothing like a vibrant new movement of Christianity appeared in her wake. By evangelical standards, she did not enjoy widespread popular success. This might be somewhat surprising, since she would seem to be well fitted for such a task. The "colored washerwoman," after all, had managed to rise above barriers of race, gender, and class to gain support and fame within the American holiness movement. Furthermore, she promoted a form of Christianity that in many ways anticipated the later success of African Pentecostalism: an enthusiastic faith of individual salvation, testimonies to inward spiritual transformations, claims of miraculous provision for daily needs, and validation of the religious abilities of relatively powerless people such as herself.[55]

But new movements of Christianity did not automatically grow from the efforts of evangelicals who discovered correct formulas, despite what famous evangelists such as Charles Finney claimed.[56] Democratized Christians could not produce popular movements wherever they went. Highly mobile itinerant evangelists in the United States, of course, had played key roles in sparking movements of evangelical Christianity since the days of George Whitefield in the 1730s. But as John Wigger notes about democratized circuit riders, "the only real distinction between a Methodist preacher and the bulk of his audience was which side of the pulpit each was on."[57] In Liberia, by contrast, the pulpit demarcated significant differences between Smith and her audience. Cultural differences mattered.

In a rather odd way, the "colored washerwoman" held an unfamiliar position of cultural power in Liberia as a representative of civilization. And it worked against her. In the United States, Smith's marginalized position of power had aided her ability to understand how whites in the holiness movement operated. African Americans lived in a society dominated by whites, which meant that they usually had no choice but to engage the white world. Smith went even further than many blacks, spending years interacting with whites in their churches, households, prayer meetings, and camp meetings. By contrast, most whites in America rarely spent time in black churches, households, prayer meetings, or camp meetings, because their position of privilege allowed them to ignore marginalized people in their society if they wished.

In Liberia, Smith was not compelled to spend extended time with any particular Americo-Liberian or Kru community. Unlike Agnes McAllister, Smith never lived in any community in Liberia longer than six months. We do not know exactly why she had such a short ministerial attention span—she might have moved on when conflicts emerged or when she felt spiritually stale or just when she saw an exciting evangelistic opportunity elsewhere—but the point is that she had the freedom to leave. Since Smith did not sit still, she was limited in how much she could learn from the people among whom she worked. It appears that she did not even learn the Kru language.[58]

In 1890, Smith left Africa and returned to the United States. Her subsequent autobiography increased her popularity among various groups within the Methodist tradition, particularly the holiness movement.[59] William Taylor not only regularly reported on how Smith preached with him on evangelistic tours in Liberia, but he also claimed, with hyperbole not unknown to him, that she had reduced the importation of alcohol into Liberia by 75 percent through her temperance campaigns.[60] By the time the General Holiness Association met in Chicago in 1901, Smith had reached the apex of that particular holiness mountain. Her portrait was included among a collection of leaders of the modern holiness movement, nearly one-fourth of whom were women.[61] The antiformalist dynamics of the holiness movement made it possible for the "colored washerwoman" to enjoy a widely popular ministry in the United States, if not in Liberia. West Africa, of course, required an individual more highly attuned to local cultural dynamics.

That individual was William Wadé Harris.[62] While missionaries such as Amanda Smith, Agnes McAllister, and William Taylor oversaw handfuls of conversions in Liberia, Harris set in motion local movements of Christianity with truly sweeping impact. As an African himself, Harris engaged the West African spiritual world in ways that the missionaries only dimly understood. At the same time, he adapted evangelical convictions, practices, and impulses that he picked up from missionary communities in Liberia.

Between 1910 and 1930, Harris traveled through Liberia, the Ivory Coast, and Ghana, where, it has been estimated, he was instrumental in bringing two hundred thousand Africans to Christianity. Ten years after Harris had itinerated through inland villages of the Ivory Coast and Ghana, Methodist and Catholic missionaries arrived for the first time to find thousands of people already baptized as Christians, asking to join their church. Many more formed their own independent "Harrist" churches. It would not be a stretch to call Harris the most significant figure in early-twentieth-century West African Christianity.[63]

As several scholars have demonstrated, Prophet Harris, as he came to be known, promoted a ministry finely tuned to issues at the center of West African cultures. He did not minister under the supervision of missionaries, and he was not connected to any Western denominational institution, at least during his

MRS. PHEBE EPPERSON,
Boone, Iowa.

FANNIE BIRDSALL,
Indianapolis, Ind.

AMANDA SMITH,
Harvey, Ill.

MARY E. EDINGER,
Demotte, Ind.

Figure 8.2. Amanda Smith, with three other leaders of the holiness movement. Photograph in S. B. Shaw, ed., *Echoes of the General Holiness Assembly, Held in Chicago, May 3–13, 1901* (Chicago: S. B. Shaw, 1901).

evangelistic years. And yet there was a missionary connection. His evangelistic ministry, African as it was, grew out of the paradoxical dynamics of evangelical missionary engagement.

Harris, who had grown up as a Kru (or Glebo) near Cape Palmas, converted to Christianity in 1881 or 1882 under the influence of an Americo-Liberian Methodist minister.[64] By the 1890s, Harris seemed to be busy attempting to shed African culture for modern Christian civilization. He had joined the Episcopalian mission as a catechist and teacher, adopting the appearance, lifestyle, and identity of a civilized Christian African. During the same time that McAllister witnessed the revival at her mission at Garraway in 1893, Harris taught Sunday school fifteen miles away at an Episcopalian mission at Half-Graway, near Cape Palmas.[65]

His stint as a respectable Episcopalian did not last. Caught up in complicated political conflicts in Liberia, Harris landed in jail in 1910 for replacing the Liberian flag with a British Union Jack. In prison, as he later proclaimed on numerous occasions, the angel Gabriel visited him in a trance. Gabriel, behaving in a rather un-Episcopalian manner, anointed Harris as "a prophet of Christ, of God the Mysterious," who would usher in a "peace of a thousand years," as spoken by John in the twentieth chapter of Revelation.

Prophet Harris then began his two-decade-long itinerant career through West Africa, a career grounded in evangelical commitments to biblical authority, the atonement, conversion, and evangelism. However, he adapted these evangelical commitments to African concerns, such as identifying and addressing the spiritual sources behind the conflicts and challenges of life. As did many Africans, the Kru believed that events did not happen by chance but were driven by spiritual agency. Ordinary people could call on the ancestors or spirits in rocks or trees, which could provoke good or evil events. Most powerful were the *deyabo* (doctors) and *we-dio* (sorcerers), who were believed to have power to control the weather, heal illnesses, identify secrets in the hearts of individuals, make charms to protect people against witchcraft, and identify people who caused particular deaths. Problems arose, however, because the spirits could be unpredictable and capricious. Disagreements arose over the proper identification of those who used witchcraft for evil.[66]

Unlike many Western missionaries, Harris saw the African belief in spirits not as ignorant superstition but as very real forces that could bring evil. The spirits, then, needed to be countered with the spiritual power of the Holy Spirit. He urged Africans to abandon their "fetishes" and worship God, who brought salvation through Jesus Christ. In a ministry accompanied by a range of signs and wonders, Harris told the people that he would "cast out from you all the influences of the fetishes and the idols, and...make of you children of God by my baptism." He claimed that the Holy Spirit gave him the power to exorcise devils from the people, heal diseases miraculously, bring rain, and produce signs and wonders that authenticated his ministry.[67]

Harris displayed the evangelical knack for simultaneously affirming and critiquing culture, but he applied this impulse to both traditional African culture and Western culture. Abandoning his Western clothes for a white robe, Harris carried a cross, a Bible, and a calabash rattle, which the Kru used to call on the spirits. In a similar manner to the Kru *deyabo*, who claimed spiritual power through possession by the spirits, Harris proclaimed that the Holy Ghost had come upon him at his conversion in the 1880s. He framed his 1910 trance with the angel Gabriel as a similar sort of spiritual possession. Displaying dissatisfaction with the civilizing mission, he dismissed the period between those two events, when he had worked as a teacher and a catechist, by claiming that he had joined the Episcopalians for money. But he also set himself up in opposition to traditional religious leaders by urging Africans to destroy their fetishes.[68] As David Shank has framed it, Harris "desacralized and then—with another Spirit—completely re-sacralized" traditional African religious practices.[69]

The Prophet Harris disparaged the spiritual significance of his years as a "civilized" Episcopalian. However, he did receive from those formalist missionaries a substantial education and familiarity with the Bible. Harris appealed to the Bible to validate all aspects of his ministry, including his message of repentance, his trances, his calling as a prophet, and his prophetic view of the future. To challenge the traditional African use of fetishes, he referred to the supernatural power accessed by Elijah, Peter, and Paul, since they challenged traditional sorcerers of their era. Harris also used the Bible to dissent from missionary conceptions of Christianity. His tacit support for polygamy, for instance, disturbed many missionaries. He traveled with several wives who assisted in his ministry, but when questioned on the Christian basis for this marital arrangement, he interpreted Isaiah 4:1 as support for African practices that removed a stigma from unattached females. For good measure, he also pointed out that Solomon had many wives.[70]

Harris received a mixed reception from missionaries in West Africa, who had not envisioned his popular brand of Christianity unfolding the way it did.[71] Methodist and Catholic missionaries readily accepted the converts who flocked to their churches as a result of his ministry, but most were not convinced that his movement represented a valid form of Christianity. Some saw his support of polygamy as a form of rebellion against God and harmful to missionary work. Catholic missionaries in the Ivory Coast supported anxious French government officials who, unsettled by the presence of an uncontrolled popular religious movement in the colony, seized and beat Harris, before expelling him from the Ivory Coast. Another missionary described the religion of Harris as "exceedingly crude and elementary." Others worried that he hypnotized followers, used terrifying methods to attract crowds, or simply worked as some sort of religious charlatan. The criticisms, however, could not prevent Harris from influencing hundreds of thousands of West Africans.[72]

Ogbu Kalu has called Harris's prophetic movement a precursor to contemporary African Pentecostalism. Indeed, Harris inspired later Ghanaian Pentecostal leaders Sampson Oppong, John Swatson, and Peter Anim. Like Harris, these African leaders sought immediate, discernible, powerful works of the Holy Spirit. The Pentecostal movements they led not only embedded themselves in local African cultures but also were driven by ordinary Christians who followed local leaders.[73] This was not just a West African phenomenon. At the same time that Harris launched his evangelistic ministry, a range of similarly decentralized, ecstatic, democratized, and culturally adaptive religious movements had emerged in regions as diverse as India, Chile, Korea, Norway, and California. Although they were local in character, these Pentecostal movements inspired and influenced one another through a web of multidirectional conduits laid by the holiness missionary network.

9

And Ever the Twain Shall Meet

In her private letters, the twenty-four-year-old Indian woman, Pandita Ramabai, called Sister Geraldine "Ajeebai," an affectionate term meaning "grandmother." Ramabai did not, however, automatically defer to Sister Geraldine in theology, even though she looked to this English missionary for spiritual guidance and insight. This stance unsettled Sister Geraldine, who considered herself to be Ramabai's spiritual mentor, a role she took very seriously. That role included a public dimension, for Ramabai already had made a name for herself in India and Great Britain. Many people were watching her.[1]

Born in 1858 to a Brahmin priest, Ramabai grew up immersed in Hindu religious practices. Her upbringing departed from the traditional paths in two very significant ways, however: her father refused to arrange a marriage for her as a child, and he educated her in the sacred language of Sanskrit. By the age of eighteen, Ramabai had deeply impressed Hindu scholars in Calcutta with her erudition and scholarly attainments. She moved to Poona (known today as Pune), where she established a reform movement, advocated female education, and wrote a book on the status of women in India. She also met several Christians, including Sister Geraldine, who belonged to an Anglican order known as the Community of St. Mary the Virgin (CSMV). Ramabai then made her way to England in 1883, so that she could expand her education and better serve the women of India. Sister Geraldine returned as well, helping Ramabai settle in with the CSMV order and enroll at Cheltenham Ladies College. After about a year in England, Ramabai converted to Christianity.[2]

Ramabai's conversion disturbed leading Hindus and thrilled leading Christians. Quite aware that many people looked with intense interest on the life of this intelligent, reform-minded young Indian woman, Sister Geraldine felt a responsibility to guide Ramabai into a mature Christian faith, which Sister Geraldine understood to be the practices and theology of high-church Anglicanism. The irrepressible convert, however, did not see the Church of England as the sole repository of mature Christian faith. Although they agreed on many points of theology, Ramabai and Sister Geraldine sparred with each other over several issues, including the Athanasian Creed, church authority, and the validity of dissenting Protestantism. Two years after her conversion, Ramabai explained to Sister Geraldine that "there is a higher power which leads us to do and believe things without doubt if we are willing to obey it," but "I am now standing between this voice and you. Will you blame me for obeying this voice?" Sister Geraldine, in fact, did blame Ramabai. "You are, as I have said before, but a babe in the Faith," she responded, "and your duty is to sit as a humble learner in the School of Christ."[3]

Much to the chagrin and general puzzlement of Sister Geraldine, Ramabai did not stay in the Church of England. Ramabai left Britain in 1888, traveled to America, and forged ties with several different Protestant bodies. She then returned to India, where she established schools for child widows, rescued famine victims, and advocated for downtrodden women in India. This all pleased British leaders, until she launched criticisms of British colonial policies.[4]

She continued to keep observers off balance. A former English acquaintance refused to visit her in India because of "the strange practices carried on in her mission." Undoubtedly, this referred to the revival that broke out in Ramabai's Mukti school near Poona. In January 1905, Ramabai had asked for volunteers to join her in praying daily for a Christian revival. At first, about seventy girls met with her twice a day for prayer. By June, the number had risen to five hundred fifty. Ramabai asked if some of the girls would preach in the surrounding villages; thirty volunteered. The real excitement began when there were reports of a burning sensation that possessed girls at prayer, who claimed that they had been baptized in the Holy Spirit. For more than a year after that, the Mukti school became a center of intense prayer and evangelism, leading to more than one thousand conversions. Many Western observers, however, did not know what to do about the reports of religious phenomena that just seemed "strange": the fire sensation, casting out of demons, speaking in tongues, and miraculous healings.[5]

Nobody predicted that an articulate, erudite, reform-minded convert to high-church Anglicanism would end up rubbing shoulders with religious enthusiasts who claimed to cast out demons. In fact, most American, British, and Indian observers quickly passed over these events, viewing the Mukti revival as anomalous and insignificant. Even today, many scholars analyze Ramabai's influence without referring to the revival or this stage in her religious journey.[6] And yet, as scholars of world Christianity now recognize, the small revival among widowed, elderly, and orphaned females at Ramabai's school played a key role in the emergence of Pentecostalism, one of the more far-reaching religious developments of the twentieth-century world.[7]

A puzzle lies therein. How did Ramabai move from engaging in theological debates over the Athanasian creed to being the leader of a popular movement known for signs and wonders? What was it about this particular evangelical movement that drew in Ramabai? The logic of that move becomes clearer when one considers her religious and cultural background in light of the evangelical missionary movement and its paradoxes of culture, power, and influence, particularly as they played out in the more radical impulses of the holiness movement.

Part of Ramabai's move to the holiness movement stemmed from earlier tensions with the Church of England, tensions that unfolded with particular cultural concerns in mind. Neither Ramabai nor Sister Geraldine worked out her theology from a culturally neutral position. Born and raised in England, Sister Geraldine understood herself to be not only a missionary but also a loyal subject of the British Empire, placing her in a position of power that deeply affected the way she related to Ramabai. She believed that she had a duty to impart both the higher spiritual truths of the Church of England and the attendant qualities of British civilization to this promising young convert from colonial India. This invested her engagement with Ramabai with a heavy custodial dynamic. In a letter to an Anglican minister in 1885, Sister Geraldine expressed her concern that an educator at Cheltenham was "mismanaging Ramabai" by letting her "see she is altogether independent of us." There was the rub. Sister Geraldine thought that Ramabai needed to be managed; Ramabai would brook no such thing. "I am always surprised," Ramabai wrote pointedly to Sister Geraldine, "when I see or hear people troubling themselves to decide my future, when My Lord...knows best to do with me whatever he likes."[8]

Deference to human authority had never been high on Ramabai's list of personal qualities. Her unorthodox upbringing in India encouraged this sensibility. At the age of twenty, she had disturbed traditional Indian leaders with critiques of the Hindu treatment of women. "The husband is said to be a woman's god," she had concluded from her study of sacred texts such as the Vedas. "This god may be the worst sinner and a great criminal; *still he is her god* and she must worship him," she objected. Ramabai embraced her identity as an educated, independent, unmarried, high-caste woman, a status that flouted traditional Hindu authority. In fact, her desire to escape Hindu patriarchy helped draw her to Christianity.[9]

Sister Geraldine did not grasp the significance of this cultural context. Convinced that deference to Anglican officials was an admirable and even necessary spiritual task, she grew alarmed when Ramabai displayed independent ways of thinking. The sister fell back on common Western perceptions of India to explain the unsettling autonomy of the young convert. Pantheism makes the "Hindu mind" illogical, Sister Geraldine wrote. Indians quickly "grasp the surface ideas," but "it is almost impossible to impress Indian people with...a sense of loyalty to the Church." Ramabai's vegetarianism, Sister Geraldine told her, showed that she still clung to "caste prejudices" and revealed a pride that prevented her from "accepting the full teaching of the Gospel." In Sister Geraldine's way of thinking,

Ramabai's later criticisms of British colonial policies in India were not just "childish" and "sensational" but also "disloyal" and "seditious."[10]

Obviously, colonialism loomed large here. Ramabai did not see why conversion from Hinduism to Christianity meant that she must declare loyalty to Great Britain, adopt an Anglican identity, or submit to the Church of England. "I like to be called a Hindoo," she wrote in response to Sister Geraldine, "for I am one, and also keep all the customs of my forefathers as far as I can." Why was she supposed to believe that "your Anglican Church is the sole treasury of truth?"[11] That treasury of truth did not seem to provide Anglican leaders with as much understanding of India as they thought. The English bishop from Bombay, for instance, objected to the prospect of Ramabai lecturing to men and women in Britain, arguing that "her influence in India will be ruined for ever in India if she is known to have taught young men." Sister Geraldine, in turn, told Ramabai that they must "accept the opinion of those who, from their knowledge of India and its people, are far better judges than ourselves." Ramabai bristled. "I know India and its people," she replied, "far better than any foreigners even if they have been staying in India from long time [sic] before I was born."[12]

She had a point. By the age of twenty-two, Ramabai not only had lectured to both men and women in India but also had been honored with the titles of Pandita ("Learned Woman") and Saraswati ("Goddess of Learning") by the Sanskrit scholars of Calcutta. It is doubtful that the bishop of Bombay could, like Ramabai, speak seven languages or explicate the Vedas, the Upanishads, and the Dharmashastras. Furthermore, Ramabai's singular childhood had provided her with a wide-ranging and intimate knowledge of India. She spent her youth traveling thousands of miles across India with her parents, who received food, clothing, and gifts in return for narrating stories at temples and sacred locations. She had seen "the sufferings of Hindu women" and had known suffering herself. Despite her high caste and extensive educational attainments, she had lived in poverty, in hardship, and on the edge of starvation as a youth, an experience that instilled in her a deep empathy for the downtrodden. When she was sixteen, Ramabai's parents and a sister died in the midst of a famine. Her brother died two years later, leaving her all alone in the world. She then took the unorthodox route of marrying outside her caste, but her husband died after sixteen months of marriage. She was left a widow with an infant daughter, Monoramabai. Forced to make her way without the kinship ties and traditional patterns of local networks, she understood quite well the challenges that unattached Indian women faced in a patriarchal culture.[13]

To their credit, both Ramabai and Sister Geraldine continued their friendship and correspondence with each other for many years after they had parted, even amid new disagreements, which usually stemmed from Ramabai's refusal to embrace high-church Anglicanism.[14] She gravitated to a broad, ecumenical form of Christianity after she left Britain for the United States in 1886, attracting intense interest from prominent American Protestants. She established the Ramabai Association in 1887, which helped raise money for her plans to educate Indian women. Formed in Boston with a large contingent of Unitarian leadership, the Ramabai Association landed some of the most influential and respected American Protestants on its board, including Phillips Brooks, Frances Willard, George A. Gordon, and Lyman Abbott.[15] To many in her American audiences, Ramabai seemed to embody the Woman's Work for Women model in missions. "Cultured audiences" listened to her explain how "the enfranchisement and elevation of her countrywomen" had become her life's goal. "Elevate the women of India, and who can tell of her power?" asked one American supporter.[16]

Ramabai returned to India and established Sharada Sadan, one of the earliest schools for high-caste widows and unmarried Hindu girls. With a local advisory board made up of influential Hindu men in Bombay and Poona, Ramabai attempted to forge a modern, liberal arrangement for handling competing religious claims. She declared that she would not teach Christianity but would let the girls study Hindu and Christian religions outside the classroom. The nonsectarian, secular policies of Sharada Sadan created new problems for her, though. Some of the Hindu girls, strongly attracted to Ramabai and curious about the Christian faith, approached her at devotions. Since they had come of their own accord outside the classroom, Ramabai let them join her. Upon hearing of this news, the men on the Bombay advisory board and an American representative of the Ramabai Association objected, particularly after a few girls expressed interest in conversion. "We consider the Christian women, who try to make inroads into our society under the garb of female education... to be enemies of our society, of Hinduism, and even of female education," one board member wrote. Ramabai argued that "perfect freedom" would allow girls and young women to explore the Christian faith of their own volition. This, after all, had been her own experience. "I would not prevent them from reading the sacred books of their own religion," Ramabai explained, "so too did I not mean to prevent them from reading the Bible if they wished to do so." The backlash set in, however. The Hindu advisory board disbanded, Unitarians resigned from the Ramabai Association, parents withdrew their girls from her school, and Sharada Sadan fell on unstable financial footing.[17]

And then Ramabai discovered Wesleyan holiness Christianity. After reading several books and listening to evangelists traveling through India, she had come to the conviction that "mine was only an intellectual belief—a belief in which there was no life." She had "failed to see the need of placing my implicit faith in Christ and His atonement." She read Amanda Smith's explanation of how she had been led out of bondage from both slavery and sin. Ramabai believed that she also had been delivered from "the bondage of man's opinions" and the "bondage of sin" but felt, as Smith did, that she needed "the abiding presence of the Holy Spirit within me." Ramabai sought out a holiness camp meeting in India, an annual event that had been established by Lucy and William Osborn. It was there where, in her words, she received the Holy Spirit. Hitching her ministry to the holiness movement, she attended annual holiness camp meetings in India, traveled to Britain to speak at the Keswick Convention, and recruited holiness missionaries to her work. She abandoned the secular model of Sharada Sadan and founded a new school, Mukti, with clear evangelistic goals as part of its program. By 1900, Mukti educated about two thousand females, including high-caste widows, elderly women, lower-caste famine victims, sexually abused females, and the blind.[18]

There were many factors at work in this move to holiness. Ramabai had always found herself restricted and hemmed in religiously by a host of systems: the patriarchy of Hinduism, British colonialism, high-church Anglicanism, the advisory board of Sharada Sadan, and the Ramabai Association. The decentralized and democratized dynamics of the holiness movement actually encouraged her to strike out on her own initiatives, without the controlling oversight of the numerous boards, agencies, and organizations. Furthermore, part of the reason Ramabai had been baptized in England in the first place was "that I had found a religion which gave its privileges equally to men and women; there was no distinction of caste, colour, or sex made in it." Of all of the varieties of Christianity in 1900, none might have exhibited these characteristics as fully as the holiness movement. Finally, the disenchanted and secular arrangement of Sharada Sadan placed her in a passive role in terms of spiritual leadership and could not help her when girls sought her out for Christian guidance. Anything but passive, the holiness movement took spiritual forces seriously.[19]

A radical wing of the holiness movement had emerged in America during the years when Ramabai established the Mukti school. Building on antiformalist impulses that had always existed within the holiness movement, this radical branch increasingly disregarded all sorts of cultural conventions for the cause of evangelism. Eventually, radical holiness produced what came to be known as Pentecostalism, but not without significant contributions from Christians around the world. Born not simply as an American but as a worldwide movement, Pentecostalism gained vitality from multidirectional influences that flowed through the conduits laid by the holiness missionary network.

No periodical in the 1890s might have done more to push the antiformalist impulses of the holiness movement than the *Revivalist,* which held one of the largest circulations among the dozens of holiness newspapers that popped up during that decade. Edited by Martin Wells Knapp, the *Revivalist* fed about twenty thousand readers each month with a diet of zealous articles laced with supernatural imagery. Knapp described revivals as dynamite, sparks, tornadoes, lightning falling from above, stupendous avalanches, and "mighty spiritual electric currents."[20] While all holiness advocates desired to see an outpouring of the

Holy Spirit, the *Revivalist* had an unsettling habit of identifying fellow Christians as barriers to that outpouring. American Christianity and the Methodist Episcopal Church in particular received criticism for their cold formality and worldly addiction to fashion. The *Revivalist* explicitly rejected laudatory encomiums praising the progress of civilization. "Nothing but Pentecost," wrote a contributor, could move the church beyond its "cloud of rose-colored idealism" about "the march of the nineteenth century," which mistakenly promoted the belief that "the world is growing better and better." Missionaries, the writer complained, would not keep up with global population growth, thanks to the "self-seeking, ease-loving, heathen-forgetting, Christ-neglecting spirit of the Church." Unless, of course, "jagged bolts of lightning" from God struck and transformed Christianity.[21]

More was afoot here than supernatural thunderstorms and interdenominational sniping. Like many holiness enthusiasts, Knapp yearned for a reestablishment of a cosmic event in history, the ancient Pentecost. In this scheme, a worldwide movement of conversion and the baptism of the Holy Spirit were absolutely essential in reclaiming the primitive Christianity of the early church. It would also usher in the end of time. Writing of "these last days," the *Revivalist* adopted a new theology of dispensationalist eschatology, which was gaining ground within some quarters of evangelicalism. Dispensationalists believed that history was poised to cross over a final threshold to an apocalyptic conclusion. Simultaneously pointing holiness advocates to an ancient past and an apocalyptic future, this theology explicitly rejected the modern faith in a progressively brighter future.[22]

These characteristics set radical-holiness enthusiasts apart from fellow Protestants, evangelicals, and moderate holiness advocates. And that was just fine with them. Although they were generally cooperative with other Protestant missionaries, radical-holiness missionaries viewed the efforts of Protestant missionaries as weak and incomplete without the baptism of the Spirit. A holiness missionary from India in 1899 explained to readers of the *Revivalist* that a "Pentecostal Revival" had not broken out in the Subcontinent because most missionaries had not been baptized in the Spirit. Logically enough, the solution to this spiritual sloth lay in sending out missionaries to the missionaries. "The editor has felt that something ought to be done by the readers of *The Revivalist*," Knapp suggested in his response, "toward reaching the missionaries on the field with the Pentecostal gospel." This way of thinking held significant implications for cultural engagement. Standard contrasts between enlightened civilization and benighted barbarism would be hard to maintain when missionaries needed missionaries.[23]

That same year, Minnie Abrams turned to the *Revivalist* to recruit missionaries for Ramabai's school in Mukti. Abrams, who was born in Minnesota, joined the Methodist Episcopal Church, attended a woman's training institute in

Chicago, and then took an assignment in India with the Women's Foreign Missionary Society as a teacher in a school for girls.[24] Yet her missionary vision did not quite fit the staid domestic program of nurturing Christian homes in India. She wanted to mobilize women to evangelize publicly in the villages. After several years in India, she heard a voice telling her to go to Ramabai's school at Mukti. She arrived unannounced in 1898. Ramabai, who had been praying for another worker, took her in.[25]

Abrams immediately began recruiting fellow holiness enthusiasts. "Without the anointing from on high, and the attending power of God," Abrams wrote in the *Revivalist*, "our preaching is all in vain. Among the evangelists who read this paper is there not someone who will offer herself for this work?" The female pronoun "herself" appeared without fanfare. It concluded an account of how Abrams and Krishnabai, an Indian Christian woman, had spent the previous year traveling from village to village to preach to men and women. Abrams simply assumed that holiness readers would support female evangelists.[26]

Never one to miss a chance at fanfare, Knapp directly addressed the issue of female preaching. And he solidly supported women like Abrams. "I know I am facing here one of the most effective fallacies that the devil has breathed from the pit," he argued with his characteristic lack of delicacy. "Men have taken the responsibility of sermonizing and theorizing, and, as a result, they have cold Churches where they ought to have hot furnaces full of fire." Justifying his arguments with biblical references, Knapp wrote that while church leaders were "scratching their heads" over women's work, the Holy Spirit went ahead and sent women overseas to evangelize the world.[27]

The *Revivalist* also dispensed with other social conventions for the cause of holiness. During the decade when Jim Crow gained ascendency and lynchings reached their peak, the newspaper included articles written by African-American holiness evangelists and suggested that revivals ought to be integrated. "In choosing His workers and material for soul-winning work God is no respecter of persons," Knapp declared. "Not the high or low, or rich or poor, man or woman." This antiformalist disregard for cultural conventions also applied to cross-cultural engagement. The *Revivalist* described the conversion of a respected reporter for a Chicago newspaper who had regularly attended church with his family in "Christian America," heard "great divines" preach, and knew the Bible well. While on business in China, though, the reporter met "native Christians" who converted him. "Why was this so?" the writer asked. "Simply because . . . the converted heathen had become Christ-men. . . . Regeneration had regenerated them."[28]

That idea challenged all sorts of categories of thought that reigned in American culture in 1900. When a man enjoying all of the benefits of Christian America was converted by Chinese Christians fresh out of "heathenism," then education, religious training, Christian nurture, and the progress of Western civilization mattered very little in the grand scheme of things. Holiness enthusiasm for evangelism readily granted religious authority to non-Western Christians who were considered "childlike" or "uncivilized" by most Americans. Holiness advocates did not find it odd to report in 1902 that an evangelist from India, "brother Joshi," helped lead a revival in Springfield, Missouri. Within the missionary conduits of the holiness movement, evangelistic energies had begun to flow in multiple directions.[29]

These antiformalist impulses help explain why Ramabai's relationship with Minnie Abrams functioned differently from her relationship with Sister Geraldine. Abrams's status at Mukti reversed the standard power relations in missionary engagement. Typically, British or American missionaries took center stage in evangelical missionary accounts, assisted by "native workers" whose names were often not given. Abrams and two dozen other missionaries relinquished this position of status to work for Ramabai. Radical-holiness periodicals introduced Abrams as "an Associate of Pandita Ramabai" and described missionaries at Mukti as Ramabai's "European helpers." The "workers" employed at the Mukti mission included twenty-five American, English, and Swedish missionaries, plus forty-five Indians, who appeared to hold equal status with the Westerners.[30]

Ramabai, in fact, helped to train Abrams in holiness spirituality. In 1910, Abrams wrote that at one time, she had opposed "faith missions," but God showed her, though Ramabai, how to trust the Holy Spirit for financial support. Ramabai had given a one-month notice to her workers that she would no longer pay them a salary. If they stayed on, the missionaries and the Indian workers would have to trust divine rather than human agency to provide for their expenses. Then, after listening for a message from God, Ramabai gave Abrams fifty dollars that had just been donated to the mission so that Abrams could take a break in the mountains. Abrams protested that she could not accept the money, especially since Mukti was short on funds. When Ramabai told her that the Lord had directed her to use the money in this way, Abrams accepted it as an act of obedience to God. The next morning, Ramabai unexpectedly received a check for one thousand dollars. Abrams saw this as evidence of the Holy Spirit responding to an act of sanctified faith. Ramabai had taught Abrams the Lord Knows Tomorrow Test. Abrams urged American audiences to adopt it, too.[31]

Ramabai and Abrams believed that the Holy Spirit worked in sudden and unpredictable ways. This kind of conviction animated a movement with key features that departed from Western culture. Holiness enthusiasts rejected claims that the world operated solely by naturalistic, mechanistic, and human causality. Primitivist desires for a return of Pentecost and hopes for the second coming of Christ derailed ideas of progress and gradual development. Under the logic of the transforming effects of the baptism of the Spirit, the highest positions of religious authority no longer belonged solely to civilized white males but were available to anyone who embraced the experience.

Just as Ramabai taught Abrams the Lord Knows Tomorrow Test, a number of key non-Western Christians helped shape these developments. Their evangelistic actions on the ground in several places around the world produced a decentralized, enthusiastic, democratized, and multidirectional set of movements. News of these events, running along the overlapping conduits laid by the holiness missionary enterprise, stirred the earliest fires of Pentecostalism.

Non-Western Christians had already broadened American holiness conceptions of supernatural activity. Like all evangelicals, American holiness advocates believed that the Holy Spirit worked through conversions, answers to prayers, and revivals. In the 1880s and '90s, some American holiness enthusiasts began testifying to divine healing, visions, and the Lord Knows Tomorrow Test. Through missionary accounts, non-Western Christians added new varieties of supernatural activity to this mix. A holiness missionary in China in 1904 reported that a woman who had been "literally possessed by demons" had them cast out after she had been told a biblical story of Jesus casting out demons. The Chinese woman became a holiness evangelist. By 1906, in the months before the famous Pentecostal revival at Azusa Street broke out, holiness missionaries in India spoke of the Spirit striking individuals dumb. Additional missionaries in China reported, without fanfare, that they saw the Holy Spirit casting out demons. Holiness advocates read that eighteen Indian girls at the Mukti school miraculously survived bites from a sudden and unprecedented influx of poisonous snakes. New movements of world Christianity had begun to bring new forms of enchantment to the American holiness movement.[32]

Nothing, though, could intensify a sense that the Holy Spirit was at work in exciting ways in regions all over the world like news of revivals. In 1904–05, a powerful revival swept over Wales. The holiness network widely reported ongoing news of this event, which included dramatic confessions, ecstatic worship, and new evidence of holy living. Revivals were also seen to be spreading to other areas, increasing interest in the works of the Holy Spirit. By early 1906, holiness enthusiasts reported revival "sparks" in Sweden, Norway, Germany, India, Uganda, Madagascar, Egypt, Persia, China, Australia, Chile, Brazil, and numerous places across the United States and Canada. Missionary reports intensified the sense that a "Latter Rain" of Pentecostal outpouring signaled the imminent return of Christ to earth.[33]

Pandita Ramabai was interested. She had already sent her daughter Monoramabai and Minnie Abrams to observe a revival in Australia in 1904 and find out what would be needed for something similar in India. Now they all paid close attention to the events in Wales. Concluding that they needed to pour out their lives in prayer, Ramabai called the females of her school together for prayer in early 1905. She also sent a letter to more than thirty-five hundred missionaries and Christians in India, asking for names of Christians so that they could pray for them. Each of the girls in the "Praying Band" prayed for hundreds of people by name, a discipline that mirrored Hindu devotion that the girls had known. "When we were Hindus, we used to repeat one or two thousand names of the gods daily and repeat several hundred verses from the so-called sacred books, in order to gain merit," Ramabai explained. "Why should we not, as Christians, be able to pray for many hundreds of people by name?"[34]

After six months of prayer, some of the girls experienced the fire sensation that they determined to be the baptism of the Holy Ghost. The Mukti revival erupted, encouraging a sense that spontaneous and miraculous activity had been poured out from heaven. Abrams wrote of girls shaking violently, getting struck down, and feeling an "actual experience of fire." Public confession of sins, expressions of deep joy, and the fire experience proved to be the primary focus of the Mukti revival, but it also included what Pentecostals would call "signs and wonders." After eighteen months, seven hundred young women had ventured out in village evangelism, and eleven hundred had been baptized.[35]

At first, Ramabai and several of the missionaries were uneasy about some of the more extreme manifestations of this revival. Ramabai attempted to order matters with established rules. "I wanted to be very proper and conduct meetings in our old civilised ways," she explained. But she soon abandoned this custodial role. Ramabai's explanation was that "God would have none of my ways." Playing into this also might have been her own lifelong aversion to authoritarian systems or the holiness tendency to take the spiritual experiences of ordinary people at face value, or both. Like William Taylor at the South African revival of 1866, Ramabai decided to take her "hand off the work." Personally, Ramabai did not speak in tongues and did not seem to be drawn to the highly ecstatic expressions. But she became convinced "more and more that those who have received the gift of tongues, have been greatly helped to lead better lives." They were "a very humble and unpretending people, walking in the fear of the Lord."[36]

The news of the Mukti revival spread quickly, provoking different sorts of reactions. The unorthodox spiritual manifestations of the event and the marginal identities of the participants made the revival suspect to some. One missionary in India pronounced it "sensuous and superstitious...pure heathenism in Christian dress." A. T. Pierson, a leading American evangelist and promoter of missions, decried the "indecencies" committed by "hysterical women" at Mukti. Ramabai responded with both a theological and a cultural critique. Like a good evangelical, she quoted passages from Isaiah and 1 Corinthians to defend tongues, before asking, "why should everything that does not reach the high standard of English and American civilization be taken as coming from the devil?" Defending the power of this "Holy Ghost revival" to move people to an "unbroken communion with God," she declared, "I, for one, do not dare to put them down as a few ignorant and 'hysterical women.'"[37]

Radical-holiness advocates in India, however, embraced the news from Mukti and prayed that it would be replicated elsewhere. A revival soon broke out at Dhond, where Albert Norton, who had arrived in India in 1872 to work with William Taylor, had established a mission for famine victims and orphaned boys. Soondarbai Powar, a former coworker of Ramabai, led a revival at her school in Poona. Enthusiastic revivals also appeared in Allahabad, Bangalore, Bombay, Aurangabad, and Manmad, after news of the Mukti revival had gone forth.[38]

But Mukti represented just one of several radical-holiness revivals around the world. A "Korean Pentecost" in Pyongyang in 1907 built on earlier holiness revivals that had started in Korea in 1903. These influenced similar revivals in Manchuria and Shandong, China, in 1909. The Welsh revival helped inspire the most famous and significant radical-holiness revival of them all, the Azusa Street revival in Los Angeles in 1906, which in turn influenced Pentecostal revivals in Norway and many other parts of the world.[39]

Minnie Abrams spread the news of the Mukti revival by way of a book titled *The Baptism of the Holy Ghost & Fire*. Part theology, part evangelistic tract, and part religious news, the book called all of its readers, including those in the United States, to seek the baptism of the Spirit that had fallen on the young Indian women at Mukti. Read in the United States and India, its most significant effect was felt in Chile. Abrams sent a copy of her book to May Hoover, a friend who had attended the Chicago Training School with her in 1888. May and her husband, Willis, had joined William Taylor's self-supporting mission in Chile after Willis heard an inner call that said, "South America, South America, South America." Steeped in holiness enthusiasm, the Hoovers wanted to build a church that fueled a constant state of revival, like one they saw on a trip to Chicago in 1894. Over the next decade, Willis Hoover sought to stir up revival enthusiasm among lower-class Chileans in the church he pastored in Valparaiso.[40]

After reading Abrams's book, the Hoovers began corresponding with Abrams and other Pentecostal leaders, including T. B. Barratt, the noted Pentecostal preacher from Norway. The Hoovers and the members of their church began to seek the baptism of the Spirit. Congregants gathered for all-night prayer vigils. A lay member gave Willis Hoover a prophecy that they were all about to be baptized by tongues of fire. When the Pentecostal revival broke out, it arrived with visions, premonitions, special revelations, and speaking in tongues. Worshippers wrestled with evil spirits and fell to the floor, writhing. Some broke out in uncontrollable fits of laughter. Willis Hoover regarded these behaviors as proof of divine power.[41]

A few fellow missionaries regarded them as proof of irrational disorder and fanaticism. The revival brought to the surface long-standing tensions among Methodists in Chile. A dispute between a Methodist missionary and a Pentecostal laywoman, who interrupted a worship service by claiming prophetic authority, resulted in a physical scuffle. The police were called. The local Methodist conference charged Willis Hoover with promoting false doctrine on the baptism of the Spirit and urged the Hoovers to return to the United States for furlough. Several Chilean Christians took matters into their own hands, abandoning the Methodist missionaries, church buildings, and financial resources to form an independent Pentecostal church. May and Willis Hoover decided to join them. Rapidly increasing its primarily working-class membership, the Iglesia Metodista Pentecostal eventually claimed nearly 1 million members.[42]

Issues of theology, ecclesiology, and supernaturalistic spirituality played key roles in this conflict. But these religious disputes also came wrapped around issues of culture and power. Inheriting a relatively meager salary from William Taylor's self-supporting system, Willis and May Hoover had lived much closer to the financial level of the Chilean people than many Methodist missionaries. Most of the Hoovers' closest friends had been Chilean preachers. Florence Smith, a Presbyterian missionary, compared her denomination's missionaries with the Hoovers' ministry by stating that the Presbyterians were more advanced in "education, sound judgment and worldly wisdom." However, she admired the "warmth of spiritual life" that she saw in Willis Hoover, a man who was "not too cultured to call the Chileans brothers," even if he was "narrow" and "bigoted" in his theology. When Pentecostal Chileans broke from the Methodist church in nearby Santiago in 1909, Willis Hoover willingly ordained a tradesman, Guillermo Toro, whom the congregation had chosen as their leader.[43]

Although the Azusa Street revival of 1906 is often described as the epicenter that influenced all other Pentecostal revivals, it is impossible to identify all of the paths of influences on the radical-holiness revivals that emerged between 1903 and 1910. The holiness missionary movement had created an international web of media reports, institutional connections, evangelistic circuits, and personal relationships that flowed in multidirectional paths. To use just one example, Pandita Ramabai's decision to pray for a revival at Mukti in 1905 can be linked to Amanda Smith's autobiography, the Osborns' camp meetings in India, traveling English evangelists in India, Keswick conferences in England, Australian revivals in 1903, and the Welsh revivals of 1904–05, to name just a few. Furthermore, Ramabai drew on the context of Indian culture for the Mukti revival, as she worked to embrace the movements of the Holy Spirit, empower downtrodden Indian females, and establish an institution free from Hindu and British control.

Nor were radical-holiness revivals simply sparked by Western missionaries bringing Pentecostalism to non-Western cultures from the United States. Although one can find American and British influences on Ramabai, she deeply influenced Soonderbai Powar, Albert Norton, and Minnie Abrams, who in turn influenced radical-holiness revivals in India, Chile, and an unknown number of places around the world. Lower-caste Indian females further shaped the Mukti revival. The fire sensation, ecstatic praying, speaking in tongues, and many more Spirit-filled manifestations all emerged from the spiritual pursuits of the lower-caste widows, famine victims, and orphans who populated the school. Similar patterns appeared in radical-holiness revivals around the world. The enthusiastic revivals that broke out in Madagascar and the Khassia and Janta hills in northeast India in 1905 started with indigenous Christians rather than the Welsh missionaries in the area. Evangelists Sun Ju Kil and Ik Du Kim pushed the Pentecostal dimensions of the Korean revivals in directions that similarly unsettled the Presbyterian missionaries there.[44]

Amid the excitement of these worldwide Pentecostal revivals, new movements of world Christianity drew American Pentecostalism further into supernaturalism. In addition to reports of miraculous healings and speaking in tongues, Pentecostal missionaries between 1906 and 1911 reported demons being cast out by local Christians in China, India, South Africa, and Chile.[45] When African and Chinese Pentecostals reported that individuals had been raised from the dead under the power of the Holy Spirit, American Pentecostal periodicals accepted the claims at face value.[46]

At no point in its history, then, was Pentecostalism solely an "American" or "Western" phenomenon. Azusa Street might have been the most influential of the Pentecostal revivals, but it marked only one part of many radical-holiness movements that emerged in several places around the world. In the century that followed, Pentecostalism proved to be a decentralized, multicultural, fragmented, democratized, multidirectional, and enthusiastic worldwide movement. Its birth was no different.[47]

The suggestion, in 1905, that Americans should seek a baptism of fire as displayed by female students in a school in India represented more than just a strange religious appeal. It turned the existing discourse of civilization on its head. This was no mean feat. At the dawn of the twentieth century, Americans could not discuss non-Westerners, and could scarcely talk about themselves, without using the term *civilization*. Academics used the concept of civilization to explain human difference in anthropology, psychology, and the history of societies. Politicians used it to justify imperialism and immigration policy. On a popular level, civilization served as an organizing framework for everything from travelogues, novels, and journalism to soap advertisements, world fairs, and mixed-race boxing matches.[48]

Awash in a sea of civilizing faith, most Americans understood missionary work as a task in which educated and spiritually mature individuals took the glories of Christian civilization to benighted souls in heathen lands. In one of his many roles as a prominent Protestant spokesperson, Lyman Abbott, who served on the board of the Ramabai Association, wrote that it was "the function of the

Anglo-Saxon race to confer these gifts of civilization, through law, commerce, and education on the uncivilized people of the world."[49] This type of civilizationist thinking reflected theological and intellectual shifts undertaken by many Protestants who had moved from evangelicalism to modernism in the late nineteenth century. Modernist Protestants such as Abbott increasingly emphasized environmental roles in religious development, defined the Christian faith in terms of social and ethical activity, and abandoned traditional concepts of atonement, biblical authority, personal evangelism, and the individual conversion experience.[50]

These shifts affected missionary activity. By 1895, the American Board of Commissioners for Foreign Missions had dropped its requirement that missionaries must believe in eternal punishment. In the annual sermon before the ABCFM that year, George Gordon, who also served on the board of the Ramabai Association, portrayed missionaries as cultural schoolteachers nurturing immature nations in a progressive task of education. "Any right conception of foreign missions" must leave the old theology behind, he preached, and build on a "principle of development" that helps nations, as one helps boys and youth "come at length to their majority." Envisioning history as a long, diverse evolution of ethics in human societies, modernists sought to aid that process through missionary goals that promoted schools, hospitals, and social service, tasks that fit quite well with the civilizing mission.[51]

The modernist formulation of civilization represented, in part, the effort by highly educated Protestants to reconcile a Christian understanding of humanity with new claims of social science, evolution, philosophical idealism, and historicist readings of the past. Anthropologists increasingly dropped divine causality in favor of wholly naturalistic explanations of cultural development in history. Darwinian anthropologists argued that white and black savages had originally been psychologically united, but through evolutionary battles, white savages had developed superior brains, enabling white cultures to progress while black "savages" remained very close to their evolutionary roots. In their studies of "primitive" or "savage" cultures, then, Darwinian anthropologists saw themselves studying the very distant origins of their very own advanced and superior civilization. Modernist Protestants such as Gordon, who accepted many, but not all, of these new ideas in anthropology, responded by linking some kind of Darwinian mechanism and a historicist interpretation of social development with ideas of progress and Christian civilization. Theologically, this encouraged the shift toward emphasizing the immanence of God, whereby the spirit of God did not work so much through personal transformation as through evolutionary development and a civilizing process of uplift.[52]

Radical-holiness advocates, of course, hiked through a very different theological landscape. The modernist impulse to link scientific progress with ethical maturity did not usually mix well with religious practices that included visions, ecstatic worship, divine healing, and speaking in tongues.[53] Radical-holiness enthusiasts spoke more of worldwide revivals, the imminent return of Christ, and the end of history itself. Who, then, had need for civilization? Indeed, Minnie Abrams did not use the term *civilization* once in her eighty-eight-page booklet, *The Baptism of the Holy Ghost & Fire*.[54]

This disregard for the concept of civilization placed holiness advocates at a different vantage point for viewing non-Westerners. In their debates over imperialism, for instance, American politicians questioned whether the uncivilized nature of the newly colonized Filipinos made them suitable candidates for membership in American society. Indiana senator Albert Beveridge reflected the dominant American perception of the uncivilized in a now-infamous speech before Congress in 1900, when he declared that Filipinos were not capable of self-government. "How shall they, in the twinkling of an eye, be exalted to the heights of a self-governing people," Beveridge intoned, "which required a thousand years for us to reach, Anglo-Saxon though we are?"[55] The rhetoric of civilization posited a gap between the civilized and the uncivilized that would take generations—or, more likely, centuries—to overcome. In the minds of many Americans, it was biologically impossible ever to bridge that gap.

As champions of the "twinkling of an eye" school of thought, radical-holiness enthusiasts believed that the gap could be bridged instantaneously. Individuals from India or Chile or Korea found it much easier to receive the baptism of the Spirit than to convince Westerners that they had climbed to the top of the ladder of civilization. When she identified the religious leaders of the world who were about to do nothing less than usher in the end of time, Abrams not only included standard holiness heroes George Mueller and Hudson Taylor, but she also listed Pandita Ramabai, "Pastor Hsi of China," three Indian girls in an Anglican school in Bombay, and those attending the Welsh and Azusa Street revivals.[56] The logic of radical holiness led an American missionary in 1906 to claim Asian evangelists as leaders in nothing less than God's plan to end the cosmic struggle against evil that had plagued humanity since the beginning of history. American politicians, meanwhile, doubted whether Asians could vote intelligently.

At the same time, cultural engagement at the turn of the century tended to strengthen national, ethnic, and racial markers. In their adaptation to American society, immigrant communities often sharpened their ethnic identities. Many native-born Americans reacted against the massive influx of non-Anglo immigration by instigating Americanization or nativist programs that sought to exclude certain ethnic and racial groups. Imperialistic ventures in the Philippines and Latin America reinforced perceptions among many Americans that their identities as whites, modern Anglo-Saxons, or civilized Christians placed them at a significant distance from the primitive identities of the colonized, while simultaneously sparking nationalistic movements of resistance among the colonized.[57]

Radical holiness could, at times, disable these powerful impulses to reify identities based on nationality, ethnicity, and race. Indian, Chinese, and African evangelists joined American missionaries in writing accounts in holiness literature, blurring lines of national, ethnic, and racial prominence.[58] More important, newly minted Pentecostals perceived the baptism of the Spirit to be the same wherever it occurred. Periodicals such as the *Apostolic Faith* reported news of revivals in Calcutta with the same descriptive language that it used in reporting revivals in Chattanooga. At that point, the Orientalism that had pervaded Western culture, as Edward Said so ably described, ceased to carry much meaning for North American Pentecostals. The image of the "exotic other" faded into obscurity when the *Bridegroom's Messenger*'s depiction of a Pentecost falling in Palestine and Liberia looked just the same as the Pentecost that fell in Indianapolis and Bellingham, Washington.[59]

Most Pentecostal leaders essentially divided the world into two major categories, the saved and the unsaved, each with its own subcategories. Under the category of the unsaved, Minnie Abrams unceremoniously lumped together the "heathen," who lived in a land that had not heard the missionary message of Christianity, with the "unconverted," who lived in Western lands but had not yielded to conversion. Under the category of the saved, those who had discovered the baptism of the Spirit rubbed shoulders with nonholiness Christians who had yet to receive its power.[60]

When radical-holiness advocates began asserting that one only needed the baptism of the Spirit in order to qualify for a prophetic anointing from God, less educated, refined, or respectable individuals often strode confidently into the limelight. Just as a poor black woman such as Amanda Smith could confound terms of race, class, and gender by attracting a following among white middle-class holiness advocates in the 1880s and '90s, the radical-holiness missionary network opened the door for a host of new charismatic leaders around the world to confound American cultural conventions. Theological or seminary education mattered less and less. So did a host of other conscious or unconscious qualifications for religious leadership. By 1910, American Pentecostals had installed several non-Western leaders into their pantheon of missionary celebrities, right alongside their American heroes. American editors regularly published letters from Chinese evangelist Mok Lai Chi, whose Pentecostal testimony read as if it might have come from a congregation in Chicago. Demonstrating that he had picked up the modern skills of the Pentecostal evangelist, Mok Lai Chi started a Chinese-language periodical called *Pentecostal Truths*. Just as American holiness missionaries did, he raised funds directly from American supporters. The *Upper Room* upheld Mok Lai Chi as proof that "God's operations are the same in China as at home" and called him "a wise, careful leader under God—a man full of faith and of the Holy Ghost."[61] D. E. Dias-Wanigasekera, an evangelist from Ceylon, also utilized holiness periodicals to raise funds directly from American Pentecostal supporters. The editor of the *Bridegroom's Messenger* gave one of Wanigasekera's letters the headline "From Ceylon: A Portion of a Letter from a Missionary—Pray for Our Brother," unselfconsciously granting Wanigasekera equal status with the two other American missionaries in India whose letters received similar titles on that same page of the periodical.[62] On a lower level of Pentecostal fame, numerous other non-Western Pentecostal evangelists published testimonies, revival news, and accounts of divine healing in American publications, although the funds they received from American supporters usually fell under the traditional missionary categories of "Native Workers" or "Native Missionaries."[63]

If Mok Lai Chi and Wanigasekera were Pentecostal heroes, Pandita Ramabai was a superstar. Already prominent within the holiness network by 1900, Ramabai sealed her hero status by sparking the Mukti revival. More widely connected within the radical-holiness periodical network than any American missionary, Ramabai drew on a wide range of early Pentecostal bodies in the United States for financial support. American Pentecostals regularly provided Ramabai with more financial support than they did many American missionaries and continued to shower her with praise and admiration right up to her death in 1922.[64] "One almost holds their breath at the magnitude of this work going on in every department without a hitch," marveled a report in the Pentecostal periodical *Trust* in 1918, "and then to realize that the head of this huge enterprise is this one, most wonderful woman, RAMABAI...." Ramabai's Mukti mission became an obligatory stop for Pentecostal missionaries traveling through India, who could boost their status by mentioning "Ramabai's work" in their correspondence. A picture of Ramabai dwarfed a small inset of Pentecostal missionary Rachel Nalder in the only image of any person to appear in the *Latter Rain Evangel*, in 1909.[65]

Unlike mainline Protestants who were fascinated by the exotic dimensions of this high-caste Indian Christian woman, American radical-holiness writers provided, at most, passing references to Ramabai's national, ethnic, or racial identity. Ramabai and her daughter Monoramabai, meanwhile, used terminology in holiness periodicals that not only ignored these cultural markers but also resonated deep with radical holiness sensibilities. "The Lord is doing deeper work in the hearts and lives of many of His children who were blessed in the revival," Ramabai wrote to one Pentecostal periodical. "Please pray that the Holy Ghost revival may be continued among us until the glorious appearing of our Lord Jesus Christ, and that we may be ready to meet Him, and be kept in a watchful and prayerful, humble spirit, and that our hearts and our lives may be flooded with His love always." She could have been a deacon from a small church in Ohio.[66]

Ramabai represented only one kind of Pentecostal evangelist, though. Pentecostalism proved to be remarkably adept at promoting local leaders who were

Figure 9.1. Pentecostal missionary Rachel Nalder (inset) and the more famous Pandita Ramabai in the *Latter Rain Evangel*. (Flower Pentecostal Heritage Center.)

not usually looked on as respectable, civilized individuals. Pentecostal evangelists between 1905 and 1910 included Chinese men, Indian girls, spirit-filled Zulus, working-class Chileans, female preachers, and African-American ministers, plus white American males. Although demanding that its followers leave "heathenism," Pentecostalism quickly granted religious authority to Chinese, American, Chilean, African, British, and Indian enthusiasts.[67] Pentecostalism, then, contained both Western and non-Western leaders at its birth.

Caught up in their antiformalist enthusiasm, early Pentecostals seemed to be blissfully unaware of the cultural, social, and structural implications of their movement, except for a few arguments about women preaching or people from all nations joining Holy Ghost revivals. Not exactly an intellectual, Minnie Abrams never indicated that she had read the Vedas, the Upanishads, or the Dharmashastras. It is likely that she had never heard of the Athanasian Creed, much less debated its merits. Abrams did not offer explanations of racial differences, theories of civilization, or systematic accounts of cultural differences. *The Baptism of the Holy Ghost & Fire* scuttled Western conventions of race, gender, nationality, progress, millennialism, and civilization, but Abrams did not point out that her book did any of this. Abrams embodied an odd antiformalist dynamic of radical-holiness thinking, in that she challenged any number of social conventions while rarely recognizing or mentioning that she did so.

At its core, radical holiness was driven not by antiracism, gender equality, or cross-cultural cooperation but by a desire for personal access to visible activity of the Holy Spirit. As a result, even though the movement always held the potential to challenge existing social conventions, these impulses could also fade quickly. Pentecostal bodies in the United States that broke down barriers of race, ethnicity, and gender often fell back into older patterns after the initial excitement of the early revivals subsided. Despite the interracial worship that existed in a number of holiness congregations and nascent Pentecostal bodies between 1880 and 1920, segregated patterns reemerged in almost all groups after that.[68]

Nor did holiness or Pentecostal groups all challenge the same social conventions. Many radical-holiness bodies contained rigid hierarchies, racial divisions, and strict gender distinctions. Female ministers thrived in some holiness bodies, such as the Pilgrim Holiness Church, where women made up as much as 30 percent of all of its ordained ministers in the 1930s, but other bodies, such as the Old Apostolic Faith Movement, opposed women in ministry. The woman who founded the Pillar of Fire Church, Alma White, believed that the Ku Klux Klan was God's instrument for maintaining order. William Seymour, the black leader of the Azusa Street revival, had previously attended a Church of God congregation in Cincinnati that was open to people of all races but set itself against middle-class members of society by forbidding its preachers to wear neckties. Female preaching, interracial worship, and the promotion of lower-class leaders, when they occurred, emerged unevenly as unintended by-products of holiness zeal rather than conscious visions of a new social order.[69]

In missionary settings, the same antiformalist impulse that minimized national, ethnic, and racial identities inadvertently steered Pentecostal advocates away from considering the significance of cultural differences. In fact, Pentecostal missionaries thought less about social systems and cultural institutions than probably any other contingent of missionaries who traveled overseas. Of course, one might not expect Pentecostal evangelists to extol the glories of social science, modern legal systems, or progressive economics. But Minnie Abrams demonstrated little indication that Americans ought to respect, learn from, or even take into account the cultures of non-Western people, despite her acceptance of the fire sensation at Mukti. She did not speak of matters such as an indigenous church, how Christianity might adapt to Indian culture, how India's social structure might be transformed by radical holiness, or how the baptism of the Holy Spirit would affect the role of women in India. In fact, Abrams made no reference to the customs, practices, or cultural characteristics of anyone she sought to evangelize, even though she addressed global evangelism, hinted at deficiencies in the current missionary methods, and titled a chapter in her book "The Evangelization of the Heathen."[70]

Even so, radical-holiness missionaries could not escape the realities of cultural differentiation. Pentecostal evangelists around the globe eventually discovered that when they got down to the day-to-day workings of their ministry, they still had to negotiate local cultural dilemmas. Mok Lai Chi wrestled with the question of whether Chinese Christians would give to "faith missions," since Chinese culture did not have a tradition of free-will offerings.[71] More famously, early Pentecostal missionaries who believed that the supernatural gift of tongues would allow them to preach without learning local languages discovered, after they actually arrived in India, China, Japan, or the Middle East, that they actually did have to buckle down and learn the vernacular.[72]

Nor could Spirit-filled missionaries ignore the cultural dilemmas that had challenged fellow evangelical missionaries for more than a century. Five years after the Mukti revival, at a fund-raising address before a Pentecostal audience in Chicago, Minnie Abrams briefly hinted at evangelistic difficulties in a culture where Hinduism reinforced powerful social hierarchies, kinship networks, and caste identities. "There is no possibility of these high caste people coming out unless God Himself separates them by cutting off all their kindred, or in some drastic way like a famine, brings about their separation," she told the Pentecostal faithful. Abrams then returned to standard Pentecostal assurances that God was "pouring out His Spirit on those who are preaching" and urged her listeners to pray for conversions. Her aside, however, spoke much about cross-cultural realities. While they did not direct much of their efforts toward examining these cultural distinctions, Pentecostal missionaries still had to negotiate very real differences in their daily lives.[73]

The same held true for building institutions. With its passion for divine agency, Pentecostalism contained antiinstitutional impulses decidedly out of step with the Gilded Age and Progressive Era projects of establishing orderly, efficient systems that humans could create and master through proper application of the scientific method. In fact, after they consciously and repeatedly made the point that they did not know what God had in store for them, some Pentecostals actually took pride in proclaiming their *lack* of organization. "This great world-wide movement did not originate with man," declared Pentecostal missionary M. L. Ryan. "It has no great earthly leader. It is not a religious organization. It will not be organized."[74]

Compared with other Protestant bodies, early Pentecostalism certainly lacked institutional organizations, centralized machinery, and financial resources. But one should not be fooled by this. Pentecostals actually did a remarkable job of linking their movement to the pragmatic systems of the modern world. "Unorganized" Pentecostal missionaries shrewdly made use of a well-connected global communications network to produce a stream of revival news that was remarkable for its scope and rapidity of transmission.[75] Azusa Street leaders in Los Angeles wasted little time in establishing a periodical filled with revival reports from around the world, the first issue coming out within a few months of the beginning of their Pentecostal revival.[76]

In fact, worldwide Pentecostalism would not have emerged without the preparatory institution-building efforts of non-Pentecostals. In the 1880s, holiness missionaries from the United States had made their way to the field through the channels of established denominational agencies, particularly the Methodist Episcopal Church. Early Pentecostals repeated the pattern. In 1908, the *Bridegroom's Messenger* proudly listed fifteen different denominational missionary agencies in India that had a Pentecostal witness within them.[77] Furthermore, non-Pentecostal institutions provided widespread levels of literacy among audiences, a high degree of mobility for its missionaries, and respectable levels of financial resources among its supporters. Most significantly, Pentecostalism all over the world grew in areas where the Bible had already been translated into the vernacular. This long, painstaking, and unglamorous translation work had already been undertaken by Christians from those "cold" denominations that holiness enthusiasts had criticized for failing to embrace the baptism of the Spirit. In a technical sense, M. L. Ryan had been correct in saying that early Pentecostalism was not a "religious organization." He did not see, however, that it was unparalleled in its ability to make use of non-Pentecostal religious organizations.

Pentecostals also discovered that they had to build some sort of ecclesiastical machinery of their own to keep their movement intact. Individual claims to divine inspiration might have empowered Pentecostals to break with established authorities, but sooner or later, and usually sooner, these claims came into conflict with one another. Like many other Pentecostal leaders, the Hoovers resolved conflicts by claiming theological authority for themselves and other indigenous pastors who had been specially anointed. And so, egalitarian Pentecostal movements that accepted prophetic claims from poor, uneducated enthusiasts often solved problems by investing hierarchical authority in charismatic leaders. Alternatively, one could fall back on the old Protestant custom of splitting off to form a new denomination, a practice that became popular within Pentecostalism, which has displayed a rather vigorous tendency toward decentralization and fragmentation.[78]

When they remained overwhelmingly interested in reaping conversions, the early Pentecostal movements failed to produce intellectuals or theologians who could identify and analyze the relationship between their religious activities and cultural, political, or structural systems. Minnie Abrams's work has been called the first theology of missions for early Pentecostalism, but Pentecostals did not explore or develop the social, racial, and cultural implications of the book. During its first decades, no Pentecostal versions of a Francis Wayland or a Rufus Anderson emerged to explore the theoretical, structural, and theological implications of what was taking place in missionary encounters around the world.[79]

The individual who probably understood the complicated dynamics of Pentecostalism better than anybody proved to be Pandita Ramabai. Ironically, Ramabai is probably better categorized, to the extent that she can be categorized, as a moderate holiness advocate than as a Pentecostal. Like so many experiences in her life, the Mukti revival placed Ramabai in the midst of religious enthusiasts pulling her in conflicting directions. As always, she was up to the task of articulating her own position. To the Christian leaders from the "civilizing mission" school who saw the revival as "pure heathenism in Christian dress," she declared that "the English and other western missionaries [should] begin to study the Indian nature, I mean the religious inclinations, the emotional side of the Indian mind." Four months after the Mukti revival had begun, she argued that missionaries should not "try to conduct revival meetings and devotional exercises altogether in western ways and conform with western etiquette." She also identified the paradoxical problem of evangelical power: "If our western teachers and foreignized Indian leaders want the work of God to be carried on among us in their own way, they are sure to stop or spoil it." Perceiving that Christianity needed to be translated into the language of the local culture, she embarked on a project of translating the Bible into the Marathi language. A Marathi translation already existed, but Ramabai observed that it contained so much Sanskrit terminology and "high-flown language" that poor Indian women found it quite inaccessible and difficult to understand. Eager to mobilize downtrodden and poorly educated Indian women, she worked also on commentaries, vocabularies, and interlinear translations of the Bible. She embarked on these projects in 1907, at the height of the Mukti revival, as part and parcel of the revival.[80]

Ramabai also faced an issue from the opposite direction. In what was often called the "evidence" debate, many American Pentecostals had begun to argue that one did not experience the baptism of the Spirit unless one spoke in tongues. That debate would ebb and flow in American Pentecostalism for many years to follow. Speaking in tongues quickly became such an important part of American Pentecostalism that it emerged as the defining feature of the movement in North America, although Pentecostals in many parts of the world did not consider it to be a necessary component of the baptism of the Spirit or a defining feature of their movement. Ramabai did not side with the majority of American Pentecostals. "The gift of tongues is certainly one of the signs of the baptism of the Holy Spirit," she wrote in 1907 after being pressed on the issue, "but there is no Scripture warrant to think that the speaking in tongues is the only and necessary sign of baptism of the Holy Spirit."[81]

Americans from both the Pentecostal and non-Pentecostal camps could not resist evaluating the Mukti revival on the basis of its ecstatic manifestations. It seemed to prove either the existence of the Holy Spirit or the existence of heathen superstition. Ramabai rejected the basis for this debate. There were those who sought out tongues and other ecstatic experiences, she explained, who did not desire God as much as some sort of selfish spiritual indulgence. There also were those who spoke in tongues and were genuinely moved by the Holy Spirit. And there were those who did not speak in tongues but were still baptized by the Holy Spirit. In the end, she argued, the key to evaluating the revival lay on different grounds. One must see whether those caught up in the revival "have been greatly helped to lead better lives, and are filled with zeal for the salvation of others, and are given to more earnest prayer than they were formerly." Ramabai was convinced that the Mukti revival, on the whole, did that.[82]

Thoughtful evangelicals had been down this path before. From 1741 to 1743, Jonathan Edwards found himself in the midst of a dispute over the validity of the First Great Awakening, with its ecstatic outbursts. Some enthusiastic supporters had accused professing Christians of knowing nothing of true religion for objecting to features of the revival, a stance that Edwards declared to be unscriptural. But even though "many errors in judgment" and "scandalous practices" occurred, the "tears, trembling, groans," and loud outcries of the revival were neither unbiblical nor necessary indications of the outpouring of the Spirit. Edwards believed that the "distinguishing marks" of the work of the Spirit lay instead in qualities such as a love for the Bible, the renunciation of worldly ambitions, and a greater love for Jesus and others. Edwards was convinced that the Great Awakening, on the whole, did that. Separated by two centuries, two continents, and innumerable cultural factors, Pandita Ramabai and Jonathan Edwards had reached very similar conclusions.[83]

The tongues debate did not matter much to non-Americans, anyway. As was typical with new movements of world Christianity, issues that vexed Christians in Western culture were often nonissues to Christians in Africa, Asia, or Latin America. In many parts of the world, supernatural activity and ecstatic religious manifestations were often seen as a common part of life, regardless of whether one were a Christian. Pentecostalism continued to grow around the world in large part because it was a religious faith that readily promoted indigenous leaders who found the spiritual power to address issues pertinent to their local culture.

Ogbu Kalu, for instance, observed that "Pentecostals take the African map of the universe very seriously." In Ghana, Pentecostal theological beliefs in miraculous healing, visions, a high creator God, and the concept of salvation all had antecedents in traditional Akan religious beliefs. Pentecostal prophets in Ghana played a role analogous to traditional elders, while the strict codes of morality enforced by Pentecostal churches expressed an ethos similar to some of the codes of morality found in traditional African villages. But Pentecostal evangelists fiercely opposed the use of charms and amulets, the mediating role of the ancestors, and any attempt to harness the power of malevolent spirits. As with American evangelicals, Ghanaian Pentecostals saw both the darkness of sin and the light of the Gospel residing in their culture.[84]

Even with the cultural diversity of worldwide Pentecostalism, it appears that different bodies shared a similar combination of characteristics: primitivism, supernaturalism, sectarian tendencies, sophisticated communication networks, individualistic conceptions of the self, and audience-driven polities. Pentecostalism grew on the peripheries in ways quite unfamiliar to many in Western culture, which may help explain why scholars failed to pay serious attention to these movements through most of the twentieth century. In the meantime, Pentecostalism continued to expand according to its own particular dynamics, paying little attention to Western culture and thriving on it all the same. In terms of evangelism, Pentecostal missionaries worked themselves out of a job more quickly than they even recognized.

Epilogue

Themes of self-sacrifice have played a central part in evangelical conceptions of missionary life ever since the First Great Awakening, when Jonathan Edwards wrote *The Life of David Brainerd*. Evangelicals recognized that missionaries left behind the familiarity and comforts of their home life to labor in challenging conditions. Missionaries sometimes gave up higher salaries or more comfortable positions for their cause. They often placed their lives at risk, particularly in the nineteenth century, when disease claimed many. Long years of toil often resulted in few converts.

Oddly, though, the missionary encounter could wed self-sacrifice to power and status. Even if they had held marginal or ordinary identities within their communities in the United States, nineteenth-century evangelical missionaries usually qualified as elites in the societies in which they ministered. William Taylor billed himself as a common street preacher in America, but in South Africa, India, and West Africa, he drew on established denominational systems and well-positioned Western contacts that audiences in these places could not. In Burma, Ann Judson, Sarah Boardman, and Deborah Wade actually enjoyed more authority and freedom as women to preach, teach, evangelize, and pursue academic activity than they did in the United States. Henry McNeal Turner's reputation as an educated black denominational leader preceded him in South Africa. Agnes McAllister attracted serious attention in Garraway, Liberia, simply by pulling out her sewing machine. Even Amanda Smith, who drew audiences to her holiness message in the United States by consciously making use of her marginal status as a poor black woman, carried an identity as a representative of Western civilization with her in India and Liberia. Evangelical missionaries consistently enjoyed more economic resources, levels of education, political contacts, and access to transportation networks than their audiences. Through the books, periodical articles, and newspaper reports they wrote, missionaries employed mass media for their cause, a feature that gave them great influence over American perceptions of missionary engagement.

The new movements of world Christianity connected to evangelicalism, however, were almost always democratized. These audiences followed popular leaders, not elites. As Nathan Hatch has stated about democratized religion in America, popular leaders derived their authority "not from their education or stature...but from the democratic art of persuasion." Democratized religion displayed "the vitality of religion among ordinary people, the continuing prominence of populist religious leaders, and the vitality of mass democratic movements that reflect the charisma and organizational skills of these leaders."[1] So it went with many new movements of world Christianity. Democratized characteristics animated Ko Tha Byu's Karen Christianity, the 1866 South African revival led by Charles Pamla, ordinary AME preachers in the postbellum American south, Pentecostal females in India, and hundreds of additional movements around the world. Audiences joined these movements by following the lead of local Christian leaders, often individuals of marginal status, ordinary education, or limited means, who directed the movements according to their own cultural sensibilities.

Arguably, then, the newly elite American evangelical missionaries had their biggest impact in the democratized forms of evangelicalism that indigenous leaders picked up from them. But these popular leaders of world Christianity did not promote these movements in quite the ways missionaries expected or always recognized. Karen evangelists appealed to their oral tradition of the lost book and prayed for demons to be cast out. Charles Pamla evoked traditional Xhosa patterns of spiritual power in his preaching. Ordinary African-American preachers employed the ring shout and enthusiastic religious practices from African culture that had persisted in African-American communities. William Wadé Harris appealed to miraculous signs and supported polygamy. Female students at Mukti sparked a Pentecostal revival by claiming an ecstatic experience that resembled lower-caste Hindu spirit possession. All of these movements grew at the hands of "uncivilized" local leaders, not the respectable missionary representatives of civilization.

These were unexpected and paradoxical results. One way to view this dynamic would be to see an "American" feature of the missionary program, democratization, playing a key role in enabling leaders to build movements with cultural features that did not stem from American culture. And yet that framework cannot quite carry the day. For one thing, democratization was not the only dynamic at work. Translation, as Lamin Sanneh has demonstrated, also played a critical role.[2] Furthermore, popular leaders of world Christianity such as Ko Tha Byu did not lead their movements with visions of American culture in mind.

Perhaps, then, it is more accurate to say that these movements of world Christianity picked up democratized features from missionaries that stemmed from evangelical or Christian dynamics rather than the workings of American or Western culture. This is a subtle but important distinction. Those of us who have been deeply shaped by modernity tend to make religious developments the handmaiden of other forces that are perceived to be fundamental starting points, such as the nation-state or political economy or civilization. As a result, scholarship often tried to fit the missionary movement into a model of cultural imperialism in which Great Britain or capitalism or Westernization loom as the starting point for understanding the cultural dynamics involved. These are all significant matters that greatly affected the missionary encounter. In the end, though, if one is discussing the evangelical missionary movement, one must start with Christianity. Viewed more broadly, we find that the democratized features of the last two centuries of world Christianity represent just one of many ways in which Christianity has been transmitted across cultural boundaries down through the centuries. As Andrew Walls, Lamin Sanneh, and others have shown, Christianity has shown a remarkable ability to adapt to different cultures throughout its history. Since its inception, Christianity never has been solely a Western religion.[3]

In the last two centuries, many, though not all, new movements of world Christianity have been driven by the evangelical characteristics of conversion, biblical authority, zeal for evangelism, and emphasis on the atoning work of Christ. Distinctively "American" characteristics proved less helpful. As he passionately sought conversions, William Wadé Harris knew far better than Agnes McAllister how to access the West African spiritual world to urge audiences to leave fetishes behind. Karen preachers not only consumed Scriptures translated into the vernacular, but they also read these ancient texts according to their sense of Karen traditions and issues. Driven by evangelical zeal, *unzondelelo* leaders in South Africa quickly outran missionaries, with a fuller understanding of local cultural conditions and a deeper affinity for their own people group. "Uncivilized" evangelists such as Ko Tha Byu, Charles Pamla, and Spirit-filled Indian females at Mukti embraced evangelical conceptions of atonement, proving to be more effective than the missionaries in convincing audiences that salvation was available to all people, regardless of their social situation.

These local or indigenous cultural dynamics placed missionaries in unaccustomed social locations. The educational background, material resources, technological expertise, links to media, and political contacts, indeed, all of the markers of "civilization" enjoyed by the missionaries, distanced them from the very audiences that they hoped to influence. Evangelical missionaries with antiformalist instincts who had been raised in popular evangelical settings in the United States were now elites. At just the point when these evangelical missionaries began to enjoy levels of power and status that they had not known before, they found themselves working amid movements that did not follow the lead of elites.

The most difficult self-sacrifice for missionaries to make, then, might have been that of giving up some aspect of their status and power as "civilized" individuals. Just by traveling to Burma, of course, George Boardman sacrificed the comfort of a familiar life in New England and probably died at an earlier age than he would have otherwise. Those were real sacrifices. However, as any evangelical of his era who read *The Life of David Brainerd* understood, these kinds of sacrifices were to be expected of missionaries. And, in fact, they helped make a hero out of "Boardman of Burma." His decision to follow the Karen evangelists into the remote hills of Burma, though, required a different kind of sacrifice or, at least, a sacrifice with unexpected implications. Boardman had to meet the Karen villagers in their communities, on their terms. That meant that he had to become willing to let uncivilized evangelists take the lead. He had to consider the possibility that his civilized status did not guarantee his mastery of all aspects of Christianity or social character. In that respect, his journey involved relinquishing some level of pride or righteousness that he saw in himself, his Yankee culture, and his civilization.

It is difficult to identify, much less relinquish, the power and sense of custodianship that come attached to one's elite status, especially if one has always considered oneself ordinary. Some missionaries, such as the Wesleyans who dealt with Mangena Mokone in South Africa, did not seem to give up much of anything. But many missionaries managed to cede status as they worked with movements that they did not fully understand. Elisha Abbott set a Baptist precedent by ordaining Karen evangelists, surrendering the implicit claim that missionaries held sole authority to baptize and supervise congregations in Burma. William Taylor persuaded Robert Lamplough to let Charles Pamla take the Annshaw revival in a much more exuberant, expressive, and African direction. Henry McNeal Turner demonstrated his willingness to sacrifice respectability by ordaining enthusiastic but poorly educated preachers in the American south. Minnie Abrams not only cast herself as an assistant and spiritual student to Pandita Ramabai but also broadcast to the world the reality that she had sought out a supernatural experience that had fallen upon young Indian women.

This challenge extended beyond individual missionaries such as Boardman. World Christianity also raised questions about whether evangelicals in the United States would be willing to relinquish perceptions of Western Christianity as the custodian of the world or American civilization as the normative standard that others needed to emulate. If it was difficult for individual missionaries to relinquish elite status, it was even harder for evangelicals in the United States collectively to give up prestige and power. Most American evangelicals did not work directly with non-Americans. Many paid little attention to missionary issues. Desires to build a Christian nation, guide American culture, achieve economic prosperity, or advance civilization inevitably lured evangelicals toward the tools of power, as they did many other Americans. With these forces at their backs, many evangelicals who took cursory glances at the missionary encounter concluded that American civilization justified a custodial missionary enterprise.

But the missionary encounter had a way of influencing American evangelicalism and American culture. Through the missionary networks, world Christianity pulled American evangelicalism in new directions, although few people recognized this process. Compelled to ordain "uncivilized" evangelists, Baptist missionaries established schools of higher education for nonwhites in Burma and in the American south at a time when the most powerful academics in America and Europe considered such attempts impossible, foolish, and perhaps dangerous. The African-American Great Awakening built on earlier black evangelical movements to solidify a black identity that maintained elements of African culture in African-American religious life. Because Christians such as Mok Lai Chi, D. E. Wanigasekera, and Pandita Ramabai convinced Pentecostal missionaries of their Spirit-baptized piety and evangelistic effectiveness, Pentecostal bodies in 1910, arguably, promoted more non-Westerners to the highest positions of status than any other movement in America.

It is questionable whether evangelical missionaries and their audiences at home would have relinquished these forms of status and power, however haltingly and imperfectly, if new movements of world Christianity had not challenged them to do so. Nor would they have been likely to do so if they had not drawn on dynamics within the Christian faith itself that pushed them in that direction. *The Life of David Brainerd* gave its readers very little in the realm of cross-cultural insight, but it did urge Christians toward self-denial and sacrifice.[4] Evangelicals could wield biblical authority in ways that exalted their own power and status, but within this text, they also encountered admonitions to act with compassion, humility, meekness, and love. Missionaries could use the evangelical goal of spreading the Gospel to exalt the righteousness of Western civilization, but movements of world Christianity raised questions about the cultural content of righteousness itself. The missionary encounter challenged missionaries, American evangelicalism, and the society that produced them, to rework many of their conceptions of how culture, power, and influence ought to work. It is a challenge that remains with us today.

NOTES

Introduction

1. Minnie Abrams, *The Baptism of the Holy Ghost & Fire* (Kedgaon, India: Mukti Mission, 1906); Gary B. McGee, "'Latter Rain' Falling in the East: Early-Twentieth-Century Pentecostalism in India and the Debate over Speaking in Tongues," *Church History* 68 (September 1999): 648–65.
2. Quoted in Gary B. McGee, "Minnie F. Abrams: Another Context, Another Founder," in James R. Goff Jr. and Grant Wacker, eds., *Portraits of a Generation: Early Pentecostal Leaders* (Fayetteville: University of Arkansas Press, 2002), 94.
3. Abrams, *The Baptism*, 3–12, 42, 64, 69–70, 72, 77, 88; McGee, "'Latter Rain'"; Meera Kosambi, *At the Intersection of Gender Reform and Religious Belief: Pandita Ramabai's Contribution and the Age of Consent Controversy* (Bombay: Research Centre for Women's Studies, 1993), 76–77.
4. The book, which scholars have called the first major work of Pentecostal theology of mission, may be the most important document in the birth of world Pentecostalism. Abrams, *The Baptism*; Gary B. McGee, "'Baptism of the Holy Ghost and Fire!' The Mission Legacy of Minnie F. Abrams," *Missiology* 27 (October 1999): 515–22; McGee, "Minnie F. Abrams," 86–104; Dana L. Robert, *American Women in Mission: A Social History of Their Thought and Practice* (Macon, Ga.: Mercer University Press, 1996), 244–54.
5. Robert Mapes Anderson, *Vision of the Disinherited: the Making of American Pentecostalism* (New York: Oxford University Press, 1979), 45; Joe Creech, "Visions of Glory: The Place of the Azusa Street Revival in Pentecostal History," *Church History* 65 (September 1996): 405–24.
6. The Westernization thesis is so pervasive that space prohibits the major part of this body of literature to be listed here. For representative examples, see Patricia Grimshaw, "'Christian Woman, Pious Wife, Faithful Mother, Devoted Missionary': Conflicts in Roles of American Missionary Women in Nineteenth Century Hawaii," *Feminist Studies* 9 (Fall 1983): 489–521; Edward H. Berman, *African Reactions to Missionary Education* (New York: Teachers College Press, 1975), 6; George Tinker, *Missionary Conquest: The Gospel and Native American Cultural Genocide* (Minneapolis: Fortress, 1993); Sylvia Jacobs, "The Historical Role of Afro-Americans in American Missionary Efforts in Africa," in Sylvia Jacobs, ed., *Black Americans and the Missionary Movement in Africa* (Westport, Conn.: Greenwood, 1982), 6; Jean Comaroff and Joan Comaroff, *Of Revelation and Revolution: Christianity, Colonialism and Consciousness in South Africa*, vols. 1 and 2 (Chicago: University of Chicago Press, 1991). Even among scholars for whom missionaries are not a primary focus of their work, the cultural-imperialism model still functions as their default explanation. See, for instance, Karen Armstrong, *Holy War: The Crusades and Their Impact on Today's World* (New York: Anchor, 2001), 411–12; Ivan Eland, "GloboCop Runs Amok: Bipartisan Foolishness in U.S. Foreign Policy," *Chronicle of Higher Education*, September 9, 2005, B14. For examples

in works of fiction, see James A. Michener, *Hawaii* (New York: Random House, 1959); Barbara Kingsolver, *The Poisonwood Bible* (New York: HarperCollins, 1998).

7. Through most of the twentieth century, scholarship in the Westernization school of thought ignored the emergence of these movements or explained them away as quirky aberrations. Shaped by modernization theories, framed by the secularizing trends of modern intellectual currents, and grounded in the assumption that religious conversion by non-Westerners must stem from some type of coercion, twentieth-century scholarship was ill equipped to anticipate the emergence of enthusiastic local leaders promoting the extensive growth of Christianity in the global South. For a reconsideration of the relationship among secularization, modernization, and religion, see José Casanova, *Public Religions in the Modern World* (Chicago: University of Chicago Press, 1994).

8. Andrew F. Walls, *The Missionary Movement in Christian History: Studies in the Transmission of Faith* (Maryknoll, N.Y.: Orbis, 1996); Lamin Sanneh, *Translating the Message: The Missionary Impact on Culture* (Maryknoll, N.Y.: Orbis, 1999); Philip Jenkins, *The Next Christendom: The Coming of Global Christianity* (Oxford: Oxford University Press, 2002); Philip Jenkins, *The New Faces of Christianity: Believing the Bible in the Global South* (Oxford, U.K., and New York: Oxford University Press, 2007); Lamin Sanneh and Joel A. Carpenter, eds., *The Changing Face of Christianity: Africa, the West, and the World* (New York: Oxford University Press, 2005); David Martin, *Tongues of Fire: The Explosion of Protestantism in Latin America* (Oxford, U.K., and Cambridge, Mass.: Blackwell, 1990); Allan Anderson, *An Introduction to Pentecostalism: Global Charismatic Christianity* (Cambridge, U.K.: Cambridge University Press, 2004); Martin Marty, *The Christian World: A Global History* (New York: Modern Library, 2007); David B. Barrett, George T. Kurian, and Todd M. Johnson, eds., *World Christian Encyclopedia: A Comparative Survey of Churches and Religions in the Modern World*, 2nd ed., vol. 1 (New York: Oxford University Press, 2001), 4.

9. I use the term *world Christianity* because it recognizes that Christian movements in Africa, Asia, and Latin America have not simply been shaped by Western Christendom. It also recognizes that since its inception two thousand years ago, Christianity has encompassed more than Western Christendom. Finally, because of the cultural diversity of these different bodies, the term *world* seems a more accurate descriptor than *global*, which can connote a centralized, homogeneous system. Walls, *The Missionary Movement*; Sanneh, *Translating the Message*; Marty, *The Christian World*; Lamin Sanneh, *Disciples of All Nations: Pillars of World Christianity* (Oxford, U.K., and New York: Oxford University Press, 2007); Dale T. Irvin and Scott W. Sunquist, *History of the World Christian Movement: Volume I: Earliest Christianity to 1453* (Maryknoll, N.Y.: Orbis, 2004); Kwame Bediako, *Christianity in Africa: The Renewal of Non-western Religion* (Edinburgh: Edinburgh University Press and Maryknoll, N.Y.: Orbis, 1995).

10. Quoted in Eric T. Love, *Race over Empire: Racism and U.S. Imperialism, 1865–1900* (Chapel Hill: University of North Carolina Press, 2004), 166; William R. Hutchison, *Errand to the World: American Protestant Thought and Foreign Missions* (Chicago: University of Chicago Press, 1987), especially 9–13.

11. *Baptist Missionary Magazine*, November 1895, 543–44, and February 1895, 42; Abrams, *The Baptism*.

12. One prominent myth about missionaries that permeated scholarship in the last decades of the twentieth century was the claim that missionaries compelled non-Western people to change their sexual practices so that sexual intercourse took place face-to-face with the man on top of the woman. This myth has produced the popular term *missionary position*. As Robert J. Priest has demonstrated, even though this claim about missionaries was widely accepted as historically accurate, it originated not from actual historical evidence of missionary engagement but from a misreading of Malinowski by Alfred Kinsey. Priest goes on to argue that the power and persistence of this myth are driven by a number of factors within modern and postmodern scholarship, including objections to Christian morality. John J. Priest, "Missionary Positions: Christian, Modernist, Postmodernist," *Current Anthropology* 42 (February 2001): 29–68.

13. On the definition of evangelicalism, see Mark A. Noll, David W. Bebbington, and George A Rawlyk, eds., *Evangelicalism: Comparative Studies of Popular Protestantism in North America, the British Isles, and Beyond, 1700–1900* (New York: Oxford University Press, 1994), 6.
14. Typical of the assumptions of those in the Westernization school of thought, Jean and John Comaroff claim that "in the context of European colonialism, 'conversion' has always been part of its apparatus of cultural coercion." Comaroff and Comaroff, *Of Revelation and Revolution*, 251.
15. Sanneh, *Translating the Message*.
16. Nathan Hatch, *The Democratization of American Christianity* (New Haven, Conn.: Yale University Press, 1989); John H. Wigger, *Taking Heaven by Storm: Methodism and the Rise of Popular Christianity in America* (New York: Oxford University Press, 1998); Vinson Synan, *The Holiness-Pentecostal Tradition: Charismatic Movements in the Twentieth Century* (Grand Rapids, Mich.: Eerdmans, 1997).
17. Andrew Walls notes that this cultural tension has actually characterized Christianity from its very beginning. Walls, *The Missionary Movement*, 3–15.
18. The closest observers of American and British evangelicalism have noted that cultural tensions have always been present within the movement. Andrew Walls, "The Evangelical Revival, the Missionary Movement, and Africa," in Noll, Bebbington, and Rawlyk, eds., *Evangelicalism*, 310–30; Hatch, *Democratization*, 219; George M. Marsden, *Fundamentalism and American Culture: The Shaping of Twentieth Century Evangelicalism, 1875–1920* (New York: Oxford University Press, 1980), 7; Grant Wacker, *Heaven Below: Early Pentecostals and American Culture* (Cambridge, Mass.: Harvard University Press, 2001), 10.
19. Nathan O. Hatch and Mark A. Nolls, eds., *The Bible in America: Essays in Cultural History* (New York: Oxford University Press, 1982); Candy Gunther Brown, *The Word in the World: Evangelical Writing, Publishing, and Reading in America, 1789–1880* (Chapel Hill: University of North Carolina Press, 2004); David Paul Nord, *Faith in Reading: Religious Publishing and the Birth of Mass Media in America* (New York: Oxford University Press, 2004); Marsden, *Fundamentalism*; Richard T. Hughes, ed., *The American Quest for the Primitive Church* (Urbana: University of Illinois Press, 1988); Paul S. Boyer, *When Time Shall Be No More: Prophecy Belief in Modern Culture* (Cambridge, Mass.: Belknap, 1994); Timothy P. Weber, *Living in the Shadow of the Second Coming: American Pre-Millennialism, 1875–1925* (New York: Oxford University Press, 1979).
20. George W. Stocking Jr., *Victorian Anthropology* (New York: Free Press, 1987); Gail Bederman, *Manliness and Civilization: A Cultural History of Gender and Race in the United States, 1880–1917* (Chicago: University of Chicago Press, 1995); Matthew Frye Jacobson, *Barbarian Virtues: The United States Encounters Foreign Peoples at Home and Abroad, 1876–1917* (New York: Hill and Wang, 2000); Robert W. Rydell, *World of Fairs: The Century-of-Progress Expositions* (Chicago: University of Chicago Press, 1993); Adam Kuper, *Culture: The Anthropologists' Account* (Cambridge, Mass.: Harvard University Press, 1999), 23–46; Michael Adas, *Dominance by Design: Technological Imperatives and America's Civilizing Mission* (Cambridge, Mass.: Belknap, 2006).
21. This is not to say that new movements of world Christianity did more than anything else to undermine racism in nineteenth-century American culture. The actions of slaves, free blacks, and abolitionists, for instance, certainly played significant roles in undermining racism. And most white evangelicals in the late nineteenth century did not face up to these challenges brought by the missionary movement. If they harbored anxieties about the stability of the American republic or cared deeply about maintaining their position of influence within American civilization, American evangelicals tended to pay very little attention to the racial challenges launched by world Christianity. See, for instance, Edward J. Blum, *Reforging the White Republic: Race, Religion and American Nationalism, 1865–1898* (Baton Rouge: Louisiana State University Press, 2007).
22. H. H. Gerth and C. Wright Mills, eds., *From Max Weber: Essays in Sociology* (New York: Oxford University Press, 1946), 139–49.
23. The diversity of evangelicalism has often been underappreciated. If one examines the full scope of evangelicalism, the simplistic equation of evangelical Christianity with American

or Western culture quickly runs into complications and contradictions. For the diversity of evangelicalism, see Mark A. Noll, *America's God: From Jonathan Edwards to Abraham Lincoln* (New York; Oxford: Oxford University Press, 2002); George M. Marsden, *Jonathan Edwards: A Life* (New Haven, Conn.: Yale University Press, 2003); Hatch, *Democratization*; Thomas S. Kidd, *The Great Awakening: The Roots of Evangelicalism in Colonial America* (New Haven, Conn.: Yale University Press, 2007); Curtis D. Johnson, *Redeeming America: Evangelicals and the Road to Civil War* (Chicago: Dee, 1993); Roger J. Carwardine, *Evangelicals and Politics in Antebellum America* (New Haven, Conn.: Yale University Press, 1993); Catherine A. Brekus, *Strangers and Pilgrims: Female Preaching in America, 1740–1845* (Chapel Hill: University of North Carolina Press, 1998); Susan Hill Lindley, *"You Have Stept Out of Your Place": A History of Women and Religion in America* (Louisville, Ky.: Westminster John Knox, 1996); Sylvia R. Frey and Betty Wood, *Come Shouting to Zion: African American Protestantism in the American South and British Caribbean to 1830* (Chapel Hill: University of North Carolina Press, 1998).

24. Curtis Johnson makes distinctions among formalist, antiformalist, and African-American evangelicals, although historians have used other terminology to describe similar dynamics. Thomas Kidd places evangelicals in the First Great Awakening along a continuum from antirevivalist to moderate to radical. Mark Noll has categorized eighteenth-century evangelicals as "Patrician," "Plebeian," and "Bourgeois," while using "formalist" and "antiformalist" to describe evangelical theological attitudes in the nineteenth century. David Martin describes evangelicalism in Latin America as falling between what he calls the "Methodist Model" and Pentecostalism. Johnson, *Redeeming America*, 6–9; Kidd, *The Great Awakening*, xiv–xv; Mark A. Noll, *The Rise of Evangelicalism: The Age of Edwards, Whitefield and the Wesleys* (Downers Grove, Ill.: Intervarsity, 2003), 234–56; Noll, *America's God*, 175–76, 193–202; David Martin, *Tongues of Fire: The Explosion of Protestantism in Latin America* (Oxford, U.K.: Blackwell, 1990). See also the poem "Methodist and Formalist" in the appendix of Hatch, *Democratization*, 239–41.

25. Jeffrey Cox, *Imperial Fault Lines: Christianity and Colonial Power in India, 1818–1940* (Stanford, Calif.: Stanford University Press, 2002); R. Pierce Beaver, ed., *To Advance the Gospel: Selections from the Writings of Rufus Anderson* (Grand Rapids, Mich.: Eerdmans, 1967); Joe M. Richardson, *Christian Reconstruction: The American Missionary Association and Southern Blacks, 1861–1890* (Athens: University of Georgia Press, 1986); William G. McLoughlin, *Cherokees and Missionaries, 1789–1839* (Norman: University of Oklahoma Press, 1995); Kevin Grant, *A Civilised Savagery: Britain and the New Slaveries in Africa, 1884–1926* (New York: Routledge, 2005), 39–78.

26. Johnson, *Redeeming America*, 7–8; Noll, *America's God*, 175–76, 193–202; Kidd, *The Great Awakening*, xiv–xv; Brekus, *Strangers and Pilgrims*; Wigger, *Taking Heaven by Storm*; Hatch, *Democratization*; Rhys Isaac, *The Transformation of Virginia, 1740–1790* (Chapel Hill: University of North Carolina Press, 1982); Ann Taves, *Fits, Trances, and Visions: Experiencing Religion and Explaining Experience from Wesley to James* (Princeton, N.J.: Princeton University Press, 1999).

Chapter 1

1. Portions of this chapter were published earlier in Jay Riley Case, "Interpreting Karen Christianity: The American Baptist Reaction to Asian Christianity in the Nineteenth Century," in Lamin Sanneh and Joel Carpenter, eds., *The Changing Face of Christianity: Africa, the West and the World* (Oxford: Oxford University Press, 2005), 135–57.

2. We do not have written sources, of course, from the members of this preliterate Karen village. This account has been reconstructed from ethnologies of traditional Karen culture and the information recorded in various journal entries by George Boardman in 1828 and 1829, during his initial contacts with the members of this Karen village. *American Baptist Magazine*, July 1829, 242–44; August 1829, 278, 281; January 1830, 22–23; February 1830, 51–52; March 1830, 87–91; Charles F. Keyes, *The Golden Peninsula: Culture and Adaptation in Mainland Southeast Asia* (Honolulu: University of Hawaii Press, 1997),

52–57; U Zan and Erville E. Sowards, "Baptist Work among the Karens," in Maung Shwe Wa and Erville E. Sowards, eds., *Burma Baptist Chronicle, Book II* (Rangoon: University Press, 1963), 305; Harry Ignatius Marshall, *The Karen People of Burma: A Study in Anthropology and Ethnology* (Columbus: Ohio State University, 1922); Anders P. Hovemyr, *In Search of the Karen King: A Study in Karen Identity with Special Reference to 19th Century Karen Evangelism in Northern Thailand* (Uppsala: Studia Missionalia Upsaliensia, 1989).
3. *American Baptist Magazine*, July 1829, 242–46; Robert G. Torbet, *Venture of Faith: The Story of the American Baptist Foreign Mission Society and the Woman's American Baptist Foreign Mission Society, 1814–1954*, (Philadelphia: Judson Press, 1955), 40–43.
4. Francis Mason, *The Karen Apostle, or Memoir of Ko Thah Byu, the First Karen Convert, with Notices concerning His Nation* (Bassein: Sgau Karen Press, 1884), 23.
5. Martin Smith, *Burma: Insurgency and the Politics of Ethnicity* (Dhaka: University Press, 1999), 44; John Frank Cady, *A History of Modern Burma* (Ithaca, N.Y.: Cornell University Press, 1958), 42–43, 73–80; Keyes, *The Golden Peninsula*, 49–57, 117–19.
6. Mason, *The Karen Apostle*, 9–22; *American Baptist Magazine*, January 1830, 22–23.
7. *American Baptist Magazine*, July 1829, 243–44.
8. Ibid.
9. *American Baptist Magazine*, January 1830, 22.
10. *American Baptist Magazine*, January 1830, 22–23.
11. *American Baptist Magazine*, May 1829, 170–71; July 1829, 242–44; August 1829, 278, 281; September 1829, 317; November 1829, 386–88; January 1830, 21–23; February 1830, 51–52; March 1830, 87–91.
12. L. P. Brockett, *The Story of the Karen Mission in Bassein, 1838–1890* (Philadelphia: American Baptist Publication Society, 1891), 149–50.
13. Joseph Chandler Robbins, *Boardman of Burma: A Biography* (Philadelphia: Judson Press, 1940), 11; Alonzo King, *Memoir of George Dana Boardman, Late Missionary to Burmah* (Boston: Gould, Kendall & Lincoln, 1839).
14. *American Baptist Magazine*, July 1829, 242–44; August 1829, 278, 281; January 1830, 22–23; February 1830, 51–52; March 1830, 87–91.
15. *American Baptist Magazine*, July 1829, 244–46.
16. *American Baptist Magazine and Missionary Intelligencer*, September 1818, 181; July 1820, 381–2; January 1821, 60; January 1823, 20; *American Baptist Magazine*, August 1825, 252; November 1825, 340; February 1826, 53–54; April 1826, 109–11; May 1826, 143–47; February 1827, 43; Francis Wayland, *A Memoir of the Life and Labors of the Rev. Adoniram Judson, D.D.*, Vol. 1 (Boston: Phillips, Sampson, 1853), 157–61; Fanny Forester, *Memoir of Sarah B. Judson, Member of the American Mission to Burmah* (New York: L. Colby, 1848), 76–77.
17. *American Baptist Magazine*, July 1829, 243; Henry Warner Bowden, *American Indians and Christian Missions: Studies in Cultural Conflict* (Chicago: University of Chicago Press, 1981); Peter Silver, *Our Savage Neighbors: How Indian War Transformed Early America* (New York: W. W. Norton, 2008).
18. George Boardman letter, January 15, 1828. Official Correspondence File, Archived Collections of the Board of International Ministries, American Baptist Historical Society, Valley Forge, Pa. (Hereafter, such correspondence will be cited as BIM Correspondence File); *American Baptist Magazine*, July 1829, 243.
19. *American Baptist Magazine*, July 1829, 242–43; Torbet, *Venture of Faith*, 43–44.
20. King, *Memoir*, 253; *American Baptist Magazine*, July 1829, 242–43; January 1830, 22–23; Marshall, *The Karen People*, 143; Keyes, *The Golden Peninsula*, 54–55, 117–19.
21. Boardman letter, January 15, 1828, BIM Correspondence File.
22. *American Baptist Magazine*, January 1830, 21–22.
23. King, *Memoir*, 220–21, 226, 235; Mason, *The Karen Apostle*, 35–38; Torbet, *Venture of Faith*, 47.
24. King, *Memoir*, 164–65; *American Baptist Magazine*, March 1830, 88–89.
25. Ibid.
26. Wayland, *A Memoir*, Vol. 1, 120, 114–19; Torbet, *Venture of Faith*, 24–30.
27. Wayland, *A Memoir*, Vol. 1, 120.

28. George W. Stocking, Jr., *Victorian Anthropology* (New York: Free Press, 1987), 105.
29. *American Baptist Magazine and Missionary Intelligencer*, May 1818, 325; Brian Stanley, *The History of the Baptist Missionary Society, 1792–1992* (Edinburgh: T&T Clark, 1992), 43–44.
30. *American Baptist Magazine*, December 1833, 425; Stanley, *The History*, 43–44; Helen G. Trager, *Burma through Alien Eyes: Missionary Views of the Burmese in the Nineteenth Century* (New York: Praeger, 1966).
31. See, for example, *American Baptist Magazine and Missionary Intelligencer*, May 1817, 95; May 1818, 411; January 1819, 14; July 1819, 135; November 1825, 337–38; *American Baptist Magazine*, December 1833, 425; Ann Taves, *Fits, Trances, and Visions: Experiencing Religion and Explaining Experience from Wesley to James* (Princeton, N.J.: Princeton University Press, 1999).
32. Wayland, *A Memoir*, Vol. 1, 187, 229, 326.
33. *American Baptist Magazine and Missionary Intelligencer*, May 1818, 325.
34. *American Baptist Magazine*, November 1835, 429; *American Baptist Magazine and Missionary Intelligencer*, January 1822, 253.
35. *American Baptist Magazine*, November 1828, 322; December 1829, 415; *Watchman and Reflector*, May 27, 1852, 86.
36. Joan Jacobs Brumberg, *Mission for Life: The Story of the Family of Adoniram Judson, the Dramatic Events of the First American Foreign Mission, and the Course of Evangelical Religion in the Nineteenth Century* (New York: Free Press, 1980); Candy Gunther Brown, *The World in the World: Evangelical Writing, Publishing and Reading in America, 1789–1880* (Chapel Hill: University of North Carolina Press, 2004), 110.
37. Quoted in Brumberg, *Mission for Life*, 21, 30; Charles E. Hambrick-Stowe, *The Practice of Piety: Puritan Devotional Disciplines in Seventeenth-Century New England* (Chapel Hill: University of North Carolina Press, 1982); Harry S. Stout, *The New England Soul: Preaching and Religious Culture in Colonial New England* (New York: Oxford University Press, 1986).
38. Wayland, *A Memoir*, Vol. 1, 28, 22; see also 11–28. Brumberg, *Mission for Life*, 20–43.
39. *New York Recorder*, April 3, 1850, 1.
40. Curtis D. Johnson, *Redeeming America: Evangelicals and the Road to Civil War* (Chicago: Dee, 1993); Mark A. Noll, *America's God: From Jonathan Edwards to Abraham Lincoln* (New York: Oxford University Press, 2002).
41. *American Baptist Magazine*, January 1835, 14.
42. Lamin Sanneh, *Translating the Message: The Missionary Impact on Culture* (Maryknoll, N.Y.: Orbis, 1999).
43. Wayland, *A Memoir*, Vol. 1, 176–77.
44. Judson's advice was reprinted in Edward Judson, *The Life of Adoniram Judson* (New York: Randolph, 1883), 578–79.
45. Sanneh, *Translating the Message*, app. B; Harvey Markowitz, "Bible Translations," in Frederick E. Hoxie, ed., *Encyclopedia of North American Indians* (Boston: Houghton Mifflin, 1996), 68–69; Reginald Horsman, *Race and Manifest Destiny: The Origins of American Racial Anglo-Saxonism* (Cambridge, Mass.: Harvard University Press, 1981); Ronald Takaki, *Iron Cages: Race and Culture in 19th-Century America* (New York: Oxford University Press, 1990), 80–107.
46. American Baptist Missionary Union, *The Missionary Jubilee: An Account of the 50th Anniversary of the American Baptist Missionary Union, at Philadelphia, May 24, 25 & 26, 1864* (New York: Shelton, 1865), 281–83.
47. Wayland, *A Memoir*, Vol. 1, 120–21. Stanley, *The History*, 49; Sanneh, *Translating the Message*.
48. *American Baptist Magazine and Missionary Intelligencer*, July 1820, 382; Judson, *The Life*, 589; Howard Malcom, *Travels in South-Eastern Asia, Embracing Hindustan, Malaya, Siam, and China; With Notices of Numerous Missionary Stations, and a Full Account of the Burman Empire; with Dissertations, Tables, etc.*, Vol. 1, (Boston: Gould, Kendall & Lincoln, 1839), 72.
49. *American Baptist Magazine*, January 1835, 14; July 1835, 288.
50. Andrew F. Walls, *The Missionary Movement in Christian History: Studies in the Transmission of Faith* (Maryknoll, N.Y.: Orbis, 1996), 47.
51. *American Baptist Magazine*, February 1826, 53–54. See also Wayland, *A Memoir*, Vol. 2, 128–53.

52. *American Baptist Magazine*, April 1826, 109–11; May 1826, 143–47.
53. *American Baptist Magazine and Missionary Intelligencer*, January 1823, 18–20.
54. Of the sixty-nine Baptist missionaries who had worked in Burma by 1844, only nine were born someplace other than New England or upstate New York. In 1845, the Triennial Convention, as the Baptist foreign missionary agency had been called up to that point, split into northern and southern organizations on the issue of slavery. The northern wing, which is the subject of this chapter, took the name of the American Baptist Missionary Union, or ABMU. *American Baptist Magazine*, July 1846, 236–37; ABMU, *The Missionary Jubilee*, 236 ff.; Edwin Scott Gaustad, *Historical Atlas of Religion in America* (New York: Harper & Row, 1962), 43, 52; Roger Torbet, *A History of the Baptists*, 3rd ed. (Valley Forge, Pa.: Judson Press, 1963), 305–19; E. Brooks Holifield, *God's Ambassadors: A History of Christian Clergy in America* (Grand Rapids, Mich.: Eerdmans, 2007), 115–16.
55. Dana Robert, *American Women in Mission: A Social History of Their Thought and Practice* (Macon, Ga.: Mercer University Press, 1996), 7–9; Kathryn Kish Sklar, *Catherine Beecher: A Study in American Domesticity* (New Haven, Conn.: Yale University Press, 1973).
56. King, *Memoir*, 193.
57. Ibid., 219–20.
58. Ibid., 226, 235; Mason, *The Karen Apostle*, 35–38; Torbet, *Venture of Faith*, 47.
59. King, *Memoir*, 278, 276.
60. Ibid., 276–77.
61. Ibid., 268.
62. Mason, *The Karen Apostle*, 68–69.
63. King, *Memoir*, 296–309; Forester, *Memoir*, 124–43.
64. Mason, *The Karen Apostle*, 43, 53–65.
65. Ibid., 58; see also 53–65.
66. Saw Doh Say, "A Brief History and Development Factors of the Karen Baptist Church of Burma (Myanmar)," master's thesis, Fuller Theological Seminary, 1990, 84; Dana Robert, "Evangelist or Homemaker? Mission Strategies of Early Nineteenth-Century Missionary Wives in Burma and Hawaii," *International Bulletin of Missionary Research* 17 (January 1993), 4–10; Torbet, *Venture of Faith*, 47–49, 61–69; Shwe Wa and Sowards, *Burma Baptist Chronicle*, 174; Brockett, *The Story*, 149–50.
67. *American Baptist Magazine*, July 1838, 154; December 1838, 301–4; *Baptist Missionary Magazine*, July 1845, 198; August 1862, 316; Smith, *Burma*; Cady, *A History*; Keyes, *The Golden Peninsula*, 56–57.
68. Letter of Rev. H. L. Van Meter, August 21, 1852, BIM Correspondence File, folder 25.
69. Saw Doh Say, "History," 41–44; Mason, *The Karen Apostle*, 127–55; *American Baptist Magazine*, May 1888, 120–21.
70. Marshall, *The Karen People*, 161; Smith, *Burma*; Cady, *A History*; Keyes, *The Golden Peninsula*, 56–57.
71. Walls, *The Missionary Movement*; Sanneh, *Translating the Message*.
72. Smith, *Burma*, 44; U Zan and Sowards, "Baptist Work," 312–13; Shwe Wa and Sowards, *Burma Baptist Chronicle*, 126; Torbet, *Venture of Faith*, 238; *American Baptist Magazine*, May 1839, 102.
73. *American Baptist Magazine*, August 1852, 327, 329.
74. David D. Hall, *Worlds of Wonder, Days of Judgment: Popular Religious Belief in Early New England* (Cambridge, Mass.: Harvard University Press, 1989); Taves, *Fits, Trances and Visions*.
75. *American Baptist Magazine*, August 1852, 327, 329.
76. Ibid.; *The Helping Hand*, August 1879, 59; Marshall, *The Karen People*, 267–78.
77. *American Baptist Magazine*, August, 1852, 327–28.
78. Ibid., 328–30.
79. Walter N. Wyeth, *A Galaxy in the Burman Sky: A Memorial* (Philadelphia: Wyeth, 1892), 32; *Baptist Missionary Magazine*, July 1846, 236–40; July 1897, 436–39. For the centrality of Burma in the Baptist missionary enterprise, see ABMU, *The Missionary Jubilee*.

80. Quoted in David Paul Nord, *Faith in Reading: Religious Publishing and the Birth of Mass Media in America* (Oxford and New York: Oxford University Press, 2004), 96.
81. American Tract Society, *Report of the Ecumenical Conference on Foreign Missions*, Vol. 1 (New York: American Tract Society), 97. See also the bibliography in Torbet, *Venture of Faith*, 599–612; N. G. Clark, "Higher Christian Education as a Missionary Agency," in James Johnston, ed., *Report of the Centenary Conference on the Protestant Missions of the World*, Vol. 2 (New York: Revell, 1888), 185; *Word and Work*, June 1899, 52.
82. Brumberg, *Mission for Life*. For a bibliography of works from 1829 to 1954 on missions in Burma, see Torbet, *Venture of Faith*, 599–612.
83. I take the term *Judsoniana* from Brumberg, *Mission for Life*, 233; see also, ix–xvi, 1–19, 102–4, 225–33. The genealogical references to Adoniram Judson are derived from an Internet search conducted in the summer of 2005.
84. Brumberg, *Mission for Life*; Torbet, *Venture of Faith*, 599–612.

Chapter 2

1. Alonzo King, *Memoir of George Dana Boardman, Late Missionary to Burmah* (Boston: Gould, Kendall & Lincoln, 1839), 165; *American Baptist Magazine*, July 1829, 243. Portions of this chapter were published earlier in Jay Riley Case, "Interpreting Karen Christianity: The American Baptist Reaction to Asian Christianity in the Nineteenth Century," in Lamin Sanneh and Joel Carpenter, eds., *The Changing Face of Christianity: Africa, the West and the World* (Oxford: Oxford University Press, 2005), 135–57.
2. *American Baptist Magazine*, December 1838, 301–3; May 1839, 101–7; September 1839, 216; April 1840, 80–81; C. H. Carpenter, *Self-Support, Illustrated in the History of the Bassein Karen Mission from 1840–1880* (Boston: Rand, Avery, 1883), 9, 20–27; John Frank Cady, *A History of Modern Burma* (Ithaca, N.Y.: Cornell University Press, 1958), 73–80.
3. *American Baptist Magazine*, September 1839, 216.
4. *American Baptist Magazine*, April 1840, 81; see also May 1839, 101–7; September 1839, 216.
5. Carpenter, *Self-Support*, 20–27; *American Baptist Magazine*, September 1840, 216.
6. *American Baptist Magazine*, January 1839, 15; September 1840, 217; February 1841, 36–37.
7. Brian Stanley, *The History of the Baptist Missionary Society, 1792–1992* (Edinburgh: T&T Clark, 1992), 47–52.
8. *American Baptist Magazine and Missionary Intelligencer*, January 1821, 36; January 1822, 254; May 1822, 346; *American Baptist Magazine*, March 1827, 77; January 1828, 14; Roger Torbet, *A History of the Baptists*, 3rd ed. (Valley Forge, Pa.: Judson Press, 1963), 247–49.
9. *American Baptist Magazine*, June 1828, 167. For similar arguments in later years, see *American Baptist Magazine*, August 1848, 306; *Baptist Missionary Magazine*, April 1853, 110–11; July 1873, 223.
10. *American Baptist Magazine*, April 1842, 87–90.
11. Carpenter, *Self-Support*, 147–48; *American Baptist Magazine*, December 1829, 414.
12. Perry Miller, *The New England Mind: From Colony to Province* (Cambridge, Mass.: Harvard University Press, 1953), 68–81; David D. Hall, *Worlds of Wonder, Days of Judgment: Popular Religious Belief in Early New England* (Cambridge, Mass.: Harvard University Press, 1990), 150–52; Charles E. Hambrick-Stowe, *The Practice of Piety: Puritan Devotional Disciplines in Seventeenth-Century New England* (Chapel Hill: University of North Carolina Press, 1982), 85–90.
13. King, *Memoir*, 220–21, 226, 235; *American Baptist Magazine*, March 1830, 89–90; Robert G. Torbet, *Venture of Faith: The Story of the American Baptist Foreign Mission Society and the Woman's American Baptist Foreign Mission Society, 1814–1954* (Philadelphia: Judson Press, 1955), 43–44.
14. *American Baptist Magazine*, February 1841, 39; Carpenter, *Self-Support*, 75.
15. Carpenter, *Self-Support*, 75.
16. *American Baptist Magazine*, April 1842, 93; Carpenter, *Self-Support*, 44.
17. Carpenter, *Self-Support*, 74.
18. Nathan Hatch, *The Democratization of American Christianity* (New Haven, Conn.: Yale University Press, 1989); Whitney R. Cross, *The Burned-over District: The Social and Intellectual*

History of Enthusiastic Religion in Western New York, 1800–1850 (New York: Harper & Row, 1950); Walter N. Wyeth, *A Galaxy in the Burman Sky: A Memorial* (Philadelphia: Wyeth, 1892), 87.

19. *Baptist Missionary Magazine*, July 1866, 251–53; October 1866, 393; Francis Mason, *The Karen Apostle, or Memoir of Ko Tha Byu, the First Karen Convert, with Notices concerning His Nation* (Bassein: Sgau Karen Press, 1884), 23; Charles F. Keyes, *The Golden Peninsula: Culture and Adaptation in Mainland Southeast Asia* (Honolulu: University of Hawaii Press, 1997), 54–56; Anders P. Hovemyr, *In Search of the Karen King* (Uppsala: S. Academiae Ubsaliensis, 1989), 76–78.
20. *American Baptist Magazine*, December 1842, 324.
21. Ibid.
22. *American Baptist Magazine*, December 1843, 302–3.
23. *American Baptist Magazine*, July 1844, 203.
24. William R. Hutchison, *Errand to the World: American Protestant Thought and Foreign Missions* (Chicago: University of Chicago Press, 1987), 62–90; Timothy L. Wood, "Kingdom Expectations: The Native American in the Puritan Missiology of John Winthrop and Roger Williams," *Fides et Historia* 32 (Winter/Spring 2000): 39–49; Mark A. Noll, *America's God: From Jonathan Edwards to Abraham Lincoln* (Oxford: Oxford University Press, 2002), 174–86; Curtis D. Johnson, *Redeeming America: Evangelicals and the Road to the Civil War* (Chicago: Dee, 1993), 18–32.
25. Hutchison, *Errand to the World*, 63–67; Stephen Neill, *A History of Christian Missions* (London: Penguin, 1990), 233–34. American Baptists occasionally reported on Duff's efforts and ideas. See, for instance, *Watchman and Reflector*, January 16, 1851, 10.
26. William G. McLoughlin, *Cherokees and Missionaries, 1789–1839* (Norman: University of Oklahoma Press, 1995), 239–65; Joe M. Richardson, *Christian Reconstruction: The American Missionary Association and Southern Blacks, 1861–1890* (Athens: University of Georgia Press, 1986).
27. Rhys Isaac, *The Transformation of Virginia, 1740–1790* (Chapel Hill: University of North Carolina Press), 1982; Hatch, *The Democratization*; Thomas S. Kidd, *The Great Awakening: The Roots of Evangelical Christianity in Colonial America* (New Haven, Conn.: Yale University Press, 2007); Noll, *America's God*; Paul William Harris, *Nothing but Christ: Rufus Anderson and the Ideology of Protestant Foreign Missions* (New York: Oxford University Press, 1999), 26.
28. Quoted in Hatch, *The Democratization*, 98; Catherine A. Brekus, *Strangers and Pilgrims: Female Preaching in America, 1740–1845* (Chapel Hill: University of North Carolina Press, 1998).
29. *American Baptist Magazine*, May 1826, 150–52.
30. *American Baptist Magazine*, February 1838, 36–38; July 1838, 154; October, 1838, 256; September 1839, 217; February 1841, 35; Dana Robert, *American Women in Mission: A Social History of Their Thought and Practice* (Macon, Ga.: Mercer University Press, 1996), 51–75; Dana Robert, "Evangelist or Homemaker? Mission Strategies of Early Nineteenth-Century Missionary Wives in Burma and Hawaii," *International Bulletin of Missionary Research* 17 (January 1993): 4–10.
31. Torbet, *A History*, 546–47; R. Laurence Moore, *Religious Outsiders and the Making of Americans* (New York: Oxford University Press, 1986).
32. *New York Recorder*, August 18, 1852, 82; Susan Hill Lindley, *"You Have Stept Out of Your Place": A History of Women and Religion in America* (Louisville, Ky.: John Knox, 1996), 90–106; Colleen McDannell, *The Christian Home in Victorian America, 1840–1900* (Bloomington: Indiana University Press, 1986); Robert, *American Women*, 81–124; Kathryn Kish Sklar, *Catherine Beecher: A Study in American Domesticity* (New Haven, Conn.: Yale University Press), 1973.
33. Richard J. Carwardine, *Evangelicals and Politics in Antebellum America* (New Haven, Conn.: Yale University Press, 1993), 137–38; Noll, *America's God*, 194–208.
34. *Baptist Missionary Magazine*, July 1846, 229; July 1848, 234; July 1850, 239; July 1851, 309; July 1855, 343; July 1857, 288; July 1859, 282; Carwardine, *Evangelicals and Politics*, 21, 40,

113, 127–31, 275–76; "George Nixon Briggs," in John A. Garraty and Mark C. Carnes, eds., *American National Biography*, Vol. 3 (New York: Oxford University Press, 1999).
35. *New York Recorder*, July 19, 1850, 58; *Watchman and Reflector*, October 2, 1851, 155.
36. Edwin Scott Gaustad, *Historical Atlas of Religion in America* (New York: Harper & Row, 1962), 43, 52; Torbet, *A History*, 305–19.
37. *New York Recorder*, April 9, 1851, 6; April 16, 1851, 10.
38. *Watchman and Reflector*, July 24, 1851, 117; *New York Recorder*, July 30, 1851, 69. See also *Watchman and Reflector*, May 22, 1851, 82; January 8, 1852, 5–6; January 15, 1852, 10; February 26, 1852, 33; *New York Recorder*, May 21, 1851, 31.
39. Mason, *The Karen Apostle*, 48.
40. *American Baptist Magazine*, April 1842, 84–85; Mason, *The Karen Apostle*, 51.
41. Mason internalized the academic conceptions of "Orientalism" more fully than other American Baptist missionaries of his era. See Francis Mason to Solomon Peck, April 4, 1842, Official Correspondence File, Archived Collections of the Board of International Ministries, American Baptist Historical Society, Valley Forge, Pa. (hereafter, each correspondence will be cited as BIM Correspondence File); Torbet, *Venture of Faith*, 238–39; "Francis Mason," in Gerald H. Anderson, ed., *Biographical Dictionary of Christian Missions* (Grand Rapids, Mich.: Eerdmans, 1998), 439; Harry Ignatius Marshall, *The Karen People of Burma: A Study in Anthropology and Ethnology* (Columbus: Ohio State University Press, 1922), 5–12; Edward W. Said, *Orientalism* (New York: Vintage, 1994).
42. Mason, *The Karen Apostle*, 48–49; Torbet, *Venture of Faith*, 64–65.
43. *American Baptist Magazine*, April 1842, 84–85.
44. Joseph Chandler Robbins, *Boardman of Burma: A Biography* (Philadelphia: Judson Press, 1940), 19–56.
45. Mason, *The Karen Apostle*, 30. See also Lamin Sanneh, *Translating the Message: The Missionary Impact on Culture* (Maryknoll, N.Y.: Orbis, 1999).
46. *American Baptist Magazine*, June 1843, 154–55.
47. *American Baptist Magazine*, April 1842, 84–85; July 1844, 203.
48. Carpenter, *Self-Support*, 76; *American Baptist Magazine*, April 1842, 84.
49. *American Baptist Magazine*, July 1844, 203; Carpenter, *Self-Support*, 73.
50. *American Baptist Magazine*, June 1843, 154–55.
51. George M. Frederickson, *The Black Image in the White Mind: The Debate on Afro-American Character and Destiny, 1817–1914* (New York: Harper & Row, 1971); Bruce Dain, *A Hideous Monster of the Mind: American Race Theory in the Early Republic* (Cambridge, Mass.: Harvard University Press, 2002), 165–69; Erskine Clarke, *Dwelling Place: A Plantation Epic* (New Haven, Conn.: Yale University Press, 2007).
52. Quoted in Charles Sellers, *The Market Revolution: Jacksonian America, 1815–1846* (New York: Oxford University Press, 1991), 427; see also 386–91; Frederick Merk, *Manifest Destiny and Mission in American History: A Reinterpretation* (New York: Vintage, 1963); Reginald Horsman, *Race and Manifest Destiny: The Origins of American Racial Anglo-Saxonism* (Cambridge, Mass.: Harvard University Press, 1981); Ronald Takaki, *Iron Cages: Race and Culture in 19th-Century America* (New York: Oxford University Press, 1990); Dain, *A Hideous Monster*, 120.
53. Quoted in Theda Perdue and Michael D. Green, eds., *The Cherokee Removal: A Brief History with Documents* (Boston: St. Martin's Press, 1995), 109, 120. See also Francis Paul Prucha, *American Indian Treaties: The History of a Political Anomaly* (Berkeley: University of California Press, 1994), 9–14, 118–19; Robert F. Berkhofer Jr., *The White Man's Indian: Images of the American Indian from Columbus to the Present* (New York: Knopf, 1978); Dain, *A Hideous Monster*, 81–83, 98–101, 121–23.
54. Quoted in Sellers, *The Market Revolution*, 422–23.
55. *Baptist Missionary Magazine*, July 1845, 153–54. For a similar sort of Baptist analysis of British imperialism in Burma, see *New York Recorder*, August 11, 1852, 78.
56. *Christian Watchman and Reflector*, August 10, 1854, 126. For further criticisms of British imperialism in India, China, and South Africa and possible American conquests of Cuba and Mexico, see *Christian Watchman and Reflector*, May 29, 1851, 86; September 16, 1852, 150; *New York Recorder*, June 15, 1853, 46.

57. *Christian Watchman and Reflector*, August 10, 1854, 126. For background on missionary work in Hawaii, see Hutchison, *Errand to the World*, 45, 62–63.
58. Quoted in Horsman, *Race and Manifest Destiny*, 127–28; see also 135–37, 142–44; Dain, *A Hideous Monster*, 197–226; George W. Stocking Jr., *Victorian Anthropology* (New York: Free Press, 1987), 26–27, 49, 64–69; Frederickson, *The Black Image*, 74–92.
59. *Baptist Missionary Magazine*, August 1848, 308. Agassiz quotes are from Horsman, *Race and Manifest Destiny*, 132.
60. Horsman, *Race and Manifest Destiny*, 178, 179; Frederickson, *The Black Image*, 98–126; Thomas F. Gossett, *Race: The History of an Idea in America* (Dallas: Southern Methodist University Press), 1963.
61. Frederickson, *The Black Image*, 37; Henry Mayer, *All on Fire: William Lloyd Garrison and the Abolition of Slavery* (New York: St. Martin's Press, 1998); Noll, *America's God*, 387; Dain, *A Hideous Monster*, 149–96.
62. Both evangelical abolitionism and evangelical missionary thinking have been largely overlooked as distinct schools of thought on race. It is quite likely that the two streams of thought influenced each other, although a systematic examination of this relationship has not been undertaken. On evangelicalism and abolition, see Charles E. Hambrick-Stowe, *Charles G. Finney and the Spirit of American Evangelicalism* (Grand Rapids, Mich.: Eerdmans, 1996), 159–75; C. C. Goen, *Broken Churches, Broken Nation: Denominational Schisms and the Coming of the American Civil War* (Macon, Ga.: Mercer University Press, 1985); Richardson, *Christian Reconstruction*.
63. Dain, *A Hideous Monster*, 112–48, 170–96.
64. *Baptist Missionary Magazine*, May 1847, 135–37.
65. *Baptist Missionary Magazine*, July 1845, 154; August 1848, 306; Carpenter, *Self-Support*, 148–64; *Western Recorder*, January 28, 1886, 4.
66. *American Baptist Magazine*, June 1843, 125–26.
67. ABMU, *The Missionary Jubilee*, 239; *Baptist Missionary Magazine*, January 1847, 5.
68. *Baptist Missionary Magazine*, December 1848, 444–46.
69. *Baptist Missionary Magazine*, August 1848, 308.
70. *Baptist Missionary Magazine*, January 1847, 5–6.
71. *Baptist Missionary Magazine*, December 1848, 448.
72. Quoted in Carpenter, *Self-Support*, 111, 112, 116.
73. *Baptist Missionary Magazine*, July 1844, 166–67; July 1846, 288.
74. *Baptist Missionary Magazine*, July 1846, 288; April 1853, 110–11.

Chapter 3

1. Frederick Douglass, *Life and Times of Frederick Douglass, Written by Himself: His Early Life as a Slave, His Escape from Bondage, and His Complete History* (New York: Macmillan, 1962), 263–64; David W. Blight, ed., *Narrative of the Life of Frederick Douglass, an American Slave, Written by Himself, with Related Documents* (Boston: Bedford/St. Martin's, 2003), 146. Portions of this chapter were published earlier in Jay Riley Case, "Interpreting Karen Christianity: The American Baptist Reaction to Asian Christianity in the Nineteenth Century," in Lamin Sanneh and Joel Carpenter, eds., *The Changing Face of Christianity. Africa, the West and the World* (Oxford: Oxford University Press, 2005), 135–57; Jay Riley Case, "From the Native Ministry to the Talented Tenth: The Foreign Missionary Origins of White Support for Black Colleges," in Daniel H. Bays and Grant Wacker, eds., *The Foreign Missionary Enterprise at Home: Explorations in North American Cultural History* (Tuscaloosa: University of Alabama Press, 2003), 60–93.
2. Kenneth R. M. Short, "Baptist Training for the Ministry: The Francis Wayland-Barnas Sears Debate of 1853," *Foundations* 11 (July-September 1968), 227–34; Glenn T. Miller, *Piety and Intellect: The Aims and Purposes of Ante-Bellum Theological Education* (Atlanta: Scholars Press, 1990).
3. Whitney R. Cross, *The Burned-over District: The Social and Intellectual History of Enthusiastic Religion in Western New York, 1800–1850* (New York: Harper & Row, 1950); Paul E. Johnson,

A Shopkeeper's Millennium: Society and Revivals in Rochester, New York, 1815–1837 (New York: Hill and Wang, 1978); Carol Sheriff, *The Artificial River: The Erie Canal and the Paradox of Progress, 1817–1862* (New York: Hill and Wang, 1996).

4. Cross, *The Burned-over District*, 73; Sheriff, *The Artificial River*, 53.
5. Cross, *Burned-over District*, 73, 114–25, 345–47; Johnson, *A Shopkeeper's Millennium*, 66–71; Charles E. Hambrick-Stowe, *Charles G. Finney and the Spirit of American Evangelicalism* (Grand Rapids, Mich.: Eerdmans, 1996), 101–14; Sheriff, *The Artificial River*, 53; Waldo E. Martin Jr., *The Mind of Frederick Douglass* (Chapel Hill: University of North Carolina Press, 1984), 31, 39, 40; Miriam Gurko, *The Ladies of Seneca Falls: The Birth of the Woman's Rights Movement* (New York: Macmillan, 1974), 156–57.
6. Cross, *Burned-over District*, 24.
7. Ibid., 24, 197, 223–24, 300–301; Nathan Hatch, *The Democratization of American Christianity* (New Haven, Conn.: Yale University Press, 1989), 134.
8. In 1845, the slavery issue had split the Baptist foreign-missionary agency, the Triennial Convention, into northern and southern agencies. The ABMU became the agency for northern Baptists. Robert G. Torbet, *A History of the Baptists*, 3rd ed. (Valley Forge, Pa.: Judson Press, 1975), 282–94; Francis Wayland and H. L. Wayland, *A Memoir of the Life and Labors of Francis Wayland, D.D., LL.D.* (New York: Sheldon, 1867, reprint New York: Arno, 1972), Vol. 1, 158–70, and Vol. 2, 58–61; Francis Wayland, *A Memoir of the Life and Labors of the Rev. Adoniram Judson, D.D.*, Vols. 1 and 2 (Boston: Phillips, Sampson, 1853).
9. *Baptist Missionary Magazine*, July 1848, 227–28.
10. Francis Wayland, *The Apostolic Ministry: A Discourse Delivered in Rochester, N.Y., before the New York Baptist Union for Ministerial Education, July 12, 1853* (Rochester: Sage, 1853). For primitivism, see Richard T. Hughes, ed., *The American Quest for the Primitive Church* (Urbana: University of Illinois Press, 1988).
11. Wayland, *The Apostolic Ministry*, 49–56.
12. Ibid., 18–19, 41, 49–52.
13. *Watchman and Reflector*, September, 23, 1852, 54; American Baptist Missionary Union, *The Missionary Jubilee: An Account of the 50th Anniversary of the American Baptist Missionary Union, at Philadelphia, May 24, 25 & 26, 1864* (New York: Shelton, 1865), 432, 436, 445; Robert G. Torbet, *Venture of Faith: The Story of the American Baptist Foreign Mission Society and the Woman's American Baptist Foreign Mission Society, 1814–1954* (Philadelphia: Judson Press, 1955), 86.
14. Barnas Sears, *An Educated Ministry: An Address Delivered Before the N.Y. Baptist Union for Ministerial Education, at its Anniversary, Held in Rochester, July 12, 1853* (New York: Lewis Colby, 1853), 4; Perry Miller, *Errand into the Wilderness* (Cambridge, Mass.: Harvard University Press, 1956).
15. Sears, *An Educated Ministry*, 8–9, 14.
16. Ibid., 11.
17. Ibid., 9, 12.
18. Ibid., 8–9, 14.
19. *Christian Watchman and Reflector*, May 22, 1851, 81; *Baptist Missionary Magazine*, July 1851, 194–95, 309.
20. See, for example, *Watchman and Reflector*, October 13, 1853, 162; October 20, 1853, 165; November 10, 1853, 177; December 22, 1853, 202; March 30, 1854, 49; April 6, 1854, 53; April 13, 1854, 57; April 20, 1854, 61; April 27, 1854, 66; May 11, 1854, 74; September 7, 1854, 142; *Home Mission Record*, May 1854, June 1854, August 1854, December 1854, January 1855, February 1855.
21. *Watchman and Reflector*, June 12, 1853; May 25, 1854, 82; Torbet, *Venture of Faith*, 127–28.
22. *Baptist Missionary Magazine*, December 1852, 470; Torbet, *Venture of Faith*, 127–28, 280, 373.
23. *Baptist Missionary Magazine*, July 1854, 233; *Watchman and Reflector*, July 6, 1854, 106.
24. *Baptist Missionary Magazine*, November 1853, 452; Torbet, *Venture of Faith*, 128–33.
25. *Baptist Missionary Magazine*, July 1854, 238. See also the October 1853, November 1853, December 1853, and January 1854 issues of *Baptist Missionary Magazine*; *Watchman and Reflector*, May 25, 1854, 82.

26. *Baptist Missionary Magazine*, July 1854, 218-26.
27. *Baptist Missionary Magazine*, July 1854, 221. R. Pierce Beaver, ed., *To Advance the Gospel: Selections from the Writings of Rufus Anderson* (Grand Rapids, Mich.: Eerdmans, 1967). See also Charles Forman, "A History of Foreign Mission Theory," in R. Pierce Beaver, ed., *American Missions in Bicentennial Perspective* (South Pasadena, Calif.: William Carey Library, 1976); William R. Hutchison, *Errand to the World: American Protestant Thought and Foreign Missions* (Chicago: University of Chicago Press, 1987); Paul William Harris, *Nothing but Christ: Rufus Anderson and the Ideology of Protestant Foreign Missions* (New York: Oxford University Press, 1999); Dana L. Robert, *American Women in Mission: A Social History of Their Thought and Practice* (Macon, Ga.: Mercer University Press, 1996), 116-23.
28. Wayland and Wayland, *A Memoir*, 327.
29. C. Peter Williams, *The Ideal of the Self-Governing Church: A Study in Victorian Missionary Strategy* (Leiden: Brill, 1990); Lamin Sanneh, *West African Christianity: The Religious Impact* (Maryknoll, N.Y.: Orbis, 1983), 60-64, 158-59, 168-73; Beaver, *To Advance the Gospel*, 98; Harris, *Nothing but Christ*, 56, 63-72; Hutchison, *Errand to the World*, 69-90; *Baptist Missionary Magazine*, June 1843, 125-26.
30. Quoted in Hennie Pretorius and Lizo Jafta, "'A Branch Springs Out': African Initiated Churches," in Richard Elphick and Rodney Davenport, eds., *Christianity in South Africa: A Political, Social and Cultural History* (Berkeley: University of California Press, 1997), 212. See also Everett N. Hunt Jr., "John Livingstone Nevius, 1829-1893: Pioneer of the Three-Self Principles in Asia," in Gerald H. Anderson et al., eds., *Mission Legacies: Biographical Studies of the Modern Missionary Movement* (Maryknoll, N.Y.: Orbis, 1994), 190-96; Wilbert R. Shenk, "The Origins and Evolution of the Three-Selfs in Relation to China," *International Bulletin of Missionary Research* 14 (January 1990): 29-30; Wade Crawford Barclay, *History of Methodist Missions, Part Two: The Methodist Episcopal Church, 1845-1939, Volume Three: Widening Horizons, 1845-95* (New York: Board of Missions of the Methodist Church, 1957), 160-61, 535-37; Jonathan D. Spence, *The Search for Modern China*, 2nd ed. (New York: Norton), 508; Janet Hodgson, "A Battle for Sacred Power: Christian Beginnings among the Xhosa," in Richard Elphick and Rodney Davenport, eds., *Christianity in South Africa: A Political, Social, and Cultural History* (Berkeley: University of California Press, 1997), 87. For a critique from an African perspective of some of the dynamics of this policy, see Isaac M. T. Mwase, "Shall They Till with Their Own Hoes? Baptists in Zimbabwe and New Patterns of Independence, 1950-2000," in Lamin Sanneh and Joel A. Carpenter, eds., *The Changing Face of Christianity: Africa, the West, and the World* (Oxford: Oxford University Press, 2005), 63-79.
31. *Watchman and Reflector*, June 2, 1853, 86; May 25, 1854, 81-82; *Baptist Missionary Magazine*, July 1853, 220.
32. *Baptist Missionary Magazine*, July 1854, 241; *Watchman and Reflector*, May 25, 1854, 82.
33. Calista V. Luther, *The Vintons and the Karens: Memorials of Rev. Justus H. Vinton and Calista H. Vinton* (Boston: Corthell, 1880), 123; *Watchman and Reflector*, May 25, 1854, 82-83; Torbet, *Venture of Faith*, 135.
34. *Baptist Missionary Magazine*, May 1855, 130-31, 151-59, 164; July 1856, 195-211, 239-40; August 1856, 331-34; Torbet, *Venture of Faith*, 134-39.
35. Mrs A. M. French, *Slavery in South Carolina and the Ex-Slaves: or, the Port Royal Mission* (1862; reprint New York: Negro Universities Press, 1969), 133-34, 214-15. The spelling and dialect of these African Americans, which were recorded by white observers, have been standardized for this account, although the grammar has remained intact. Daniel W. Stowell, *Rebuilding Zion: The Religious Reconstruction of the South, 1863-1877* (New York: Oxford University Press, 1988), 70; Vincent Harding, *There Is a River: The Black Struggle for Freedom in America* (San Diego: Harcourt Brace, 1981), 219-35; Willie Lee Rose, *Rehearsal for Reconstruction: The Port Royal Experiment* (London: Oxford University Press, 1964).
36. Rose, *Rehearsal for Reconstruction*; Leon F. Litwack, *Been in the Storm So Long: The Aftermath of Slavery* (New York: Vintage, 1980), 68-69; Eric Foner, *Reconstruction: America's Unfinished Revolution, 1863-1877* (New York: Harper & Row, 1988), 50-54.

37. Rose, *Rehearsal for Reconstruction*, 97–100; Albert J. Raboteau, *Slave Religion: The "Invisible Institution" in the Antebellum South* (Oxford: Oxford University Press, 1978); Mechal Sobel, *Trabelin' On: The Slave Journey in Afro-Baptist Faith* (Princeton, N.J.: Princeton University Press, 1988).
38. *Third Series of Extracts from Letters Received by the Educational Commission for Freedmen, from Teachers and Superintendents at Port Royal and Its Vicinity*, printed by order of the General Committee, Boston, June 17, 1863.
39. French, *Slavery in South Carolina*, 260; Rupert Sargent, ed., *Letters and Diary of Laura M. Towne: Written from the Sea Islands of South Carolina, 1862–1884* (1912; reprint New York: Negro Universities Press, 1969), 32.
40. Rose, *Rehearsal for Reconstruction*, 64–68, 177, 240. See also Erskine Clarke, *Dwelling Place: A Plantation Epic* (New Haven, Conn., and London: Yale University Press, 2007).
41. French, *Slavery in South Carolina*, 177; Rose, *Rehearsal for Reconstruction*, 64–67, 84–86.
42. Thirty of the fifty ordained ministers appointed by the ABHMS by 1867 were black. Peck reported that he instructed African-American ministers as part of his work in South Carolina, so it is likely that Wilkins was African-American. *Home Evangelist*, July 1863, 26; *Macedonian and Home Mission Record*, July 1867, 26; American Baptist Home Mission Society, *Baptist Home Missions in North America; Including a Full Report of the Proceedings and Addresses of the Jubilee Meeting, and a Historical Sketch of the American Baptist Home Mission Society, Historical Tables, etc., 1832–1882* (New York: Baptist Home Mission Rooms, 1883), 405, 408; French, *Slavery in South Carolina*, 30–33; Rose, *Rehearsal for Reconstruction*, 88; Heather Andrea Williams, *Self-Taught: African American Education in Slavery and Freedom* (Chapel Hill: University of North Carolina Press, 2005), 35.
43. Rose, *Rehearsal for Reconstruction*, 73, 75; Robert C. Morris, *Reading, 'Riting, and Reconstruction: The Education of the Freedmen in the South, 1861–1870* (Chicago: University of Chicago Press, 1981), 61; Joe M. Richardson, *Christian Reconstruction: The American Missionary Association and Southern Blacks, 1861–1890* (Athens: University of Georgia Press, 1986), 74.
44. Quoted in Rose, *Rehearsal for Reconstruction*, 71, 75, 220, 223.
45. *Home Evangelist*, March 1863, 10; July 1863, 26; May 1865, 18; January 1866, 2; *National Baptist*, January 12, 1865, 1.
46. *Macedonian and Home Mission Record*, May 1870, 17; June 1870, 22; July 1867, 26, 28; October 1869, 37; December 1869, 46; ABHMS, *Baptist Home Missions*, 405.
47. *Home Evangelist*, July 1863, 26; *Macedonian and Home Mission Record*, July 1867, 26; ABHMS, *Baptist Home Missions*, 405, 408.
48. *Macedonian and Home Mission Record*, July 1868, 28; July 1870, 26; see also July 1863, 26; January 1866, 1; July 1868, 25–26.
49. *Home Evangelist*, July 1863, 26; May 1865, 18; September 1865, 34; January 1866, 2; March 1866, 1; *Macedonian and Home Mission Record*, March 1867, 9; July 1867, 26, 28; December 1867, 50; March 1868, 5; July 1868, 25, 27, 28; October 1868, 41; June 1869, 21; July 1869, 25, 26; September 1869, 34; October 1869, 37–38; November 1869, 42; December 1869, 46; April 1870, 14; May 1879, 17; June 1870, 22; July 1870, 25–26; August 1870, 29; January 1871, 4; February 1871, 8; March 1871, 12; April 1871, 15; July 1871, 28; October 1871, 39; January 1872, 4; April 1872, 15; February 1872, 7; November 1872, 44; *National Baptist*, February 15, 1872.
50. ABHMS, *Baptist Home Missions*, 406. The larger policy decisions are described on pp. 402–9.
51. *Macedonian and Record*, July 1868, 25; *Home Mission Monthly*, December 1881, 254. See also *Home Evangelist*, March 1863, 10; *Macedonian and Home Mission Record*, July 1870, 26; December 1869, 46; December 1867, 50.
52. *Baptist Missionary Magazine*, February 1867, 39. See also *Macedonian and Home Mission Record*, April 1871, 65.
53. *Home Mission Monthly*, August 1881, 170; January 1879, 100; June 1879, 190; August 1880, 149; *Home Evangelist*, July 1863, 26; March 1866, 9; *Macedonian and Home Mission Record*, July 1868, 27; February 1872, 7; *National Baptist*, January 12, 1865, 1.
54. *Home Mission Monthly*, August 1880, 148–49.

55. Robert Wiebe, *The Search for Order, 1877–1920* (New York: Hill & Wang, 1967); Thomas P. Hughes, *American Genesis: A Century of Invention and Technological Enthusiasm, 1870–1970* (New York: Penguin, 1989); Michael Adas, *Dominance by Design: Technological Imperatives and America's Civilizing Mission* (Cambridge, Mass.: Harvard University Press, 2006).
56. See ABHMS, *Baptist Home Missions*, 547–49. ABMU officers are found in the annual reports of the *Baptist Missionary Magazine*.
57. *Baptist Missionary Magazine*, August 1867, 235.
58. Ibid., 240–41, 323–28; see also February 1863, 56–57.
59. *Macedonian and Home Mission Record*, July 1867, 28; see also October 1869, 37; June 1870, 22; July 1870, 25; *Home Evangelist*, May 1865, 18; January 1866, 2; March 1866, 1.
60. *Macedonian and Home Mission Record*, July 1867, 28.
61. R. Pierce Beaver, *American Protestant Women in World Mission: History of the First Feminist Movement in North America* (Grand Rapids, Mich.: Eerdmans, 1968), 91–103; Patricia R. Hill, *The World Their Household: The American Woman's Foreign Mission Movement and Cultural Transformation, 1870–1920* (Ann Arbor: University of Michigan Press, 1985), 47–53; Robert, *American Women in Mission*, 125–29.
62. *Helping Hand*, June 1882, 45; *Heathen Woman's Friend*, August 1869, 20; Hill, *The World Their Household*; Robert, *American Women in Mission*, 125–49; Susan Hill Lindley, *"You Have Stept Out of Your Place": A History of Women and Religion in America* (Louisville, Ky.: John Knox, 1996), 83–87.
63. Nancy F. Cott, *The Bonds of Womanhood: "Women's Sphere" in New England, 1780–1835* (New Haven, Conn., and London: Yale University Press, 1977), 7–8, 128, 132; Robert, *American Women in Mission*.
64. Wayland, *The Apostolic Ministry*, 49–56.
65. Robert, *American Women in Mission*, 81–114; Colleen McDannell, *The Christian Home in Victorian America, 1840–1900* (Bloomington: Indiana University Press, 1986).
66. *Baptist Missionary Magazine*, August 1867, 323–28, 235; *Macedonian and Home Mission Record*, March 1867, 9; see also *Home Mission Monthly*, December 1878, 90.
67. *Western Recorder*, January 28, 1886, 4.
68. Dana L. Robert, "Adoniram Judson Gordon, 1836–1895: Educator, Preacher, and Promoter of Missions," in Gerald H. Anderson et al., eds., *Missionary Legacies: Biographical Studies of Leaders of the Modern Missionary Movement* (Maryknoll, N.Y.: Orbis, 1994), 18–26.
69. *Missionary Review of the World*, August 1893, 584–89; December 1893, 881–88; *Baptist Missionary Magazine*, November 1895, 543–45.
70. *Baptist Missionary Magazine*, May 1868, 158; June 1870, 166–67; July 1879, 228; July 1871, 227–28; October 1871, 371–73; August 1873, 312; February 1874, 52–53; July 1875, 225–26; August 1875, 305; October 1875, 439; March 1876, 74–75; May 1878, 140–41; March 1885, 72–73; *Helping Hand*, June 1872, 217–18; July 1872, 315.
71. *Baptist Missionary Magazine*, December 1894, 910–14.
72. For examples of missionary work as institution and civilization building, see *Baptist Missionary Magazine*, July 1869, 259–60; October 1870, 371; May 1871, 138–39; July 1871, 194; September 1874, 323–26; August 1875, 395–99; January 1877, 3; June 1880, 147–49; November 1893, 490–91; January 1894, 1.
73. *Baptist Missionary Magazine*, July 1866, 222, 223.
74. Quoted in Sandy Dwayne Martin, "The American Baptist Home Mission Society and Black Higher Education in the South, 1865–1900," in Donald G. Nieman, ed., *African Americans and Education in the South* (New York: Garland, 1994), 234, 239. See also ABHMS, *Baptist Home Missions*, 549; *Macedonian and Home Mission Record*, July 1867, 28; May 1870, 17; Charles H. Corey, *A History of the Richmond Theological Seminary, with Reminiscences of Thirty Years' Work among the Colored People of the South* (Richmond, Va.: Randolph, 1895), 55–57, 64.
75. *Macedonian and Home Mission Record*, February 1872, 7. See also *Baptist Missionary Magazine*, October 1874, 367–68.
76. *Macedonian and Home Mission Record*, July 1868, 25; James Melvin Washington, *Frustrated Fellowship: The Black Baptist Quest for Social Power* (Macon, Ga.: Mercer University Press, 1986), 70–81, 95–105.

77. *Baptist Missionary Magazine*, July 1866, 251–53; October 1866, 393, August 1867, 258–63; November 1870, 412; Torbet, *Venture of Faith*, 128, 136, 138, 214–15, 239–40; H. L. Van Meter to ABMU, December 17, 1852, Official Correspondence File, Archived Collections of the Board of International Ministries, American Baptist Historical Society, Valley Forge, Pa. (Hereafter, correspondence will be cited as BIM Correspondence File.)
78. *Baptist Missionary Magazine*, August 1867, 262; J. L. Douglass to J. G. Warren, May 11, 1866, and January 9, 1867, BIM Correspondence File; "Abbott, Elisha Litchfield," ABMU Missionary Register, Archived Collections of the Board of International Ministries, American Baptist Historical Society, Valley Forge, Pa.; *Baptist Missionary Magazine*, July 1866, 251–53; October 1866, 393; August 1867, 258–63.
79. John F. Cady, *A History of Modern Burma* (Ithaca, N.Y.: Cornell University Press, 1958), 73, 88, 137–41.
80. *Baptist Missionary Magazine*, May 1855, 172–73; October 1866, 393; August 1867, 258–62. For examples of Baptist missionary discussions of self-support, see *Baptist Missionary Magazine*, July 1869, 232; July 1870, 221; September 1870, 342–43; November 1870, 411–15; May 1871, 138; March 1874, 68–72; September 1875, 398–99; January 1876, 10–12; January 1877, 6–9; C. H. Carpenter, *Self-Support, Illustrated in the History of the Bassein Karen Mission from 1840–1880* (Boston: Rand, Avery, 1883).
81. *Baptist Missionary Magazine*, July 1866, 252; October 1866, 393; Nieman, *African Americans and Education*, vii–viii; James M. McPherson, *The Abolitionist Legacy: From Reconstruction to the NAACP* (Princeton, N.J.: Princeton University Press, 1995), 143–48.
82. *Baptist Missionary Magazine*, July 1866, 225; July 1873, 223–24.
83. Darlene Clark Hine, "The Anatomy of Failure: Medical Education Reform and the Leonard Medical School of Shaw University, 1882–1920," in Nieman, *African Americans and Education*, 130–43; James McPherson, "White Liberals and Black Power in Negro Education, 1865–1915," in Nieman, *African Americans and Education*, 250; Adolph H. Grundman, "Northern Baptists and the Founding of Virginia Union University: The Perils of Paternalism," *Journal of Negro History* 63 (January 1978): 26–41.
84. L. P. Brockett, *The Story of the Karen Mission in Bassein, 1838–1890: or, the Progress and Education of a People from a Degraded Heathenism to a Refined Christian Civilization* (Philadelphia: American Baptist Publication Society, 1891).
85. *Home Evangelist*, January 1866, 2; *Macedonian and Home Mission Record*, February 1869, 6; November 1869, 41; June 1870, 22; October 1871, 39.
86. *Baptist Missionary Magazine*, April 1873, 97.
87. Edward J. Blum, *Reforging the White Republic: Race, Religion and American Nationalism, 1865–1898* (Baton Rouge: Louisiana State University Press, 1995).
88. In 1964, Willie Lee Rose pointed out that "nearly all that would be done in the future by the North for Negro education would come through the American Missionary Association and other denominational groups." In 1975, James McPherson argued that "most histories of black education have slighted the role of the mission societies." Some historians in the 1980s and 1990s recognized these points, while others ignored McPherson and the evangelical sources, continuing to argue either that all northern support for black education ended after Reconstruction or else that all northerners lost faith in the ability of blacks to achieve an education more advanced than industrial education. None has considered the role that the foreign-missionary movement might have played in these movements. Rose, *Rehearsal for Reconstruction*, 387–88; McPherson, *The Abolitionist Legacy*, 145. For examples of historians who, to various degrees, have paid attention to evangelical agencies, see Richardson, *Christian Reconstruction*; Morris, *Reading, 'Riting and Reconstruction*. For examples of works that have not carefully considered sources that demonstrate long-term white evangelical support for black higher education and black capabilities, see Ronald E. Butchart, *Northern Schools, Southern Blacks and Reconstruction: Freedmen's Education, 1862–1875* (Westport, Conn.: Greenwood, 1980), especially 15, 49, 205; Roy E. Finkenbine, "'Our Little Circle': Benevolent Reformers, the Slater Fund, and the Argument for Black Industrial Education, 1882–1908," in Nieman, *African Americans and Education*, 70–86; J. M. Stephen Peeps, "Northern Philanthropy and the Emergence of Black Higher

Education—Do-Gooders, Compromisers, or Co-conspirators?" in Nieman, *African Americans and Education*, 293–311; Foner, *Reconstruction*, 96–102, 142–48, 367–69, 524–28, and 605–6.
89. ABHMS, *Baptist Home Missions*, 77–81; *Home Mission Monthly*, July 1892, 250–51.
90. Howard University would be the institutional exception, since it was created by an act of the federal government. But even here, missionary-minded evangelicals proved to be the driving force behind the congressional action that produced Howard. Atlanta University and Leland University, technically independent of any missionary agency, still had strong ties to evangelical agencies. See McPherson, *The Abolitionist Legacy*, 143–54 and app. B; Richardson, *Christian Reconstruction*, 75–78, 123, 146–51, 189–91.
91. Butchart, *Northern Schools, Southern Blacks*, 205.
92. Foner, *Reconstruction*; Blum, *Reforging the White Republic*.
93. Carol A. Horton, *Race and the Making of American Liberalism* (Oxford: Oxford University Press, 2005), 15–35; McPherson, *The Abolitionist Legacy*.
94. McPherson, *The Abolitionist Legacy*, 144–45.
95. *Home Mission Monthly*, June 1889, 145; November 1888, 301; James D. Anderson, *The Education of Blacks in the South, 1860–1935* (Chapel Hill: University of North Carolina Press, 1988), 132–37, 252–55.
96. *Home Mission Monthly*, November 1888, 279; see also, July 1886, 166.
97. *Home Mission Monthly*, November 1888, 304; August 1896, 277; *Baptist Missionary Magazine*, August 1848, 308.
98. W. E. B. DuBois, "The Talented Tenth," in *The Negro Problem* (Miami: Mnemosyne, 1969, reprint of 1903 ed.), 75.
99. *Home Mission Monthly*, March 1884, 61; June 1889, 144–45; American Baptist Home Mission Society, *Baptist Home Missions in North America* (New York: Baptist Home Mission Rooms, 1883), 72, 93.

Chapter 4

1. *Wesleyan Methodist Magazine*, October 1862, 934–35; October 1866, 928–29; William Taylor, *Christian Adventures in South Africa* (New York: Phillips & Hunt, 1880), 117; Janet Hodgson, "A Battle for Sacred Power: Christian Beginnings among the Xhosa," in Richard Elphick and Rodney Davenport, eds., *Christianity in South Africa: A Political, Social, and Cultural History* (Berkeley: University of California Press, 1997), 68–88.
2. J. B. Peires, *The House of Phalo: A History of the Xhosa People in the Days of Their Independence* (Berkeley: University of California Press, 1982), 4, 64–69, 74–76; J. B. Peires, *The Dead Will Arise: Nongqawuse and the Great Xhosa Cattle Killing Movement of 1856-7* (Johannesburg: Ravan, 1989) 104–5, 125–28; Janet Hodgson, *The God of the Xhosa* (Cape Town: Oxford University Press, 1982), 32–37; John S. Mbiti, *African Religions and Philosophy* (Garden City, N.Y.: Anchor, 1970); E. Bolaji Idowu, *African Traditional Religion, A Definition* (Maryknoll, N.Y.: Orbis, 1973).
3. Quoted in Peires, *The Dead Will Arise*, 6.
4. Ibid., 12–37.
5. Ibid., 241–45, 319–21.
6. Quoted in ibid., 247, 263.
7. Historians have debated the origins and original composition of the Mfengu. See Carolyn Hamilton, ed., *The Mfecane Aftermath: Reconstructive Debates in Southern African History* (Johannesburg: Witwatersrand University Press, 1995); Peires, *The Dead Will Arise*, 55–56.
8. Peires, *The Dead Will Arise*, 249.
9. Peires, *The House of Phalo*, 64–74; Peires, *The Dead Will Arise*, 123; Hodgson, *The God of the Xhosa*, 8–11; Hodgson, "A Battle for Sacred Power," 69–73; Taylor, *Christian Adventures*, 274–77.
10. Hodgson, "A Battle for Sacred Power"; Peires, *The Dead Will Arise*, 263–64.
11. Peires, *The Dead Will Arise*; Wallace G. Mills, "The Taylor Revival of 1866 and the Roots of African Nationalism in the Cape Colony," *Journal of Religion in Africa* 8 (1976): 105–22;

Wallace G. Mills, "The Role of African Clergy in the Reorientation of Xhosa Society to the Plural Society in the Cape Colony, 1850–1915," PhD dissertation, University of California, Los Angeles, 1975; *Wesleyan Methodist Magazine,* June 1866, 557.
12. *Wesleyan Methodist Magazine,* October 1866, 928–29; Taylor, *Christian Adventures,* 96–97.
13. *Wesleyan Methodist Magazine,* October 1866, 928–29. Taylor, *Christian Adventures,* 96–97, 103–4, 118–26, 128–29, 135.
14. Peires, *The House of Phalo*; Peires, *The Dead Will Arise*; Hodgson, *The God of the Xhosa.*
15. Craig M. Gay, *The Way of the (Modern) World: Or Why It Is Tempting to Live as if God Doesn't Exist* (Grand Rapids, Mich.: Eerdmans, 1998).
16. Taylor, *Christian Adventures,* 135, 234–35.
17. And he wrote books about it all. At forty-eight chapters and 770 pages, his magnum opus, *Story of My Life,* reads like a very long, though rather entertaining, sermon illustration on global evangelism. William Taylor, *Story of My Life: An Account of What I Have Thought and Said and Done in My Ministry of More than Fifty-Three Years in Christian Lands and among the Heathen* (New York: Eaton & Mains, 1895); William Taylor, *Seven Years' Street Preaching in San Francisco, California: Embracing Incidents, Triumphant Death Scenes, etc.* (New York: Carleton & Porter, 1857); William Taylor, *California Life Illustrated, by William Taylor of the California Conference* (New York: Carleton & Porter, 1858).
18. Taylor, *Story of My Life.*
19. Ibid., 213; Taylor, *Seven Years' Street Preaching;* David Bundy, "Bishop William Taylor and Methodist Mission: A Study in Nineteenth Century Social History," *Methodist History* 27 (July 1989): 197–210.
20. Taylor, *Story of My Life,* 59–64, 87, 102; John H. Wigger, *Taking Heaven by Storm: Methodism and the Rise of Popular Christianity in America* (New York: Oxford University Press, 1998), 56–57; Donald E. Byrne Jr., *No Foot of Land: Folklore of American Methodist Itinerants* (Metuchen, N.J.: Scarecrow, 1975).
21. Taylor, *Story of My Life;* Wigger, *Taking Heaven by Storm.*
22. Mark A. Noll, *America's God: From Jonathan Edwards to Abraham Lincoln* (New York: Oxford University Press, 2002), 236; Charles E. Hambrick-Stowe, *Charles G. Finney and the Spirit of American Evangelicalism* (Grand Rapids, Mich.: Eerdmans, 1996), 155–59.
23. Taylor, *Christian Adventures,* 38.
24. Ibid., 40–44.
25. Ibid., 54–55, 59.
26. Ibid., 46–47, 84, 94–95.
27. Ibid., 118.
28. Hodgson, "A Battle for Sacred Power," 70.
29. Taylor, *Christian Adventures,* 119–21, 124.
30. Ibid., 124–25; *Wesleyan Methodist Magazine,* December 1861, 1131; Hodgson, "A Battle for Sacred Power," 76.
31. Ann Taves, *Fits, Trances, and Visions: Experiencing Religion and Explaining Experience from Wesley to James* (Princeton, N.J.: Princeton University Press, 1999); George M. Marsden, *Jonathan Edwards: A Life* (New Haven, Conn., and London: Yale University Press, 2003); Thomas S. Kidd, *The Great Awakening: The Roots of Evangelical Christianity in Colonial America* (New Haven, Conn., and London: Yale University Press, 2007).
32. Quoted in George W. Stocking Jr., *Victorian Anthropology* (New York: Free Press, 1987), 153; Bruce Dain, *A Hideous Monster of the Mind: American Race Theory in the Early Republic* (Cambridge, Mass.: Harvard University Press, 2002), 2; George M. Frederickson, *The Black Image in the White Mind: The Debate on Afro-American Character and Destiny, 1817–1914* (New York: Harper & Row, 1971), 99–101.
33. A carefully planned, restrained style of evangelism characterized middle-class British Methodism. D. W. Bebbington, *Evangelicalism in Modern Britain: A History from the 1730s to the 1980s* (London: Unwin Hyman, 1989), 116–17; Taylor, *Christian Adventures,* 124.
34. *Wesleyan Methodist Magazine,* October 1866, 928–29; Taylor, *Christian Adventures,* 97, 125.
35. Taylor, *Story of My Life,* 47–48.
36. Taylor, *Christian Adventures,* 124–25.

37. *Wesleyan Methodist Magazine,* October 1866, 928.
38. *Wesleyan Methodist Magazine,* November 1866, 1036; Taylor, *Christian Adventures,* 157, 162, 167, 200, 218, 227–28, 240, 242, 295, 359, 470, 475.
39. Taylor, *Christian Adventures,* 248, 512.
40. Ibid., 478.
41. Ibid., 479–80; Taylor, *Story of My Life,* 482–84.
42. Stocking, *Victorian Anthropology,* 188–91; Paul A. Carter, *The Spiritual Crisis of the Gilded Age* (DeKalb: Northern Illinois University Press, 1971); James Turner, *Without God, Without Creed: The Origins of Unbelief in America* (Baltimore: Johns Hopkins University Press, 1985).
43. Stocking, *Victorian Anthropology*; Jean Comaroff and John Comaroff, *Of Revelation and Revolution: Christianity, Colonialism, and Consciousness in South Africa* (Chicago: University of Chicago Press, 1991).
44. While the term *kaffir* became a very insulting word in South Africa, whites and blacks alike in the 1860s often used it in reference to the Xhosa people. Some of these may not have intended to attach derogatory meanings to the term, although it certainly carried baggage related to race and civilization. A bilingual black in 1866 with extensive interactions with whites probably would have sensed when a white consciously or unconsciously loaded the word with patronizing or derogatory meaning. Peires, *The Dead Will Rise,* xii.
45. Taylor, *Christian Adventures,* 471–75.
46. James T. Campbell, *Songs of Zion: The African Methodist Episcopal Church in the United States and South Africa* (New York: Oxford University Press, 1995), 107–9; Mills, "The Role of African Clergy," 24–27.
47. Hodgson, "A Battle for Sacred Power," 75–77.
48. Quoted in Peires, *The Dead Will Arise,* 290–91.
49. *Wesleyan Methodist Magazine,* October 1866, 927–28; November 1866, 1035–36; June 1867, 558; Taylor, *Christian Adventures,* viii, 310, 335, 450; Mills, "The Role of African Clergy," 24–27; Mills, "The Taylor Revival," 108–9.
50. *Wesleyan Methodist Magazine,* June 1866, 557–58; June 1867, 558–59; Taylor, *Christian Adventures,* 338–39.
51. Taylor, *Christian Adventures,* 310; Lamplough quoted in Mills, "The Role of African Clergy," 26–27; Mills, "The Taylor Revival," 110.
52. Campbell, *Songs of Zion,* 104–25; Mills, "The Role of African Clergy," 16–42.
53. Taylor, *Christian Adventures,* 450; Taylor, *Story of My Life,* 247–49; Taylor, *Seven Years' Street Preaching,* 220; Mills, "The Taylor Revival," 108–9; Wigger, *Taking Heaven by Storm*; Nathan Hatch, *The Democratization of American Christianity* (New Haven, Conn.: Yale University Press, 1989).
54. Taylor, *Christian Adventures,* 227, 230, 231, 249.
55. Ibid., 510; Wigger, *Taking Heaven by Storm*; Hatch, *The Democratization*.
56. In a feature that might be unique among nineteenth-century European or American travelers to Africa, Taylor produced a 557-page description of South Africa while using the term *civilize* or *civilization* a total of only seven times, five of which came while he was explaining the theories put forth by the British missionaries. The term *civilize* or *civilization* doesn't appear anywhere in the 416 pages of Taylor's subsequent work about India. Taylor, *Christian Adventures,* 215, 254, 351, 507–9, 514; William Taylor, *Four Years' Campaign in India* (New York: Phillips & Hunt, n.d.).
57. Taylor, *Christian Adventures,* 110, 193–95, 255, 262, 277–78, 330–32, 336, 47.5.
58. Ibid., 505–19. Scholars today are often, in similar ways, critical of these mission stations in South Africa. Campbell, *Songs of Zion,* 106; Hodgson, "A Battle for Sacred Power," 76–77.
59. Taylor, *Christian Adventures,* 513–14; Wigger, *Taking Heaven by Storm.*
60. Taylor, *Christian Adventures,* 282–83.
61. Ibid., 391; Lamin Sanneh, *Translating the Message: The Missionary Impact on Culture* (Maryknoll, N.Y.: Orbis, 1999), 157–72.
62. Taylor, *Christian Adventures,* 391, 418; see also 391–420.
63. *Wesleyan Methodist Magazine,* October 1866, 928; Taylor, *Christian Adventures,* 394.

64. Andrew F. Walls, *The Missionary Movement in Christian History: Studies in the Transmission of Faith* (Maryknoll, N.Y.: Orbis, 1996), xiii.
65. Taylor, *Christian Adventures*, 82, 165, 170, 229, 264, 305, 339, 505–19.
66. Hodgson, "A Battle for Sacred Power"; Campbell, *Songs of Zion*.
67. Campbell, *Songs of Zion*, 107; Jane M. Sales, *The Planting of Churches in South Africa* (Grand Rapids, Mich.: Eerdmans, 1971), 129.
68. Campbell, *Songs of Zion*; Mills, "The Role of African Clergy"; Mills, "The Taylor Revival."
69. Taylor, *Four Years' Campaign*, 25; Taylor, *Christian Adventures*, 390–423, 509–10; William Taylor, *Ten Years of Self-Supporting Missions in India* (New York: Phillips & Hunt, 1882), 71, 101, 234; Taylor, *Story of My Life*, 490.
70. Taylor, *Christian Adventures*, 126, 450–51; Taylor, *Story of My Life*, 494–95.

Chapter 5

1. *Christian Advocate* (New York), July 10, 1873, 217; William Taylor, *Four Years' Campaign in India* (New York: Phillips & Hunt, n.d.), 3.
2. Wade Crawford Barclay, *The History of Methodist Missions: The Methodist Episcopal Church: Widening Horizons, 1845–95* Vol. 3 (New York: Board of Missions of the Methodist Church, 1957), 532–34; Taylor, *Four Years' Campaign;* William Taylor, *Ten Years of Self-Supporting Missions in India* (New York: Phillips & Hunt, 1882).
3. Taylor, *Four Years' Campaign*, 27–28; Barclay, *The History*, Vol. 3, 512–13.
4. Taylor, *Four Years' Campaign*, 27–28, 40–41.
5. Ibid., 20–23.
6. Ibid., 100–101. Like all of his favorite anecdotes, Taylor repeated this one in *Story of My Life*, 546. For differences between Methodists and Calvinists on conceptions of revivals, see Kathryn Long, *The Revival of 1857–8: Interpreting an American Religious Awakening* (New York: Oxford University Press, 1998).
7. Taylor, *Four Years' Campaign*, 76, 100–103, 134, 140–41.
8. Ibid., 106, 112, 113. Taylor demonstrated a feature of early American Methodism that, in the words of John Wigger, gave lay members "a remarkable degree of input in shaping the character of the church." John H. Wigger, *Taking Heaven by Storm: Methodism and the Rise of Popular Christianity in America* (New York: Oxford University Press, 1998), 80; see also 80–103.
9. *Christian Advocate* (New York), May 9, 1872, 151; Taylor, *Four Years' Campaign*, 150–67; Barclay, *The History*, Vol. 3, 514–20.
10. Taylor, *Ten Years of Self-Supporting Missions*, 383; *Zion's Herald*, March 28, 1872, 154; April 11, 1872, 178.
11. See *Christian Advocate* (New York), August 18, 1870, 257; August 25, 1870, 268; December 15, 1870, 393; May 4, 1871, 140; May 11, 1871, 148; August 17, 1871, 260; August 31, 1871, 274; April 25, 1872, 130; Barclay, *The History*, Vol. 3, 166–70, 877–85; Sylvia Jacobs, "Francis Burns, First Missionary Bishop of the Methodist Episcopal Church, North," in David W. Wills and Richard Newman, eds., *Black Apostles at Home and Abroad: Afro-Americans and the Christian Mission from the Revolution to Reconstruction* (Boston: G. K. Hall, 1982), 255–64.
12. Taylor, *Four Years' Campaign*, 151, 161–67; *Christian Advocate* (New York), May 9, 1872, 151; Barclay, *The History*, Vol. 3, 514–20.
13. *Christian Advocate* (New York), May 15, 1873, 153. Taylor published his complete theory in a separate book, William Taylor, *Pauline Methods of Missionary Work* (Philadelphia: National Publishing Association for the Promotion of Holiness, 1879). See also Taylor, *Ten-Years*, 357; William Taylor, *Our South American Cousins* (New York: Nelson and Phillips, 1879), 129.
14. *Christian Advocate* (New York), November 14, 1872, 364; see also April 25, 1872, 130; May 2, 1872, 138; May 9, 1872, 151; December 19, 1872, 401; *Advocate of Christian Holiness*, April 1872, 194; June 1872, 235; November 1872, 116.
15. Wigger, *Taking Heaven by Storm*; Nathan O. Hatch, *The Democratization of American Christianity* (New Haven, Conn.: Yale University Press, 1989); Catherine A. Brekus, *Strangers*

and *Pilgrims: Female Preaching in America, 1740–1845* (Chapel Hill: University of North Carolina Press, 1998).

16. Wigger, *Taking Heaven by Storm*; Russell E. Richey, "Organizing for Missions: A Methodist Case Study," in Daniel H. Bays and Grant Wacker, eds., *The Foreign Missionary Enterprise at Home: Explorations in North American Cultural History* (Tuscaloosa: University of Alabama Press, 2003), 75–93.

17. Edwin Scott Gaustad, *Historical Atlas of Religion in America* (New York: Harper & Row, 1962), 76–81; Wigger, *Taking Heaven by Storm*, 3–7; Hatch, *The Democratization*, 3–4; Barclay, *The History*, Vol. 3, 1–2.

18. Nathan O. Hatch, "The Puzzle of American Methodism," *Church History* 63 (June 1994): 181.

19. Walter W. Benjamin, "The Methodist Episcopal Church in the Postwar Era," in Emory Stevens Bucke, ed., *The History of American Methodism*, Vol. 2 (New York: Abingdon, 1964), 318–23; Wigger, *Taking Heaven by Storm*, 173–95; Richard Carwardine, "Methodist Ministers and the Second Party System," in Russell E. Richey and Kenneth E. Rowe, eds., *Rethinking Methodist History: A Bicentennial Historical Consultation* (Nashville, Tenn.: Kingswood, 1985), 134–47; Donald B. Marti, "Rich Methodists: The Rise and Consequences of Lay Philanthropy in the Mid-19th Century," in Richey and Rowe, *Rethinking Methodist History*; Brekus, *Strangers and Pilgrims*, 284-98. For an example of the Methodist debate over respectability and educated ministry, see *Christian Advocate* (New York), February 1, 1872, 33.

20. William McGuire King, "Denominational Modernization and Religious Identity: The Case of the Methodist Episcopal Church," *Methodist History* 20 (January 1982): 343–55; Robert Wiebe, *The Search for Order, 1877–1920* (New York: Hill & Wang, 1967); Thomas P. Hughes, *American Genesis: A Century of Invention and Technological Enthusiasm, 1870–1970* (New York: Penguin, 1989).

21. Quoted in King, "Denominational Modernization." See also Richey, "Organizing for Missions."

22. *Christian Advocate* (New York), July 25, 1872, 237; Taylor, *Four Years' Campaign*, 238; Grant Wacker, *Heaven Below: Early Pentecostals and American Culture* (Cambridge, Mass.: London: Harvard University Press, 2001), 130–33; William Lawrence Svelmoe, *A New Vision for Missions: William Cameron Townsend, the Wycliffe Bible Translators, and the Culture of Early Evangelical Faith Missions, 1896–1945* (Tuscaloosa: University of Alabama Press, 2008), 58–67.

23. Taylor, *Ten Years*, 384; Taylor, *Four Years' Campaign*, 141, 237–38, 240; Barclay, *The History*, Vol. 3, 517n.

24. *Christian Advocate* (New York), May 15, 1873, 153; June 5, 1873, 180; see also July 10, 1873, 217.

25. *Christian Advocate* (New York), June 5, 1873, 180; Taylor, *Four Years' Campaign*, 293; Barclay, *The History*, Vol. 3, 527–28. See also *Christian Advocate* (New York), July 17, 1873, 228; September 3, 1874, 284.

26. Quoted in Carol A. Horton, *Race and the Making of American Liberalism* (Oxford: Oxford University Press, 2005), 47; Edward J. Blum, *Reforging the White Republic: Race, Religion and American Nationalism, 1865–1898* (Baton Rouge: Louisiana State University Press, 2007).

27. Quoted in Eric Foner, *Reconstruction: America's Unfinished Revolution, 1863–1877* (New York: Harper & Row, 1988), 525–26; see also 512–34; James M. McPherson, *The Abolitionist Legacy: From Reconstruction to the NAACP* (Princeton, N.J.: Princeton University Press, 1975), 37–40; Horton, *Race*, 46–49.

28. Foner, *Reconstruction*; Blum, *Reforging the White Republic*.

29. Quoted in Ronald Takaki, *A Different Mirror: A History of Multicultural America* (Boston: Little, Brown, 1993), 205. Ronald Takaki, *Iron Cages: Race and Culture in 19th Century America* (New York: Oxford University Press, 1990), 175–88; Thomas J. Archdeacon, *Becoming American: An Ethnic History* (New York: Free Press, 1983), 146–49; Matthew Frye Jacobson, *Barbarian Virtues: The United States Encounters Foreign Peoples at Home and Abroad, 1876–1917* (New York: Hill & Wang, 2000), 73–80.

30. Quoted in Foner, *Reconstruction*, 340.
31. Quoted in George W. Stocking Jr., *Victorian Anthropology* (New York: Free Press, 1987), 163, 226; see also chaps. 5 and 6. Thomas F. Gossett, *Race: The History of an Idea in America* (Dallas: Southern Methodist University Press, 1963); George M. Frederickson, *The Black Image in the White Mind: The Debate on Afro-American Character and Destiny, 1817–1914* (Middletown, Conn.: Wesleyan University Press, 1971), 228–45.
32. Horton, *Race*, 22–25; Foner, *Reconstruction*, 553–56; McPherson, *The Abolitionist Legacy*, 13–52.
33. George M. Marsden, *The Soul of the American University: From Protestant Establishment to Established Nonbelief* (New York: Oxford University Press), 93.
34. Barclay, *The History*, Vol. 3, 481–82.
35. *Methodist Quarterly Review*, January 1869, 33–34, 38–40.
36. Stocking, *Victorian Anthropology*, 117–28, 205–8, 236–37; Barclay, *The History*, 481–82, 613, 644.
37. Stocking, *Victorian Anthropology*.
38. Taylor, *Four Years' Campaign*, 240; Taylor, *Ten Years*, 121–24, 226.
39. Taylor, *Four Years' Campaign*, 240; Taylor, *Ten Years*, 122–23; *Christian Advocate* (New York), May 9, 1872, 151.
40. Barclay, *The History*, Vol. 3, 532–34; Taylor, *Four Years' Campaign*, 328–31; *Advocate of Christian Holiness*, August 1877, 185.
41. Taylor, *Pauline Methods*, 46–47.
42. *Christian Advocate* (New York), August 14, 1873, 258; see also August 6, 1874, 249; Taylor, *Our South American Cousins*; Taylor, *Pauline Methods*.
43. Taylor, *Ten Years*, 355–57.
44. Quoted in Barclay, *The History*, Vol. 3, 810; and Taylor, *Ten Years*, 360; see also 357–58.
45. Barclay, *The History*, Vol. 3, 810–11; Taylor, *Ten Years*, 359.
46. *Christian Advocate* (New York), July 17, 1879, 456; see also July 17, 1873, 228.
47. *Christian Advocate* (New York), February 9, 1882, 84; March 9, 1882, 147–48.
48. Wade Crawford Barclay, *The History of Methodist Missions: Part One, Early American Methodism, 1769–1844*, Vol. 1 (New York: Board of Missions and Church Extension of the Methodist Church, 1949), 206; see also 100–101, 166, 205–6; William G. McLoughlin, *Cherokees and Missionaries, 1789–1839* (Norman: University of Oklahoma Press, 1995), 164–66.
49. *Christian Advocate* (New York), March 9, 1882, 148. See also Barclay, *The History*, Vol. 3, 226; Richey, "Organizing for Missions."
50. Chandra Mallampalli, *Christians and Public Life in Colonial South India, 1863–937: Contending with Marginality* (London and New York: RoutledgeCurzon, 2004).
51. Taylor, *Story of My Life*, 219–20; see also 69, 71, 78, 80, 220; Taylor, *Four Years' Campaign*, 159. Taylor described the actions of a man named Krishna Chowey as an example of how he believed a convert from Hinduism could negotiate these challenges. Taylor, *Four Years' Campaign*, 159–60, 192–95, 248–51.
52. Taylor, *Ten Years*, 222, 225–26, 230–31, 235, 429–30, 432.
53. Donald W. Dayton, *Theological Roots of Pentecostalism* (Grand Rapids, Mich.: Francis Asbury, 1987), 39–78; Melvin Easterday Dieter, *The Holiness Revival of the Nineteenth Century* (Lanham, Md.: Scarecrow, 1996); Vinson Synan, *The Holiness-Pentecostal Tradition: Charismatic Movements in the Twentieth Century* (Grand Rapids, Mich.: Eerdmans, 1997); Charles Edwin Jones, *Perfectionist Persuasion: The Holiness Movement and American Methodism, 1867–1936* (Metuchen, N.J.: Scarecrow, 1974); Charles Edward White, "The Beauty of Holiness: The Career and Influence of Phoebe Palmer," *Methodist History* 25 (January 1987): 67–75.
54. Donald W. Dayton, "From 'Christian Perfection' to the 'Baptism of the Holy Ghost,'" in Russell E. Richey, Kenneth E. Rowe, Jean Miller Schmidt, eds., *Perspectives on American Methodism, Interpretive Essays* (Nashville, Tenn.: Kingswood, 1993), 289–97; White, "The Beauty of Holiness"; Long, *The Revival of 1857–8*.
55. Long, *The Revival of 1857–8*; Randall J. Stevens, *The Fire Spreads: Holiness and Pentecostalism in the American South* (Cambridge, Mass.: Harvard University Press, 2008); David

Bundy, "The Historiography of the Wesleyan/Holiness Tradition," *Wesleyan Theological Journal* 30 (Spring 1995): 55–77.
56. *Advocate of Christian Holiness*, December 1881, 270; August 1870, 34; December 1873, 137; January 1877, 5.
57. *Proceedings of Holiness Conferences Held at Cincinnati, November 26th, 1877 and at New York, December 17, 1877* (Philadelphia: National Publishing Association for the Promotion of Holiness, 1878), 86; Dieter, *The Holiness Revival*, 183–88, 189–90, 201–2; A. Gregory Schneider, "Objective Selves versus Empowered Selves: The Conflict over Holiness in the Post-Civil War Methodist Episcopal Church" *Methodist History* 32 (July 1994): 238–39.
58. Wacker, *Heaven Below*, 130–33.
59. Oscar von Barchwitz Krauser, *Six Years with William Taylor in South America* (Boston: McDonald & Gill, 1885), 11–85.
60. Krauser, *Six Years*.
61. Quoted in Timothy L. Smith, *Called unto Holiness: The Story of the Nazarenes, the Formative Years* (Kansas City: Nazarene Publishing House, 1962), 38. See also E. Dale Dunlap, "Tuesday Meetings, Camp Meetings, and Cabinet Meetings: A Perspective on the Holiness Movement in the Methodist Church in the United States in the Nineteenth Century," *Methodist History* 13 (April 1975): 97.
62. *Advocate of Christian Holiness*, April 1882, 98; see also January 1882, 4–5.
63. Taylor, *Ten Years*, 389, 457, 464; Taylor, *Story of My Life*, 69, 73, 100, 218.
64. *Advocate of Christian Holiness*, July 1878, 164; see also March 1882, 82–83; Schneider, "Objective Selves," 242–44.
65. See the introduction in George Hughes, *Fragrant Memories of the Tuesday Meeting and the Guide to Holiness, and their Fifty Years' Work for Jesus* (New York: Palmer and Hughes, 1886); Taylor, *Pauline Methods*, 5, 80–82.
66. Quoted in Barclay, *The History*, Vol. 3, 797. Goodsil F. Arms, *History of the William Taylor Self-Supporting Missions in South America* (New York: Methodist Book Concern, 1921), 36–42.
67. Arms, *History*, 12, 49, 73, 86, 124, 210. David Martin, *Tongues of Fire: The Explosion of Protestantism in Latin America* (Oxford: Basil Blackwell, 1990).
68. *Christian Advocate* (New York), January 10, 1884, 17; Barclay, *The History*, Vol. 3, 812.
69. *Christian Advocate* (New York), May 15, 1884, 321, 324; May 22, 1884, 335–36; May 29, 1884, 351. See also *Western Christian Advocate*, March 31, 1880, 102; *Christian Advocate* (New York), September 9, 1880, 579; Barclay, *The History*, Vol. 3, 177; Reginald F. Hildebrand, *The Times Were Strange and Stirring: Methodist Preachers and the Crisis of Emancipation* (Durham, N.C.: Duke University Press, 1995), 75–117; David Bundy, "Bishop William Taylor and Methodist Mission: A Study in Nineteenth Century Social History," *Methodist History* 27 (July 1989): 197–210; Jacobs, "Francis Burns."
70. Taylor, *Story of My Life*, 695.
71. *Christian Advocate* (New York), May 29, 1884, 349; July 24, 1884; William Taylor, *African News*, May 1889, 175; David Bundy, "Bishop William Taylor and Methodist Mission: A Study in Nineteenth Century Social History," *Methodist History* 28 (October 1989), 3–21; Jacobs, "Francis Burns," 256–57.
72. Davies, Rev. E., *The Life of William Taylor, D.D., with an Account of the Congo Country, and Mission* (Reading, Mass.: Holiness Book Concern, 1885), 94–95; *Christian Advocate* (New York), May 29, 1884, 349.
73. Jacobs, "Francis Burns," 258; Barclay, *The History*, Vol. 3, 171–80.
74. *Christian Advocate* (New York), July 16, 1885, 455. Questions about his authority as missionary bishop dogged Taylor through his twelve-year term. See the following issues of the *Christian Advocate* (New York): May 3, 1888, 295–96; January 9, 1890, 26; January 16, 1890, 41; June 16, 1892, 404.
75. *Christian Advocate* (New York), January 9, 1890, 26.
76. *Christian Advocate* (New York), September 17, 1885, 601; Barclay, *The History*, Vol. 3, 896, 904–5, 917.
77. *African News*, April 1889, 149–50; Barclay, *The History*, Vol. 3, 915–18.

78. William Taylor, *The Flaming Torch in Darkest Africa* (New York: Eaton & Mains, 1889), 5.
79. *African News*, May 1889, 175–78.
80. See, for instance, Agnes McAllister, *The Lone Woman in Africa: Six Years on the Kroo Coast* (New York: Eaton & Mains, 1896); *African News*, April 1889, 151, 164–65; Jessica L. Rousselow and Alan H. Winquist, *God's Ordinary People: No Ordinary Heritage* (Upland, Ind.: Taylor University Press, 1996), 47–57.
81. *Christian Advocate* (New York), January 12, 1888, 17; January 19, 1888, 36–37; February 9, 1888, 85, 88; March 1, 1888, 140; April 5, 1888, 221.
82. *New York Times*, April 10, 1885, 4.
83. *Baptist Missionary Magazine*, October 1889, 394.
84. *Christian Advocate* (New York), June 7, 1888, 377; June 16, 1892, 404; Barclay, *The History*, Vol. 3, 817–18.
85. J. Tremayne Copplestone, *The History of Methodist Missions: Twentieth-Century Perspectives*, Vol. 4 (New York: Board of Global Ministries of the Methodist Church, 1973), 3–4, 519.

Chapter 6

1. *Christian Recorder*, November 24, 1866, 185; Stephen Warder Angell, *Bishop Henry McNeal Turner and African American Religion in the South* (Knoxville: University of Tennessee Press, 1992), 68–69. Much of this chapter can be found in Jay Case, "New Directions: Emancipation and the African American Great Awakening, 1866–1880," in Kurt W. Peterson, Thomas S. Kidd, and Darren Dochuk, eds., *American Evangelicalism: George Marsden and the Shape of American Religious History* (Notre Dame, Ind.: University of Notre Dame Press, forthcoming).
2. *Christian Recorder*, September 29, 1866, 154; November 24, 1866, 185; December 1, 1866, 189; Angell, *Bishop Henry McNeal Turner*, 68–69.
3. Eric Foner, *Reconstruction: America's Unfinished Revolution, 1863–1877* (New York: Harper & Row, 1988), 261–64.
4. *Christian Recorder*, September 29, 1866, 154; June 23, 1866, 97.
5. Ibid., July 7, 1855, 105.
6. Ibid., May 6, 1866, 70; September 29, 1866, 154; August 4, 1866, 122; August 18, 1866, 129; September 8, 1866, 142; November 24, 1866, 185; December 1, 1866, 189; see also February 17, 1866, 26; June 2, 1866, 85; June 16, 1866, 93; September 15, 1866, 145; November 3, 1866, 174; December 15, 1866, 198; March 8, 1867, 37; March 16, 1867, 42; March 23, 1867, 45–46.
7. The term *Great Awakening* here does not mean exactly the same thing for the African-American situation as it does for whites who converted in the First and Second Great Awakenings. The original meaning of the term referred to the "reawakening" of a slumbering church. Since most of the African Americans who converted were not previously members of the Christian faith, *awakening* in this sense is not a fully accurate term. Framed another way, though, *Great Awakening* is a helpful way to describe the African-American situation. First of all, this postwar religious movement shared many characteristics with earlier evangelical movements. Second, black evangelists such as Henry McNeal Turner used the term *revival*, while being fully aware that this was more than simply the reviving of a slumbering church. As common evangelical words, *revival* and *awakening* might be the best terms at hand to explain a phenomenon that included both those who had identified with the Christian faith and those who had not. Third, the first significant numbers of African-American conversions occurred as a result of the First and Second Great Awakenings. Times of rapid evangelical growth often brought conversion experiences to nominal Christians who identified with Christianity and also to those, like many eighteenth- and nineteenth-century African Americans, who had not previously identified with the Christian faith.
8. Thomas S. Kidd, *The Great Awakening: The Roots of Evangelicalism in Colonial America* (New Haven, Conn.: Yale University Press, 2007); Sylvia R. Frey and Betty Wood, *Come Shouting to Zion: African American Protestantism in the American South and British Caribbean to 1830* (Chapel Hill: University of North Carolina Press, 1998).

9. Clarence E. Walker, *A Rock in a Weary Land: The African Methodist Episcopal Church during the Civil War and Reconstruction* (Baton Rouge: Louisiana State University Press, 1982); William E. Montgomery, *Under Their Own Vine and Fig Tree: The African-American Church in the South, 1865–1900* (Baton Rouge: Louisiana State University Press, 1993); Reginald F. Hildebrand, *The Times Were Strange and Stirring: Methodist Preachers and the Crisis of Emancipation* (Durham, N.C.: Duke University Press, 1995); James T. Campbell, *Songs of Zion: The African Methodist Episcopal Church in the United States and South Africa* (New York: Oxford University Press, 1995); Daniel W. Stowell, *Rebuilding Zion: The Religious Reconstruction of the South, 1863–1877* (New York: Oxford University Press, 1998); Paul Harvey, *Redeeming the South: Religious Cultures and Racial Identities among Southern Baptists, 1865–1925* (Chapel Hill: University of North Carolina Press, 1997); Edward J. Blum and W. Scott Poole, eds., *Vale of Tears: New Essays on Religion and Reconstruction* (Macon, Ga.: Mercer University Press, 2005); Angell, *Bishop Henry McNeal Turner*.
10. *Christian Recorder*, September 29, 1866, 154; November 24, 1866, 185; December 1, 1866, 189; Angell, *Bishop Henry McNeal Turner*, 79.
11. Stowell, *Rebuilding Zion*, 90; Angell, *Bishop Henry McNeal Turner*, 79.
12. *Census of Religious Bodies: 1906* (Washington, D.C., 1910), Vol. 1, 139; Montgomery, *Under Their Own Vine*, 117; Stowell, *Rebuilding Zion*, 94; American Baptist Home Mission Society (ABHMS), *Baptist Home Missions in North America; including a Full Report of the Proceedings and Addresses of the Jubilee Meeting, and a Historical Sketch of the American Baptist Home Mission Society, Historical Tables, etc., 1832–1882* (New York: Baptist Home Mission Rooms, 1883), 421; Mechal Sobel, *Trabelin' On: The Slave Journey to an Afro-Baptist Faith* (Princeton, N.J.: Princeton University Press, 1988), 182.
13. *Census of Religious Bodies*, Vol. 1, 137–39; Harvey, *Redeeming the South*, 46; Michael A. Gomez, *Exchanging Our Country Marks: The Transformation of African Identities in the Colonial and Antebellum South* (Chapel Hill: University of North Carolina Press, 1998), 260–61; Frey and Wood, *Come Shouting to Zion*, 149; Harvey, *Redeeming the South*, 46.
14. Frey and Wood, *Come Shouting to Zion*, xi.
15. Frey and Wood, *Come Shouting to Zion*; Gomez, *Exchanging Our Country Marks*; Eugene D. Genovese, *Roll, Jordan, Roll: The World the Slaves Made* (New York: Pantheon, 1974).
16. Frey and Wood, *Come Shouting to Zion*; Kidd, *The Great Awakening*; Nathan Hatch, *The Democratization of American Christianity* (New Haven, Conn.: Yale University Press, 1989); John H. Wigger, *Taking Heaven by Storm: Methodism and the Rise of Popular Christianity in America* (New York: Oxford University Press, 1998), 130.
17. Hatch, *The Democratization*, 106–7.
18. Donald G. Mathews, *Religion in the Old South* (Chicago: University of Chicago Press, 1977); Hatch, *The Democratization*, 107; Wigger, *Taking Heaven by Storm*, 125–50; Erskine Clarke, *Dwelling Place: A Plantation Epic* (New Haven, Conn.: Yale University Press, 2007).
19. Erskine Clark, *Dwelling Place*; Mark Noll, *The Civil War as a Theological Crisis* (Chapel Hill: University of North Carolina Press, 2006); Anne C. Loveland, *Southern Evangelicals and the Social Order, 1800–1860* (Baton Rouge: Louisiana State University Press, 1980); Genovese, *Roll, Jordan, Roll*; Mathews, *Religion in the Old South*.
20. Mrs. A. M. French, *Slavery in South Carolina and the Ex-Slaves: or, the Port Royal Mission* (1862; reprint New York: Negro Universities Press, 1969), 126–27, 133; Rupert Sargent, ed., *Letters and Diary of Laura M. Towne: Written from the Sea Islands of South Carolina, 1862–1884* (1912; reprint New York: Negro Universities Press, 1969), 81; Willie Lee Rose, *Rehearsal for Reconstruction: The Port Royal Experiment* (London: Oxford University Press, 1964), 86–87; Angell, *Bishop Henry McNeal Turner*, 20.
21. Genovese, *Roll, Jordan, Roll*, 162; Albert J. Raboteau, *Slave Religion: The "Invisible Institution" in the Antebellum South* (Oxford: Oxford University Press, 1978); Clark, *Dwelling Place*; Charles F. Irons, *The Origins of Proslavery Religion: White and Black Evangelicals in Colonial and Antebellum Virginia* (Chapel Hill: University of North Carolina Press, 2008).
22. *Census of Religious Bodies*, Vol. 1, 137; Montgomery, *Under Their Own Vine*, 121–27; Sobel, *Trabelin' On*, 182–83; Edward J. Blum, *Reforging the White Republic: Race, Religion and American Nationalism, 1865–1898* (Baton Rouge: Louisiana State University Press, 2005);

David T. Gleeson, "'No Disruption of Union': The Catholic Church in the South and Reconstruction," in Blum and Poole, *Vale of Tears*, 164–86; Cyprian Davis, *The History of Black Catholics in the United States* (New York: Crossroad, 1990).

23. Rose, *Rehearsal for Reconstruction*, 73–75; Robert C. Morris, *Reading, 'Riting, and Reconstruction: The Education of the Freedmen in the South, 1861–1870* (Chicago: University of Chicago Press, 1981), 61; Foner, *Reconstruction*, 145–47.

24. W. E. B. DuBois, *The Souls of Black Folk* (1903; reprint New York: Bantam, 2005), 73–75; Joe M. Richardson, *Christian Reconstruction: The American Missionary Association and Southern Blacks* (Athens: University of Georgia Press, 1986), 74; James M. McPherson, *The Abolitionist Legacy: From Reconstruction to the NAACP* (Princeton, N.J.: Princeton University Press, 1975), especially app. B, 409–16.

25. *Macedonian and Home Mission Record*, May 1870, 17; June 1870, 22; July 1867, 26, 28; October 1869, 37; December 1869, 46; James Melvin Washington, *Frustrated Fellowship: The Black Baptist Quest for Social Power* (Macon, Ga.: Mercer University Press, 1986).

26. Edwin S. Redkey, *Black Exodus: Black Nationalist and Back-to-Africa Movements, 1890–1910* (New Haven, Conn.: Yale University Press, 1969), 30; Angell, *Bishop Henry McNeal Turner*, 72–76.

27. *Christian Recorder*, February 20, 1869, 21; Wilson Jeremiah Moses, *The Golden Age of Black Nationalism, 1850–1925* (Hamden, Conn.: Archon, 1978); Kevin K. Gaines, *Uplifting the Race: Black Leadership, Politics, and Culture in the Twentieth Century* (Chapel Hill: University of North Carolina Press, 1996); Walter Williams, *Black Americans and the Evangelization of Africa, 1877–1900* (Madison: University of Wisconsin Press, 1982).

28. Daniel Alexander Payne, *Recollections of Seventy Years* (Nashville, Tenn.: Publishing House of the A.M.E. Sunday School Union, 1888; reprint New York: Arno, 1968), 17–20.

29. Payne, *Recollections*, 50.

30. *Christian Recorder*, February 28, 1898, 2; Payne, *Recollections*, 67–68; William J. Simmons, *Men of Mark: Eminent, Progressive and Rising* (Cleveland, Ohio: Geo. M. Rewell, 1887; reprint New York: Arno, 1968), 1084; David W. Wills, "Womanhood and Domesticity in the A.M.E. Tradition: The Influence of Daniel Alexander Payne," in David W. Wills and Richard Newman, eds., *Black Apostles at Home and Abroad: Afro-Americans and the Christian Mission from the Revolution to Reconstruction* (Boston: G. K. Hall, 1982), 133–46; Campbell, *Songs of Zion*, 37–39.

31. Quoted in Paul R. Griffin, *Black Theology as the Foundation of Three Methodist Colleges: The Educational Views and Labors of Daniel Payne, Joseph Price, Isaac Lane* (Lanham, Md.: University Press of America, 1984), 37–38.

32. Quoted in Moses, *The Golden Age*, 158.

33. Payne, *Recollections*, 161–65; Harry S. Stout, *Upon the Altar of the Nation: A Moral History of the Civil War* (New York: Viking, 2006), 185; William Wells Brown, *Black Man: His Antecedents, His Genius, and His Achievements* (New York: Thomas Hamilton, 1863), 209.

34. Simmons, *Men of Mark*, 1084; Wills, "Womanhood and Domesticity," 133–46; Campbell, *Songs of Zion*, 37–39.

35. Payne, *Recollections*, 253–54.

36. Daniel A. Payne, "The Christian Ministry: Its Moral and Intellectual Character," in Daniel Alexander Payne, *Sermons and Addresses, 1853–1891* (New York: Arno, 1972), 15; Daniel A. Payne, "Organization Essential to Success for Quarto Centennial of African Methodism in the South," in Payne, *Sermons and Addresses*, 42.

37. Charles Joyner, *Down by the Riverside: A South Carolina Slave Community* (Urbana: University of Illinois Press, 1984); Jon Butler, *Awash in a Sea of Faith: Christianizing the American People* (Cambridge, Mass.: Harvard University Press, 1990); Montgomery, *Under Their Own Vine*, 22; Genovese, *Roll, Jordan, Roll*; Frey and Wood, *Come Shouting to Zion*; Gomez, *Exchanging Our Country Marks*.

38. Gomez, *Exchanging Our Country Marks*; Raboteau, *Slave Religion*, 44–75; Sobel, *Trabelin' On*; Frey and Wood, *Come Shouting to Zion*; Ann Taves, *Fits, Trances, and Visions: Experiencing Religion and Explaining Experience from Wesley to James* (Princeton, N.J.: Princeton University Press, 1999), 99–104.

39. Harvey, *Redeeming the South*, 112; Montgomery, *Under Their Own Vine*; Moses, *The Golden Age*, 10, 20–23; Edward L. Wheeler, *Uplifting the Race: The Black Minister in the New South, 1865–1902* (Lanham, Md.: University Press of America, 1986); Gaines, *Uplifting the Race*.
40. David D. Hall, *Worlds of Wonder, Days of Judgment: Popular Religious Belief in Early New England* (Cambridge, Mass.: Harvard University Press, 1990); H. H. Gerth and C. Wright Mills, eds., *From Max Weber: Essays in Sociology* (New York: Oxford University Press, 1946), 139–49; Taves, *Fits, Trances, and Visions*; Henry F. May, *The Enlightenment in America* (Oxford: Oxford University Press, 1976).
41. For an excellent explanation of how democratized Christianity provoked a crisis of authority for New England ministers such as Lyman Beecher and Timothy Dwight, see Hatch, *The Democratization*, 17–22.
42. DuBois, *The Souls of Black Folk*, 140–41; Allen Dwight Callahan, *The Talking Book: African Americans and the Bible* (New Haven, Conn.: Yale University Press, 2006), 62–63; Harvey, *Redeeming the South*, 114–23.
43. Gomez, *Exchanging Our Country Marks*, 269–70; Campbell, *Songs of Zion*, 39–44; Montgomery, *Under Their Own Vine*, 266–68; Moses, *The Golden Age*, 41.
44. Harvey, *Redeeming the South*, 108; Heather Andrea Williams, *Self-Taught: African American Education in Slavery and Freedom* (Chapel Hill: University of North Carolina Press, 2005); Richardson, *Christian Reconstruction*; Foner, *Reconstruction*.
45. Payne, *Recollections*, 253–54.
46. Kidd, *The Great Awakening*; George M. Marsden, *Jonathan Edwards: A Life* (New Haven, Conn.: Yale University Press, 2005), 268–84.
47. Angell, *Bishop Henry McNeal Turner*.
48. Ibid.
49. *Christian Recorder*, February 25, 1865, 29; October 8, 1864, 161; March 18, 1865, 42; August, 5, 1865, 121; see also May 27, 1865, 83; July 1, 1865, 102.
50. *Christian Recorder*, July 1, 1865, 102. For a similar impact on northern missionaries, see Blum, *Reforging the White Republic*, 52–53.
51. *Christian Recorder*, January 20, 1866, 9; June 10, 1865, 89; see also February 25, 1865, 29; August 5, 1865, 121.
52. Ibid., August 5, 1865, 121.
53. Ibid., June 2, 1855, 85; June 9, 1866; Angell, *Bishop Henry McNeal Turner*, 68–69.
54. *Christian Recorder*, November 24, 1866, 185; December 1, 1866, 189; November 24, 1866, 185; December 1, 1866, 189; Angell, *Bishop Henry McNeal Turner*, 21–22.
55. *Christian Recorder*, August 5, 1865, 121; *Respect Black: The Writings and Speeches of Henry McNeal Turner*, ed. Edwin S. Redkey (New York: Arno, 1971), 30; Angell, *Bishop Henry McNeal Turner*, 72–76.
56. Angell, *Bishop Henry McNeal Turner*, 75–76. See also Hildebrand, *The Times Were Strange*, 6–17.
57. Ronald E. Butchart, *Northern Schools, Southern Blacks, and Reconstruction: Freedmen's Education, 1862–1875* (Westport, Conn.: Greenwood, 1980), 205; Rose, *Rehearsal for Reconstruction*, 74, 92–93, 180–81.
58. Blum, *Reforging the White Republic*.
59. Benjamin T. Tanner, *An Apology for African Methodism* (Baltimore, n.p., 1867), 414–15; Angell, *Bishop Henry McNeal Turner*, 76.
60. Angell, *Bishop Henry McNeal Turner*, 76, 100–101.
61. Quoted in ibid., 184; Wills, "Womanhood and Domesticity," 133–46; Campbell, *Songs of Zion*, 43–52.
62. *Christian Recorder*, June 10, 1865, 89; Angell, *Bishop Henry McNeal Turner*, 61–62, 68, 82–90.
63. Quoted in Angell, *Bishop Henry McNeal Turner*, 90; see also 82–90; *Christian Recorder*, June 10, 1865, 89.
64. Callahan, *The Talking Book*, 163.
65. DuBois, *The Souls of Black Folk*, 3; Blum, *Reforging the White Republic*; David R. Roediger, *Working toward Whiteness: How America's Immigrants Became White: The Strange Journey*

from *Ellis Island to the Suburbs* (New York: Basic Books, 2005); Noel Ignatiev, *How the Irish Became White* (New York: Routledge, 1995); Foner, *Reconstruction*.
66. Monroe Fordham, *Major Themes in Northern Black Religious Thought, 1800–1860* (Hicksville, N.Y.: Exposition, 1975), 139–50; Wheeler, *Uplifting the Race*, 37–51; Daniel Alexander Payne, *History of the African Methodist Episcopal Church* (Nashville, Tenn.: Publishing House of the A.M.E. Sunday-School Union, 1891), 483; Callahan, *The Talking Book*; Gomez, *Exchanging Our Country Marks*, 15.
67. *Voice of Missions*, March 1893; Turner, *Respect Black*, 189–90.
68. *Voice of Missions*, August 1900; Turner, *Respect Black*, 189; Leon F. Litwack, *Trouble in Mind: Black Southerners in the Age of Jim Crow* (New York: Vintage, 1998), 284.

Chapter 7

1. James T. Campbell, *Songs of Zion: The African Methodist Episcopal Church in the United States and Africa* (Chapel Hill: University of North Carolina Press, 1998), 116–17; T. D. Mweli Skota, ed., *The African Who's Who: An Illustrated Classified Register and National Biographical Dictionary of the Africans in the Transvaal*, 3rd ed. (Johannesburg: Central News Agency, 1960s), 14–15.
2. Campbell, *Songs of Zion*, 116–17; Skota, *The African Who's Who*, 14–15.
3. Mokone interpreted biblical references to Ethiopia to mean that the Christian God would fully address the circumstances of all black Africans, not just a specific people group or nation in Africa. Ethiopianism reflects not only how black nationalism developed under the racist structures of South Africa but also how evangelicalism facilitated that nationalism and became a means for reconstituting communal identities.
4. J. Mutero Chirenje, *Ethiopianism and Afro-Americans in Southern Africa, 1883–1916* (Baton Rouge: Louisiana State University Press, 1987), 66; Hennie Pretorius and Lizo Jafta, "'A Branch Springs Out': African Initiated Churches," in Richard Elphick and Rodney Davenport, eds., *Christianity in South Africa: A Political, Social and Cultural History* (Berkeley: University of California Press, 1997), 211–26; Campbell, *Songs of Zion*, 117–19.
5. The story of the encounter between the Ethiopian church and the AME through 1910 is told in great detail and excellent manner by James Campbell in *Songs of Zion*. Campbell tends to place these developments in the context of politics and race rather than the dynamics of evangelicalism and world Christianity.
6. *Christian Recorder*, June 2, 1855, 85; September, 29, 1866, 154; Stephen Warder Angell, *Bishop Henry McNeal Turner and African American Religion in the South* (Knoxville: University of Tennessee Press, 1992), 68–69; Edwin S. Redkey, ed., *Respect Black: The Writings and Speeches of Henry McNeal Turner* (New York: Arno, 1971); Edwin S. Redkey, *Black Exodus: Black Nationalist and Back-to-Africa Movements, 1890–1910* (New Haven, Conn.: Yale University Press, 1969).
7. Redkey, *Respect Black;* Melbourne S. Cummings, "The Rhetoric of Bishop Henry McNeal Turner," *Journal of Black Studies* 12 (June 1982): 457–67; C. Erick Lincoln and Lawrence H. Mamiya, *The Black Church in the African American Experience* (Durham, N.C.: Duke University Press, 1980), 177.
8. Since evangelical conversion played a critical role in facilitating the emergence of black racial identity in the Americas and South Africa, it is quite conceivable that evangelicalism could also promote forms of black nationalism. Sylvia R. Frey and Betty Wood, *Come Shouting to Zion: African American Protestantism in the American South and British Caribbean to 1830* (Chapel Hill: University of North Carolina Press, 1998); Michael A. Gomez, *Exchanging Our Country Marks: The Transformation of African Identities in the Colonial and Antebellum South* (Chapel Hill: University of North Carolina Press, 1998).
9. *Voice of Missions*, February 1898; Andrew F. Walls, *The Missionary Movement in Christian History: Studies in the Transmission of Faith* (Maryknoll, N.Y.: Orbis, 1996), 47. See also Lamin Sanneh, *Translating the Message: The Missionary Impact on Culture* (Maryknoll, N.Y.: Orbis, 1999).
10. *Voice of Missions*, February 1898.

11. Redkey, *Black Exodus*; Campbell, *Songs of Zion*, 78–83; Walter Williams, *Black Americans and the Evangelization of Africa, 1877–1900* (Madison: University of Wisconsin Press, 1982), 39–40; William E. Montgomery, *Under Their Own Vine and Fig Tree: The African-American Church in the South, 1865–1900* (Baton Rouge: Louisiana State University Press, 1993), 195–225.
12. Redkey, *Respect Black*, 13; Redkey, *Black Exodus*, 73–126. This suspicion of American civil religion has persisted within some quarters of African-American Christianity through the years. See David L. Chappell, *A Stone of Hope: Prophetic Religion and the Death of Jim Crow* (Chapel Hill: University of North Carolina Press, 2004); Allen Dwight Callahan, *The Talking Book: African Americans and the Bible* (New Haven, Conn.: Yale University Press, 2006), 114–16.
13. *Christian Recorder*, November 24, 1866, 185; Angell, *Bishop Henry McNeal Turner*, 31.
14. David W. Wills and Richard Newman, eds., *Black Apostles at Home and Abroad: Afro-Americans and the Christian Mission from the Revolution to Reconstruction* (Boston: G. K. Hall, 1982); Lamin Sanneh, *Abolitionists Abroad: American Blacks and the Making of Modern West Africa* (Cambridge, Mass.: Harvard University Press, 1999); Gayraud S. Wilmore, "Black Americans in Mission: Setting the Record Straight," in Martin E. Marty, ed., *Modern American Protestantism and Its World: Historical Articles on Protestantism in American Religious Life, Vol. 9: Native American Religion and Black Protestantism* (Munich: K. G. Saur, 1993), 81–91.
15. *Christian Recorder*, June 18, 1870, 1; July, 16, 1870, 1; July 23, 1870, 1; June 5, 1873, 1; June 4, 1874, 2; Daniel Alexander Payne, *History of the African Methodist Episcopal Church* (Nashville, Tenn.: Publishing House of the A.M.E. Sunday-School Union, 1891), 478–92.
16. *Christian Recorder*, December 8, 1887, 3. For representative examples of AME leaders linking foreign- and home-missionary work, see *Christian Recorder*, July 21, 1866, 114; April 23, 1870, 2; January 24, 1878, 1; December 7, 1882, 1; December 8, 1887, 3; June 14, 1888, 1; February 14, 1889, 2; November 7, 1889, 2; March 2, 1893, 6; February 24, 1898, 7; September 21, 1899, 2; *Voice of Missions*, November 1895; *AME Church Review*, January 1898, 364.
17. Redkey, *Respect Black*, 13; Redkey, *Black Exodus*, 73–126.
18. *Christian Recorder*, September 29, 1866, 154; November 24, 1866, 185; Eric Foner, *Reconstruction: America's Unfinished Revolution, 1863–1877* (New York: Harper & Row, 1988), 78–84.
19. *Christian Recorder*, April 11, 1878, 2. For similar claims of African-American inexperience as "leaders of civilization," the promises of American prosperity, and the priority of the American situation over the African, see *Christian Recorder*, July 4, 1878, 2; August 8, 1878, 2; February 10, 1881, 1; January 25, 1883, 1; September 22, 1887, 4; October 4, 1877, 2; January 20, 1881, 2; March 10, 1881, 1; November 9, 1882, 2; March 22, 1883, 1; February 16, 1881, 2; September, 9, 1882, 2; December, 14, 1882, 1; May 23, 1882, 1; July 2, 1882, 2.
20. Ibid., April 18, 1878, 1.
21. Ibid., July 25, 1878, 2.
22. Ibid., August 22, 1878, 2; September 26, 1878, 2. See also, August 8, 1878, 2; September 12, 1878, 2; December 5, 1878, 2. Some of the issues from the *Christian Recorder* in which Payne's letters appeared are missing, and Payne's sixth and eighth articles might not be extant. See also *AME Church Review*, April 1885, 314–20.
23. *Christian Recorder*, August 8, 1878, 2; July 25, 1878, 2; September 26, 1878, 2; see also August 22, 1878, 2; September 12, 1878, 2; December 5, 1878, 2; *AME Church Review*, April 1885, 314–20.
24. *Christian Recorder*, August 23, 1877, 4.
25. Ibid., July 25, 1878, 2; see also November 8, 1877, 1; Campbell, *Songs of Zion*, 26–62; Reginald F. Hildebrand, *The Times Were Strange and Stirring: Methodist Preachers and the Crisis of Emancipation* (Durham, N.C.: Duke University Press, 1995), 31–72; Clarence E. Walker, *A Rock in a Weary Land: The African Methodist Episcopal Church during the Civil War and Reconstruction* (Baton Rouge: Louisiana State University Press, 1982), 7–24.
26. Payne, *History*, 483; Daniel Alexander Payne, *Recollections of Seventy Years* (Nashville, Tenn.: Publishing House of the A.M.E. Sunday-School Union, 1888; reprint New York: Arno, 1968), 161–65.

27. Angell, *Bishop Henry McNeal Turner*, 165–67.
28. Campbell, *Songs of Zion*, 90–91.
29. *Christian Recorder*, August 8, 1878, 2; see also August 22, 1878, 2; September 12, 1878, 2; September 26, 1878, 2; December 5, 1878, 2; *AME Church Review*, April 1885, 314–20.
30. *Christian Recorder*, July 2, 1885, 2; September 22, 1887, 4; *AME Church Review*, July, 1885, 71; April 1885, 314–20.
31. *Christian Recorder*, December 8, 1881, 1.
32. Josephus Roosevelt Coan, "The Expansion of Missions of the African Methodist Episcopal Church in South Africa, 1896–1908," PhD dissertation, Hartford Seminary Foundation, 1961, 54–55; Williams, *Black Americans*, 49; Angell, *Bishop Henry McNeal Turner*, 145–55, 172, 216.
33. *Christian Recorder*, September 9, 1899, 8; *Voice of Missions*, November 1895; November 1899.
34. *Voice of Missions*, March 1893.
35. Ibid., May 1895.
36. Quoted in Campbell, *Songs of Zion*, 90–91.
37. Ibid., 134; Angell, *Bishop Henry McNeal Turner*, 201.
38. Quoted in Angell, *Bishop Henry McNeal Turner*, 192–93, 201.
39. Quoted in ibid., 196. See also *Christian Recorder*, December 6, 1888, 2; May 21, 1891, 1.
40. *Christian Recorder*, November 29, 1888, 2. See also Angell, *Bishop Henry McNeal Turner*, 199.
41. Henry McNeal Turner, *The Negro in All Ages* (Savannah, Ga.: D. G. Patton, 1878), 29. For examples of those arguing that Africa had been misrepresented, see *Christian Recorder*, January 17, 1878, 1; January 24, 1878, 1; February 14, 1884, 2; March 27, 1884, 1. See also Wilson Jeremiah Moses, *The Golden Age of Black Nationalism, 1850–1925* (Hamden, Conn.: Archon, 1978), 76; Campbell, *Songs of Zion*, 74–81; Angell, *Bishop Henry McNeal Turner*, 174.
42. Angell, *Bishop Henry McNeal Turner*, 4, 62–68, 76, 100–102, 107, 140–44.
43. *AME Church Review*, April 1892, 466–67. See, by comparison, *Christian Recorder*, July 1, 1865, 102; August 5, 1865, 121.
44. *AME Church Review*, April 1892, 467–68, 475, 482.
45. Michael Adas, *Dominance by Design: Technological Imperatives and America's Civilizing Mission* (Cambridge, Mass.: Harvard University Press, 2006).
46. Redkey, *Black Exodus*, 177; Angell, *Bishop Henry McNeal Turner*, 219.
47. C. S. Smith, *Glimpses of Africa: West and Southwest Coast* (Nashville:, Tenn. Publishing House, AME Church School Union, 1895), 11–12; *Voice of Missions*, July 1896; June 1893; July 1895; February 1896; July 1896; August 1896; October 1896; April 1897; August 1897; September 1897; December 1897; January 1899.
48. Angell, *Bishop Henry McNeal Turner*, 202. See also Edward J. Blum, *Reforging the White Republic: Race, Religion and American Nationalism, 1865–1898* (Baton Rouge: Louisiana State University Press, 2005).
49. *AME Church Review*, April 1892, 492–93; *Voice of Missions*, July 1895, August 1896; November 1896; September 1900.
50. *Voice of Missions*, February 1896.
51. Quoted in Williams, *Black Americans*, 169; *Voice of Missions*, May 1898; March 1899; June 1897.
52. Campbell, *Songs of Zion*, 128–34.
53. Ibid., 136.
54. Ibid., 118; Pretorius and Jafta, "A Branch Springs Out"; Elizabeth Isichei, *A History of Christianity in Africa: From Antiquity to the Present* (Grand Rapids, Mich.: Eerdmans, 1995), 125–27; Adrian Hastings, *The Church in Africa, 1450–1950* (Oxford: Clarendon, 1994), 478–81, 497–99.
55. Quoted in Campbell, *Songs of Zion*, 118.
56. *Voice of Missions*, December 1, 1897; Campbell, *Songs of Zion*, 119–24.
57. N. A. Etherington, "The Historical Sociology of Independent Churches in South East Africa," *Journal of Religion in Africa* 10 (1979): 115–16.

58. J. Whiteside, *History of the Wesleyan Methodist Church of South Africa* (London: Elliot Stock, 1906), 399; Etherington, "The Historical Sociology"; John H. Wigger, *Taking Heaven by Storm: Methodism and the Rise of Popular Christianity in America* (New York; Oxford University Press, 1998), 21.
59. Campbell, *Songs of Zion,* 109–19; Chirenje, *Ethiopianism,* 42–43.
60. Campbell, *Songs of Zion,* 109–19; Chirenje, *Ethiopianism,* 42–44.
61. Chirenje, *Ethiopianism,* 43.
62. Quoted in Campbell, *Songs of Zion,* 112; George W. Stocking Jr., *Victorian Anthropology* (New York: Free Press, 1987).
63. Campbell, *Songs of Zion,* 109–18, 183.
64. Wesleyan Methodist Church, *Minutes of Several Conversations at the One Hundred and Fifty-Fourth Yearly Conference of the People Called Methodists* (London: Methodist Book Concern, 1897), 598; J. Du Plessis, *A History of Christian Missions in South Africa* (New York: Longmans, Green, 1911), 464; John W. De Gruchy, "Grappling with a Colonial Heritage: The English-speaking Churches under Imperialism and Apartheid," in Richard Elphick and Rodney Davenport, eds., *Christianity in South Africa: A Political, Social and Cultural History* (Berkeley: University of California Press, 1997), 155–72.
65. *Voice of Missions,* December 1895; March 1896; April 1896. See also Chirenje, *Ethiopianism*; Campbell, *Songs of Zion.*
66. *Voice of Missions,* June 1898; *Christian Recorder,* February 24, 1898, 7.
67. *Voice of Missions,* December 1898.
68. Ibid., September 1899. See also *Christian Recorder,* March 23, 1899, 1, 3.
69. *Voice of Missions,* September 1895; August 1898.
70. The letters that AME missionary J. R. Frederick sent home for publication testify to this. Frederick's extended missionary service in Sierra Leone led him to help form the Dress Reform Society in 1887, to help "develop a national dress for Africa." Yet in the seventeen letters that he sent home for publication in the *Christian Recorder,* he never directly addressed the issue of promoting various forms of African culture or spoke of his activities in that regard. He did, however, discuss hopes for "negro advancement," love for Africa, excitement for African conversions, criticism of racism among white missionaries, plans for schools, efforts to prevent warfare among two tribes, goals for indigenous independence, and the need for AME members in America to give greater support to the evangelization of "our fatherland." See *Christian Recorder* February 17, 1887, 2; June 23, 1887, 1; October 6, 1887, 1; December 8, 1887, 2; January 12, 1888, 5; June 28, 1888, 1–2; February 28, 1889, 2; April 25, 1889, 1–2; May 30, 1889, 2–3; December 5, 1889, 1; December 19, 1889, 1; September 11, 1890, 1; March 12, 1891, 1–2; April 23, 1891, 2; February 23, 1893, 2; June 22, 1893, 1; October 19, 1893, 4; Hollis R. Lynch, *Edward Wilmont Blyden: Pan-Negro Patriot, 1832–1912* (London: Oxford University Press, 1967), 218–19; Williams, *Black Americans,* 46–47; Campbell, *Songs of Zion,* 89–90.
71. *Christian Recorder,* December 1, 1898, 3; December 29, 1898, 1.
72. W. J. Gaines, *The Negro and the White Man* (Philadelphia: AME Publishing House, 1897; reprint New York: Negro Universities Press, 1969), 79–87, 138, 178–83, 206–7. See also Kevin K. Gaines, *Uplifting the Race: Black Leadership, Politics, and Culture in the Twentieth Century* (Chapel Hill: University of North Carolina Press, 1996).
73. Gaines, *The Negro,* 97–99, 132–34, 206–7.
74. *AME Church Review,* January 1898, 362.
75. Quoted in Chirenje, *Ethiopianism,* 58; Campbell, *Songs of Zion,* 217–18.
76. *Christian Recorder,* December 7, 1899, 1; Coan, "The Expansion of Missions," 189–91, 236; Angell, *Bishop Henry McNeal Turner,* 235; Campbell, *Songs of Zion,* 218–27.
77. Campbell, *Songs of Zion,* 138.
78. Ibid., 226–39.
79. Quoted in ibid., 239.
80. Ibid., 139; see also chaps. 8 and 9 in Campbell.
81. By 1991, AICs included 9.2 million people and 47 percent of the black Christians in South Africa alone. Pretorius and Jafta, "A Branch Springs Out."

82. Pretorius and Jafta, "A Branch Springs Out"; Bengt Sundkler, *Zulu Zion and Some Swazi Zionists* (London: Oxford University Press, 1976); Walls, *The Missionary Movement*, 111–18.
83. Campbell, *Songs of Zion*.

Chapter 8

1. William R. Hutchison, *The Modernist Impulse in American Protestantism* (New York: Oxford University Press, 1982); Robert T. Handy, *A Christian America: Protestant Hopes and Historical Realities* (London: Oxford University Press, 1971).
2. Agnes McAllister, *A Lone Woman in Africa: Six Years on the Kroo Coast* (New York: Hunt & Eaton, 1896); Andrew F. Walls, "The American Dimension in the History of the Missionary Movement," in Joel A. Carpenter and Wilbert R. Shenk, eds., *Earthen Vessels: American Evangelicals and Foreign Missions, 1880–1980* (Grand Rapids, Mich.: Eerdmans, 1990), 1–25.
3. McAllister, *A Lone Woman*, 22–28.
4. Ibid., 32; see also 31, 47–55, 60, 78, 98–99.
5. Ibid., 133.
6. Technically, it might be more accurate to refer to the African people who lived around the town of Harper at Cape Palmas as Glebo (sometimes spelled "Grebo") rather than Kru, but this designation threatens to complicate such a short summary given in this chapter. The Glebo are usually considered a subgroup of the Kru, although scholars present different classifications of just who fit under the designation of Kru. For the purposes of this chapter, it seems reasonable to include the people of Garraway and the Glebo at Cape Palmas under the Kru designation. They shared very similar linguistic, religious, and cultural characteristics, faced similar changes brought by contact with the West, and felt the encroachments of the Americo-Liberians. Ronald W. Davis, *Ethnohistorical Studies on the Kru Coast* (Newark, Del.: Liberian Studies, 1976), 5–12; Andreas Massing, *The Economic Anthropology of the Kru (West Africa)* (Wiesbaden: Franz Steiner Verlag, 1980), 16–19.
7. Gordon MacKay Haliburton, *The Prophet Harris: A Study of an African Prophet and His Mass Movement in the Ivory Coast and the Gold Coast, 1913–15* (New York: Oxford University Press, 1973), 10–13; David A. Shank,*Prophet Harris: The "Black Elijah" of West Africa* (Leiden: Brill, 1994), 36–38, 191–92; Julia C. Emery, *A Century of Endeavor, 1821–1921: A Record of the First Hundred Years of the Domestic and Foreign Missionary Society of the Protestant Episcopal Church in the United States of America* (New York: Department of Missions, 1921), 300–301.
8. McAllister, *Lone Woman*, 168.
9. Ibid., 126–27.
10. Writing more than two years later, McAllister might have seen the significance of this epiphany more clearly than she did when she first considered Kru oral traditions. Given the ferment of wide-ranging actions that she had taken in the previous four years, it is possible that her new appreciation for the Kru oral traditions represented, at first, another in a long line of pragmatic attempts to affect her audience with her Christian message. Or she might truly have been struck with a profound sense that she had stumbled on a new view of the people around her. McAllister, *Lone Woman*, 126–27, 270–72.
11. Nathan Hatch, *The Democratization of American Christianity* (New Haven, Conn.: Yale University Press, 1989); John H. Wigger,*Taking Heaven by Storm: Methodism and the Rise of Popular Christianity in America* (New York: Oxford University Press, 1998); Thomas S. Kidd,*The Great Awakening: The Roots of Evangelicalism in Colonial America* (New Haven, Conn.: Yale University Press, 2007).
12. McAllister, *Lone Woman*, 272–73.
13. Ibid., 279, 282; see also 276–85.
14. The phrase about "walking and leaping" comes from Acts 3:8, describing the reactions of a crippled beggar who had been healed by Peter. Although she did not give the specific biblical reference, McAllister put the phrase in quotes. This illustrates a common evangelical narrative pattern; McAllister alerted readers to a biblical reference that they would have been familiar with in order to provide biblical authority for the legitimacy of behavior that

might have seemed strange to them. This would have strengthened bonds of identification with the Kru converts. Ibid., 281; see also 276–85.
15. Ibid., 275.
16. Ibid., 289.
17. Ibid., 293; Randall J. Stevens, *The Fire Spreads: Holiness and Pentecostalism in the American South* (Cambridge, Mass.: Harvard University Press, 2008), 12, 219–20; Vinson Synan,*The Holiness-Pentecostal Tradition: Charismatic Movements in the Twentieth Century* (Grand Rapids, Mich.: Eerdmans, 1997), 187–88.
18. McAllister, *A Lone Woman,* 282.
19. Catherine A. Brekus, *Strangers and Pilgrims: Female Preaching in America, 1740–1845* (Chapel Hill: University of North Carolina Press, 1998), 271; Kidd, *The Great Awakening*, xv, 127–28, 250, 262, 317–18; Susan Hill Lindley,*"You Have Stept Out of Your Place": A History of Women and Religion in America* (Louisville, Ky.: Westminster John Knox, 1996), 59–69.
20. *Helping Hand*, June 1882, 45; *Heathen Woman's Friend*, August 1869, 20; Lindley, "You Have Stept," 70.
21. See, for example, the following articles in *Heathen Woman's Friend*: May 1869, 1–2; August 1869, 20; January 1874, 588; March 1875, 807; November 1876, 109; July 1883, 12; January 1887, 178–79.
22. Ibid., November 1871, 198–99; November 1876, 109–10; January 1881, 152; October 1881, 78; September 1882, 50–52; January 1886, 154.
23. Ibid., April 1874, 629–30; June 1874, 666–67; April 1876, 225; July 1889, 13.
24. Lindley, *"You Have Stept,"* 118–22; Synan, *The Holiness-Pentecostal Tradition,* 17; Charles Edward White, "The Beauty of Holiness: The Career and Influence of Phoebe Palmer,"*Methodist History* 25 (January 1987): 67–75.
25. Stephens, *The Fire Spreads*, 62–64, 120, 133–35; Synan, *The Holiness-Pentecostal Tradition*, 68–69.
26. *African News*, March 1889, 98; *Advocate of Christian Holiness*, February 1880, 46;Charles Edwin Jones,*Perfectionist Persuasion: The Holiness Movement and American Methodism, 1867–1936* (Metuchen, N.J.: Scarecrow, 1974), 51, 54–55.
27. *African News*, January 1889, 20; March 1889, 98; Brooklyn Institute bulletins, 1891, 16–17, Taylor University Archives. Similar gender patterns emerged in holiness missionary schools founded in these decades. See *Michigan Holiness Record,* August 1884, 34; June 1885, 44; Byron L. Osborne,*The Malone Story: The Dream of Two Quaker Young People* (Newton, Kan.: United Printing, 1970), 31–37; Virginia Lieson Brereton,*Training God's Army: The American Bible School, 1880–1940* (Bloomington: Indiana University Press, 1990), 71.
28. *Advocate of Christian Holiness*, July 1878, 137–38. See also Maria Woodworth Etter, *A Diary of Signs and Wonders* (Tulsa, Okla.: Harrison House, n.d.); Thomas D. Hamm,*The Quakers in America* (New York: Columbia University Press, 2003) 184–89.
29. The figures for female missionary recruits are from 1878 to 1881. Wade Crawford Barclay,*The History of Methodist Missions: The Methodist Episcopal Church*, Vol. 3 (New York: Board of Missions of the Methodist Church, 1957), 509, 537–38, 607.
30. Brooklyn Institute bulletin, 1891, 38–39.
31. Brooklyn Institute bulletin, 1891, 15–17, 23; Grant Wacker, *Heaven Below: Early Pentecostals and American Culture* (Cambridge, Mass.: Harvard University Press, 2001), 130–33.
32. Amanda Smith, *An Autobiography: The Story of the Lord's Dealings with Mrs. Amanda Smith, the Colored Evangelist* (reprint New York: Oxford University Press, 1988), 42–49, 57–92; Adrienne M. Israel, *Amanda Berry Smith: From Washerwoman to Evangelist* (Lanham, Md.: Scarecrow, 1998), 19–24.
33. Smith, *An Autobiography,* 76.
34. Ibid., 79; see also 73–91. Smith's verbal outburst in the midst of a white congregation replicated a particular dynamic of biracial evangelicalism that dated back to 1740. Sylvia R. Frey and Betty Wood,*Come Shouting to Zion: African American Protestantism in the American South and British Caribbean to 1830* (Chapel Hill: University of North Carolina Press, 1998), 109–10.
35. Smith, *An Autobiography*, 79.

36. Ibid., 84, 109–12.
37. Ibid., 1–149; Israel, *Amanda Berry Smith*.
38. Brekus, *Strangers and Pilgrims*, 183–86.
39. The antiformalist impulses of the holiness movement could also create familial problems. Charismatic preachers could become so consumed by the desire to preach that they neglected family members. Smith seems to fall into this category. As she described her many internal and evangelistic adventures, Smith did not usually clarify exactly what she did with her children. On her first evangelistic trip to Salem, New Jersey, she left her daughter with her father in Philadelphia. It is a measure of the consuming nature of her passion for evangelism that she rarely explained the status of her children in her autobiography. Smith, *An Autobiography*, 96, 137, 149–52; Israel, *Amanda Berry Smith*, 50–52.
40. Andrew Carnegie, "Wealth," *North American Review*, June 1889, 653.
41. Smith was writing more than two decades after this event, and her memory of the details runs into snags at several points. Her autobiography dates her trip to Salem at November 1869 (the same month her husband died), October 1870, and even November 1890, although the last date is clearly a typographical error. Most likely, she went to Salem in late 1870. Smith, *An Autobiography*, 132, 135, 147, 152.
42. Ibid., 147–59.
43. Brekus, *Strangers and Pilgrims*; Lindley, *"You Have Stept,"* 117–28; Dana L. Robert, *American Women in Mission: A Social History of Their Thought and Practice* (Macon, Ga.: Mercer University Press, 1996), 125–36.
44. Smith, *An Autobiography*, 198–204.
45. Ibid., 84–85; 193–98, 226; see also 477–78.
46. Before her reputation had been established, Smith might have accepted these gifts in an unspoken exchange for housekeeping work at the camp meetings. She reported that she "often brushed and settled up their tents, or got them a pitcher or bucket of water," because "I never felt it hurt my dignity." In later years, however, whites gave her money and gifts without any expectation of manual service in return, because they saw Smith as an evangelist and missionary. Ibid., 176, 196, 207–8, 218, 222, 262, 496.
47. *Christian Recorder*, February 28, 1878, 2; Smith, *An Autobiography*, 236–40.
48. Smith, *An Autobiography*, vi, 183–84, 242, 252, 255, 264, 267, 280; Brekus, *Strangers and Pilgrims*, 190.
49. Smith, *An Autobiography*, 242–43.
50. *Christian Recorder*, September 23, 1880, 1; Smith, *An Autobiography*, 283–85.
51. *Advocate of Christian Holiness*, February 1880, 46. The *Advocate of Christian Holiness* reprinted the article from the *Bombay Guardian*.
52. Smith, *An Autobiography*, v–vi.
53. Ibid., viii–ix.
54. Ibid., 308.
55. Ogbu Kalu, *African Pentecostalism: An Introduction* (Oxford: Oxford University Press, 2008).
56. Charles E. Hambrick-Stowe, *Charles G. Finney and the Spirit of American Evangelicalism* (Grand Rapids, Mich.: Eerdmans, 1996), 155–59.
57. Wigger, *Taking Heaven by Storm*, 49.
58. Smith, *An Autobiography*, 342, 349–50, 353, 356, 362–65, 431–41; Barclay, *The History*, Vol. 3, 882, 884, 887–88, 89.
59. See, for example, *Christian Advocate* (New York), July 19, 1888, 480; *Christian Recorder*, October 28, 1886, 1; September 23, 1880, 1; October 1, 1885, 1; *Advocate of Christian Holiness*, June 1880, 132–33; June 1882, 165; *Michigan Holiness Record*, October 1886, 43; *Highway of Holiness*, April 1880, 83–84; *Christian Witness*, July 11, 1889; *African News*, June 1889, 244–47; September 1889 397–98; *Revivalist*, June 1893, 1; Marshall W. Taylor, *The Life, Travels, Labors and Helpers of Mrs. Amanda Smith: The Famous Negro Missionary Evangelist* (Cincinnati, Ohio: Cranston and Stowe, 1886). She was not admired as much by some black-nationalist evangelicals, who accused her of being more concerned with the souls of whites than those of blacks. *Voice of Missions*, July 1895.

60. *African News*, October 1889, 404, 407–8.
61. S. B. Shaw, ed., *Echoes of the General Holiness Assembly, Held in Chicago, May 3–13, 1901* (Chicago: S. B. Shaw). See also the advertisement "A Fine Group for Framing" at the end of Shaw's book.
62. The name Wadé is pronounced "Waddy." It is a Glebo name meaning "consolation." It was common for Glebo (Kru) Christians in the Cape Palmas area to add an Anglo name after they converted, while keeping their Glebo name. Wadé apparently added William and Harris to his Glebo name after his baptism, when he was about fourteen years old. Shank, *Prophet Harris*, 42n, 49.
63. Lamin Sanneh, *Disciples of all Nations: Pillars of World Christianity* (New York: Oxford University Press, 2008), 193–200; Kalu, *African Pentecostalism*, 36–38; Shank, *Prophet Harris*, 15–16; Haliburton, *The Prophet Harris*, 121.
64. For Kru and Glebo identities, see note 5 above.
65. Shank, *Prophet Harris*.
66. Massing, *The Economic Anthropology*, 60–61; Shank, *Prophet Harris*, 31–36, 87–88; Davis, *Ethnohistorical Studies*, 192–95.
67. Quoted in Shank, *Prophet Harris*, 178.
68. Ibid., 58–59, 63–64, 105–19, 154; Haliburton, *The Prophet Harris*, xiii–xv.
69. Shank, *Prophet Harris*, 219.
70. Ibid., 117–19, 154–55, 161–73, 225.
71. One century after Harris's remarkable ministry, the African Christian approach to the spiritual world and reading of the Bible continues to challenge Christians in Europe and North America. See Mark A. Noll, *The New Shape of World Christianity: How American Experience Reflects Global Faith* (Downers Grove, Ill.: IVP Academic, 2009), 33–37.
72. W. B. Williams, a Methodist missionary in Liberia, came as close as any in affirming the full religious validity of Harris's missionaries. Haliburton, *The Prophet Harris*, 124; see also 94, 121–27; Shank, *Prophet Harris*, 15–16, 20–22.
73. Kalu, *African Pentecostalism*, 31, 71.

Chapter 9

1. Portions of this chapter have been published earlier in Jay Riley Case, "And Ever the Twain Shall Meet: The Holiness Missionary Movement and the Birth of World Pentecostalism, 1870–1920," *Religion and American Culture* 16 (Summer 2006): 125–59. See also A. B. Shah, ed., and Sister Geraldine, comp., *The Letters and Correspondence of Pandita Ramabai* (Bombay: Maharashtra State Board for Literature and Culture, 1977); Uma Chakravarti, *Rewriting History: The Life and Times of Pandita Ramabai* (New Delhi: Kali for Women, 2000), 316.
2. Shah, *The Letters*, xi–xv; Pandita Ramabai, *A Testimony* (Kedgoan, India: Ramabai Mukti Mission, 1968), 4–21; Chakravarti, *Rewriting History*, 303–21; Edith L. Blumhofer, "Consuming Fire: Pandita Ramabai and the Global Pentecostal Impulse," in Ogbu U. Kalu, ed., *Interpreting Contemporary Christianity: Global Processes and Local Identities* (Grand Rapids, Mich.: Eerdmans, 2008), 207–37.
3. Shah, *The Letters*, 89, 99; see also 7–9, 59, 68, 69, 80, 87, 99, 102, 104, 105; Chakravati, *Rewriting History*, 316.
4. Shah, *The Letters*, 338; Blumhofer, "Consuming Fire," 207–18.
5. Shah, *The Letters*, 423; *Indian Witness*, January 4, 1906, 3–4; Jennie Chappell, *Pandita Ramabai: A Great Life in Indian Missions* (London: Pickering & Inglis, n.d.); Allan Anderson, *Spreading Fires: The Missionary Nature of Early Pentecostalism* (Maryknoll, N.Y.: Orbis, 2007), 79–80.
6. See, for example, Meera Kosambi, ed., *Pandita Ramabai through Her Own Words: Selected Works* (New York: Oxford University Press, 2000); Meera Kosambi, *Pandita Ramabai's American Encounter: The Peoples of the United States (1889)* (Bloomington: Indiana University Press, 2003); Gauri Viswanathan, *Outside the Fold: Conversion, Modernity and Belief* (Princeton, N.J.: Princeton University Press, 1998), 118–52; Chakravarti, *Rewriting History*.

7. Pentecostalism, with all of its diversity, has been particularly difficult to define in the global context. Unlike Pentecostalism in America, worldwide Pentecostalism can be defined not simply as groups that speak in tongues but as a collection of diverse evangelical movements that place particular emphasis on the work and gifts of the Holy Spirit. See Allan Anderson, *An Introduction to Pentecostalism: Global Charismatic Christianity* (Cambridge, U.K.: Cambridge University Press, 2004), 1–15.
8. Shah, *The Letters*, 25, 71–72.
9. Ramabai, *A Testimony*, 13, 15; Blumhofer, "Consuming Fire."
10. Shah, *The Letters*, 404–5, 101, 348; see also 107, 317, 404.
11. Ibid., 109, 112; see also 25, 39–43, 51–61, 109, 111–12, 124, 178.
12. Ibid., 44, 48, 50; see also 38–50.
13. Ibid., 17; Blumhofer, "Consuming Fire," 209; Chakravati, *Rewriting History*, 307–10; Viswanathan, *Outside the Fold*, 118–19.
14. Shah, *The Letters*, 423; Ramabai, *A Testimony*, 19.
15. *Minutes of the Ramabai Association, 1891*, Garrett-Evangelical Theological Seminary Archives; *Heathen Woman's Friend*, February 1884, 182; Helen S. Dyer, *Pandita Ramabai: The Story of Her Life* (New York: Fleming H. Revell, 1900), 62; Blumhofer, "Consuming Fire," 215.
16. *Heathen Woman's Friend*, July 1883, 12–13; April 1886, 247–48; *Indian Witness*, January 4, 1906, 3–4: Edith L. Blumhofer, "'From India's Coral Strand': Pandita Ramabai and U.S. Support for Foreign Missions," in Daniel H. Bays and Grant Wacker, eds., *The Foreign Missionary Enterprise at Home: Explorations in North American Cultural History* (Tuscaloosa: University of Alabama Press, 2003), 152–70.
17. Quoted in Robert Eric Frykenberg, *Christianity in India: From Beginnings to the Present* (Oxford: Oxford University Press, 2008), 396–97; Shah, *The Letters*, xxiv, 264–69; Chakravarti, *Rewriting History*, 327–32; Blumhofer, "Consuming Fire," 218.
18. Quoted in Dyer, *Pandita Ramabai*, 86–90. See also Ramabai, *A Testimony*, 22–24; Blumhofer, "Consuming Fire," 217–18.
19. Ramabai, *A Testimony*, 23.
20. *Revivalist*, August 1897; see also July 1890; June 1890; December 21, 1899, 9; Randall J. Stephens, *The Fire Spreads: Holiness and Pentecostalism in the American South* (Cambridge, Mass.: Harvard University Press, 2008), 112–13.
21. *Revivalist*, August 1897, 1; July 1890; June 1890; December 21, 1899, 9; Charles Edwin Jones, *Perfectionist Persuasion: The Holiness Movement and American Methodism, 1867–1936* (Metuchen, N.J.: Scarecrow, 1974), 99–105, 115–19.
22. Paul Boyer, *When Time Shall Be No More: Prophecy Belief in Modern American Culture* (Cambridge, Mass.: Harvard University Press, 1992); Timothy P. Weber, *Living in the Shadow of the Second Coming: American Premillennialism, 1875–1925* (New York: Oxford University Press, 1979).
23. *Revivalist*, January 5, 1899, 9; January 12, 1899, 9; February 9, 1899, 9.
24. Abrams had attended the Chicago Training School for City, Home and Foreign Missions, founded by Lucy Rider Meyer, who had been influenced early in her career by holiness doctrine and spirituality. Lucy Rider Meyer, *Deaconesses and Their Work: Biblical, Early Church, European, American* (Chicago: Deaconess Advocate, 1897); Lucy Rider, "Why Are We Not Filled with the Spirit?" CTS scrapbook, Garrett Theological Seminary Archives.
25. Dyer, *Pandita Ramabai*, 114–16.
26. *Revivalist*, February 16, 1899, 9; Stephens, *The Fire Spreads*, 82–84, 112–13.
27. *Revivalist*, December 28, 1899, 9.
28. Ibid., December 28, 1899, 9; May 4, 1899, 9; Stephens, *The Fire Spreads*, 82–83.
29. *Word and Work*, November 1902, 338.
30. *Trust*, March 1918, 16; *Latter Rain Evangel*, July 1909, 6; Anderson, *Spreading Fires*, 78.
31. *Latter Rain Evangel*, March 1910, 13–18.
32. *Reality*, July 1904, 167–69; *Word and Work*, October 1905, 245; April 1906, 117; February 1906, 56; Jonathan R. Baer, "Redeemed Bodies: The Functions of Divine Healing in Incipient Pentecostalism," *Church History* 70 (December 2001): 735–71.

33. *Reality,* May 1905, 107; June 1905, 121; *Word and Work,* January 1905, 18; February 1905, 53; March 1905, 82; April 1905, 114; July 1905, 181; August/September 1905, 210; October/September 1905, 244; January 1906, 21; February 1906, 51; March 1906, 82; April 1906, 116; May 1906, 145; *Triumphs of Faith,* March 1906, 57; Joe Creech, "Visions of Glory: The Place of the Azusa Street Revival in Pentecostal History," *Church History* 65 (September 1996): 405–24; Robert Mapes Anderson, *Vision of the Disinherited: The Making of American Pentecostalism* (New York: Oxford University Press, 1979), 45.
34. Quoted in S. M. Adhav, *Pandita Ramabai* (Madras: Christian Literature Society, 1979), 216; Anderson, *Spreading Fires,* 79.
35. Blumhofer, "Consuming Fire," 232–33.
36. Quoted in Adhav, *Pandita Ramabai,* 217, 221, 222.
37. Quoted in Gary B. McGee, "Minnie F. Abrams: Another Context, Another Founder," in James R. Goff Jr., and Grant Wacker, eds., *Portraits of a Generation: Early Pentecostal Leaders* (Fayetteville: University of Arkansas Press, 2002), 94; Adhav, *Pandita Ramabai,* 219–20, 223; Anderson, *Spreading Fires,* 84.
38. Minnie Abrams, *The Baptism of the Holy Ghost & Fire* (Kedgaon, India: Mukti Mission, 1906); 7–9, 70, 82–83; Anderson, *Spreading Fires,* 79–81, 99–100; Blumhofer, "Consuming Fire," 223–25.
39. Anderson, *Spreading Fires,* 29–30.
40. Vinson Synan, *The Holiness-Pentecostal Tradition: Charismatic Movements in the Twentieth Century* (Grand Rapids, Mich.: Eerdmans, 1997), 136–37; J. B. A. Kessler Jr., *A Study of the Older Protestant Missions and Churches in Peru and Chile: With Special Reference to the Problems of Division, Nationalism and Native Ministry* (Goes: Oosterbaan & Le Cointre, 1967), 108–11; Christian Lalive D'Epinay, *Haven of the Masses: A Study of the Pentecostal Movement in Chile* (London: Lutterworth, 1969), 7–8.
41. Kessler, *A Study,* 111–15; D'Epinay, *Haven of the Masses,* 7–8; J. Treymayne Copplestone, *The History of Methodist Missions: Twentieth Century Perspectives,* Vol. 4 (New York: Board of Global Ministries of the United Methodist Church, 1973), 604.
42. Walter J. Hollenweger, "Methodism's Past in Pentecostalism's Present: A Case Study of a Cultural Clash in Chile," *Methodist History* 20 (July 1982): 169–82; Kessler, *A Study,* 116–30; D'Epinay, *Haven of the Masses,* 9–12.
43. Copplestone, *The History,* Vol. 4, 603–4; Kessler, *A Study,* 105, 110, 288.
44. Anderson, *Spreading Fires,* 28–31.
45. When scholars began to explain the origins of Pentecostalism, they followed the lead of American Pentecostals from the mid-twentieth century who placed the Azusa Street revival at the epicenter of the movement. In this narrative, Pentecostalism moved from its base in Los Angeles across the United States, before blazing a west-to-east missionary path around the world. Joe Creech, however, has demonstrated that this obscured the reality that Pentecostalism actually emerged in numerous places within the United States. When one gives further consideration to the radial-holiness revivals around the world during the same time period, the birth of Pentecostalism takes on a decidedly international character. Americans might have made up a majority of Pentecostals in its first decades, but they were in the minority as early as 1950. Creech, "Visions of Glory"; Gary B. McGee, "'Latter Rain' Falling in the East: Early-Twentieth-Century Pentecostalism in India and the Debate over Speaking in Tongues," *Church History* 68 (September 1999): 648–65; Everett A. Wilson, "They Crossed the Red Sea, Didn't They? Critical History and Pentecostal Beginnings," in Murray W. Dempster, Byron D. Klaus, and Douglas Petersen, eds., *The Globalization of Pentecostalism: A Religion Made to Travel* (Oxford: Regnum, 1999), 85–115; Anderson, *An Introduction to Pentecostalism.*
46. *Bridegroom's Messenger,* July 1, 1909, 2; February 15, 1910, 4; March 1, 1910, 4; October 1, 1910, 2; November 1, 1911, 4; *Upper Room,* August 1909, 5; January 1911, 6.
47. *Bridegroom's Messenger,* May 1, 1908, 1; September 1, 1909, 2; *Upper Room,* August 1909, 6.
48. George W. Stocking, Jr., *Victorian Anthropology* (New York: Free Press, 1987); Gail Bederman, *Manliness and Civilization: A Cultural History of Gender and Race in the United States, 1880–1917* (Chicago: University of Chicago Press, 1995); Matthew Frye Jacobson,

Barbarian Virtues: The United States Encounters Foreign Peoples at Home and Abroad, 1876–1917 (New York: Hill & Wang), 2000; Robert W. Rydell, *World of Fairs: The Century-of-Progress Expositions* (Chicago: University of Chicago Press, 1993); Adam Kuper, *Culture: The Anthropologists' Account* (Cambridge, Mass.: Harvard University Press, 1999), 23–46.

49. Quoted in Robert T. Handy, *A Christian America: Protestant Hopes and Historical Realities* (London: Oxford University Press, 1971), 126; Jonathan J. Bonk, *"Not the Bloom, but the Root . . .": Conversion and Its Consequences in Nineteenth-Century Protestant Missionary Discourse* (New Haven, Conn.: Yale Divinity School Library, 2003).

50. For the liberal Protestant move away from conversion toward developmental understanding of Christianity, see Horace Bushnell, "Christian Nurture," in David A. Hollinger and Charles Capper, eds., *The American Intellectual Tradition: A Sourcebook, Volume I: 1630–1865* (New York: Oxford University Press, 1993), 336; George A. Gordon, "The Gospel for Humanity," in William R. Hutchison, ed., *American Protestant Thought in the Liberal Era* (Lanham, Md.: University Press of America, 1968), 104, 105; William R. Hutchison, *The Modernist Impulse in American Protestantism* (New York: Oxford University Press, 1982).

51. Hutchison, *American Protestant Thought*, 98–107; Hutchison, *The Modernist Impulse*, 40, 133; William Hutchison, *Errand to the World: American Protestant Thought and Foreign Missions* (Chicago: University of Chicago Press, 1987), 91–111.

52. Hutchison, *American Protestant Thought*, 105; Stocking, *Victorian Anthropology*, 149–85; Bederman, *Manliness and Civilization*, 126–27; Jacobson, *Barbarian Virtues*, 49.

53. Compare Abrams's supernaturalistic description of missionary activity with the organizational and structural language of missionary work that emerged in the Student Volunteer Movement after World War I. Abrams, *Baptism of the Holy Ghost*, 5–12, 88; Clifton J. Philips, "Changing Attitudes in the Student Volunteer Movement of Great Britain and North America, 1886–1928," in Torben Christensen and William R. Hutchison, eds., *Missionary Ideologies in the Imperialist Era: 1880–1920* (Aarhus, Denmark: Aros, 1982), 131–45.

54. See issues of *Apostolic Faith, Revivalist, Michigan Holiness Record, Word and Work, Upper Room, Trust, Bridegroom's Messenger*. Abrams, *Baptism of the Holy Ghost*, 4, 71–73; Gary B. McGee, "Pentecostal Phenomena and Revivals in India: Implications for Indigenous Church Leadership," *International Bulletin of Missionary Research* 20 (July 1996): 112–17.

55. Quoted in Jacobson, *Barbarian Virtues*, 221.

56. Abrams, *Baptism of the Holy Ghost*, 4, 69.

57. Roger Daniels, *Coming to America: A History of Immigration and Ethnicity in American Life* (New York: HarperPerennial, 1991), 218; Philip Gleason, "American Identity and Americanization," in Stephan Thernstrom et al., *Harvard Encyclopedia of American Ethnic Groups* (Cambridge, Mass.: Harvard University Press, 1980), 31–57; George J. Sanchez, *Becoming Mexican American: Ethnicity, Culture and Identity in Chicano Los Angeles, 1900–1945* (New York: Oxford University Press, 1993); John Higham, *Strangers in the Land: Patterns of American Nativism, 1860–1925* (New York: Atheneum, 1963); Frank Ninkovich, *The United States and Imperialism* (Malden, Mass.: Blackwell, 2001).

58. *Bridegroom's Messenger*, March 1, 1912, 1; May 1, 1914, 3; *Upper Room*, August 1909, 5.

59. *Apostolic Faith*, April 1907, 1; *Bridegroom's Messenger*, June 15, 1908, 1; Edward W. Said, *Orientalism* (New York: Vintage, 1979).

60. Abrams, *Baptism of the Holy Ghost*, 65, 69–73.

61. *Upper Room*, April 1910, 5; see also August 1909, 5; October/November 1909, 7; June 1910, 5; *Bridegroom's Messenger*, May 15, 1909, 2; September 15, 1909, 1; December 15, 1909, 4; January 1, 1910, 2; *Trust*, May 1910, 17; March 1911, 11; *Latter Rain Evangel*, December 1909, 22–23.

62. *Bridegroom's Messenger*, May 1, 1910, 4; see also October 1, 1910, 2; March 1, 1912, 1; May 1, 1912, 4; October 15, 1912, 3; November 1, 1913, 3.

63. Ibid., April 1, 1910, 2; August 1, 1910, 3; April 15, 1912, 2; April 1, 1914, 3; February 1, 1914, 2; May 1, 1914, 3; *Trust*, May 1910, 17; May 1911, 16; *Upper Room*, October/November 1909, 6; January 1910, 5; May 1910, 6; June 1910, 5–6; July 1910, 5; *Word and Work*, October 1914, 316–17.

64. After the 1905–06 revival, the more ecstatic features of the Mukti revival faded away, and the mission returned to a more sedate style of worship. Still, Ramabai continued to inspire American Pentecostals. A number of Pentecostal periodicals carried obituaries or memorial accounts of Ramabai upon her death. *Triumphs of Faith,* June 1922, 138–39; *Word and Work,* May 1922, 12; Chakravarti, *Rewriting History,* 340.
65. *Trust,* March 1918, 15–16; *Latter Rain Evangel,* January 1909, 13. Pentecostal periodicals produced an overwhelming number of references to Ramabai. For representative examples, see *Latter Rain Evangel,* January 1909, 13–17; *Bridegroom's Messenger,* May 1, 1908, 1; *Trust,* May 1910, 18; *Upper Room,* August 1909, 4; *Word and Work,* March 1909, 74; *Triumphs of Faith,* February 1908, 42–44; *Apostolic Faith,* May 1908, 1; *Latter Rain Evangel,* November 1908, 7–12.
66. *Bridegroom's Messenger,* February 15, 1909, 1; see also August 1, 1908, 4; *Upper Room,* August 1909, 4; September 1909, 5; *Trust,* May 1912, 19; *Triumphs of Faith,* February 1908, 42–44; *Word and Work,* March 1909, 74.
67. Scholars have noted the relative ease with which local or indigenous leaders have been able to reach positions of authority within Pentecostalism. David Martin, *Tongues of Fire: The Explosion of Protestantism in Latin America* (Oxford: Blackwell, 1990), 5, 180, 231; Harvey Cox, *Fire from Heaven: The Rise of Pentecostal Spirituality and the Reshaping of Religion in the Twenty-First Century* (Reading, Mass.: Addison Wesley, 1995); Philip Jenkins, *The Next Christendom: The Coming of Global Christianity* (Oxford: Oxford University Press, 2002); John Burdick, *Looking for God in Brazil: The Progressive Catholic Church in Brazil's Urban Arena* (Berkeley: University of California Press, 1996).
68. Edith Blumhofer, *Restoring the Faith: The Assemblies of God, Pentecostalism and American Culture* (Urbana: University of Illinois Press, 1993); Anderson, *An Introduction to Pentecostalism,* 270–76; Synan, *The Holiness-Pentecostal Tradition,* 180–83; Grant Wacker, *Heaven Below: Early Pentecostals and American Culture* (Cambridge, Mass.: Harvard University Press, 2001), 226–35.
69. Susan Hill Lindley, *"You Have Stept Out of Your Place": A History of Women and Religion in America* (Louisville, Ky.: Westminster John Knox, 1996), 328–29; Creech, "Visions of Glory"; Jones, *Perfectionist Persuasion,* 135; Synan, *The Holiness-Pentecostal Tradition,* 28–30, 93–95, 167–70, 182.
70. Abrams, *The Baptism of the Holy Ghost,* 4, 12, 68–73.
71. *Upper Room,* October/November 1909, 7.
72. Wacker, *Heaven Below,* 44–51; McGee, "'Latter Rain' Falling in the East," 650–51.
73. *Latter Rain Evangel,* March 1910, 18.
74. Quoted in Wacker, *Heaven Below,* 142.
75. *The Baptism of the Holy Ghost and Fire,* in fact, was published in installments by the Methodist periodical in India, the *Indian Witness.* See the following 1906 issues of *Indian Witness*: April 26, May 3, May 24, June 14, June 21, June 28, December 27; Gary B. McGee, "'Baptism of the Holy Ghost & Fire!' The Mission Legacy of Minnie F. Abrams," *Missiology: An International Review* 27 (October, 1999): 515–22.
76. See the first issues of *Apostolic Faith,* September 1906–April 1907.
77. *Bridegroom's Messenger,* December 1, 1908, 2.
78. Kessler, *A Study,* 295–307; Kalu, *African Pentecostalism,* 136–37; Anderson, *Spreading Fires,* 201–05.
79. Wacker, *Heaven Below,* 226–35; McGee, "'Baptism of the Holy Ghost & Fire!'"; Dana L. Robert, *American Women in Mission: A Social History of Their Thought and Practice* (Macon, Ga.: Mercer University Press, 1996), 244–54.
80. Quoted in Adhav, *Pandita Ramabai,* 217; Blumhofer, "Consuming Fire."
81. Quoted in Adhav, *Pandita Ramabai,* 223.
82. Ibid., 221, 223, 224.
83. George Marsden, *Jonathan Edwards: A Life* (New Haven, Conn., and London: Yale University Press, 2003), 233–35.
84. Kalu, *African Pentecostalism,* 80; E. Kingsley Larbi, *Pentecostalism: The Eddies of Ghanaian Christianity* (Accra: Centre for Pentecostal and Charismatic Studies, 2001).

Epilogue

1. Nathan Hatch, *The Democratization of American Christianity* (New Haven, Conn.: Yale University Press, 1989), 211.
2. Lamin Sanneh, *Translating the Message: The Missionary Impact on Culture* (Maryknoll, N.Y.: Orbis, 1999).
3. Andrew F. Walls, *The Missionary Movement in Christian History: Studies in the Transmission of Faith* (Maryknoll, N.Y.: Orbis, 1996); Lamin Sanneh, *Disciples of All Nations: Pillars of World Christianity* (Oxford and New York: Oxford University Press, 2007); Dale T. Irvin and Scott W. Sunquist, *History of the World Christian Movement, Vol. 1: Earliest Christianity to 1453* (Maryknoll, N.Y.: Orbis, 2004); Kwame Bediako, *Christianity in Africa: The Renewal of Non-western Religion* (Edinburgh: Edinburgh University Press, 1995).
4. Joseph Conforti, "Jonathan Edwards' Most Popular Work: 'The Life of David Brainerd' and Nineteenth-Century Evangelical Culture," *Church History* 54 (June 1985): 188–201; George M. Marsden, *Jonathan Edwards: A Life* (New Haven, Conn.: Yale University Press, 2006), 331–33.

INDEX

Abbott, Elisha, 45, 72, 81, 87, 94–5; evaluations of Karen Christianity, 48–50, 60, 63; promotion of Karen ordination, 51–55, 63, 69–70, 259

Abbott, Lyman, 235, 244–45

abolitionism, 12, 59, 67–9, 74, 75–6, 97, 169–70, 177, 179, 180

Abrams, Minnie, 6, 247, 251; and *Baptism of the Holy Ghost & Fire,* 4, 242, 246, 249–53; early ministry, 237–38; relationship with Pandita Ramabai, 237–40, 243, 259

Adventism, 75

Advocate of Christian Holiness 145, 147, 219, 224

African-American evangelicalism (*see also,* African Methodist Episcopal Church): African culture as component, 171–73, 177, 257; and the American nation-state, 179–82, 186–88; anti-formalist impulses within, 164–65, 171–73, 176–77, 178–79, 192–93; and black colleges, 88, 97–9, 167; early missionary efforts of, 187–88; and evangelism, 86, 160–63, 167; and emigration to Africa, 186–88; formalist impulses within, 170–74, 178–79, 188; issues of autonomy, 95–6, 167; as a part of world Christianity, 14, 159–160, 172, 257; racial dynamics of, 159–60, 168–70, 260; role of conversion within, 163–64

African American Great Awakening: characteristics of, 163–64, 167, 174, 260; and democratization, 167, 172–73, 192; influence on Henry McNeal Turner, 175, 191, 193; relationship to American culture, 179–82, 260

African Independent Churches (AICs), 83, 205

African Methodist Episcopal Church (AME), (*see also,* African-American evangelicalism; Methodists, American): 160, 174–75; antiformalist impulses within, 171–73, 192–93; civilizing mission within, 188, 190–91, 202–04; and conceptions of Africa, 188–89, 193–96, 201–05; emigration debate, 186–88; merger with Ethiopian movement, 184–85, 200; formalist impulses within, 170–74, 188–90, 192; ordination issue, 168, 178–79, 202–04; racial views of leaders, 68–9, 179–82, 188–90, 202–03; role of education, 169, 192–93, 196–97, 201, 206; in South Africa, 184, 201–205

African Presbyterian Church, 83

African religions, traditional, 105–09, 114–15, 124–25, 212–13, 229, 254

Agassiz, Louis, 67

Alabama, 161, 179, 180

Allahabad, 242

Allen, Richard, 184

AME Church Review, 191

American Baptist Home Missionary Society (ABHMS), 75, 87–90, 92–4, 96–7

American Baptist Magazine (see also, *Baptist Missionary Magazine*), 30, 31, 55, 57, 63

American Baptist Missionary Union (ABMU), (*see also,* Triennial Convention; Baptists, American): 59, 91, 94; administration of, 77, 87, 92; board and committee statements, 65–6, 70, 71, 73, 82, 96; debates within, 83–5; financial issues, 95, 98; and the Moulmein Convention, 81–4; ordination of non western Christians, 51–5, 63, 70, 91

American Baptists. *See* Baptists, American

American Board of Commissioners for Foreign Missions (ABCFM), 58, 82–3, 90, 91, 120, 130, 136, 245; "civilization first- policies, 56–7, 83

American Colonization Society, 187

American Freedman's Union Commission (AFUC), 87, 97, 167, 177

American Indians. *See* Native Americans

American Missionary Association, 170

American Oriental Society, 61

American Tract Society, 45

Americo-Liberians, 226, 227

301

Anderson, Rufus, 82–3, 123
Andover Seminary, 62, 195
Andrews, Edward, 150
Anglicanism (*see also*, Episcopalianism), 83, 106, 117, 121, 130–31, 195, 203, 231–34, 236
Anglican Society for the Propagation of the Gospel in Foreign Parts, 164
Angola, 128, 152, 154
Anim, Peter, 230
Annshaw mission station, 108, 114–16, 197, 259
Anthony, Susan B., 75
antiformalists: and Baptists, 53, 55–60, 89; and black evangelicalism, 164–65, 171–73, 176–77, 178–79, 192–93; definition, 13–14; within holiness movement, 216–19, 227, 236–40; within Methodism, 112, 133–34, 216–17; within Pentecostalism, 249–52; among South Africans, 205; and William Taylor, 103, 112, 116, 119, 126–27, 129–32, 152; in the United States, 33, 217–19, 227, 258
Anti-Masonic Party, 75
Anti-Slavery Society, 169
Apostolic Faith, 246
Apostolic Ministry, 74, 81, 85
Appeal for Africa, 191
A-Pyah Thee, 19–23, 26, 28, 30, 40, 52
Arizona, 217
Arms, Goodsil, 148
Arnett, B.W., 169
Asbury, Francis, 134, 165
Ashburn, George, 180
Assemblies of God, 209
Asiatic Society of Bengal, 61
Atlantic Monthly, 137
atonement, evangelical conceptions of: 7, 9, 31, 32, 37, 122, 125, 235
Augustine, 79
Aurangabad, 242
Australia, 111, 113, 128, 240, 243
Azor expedition, 186, 188, 191
Azusa Street revival, 210, 240, 242, 243, 246, 250, 252

Bahamas, 187
Baltimore, 175
Bancroft, George
Bangalore, 129, 242
Bangs, Nathan, 142, 145
Baptism of the Holy Ghost & Fire, 4, 242, 246, 249–53
Baptist General Tract Society, 75
Baptist Missionary Magazine, 6, 45, 61, 69, 77, 89, 92
Baptist Missionary Society (*see also*, Baptists, English), 50
Baptists, American, (*see also*, American Baptist Missionary Union): 120, 154, 165, 166, 167, 219, 259; African American, 59, 86, 92–9, 163; and the American establishment, 8, 36, 57–60, 165–66; and civilization, 6, 36, 48, 89–91; democratization among, 12, 13, 53–5, 57, 75, 77, 80–1, 164–65; during the early republic, 53–5, 57, 74–5, 164–65; and education, 37, 58–60, 67, 74–81, 86, 260; issues of autonomy, 53–4, 81–5, 92–6; missionary efforts in American South, 87–90, 98; perceptions of Burma, 28–31, 36–7, 39; perceptions of the Karen, 25–7, 48–55, 60–4, 76–80; and print media, 30, 43, 45–6; Triennial Convention board, 33, 35–6, 55, 267 n. 54
Baptists, British, 29, 30, 50
Bareilley Theological Seminary, 139
Barratt, T.B., 242
Bassein, 38, 94
Beecher, Henry Ward, 176, 223
Beecher, John, 94
Beecher, Lyman, 172
Beirut, 111
Bellingham, Washington, 246
Bennett, Cephas, 40–1
Benton, Thomas Hart, 65
Berry, Amanda. *See* Smith, Amanda Berry
Beveridge, Albert, 246
Bible: African-American use of, 165, 166, 180; role in American evangelicalism, 7, 9, 32, 45, 63, 69, 86, 117–19, 125, 212; and translations by missionaries, 33–5, 43, 252, 253, 257; use by Karen Christians, 41–5, 258; use of in world Christianity, 9, 11, 12, 41, 117–18, 198, 230, 241
Binkley, Clara, 210–12
Binney, Joseph, 70–2, 95
Blair, Frank, 138
Bleh Poh, 54, 55, 63
Blyden, Edward, 193
Boardman, George: 60, 62, 258–59; death of, 39–40, 58; educational efforts of, 27, 37, 56; engagement with Karen, 20–23; fame in America, 23, 40; plans for Burma, 20, 24–5, 27, 37; perceptions of the Karen 25–7, 37–8, 48, 52
Boardman, George, Jr., 40
Boardman, Sarah: 27, 38, 40, 256; educational efforts of, 26, 40, 56; engagement with Karen, 20–21; evangelistic activities, 58, 91; marriage to Adoniram Judson, 46
Boers, 109, 113–14, 116, 154
Bombay, 129, 130–32, 135–36, 234, 235, 242
Bombay Guardian, 224–25
Booth, Catherine, 145
Boston, 235
Boston University School of Theology, 148
Bowen, George, 136

Boyle, E. Mayfield, 195
Brainerd, David, 39
Brazil, 29, 128, 240
Brekus, Catherine, 216
Bridegroom's Messenger, 246, 248, 252
Briggs, George N., 59
British East India Company, 29
British Guinea, 187
Brooks, Phillips, 235
Brown University, 74, 99
Bucknell University, 99
Bucknell, William, 58–9
Buddhism, 20–1, 24–5, 29, 30, 33, 35, 37, 41, 49
Burma: 14, 29, 40, 120; and British imperialism, 19, 27, 41, 46, 49–50
Burmah Baptist Missionary Convention, 92, 95
Burman (people group): Christians among, 26, 27, 31, 37, 40, 42, 50; and gender, 37; missionary efforts among, 20, 24–5, 29, 30, 33, 35, 37, 79; and relationship with the Karen, 19, 20–1, 49, 54, 95
Burns, Francis, 151

Calcutta, 29, 129, 136, 225, 231, 234, 246
California, 111, 113, 132, 217, 230
Callahan, Allen Dwight, 180
Calvinism. *See* evangelical Calvinism; Dutch Reformed; Puritanism
Calvin, John, 79
Campbell, James, 203
Canada, 111, 219, 240
Cape Palmas, 211, 226, 228
Capetown, 200
Carey, William, 50, 66
Carnegie, Andrew, 98, 222
Cartwright, Peter, 121
Cass, Lewis, 65
Catholicism, 59, 113, 167, 227, 230
Ceylon, 29, 128, 247
Charleston, South Carolina, 168, 170, 186
Chattanooga, 246
Cheltenham Ladies College, 231
Cherokee, 56–7, 65
Chicago, 89, 93, 194, 238, 242, 251
Chicago Training School, 237–38, 242
Chile, 4, 140–42, 146, 148, 230, 242–3, 244
China, 45, 75, 85, 191, 196, 219, 240, 242, 244, 247, 251
Christian Adventures in South Africa, 110, 129, 132
Christian Advocate, 132, 136
Christian Recorder, 161, 175, 176, 187, 191
Christian Watchman & Reflector, 66
Chubbock, Emily. *See* Forrester, Fanny
Church Missionary Society, 83, 120
Church of England. *See* Anglicanism
Church of God (Anderson), 217
civilization (*see also,* civilizing mission): and African-Americans, 164, 169–70, 175, 177, 188–91, 194, 202–04; American conceptions of, 4, 6, 9–10, 65, 89, 137, 189, 244–46, 258; black South African challenges to, 109, 185; criticisms of, 6, 145, 180–81, 237, 241; and disenchantment, 10–12, 245; and education, 10–12, 60–1, 89–92; ignoring discourse of, 4, 6, 14, 123, 126–27, 209–10, 245–46; Karen Christian challenges to, 28, 37, 54; missionary conceptions of, 6, 25, 36–7, 51–2, 56–7, 78, 83, 89–92, 115, 120, 199, 244–45; and modernist Protestantism, 245; and Pentecostalism, 245–46; and race, 10, 64–9, 90, 137–40, 142–44, 189, 194, 199, 202–04; relationship to Christianity, 4, 6, 36–7, 55, 91–2, 135, 142–44, 199, 216–7, 259
civilizing mission, 4, 96, 135, 253; and African Americans, 169–70, 175, 188–91, 194, 202–04; in Burma, 27, 60–4, 69–70; in Liberia, 210, 211, 228; as a missionary theory, 27, 56, 83, 90; and modernist Protestantism, 244–45
Civil Rights Act of 1875, 190
Civil War, American: 85–8, 161, 162, 166, 170, 175, 179
Colby College, 62
Colenso, John, 117–19, 122
Colgate, William, 58
colonialism. *See* imperialism
Columbian College, 70, 75
Columbus Weekly Sun, 180
communism, 83
Community of St. Mary the Virgin (CSMV), 231
Congo, 128, 152–54
Congregationalism, 32, 57, 59, 87, 90, 98, 167, 170, 209, 219
Connecticut, 69
Consolidated American Baptist Missionary Convention (CABMC), 93–4
conversion: and African American evangelicalism, 160, 163–64, 187, 195; and antiformalists, 13–14, 133, 238; cultural dynamics of, 7–9; 31–2, 122, 151, 234; as experience of missionaries, 7, 31–2, 125, 174, 213; of non-westerners, 3, 27, 108, 197, 234, 235, 238; resistance to, 7, 30–1, 33, 37, 104, 106; role in missionary activities, 7, 27, 31, 122, 133, 154
Coppinger, William, 187
Coppin, Levi, 204
Crania Aegyptiaca, 67
Crania Americana, 67
Crowther, Samuel Ajayi, 83
Crozer, John, 58
Curry, Daniel, 136

Damasi, 116
Darwin, Charles, 118

Darwinian thought (*see also*, Social Darwinism), 118, 138, 245
Dawlly, Helen, 219
Delany, Martin, 193
Democratic Party, 59
democratization, 12, 13, 226; within African-American evangelicalism, 164–66, 167, 192–93; among American Baptists, 53–5, 60, 77, 80–1; and William Taylor, 114, 121, 131, 136–37; within world Christianity, 8–9, 205, 256–57
Denmark, 73
Dew, Thomas Roderick, 64
disenchantment: and cross-cultural engagement, 44; definition of, 10; holiness critique of, 146, 236, 239–40; among missionaries, 44, 215
dispensationalism, 237
Douglass, Frederick, 74, 75
Dow, "Crazy" Lorenzo, 172
Drake, Lucy. *See* Lucy Drake Osborn
Drew, Daniel, 134
DuBois, W.E.B., 98–9, 172–73, 180
Duff, Alexander, 56, 82
Durban, 116, 183
Dutch Reformed, 113
Dwane, James Mata, 184, 196–203, 204

East Indian Railroad Company, 225
Easton, Hosea, 69
Ecumenical Missionary Conference, 1900, 45
Edendale, South Africa, 198
Edinburgh, 120
Educated Ministry, 78, 85
Education: and African Americans, 86, 88–90, 192–93, 260; and autonomy issues, 95–6, 167; of missionaries, 37, 62; in missionary policy, 10–12, 30, 60–2, 67, 70–3, 82, 119–20, 192–93; and non-western Christians, 11–12, 67, 70–3, 119–20, 196–97, 201, 206; role of seminary education, 74–82, 134
Edwards, Jonathan, 28, 79, 115, 254, 256
Egypt, 240
emancipation, 85–8, 161, 163, 166
Emerson, Ralph Waldo
Enlightenment, 48; and African American Christianity, 172; assumptions of religious superstition, 11, 30, 115; conceptions of rationality, 30, 44, 56, 115, 172–73, 190; influence on evangelicals, 30, 56
Episcopalianism, 86, 166, 209, 211, 228, 229, 230
Ethiopian movement, 103, 184–85, 196–97, 199–200, 203, 205
evangelical Calvinism, 12, 32, 51, 56, 59, 130
evangelicalism (*see also*, atonement, evangelical conceptions of; Bible; conversion; evangelism): and abolitionism, 12, 67–9, 76; and African American culture, 159, 60, 164, 179–82, 195–96, 201; and American culture, 31–3, 54, 58–9, 89, 96–7, 112, 138–9, 219–20, 250; antiformalist impulses within, 13–14, 33, 53, 55, 89, 129, 216–20, 249–52; and Burmese culture, 33–7; cultural dynamics of, 7–9, 69, 82, 90–2, 117–18; and cultures of world Christianity, 250–53, 257–60; definition and characteristics of, 7, 8–9, 12–14; formalist impulses within, 13–14, 27, 32–3, 55–7, 66, 89, 143, 188–90; influenced by world Christianity, 9–12, 45–7, 48–55, 69, 74, 174; and Karen culture, 42–5, 54; and Liberian culture, 213–14; power dynamics of, 7–8, 34–5, 141–2, 243; and power among African Americans, 92–6, 159–60, 164–65, 166; and power in Burma, 23, 35, 42–5, 48–50, 54, 92–6; and power in India, 239–40; and power in Liberia, 211–12, 226–27; and power in South Africa, 184, 202–04; and power within world Christianity, 254–60; and use of print media, 34, 43, 45–6, 75, 129, 256
evangelism (*see also*, Karen Christianity, evangelism by; Xhosa Christianity, and the 1866 revival): in African-American evangelicalism, 163, 188–89, by indigenous Christians, 3, 4, 8, 11, 27, 40–1, 126, 196–98, 232; limited by slavery, 165–66; by missionaries, 7–9, 35–6, 82; within the United States, 33, 75–8, 88, 163–65

Fifteenth Amendment, 137
Finney, Charles, 68, 75, 112, 226
First Anglo-Burmese War, 49
First Great Awakening, 13, 164, 205, 216, 254, 256
Fisk University, 97
Flaming Torch in Darkest Africa, 153
Florida, 190
formalists: and Baptists, 27, 55–7, 89; and black evangelicals, 170–74, 178–79, 188–90, 192; definition, 13–14; in India, 129–31, 143; among South Africans, 205; in the United States, 32–3, 56–7
Forrester, Fanny, 46
Fourteenth Amendment, 137, 161, 180
Four Years' Campaign in India, 140
Fowler, Charles, 142
France, 72–3, 230
Free Church of Scotland, 120, 121, 131
Freedman's Bureau, 160, 161, 179–80
French, Austa, 87
Frey, Sylvia, 163–64
Friends. *See* Quakers
Fullwood, C.A., 161–62

Gaines, Wesley, 178, 202–03, 204
Galusha, Elon, 75
Garrison, William Lloyd, 68

Index 305

Garvey, Marcus, 185
gender: antiformalist impulses toward, 91–2, 216; and Baptists, 57–9; in Burma, 36–7, 51, 71; and civilization, 36–7, 90, 216–17; and education, 36–7, 71, 218; formalist impulses toward, 91–2; within the holiness movement, 146, 215–18; in India, 37, 90, 233–35, 236; female ordination issue, 178–79; forms of patriarchy, 91, 212, 233–34; increase in female missionaries, 91, 216; within Methodism, 90, 133, 216; and missionary roles, 58, 90–2, 256; within Pentecostalism, 249–50; women evangelists, 58, 92, 146, 172, 178–79, 215–16, 222–23, 238; Woman's Work for Woman missionary theory, 90, 216, 219, 223, 235; women's missionary societies, 90–1, 191, 194, 216–17
General Conference, African Methodist Episcopal Church, 178, 191, 192, 196, 202, 204, 206
General Conference, Methodist Episcopal Church, 131–32, 135, 148–51
General Holiness Association, 227
Genovese, Eugene, 166
Georgia (United States), 57, 160–62, 174, 178, 180, 187
Germany, 72–3, 77, 78, 240
Gettysburg Seminary, 169
Ghana, 227, 230, 254–55
Goddard, Josiah, 73
Gordon, Adoniram Judson, 91–2
Gordon, George A., 235, 245
Gracey, John, 136
Grahamstown, South Africa, 106–7
Granger, James, 81–2, 84
Graves, Hiram, 66
Gray, Sir George, 106–7, 123
Great Britain (*see also*, Baptists, British; Methodists, British), 61, 66, 121, 128, 224, 236; and colonists in South Africa, 109, 116, 117–18, 199; imperialism in Burma, 19, 27, 35, 41, 46, 49–50, 61, 95; imperialism in India, 232–34, 236; imperialism in South Africa, 105–7, 120, 123, 126–27, 199, 203; missionaries from, 29, 30, 50, 55, 56, 189, 197–200, 231–34, 239, 243, 244
Greece, 72–3
Greek Orthodox Church, 73
Guide to Holiness, 145

Hague, William, 89–90
Haiti, 187
Hamilton College, 75, 78
Harper's, 137
Harris, William (Methodist Episcopal Church bishop), 136
Harris, William Wadé (African evangelist), 227–30, 257, 258
Hartzell, Joseph, 154
Harvard University, 67
Hastings, Warren, 66
Haswell, James, 31
Hatch, Nathan, 15, 134, 165, 257
Hawaii, 66, 83, 120
Healdtown mission station, 121, 183
Heathen Woman's Friend, 90, 216
Heavenly Recruit Church, 218
Helping Hand, 90
Hinduism, 3–4, 30, 130, 143, 225, 231–36, 241, 257
holiness movement, 3–4, 14, 103, 128–29, 135, 155, 209; antiformalist impulses within, 216–19, 227, 236–40; characteristics of, 144–46, 149; critique of mainstream Christianity, 237, 252; and gender, 217–19; 237–38; in India, 235–36, 237; influenced by world Christianity, 214–15; origins of, 144–45; promotion of marginalized individuals, 220; and race, 238; radical branch, 11, 14, 210, 236–39, 242; rejection of disenchantment, 11, 146, 237, 239–40
Holland (AME minister), 222
Homestead Act of 1862, 180
Hoover, May, 242–43, 252
Hoover, Willis, 242–43, 252
Hosier, Harry, 165
Hough, George, 30, 31
Hsi, (Pentecostal leader in China), 246
Hughes, Sarah Ann, 178
Hume, David, 115

Iglesia Metodista Pentecostal, 243
Ik Du Kim, 244
Illinois, 121
immigration, 137–38, 146, 180, 246
imperialism, 4, 13, 152; in Burma, 19, 35, 41, 46, 49–50, 61, 95; in India, 231–34; in Ivory Coast, 230; missionary views of, 66, 139, 199; in the Philippines, 246; in South Africa, 105–7, 126–27, 199
India, 29, 30, 45, 50, 56, 139, 141, 218, 219, 230, 239, 240, 248, 251; and gender, 37; evangelism within, 128, 129–132, 237; and the Mukti revival, 3–4, 232, 240–42, 244; and Pandita Ramabai, 231–36, 240–2 253; and Amanda Smith, 224–25, 256
Indiana, 121, 146, 246
Indianapolis, 247
Indian removal, 13, 33, 56–7, 65
Indians, American. *See* Native Americans.
Indigenous leaders, 239; as cultural experts, 8, 11, 35–6, 50, 62, 96, 205, 234; evangelism by, 5, 8, 27, 35–6, 50, 126, 196–98, 205, 214, 227, 232, 248–49, 257; higher education of, 11, 50, 70–3, 88–9, 196–97; ordination of, 50–55, 70, 91, 127, 202–04, 243

Indonesia, 29
Ingalls, Murilla, 92
Inskip, John, 220–21, 223
Iowa, 217
Islam, 130, 143, 225
Ivory Coast, 227, 230

Jackson, Andrew, 65
Jamaica, 187
Japan, 29, 45
Jennings, Joseph H., 176
Johnson, John Albert, 206
Jones, Joseph E., 89
Joshi, (Indian evangelist in America), 239
Judson, Adoniram, 26, 69, 77, 79, 81; arrival in Burma, 29; Bible translation work of, 34–5; conversion narrative of, 31–2; early perceptions of Burma, 29; engagement with Burmese culture, 25, 30, 34–5; as evangelical celebrity, 46; issue of Burman ordination, 50–1
Judson, Ann, 25, 26, 31, 256; arrival in Burma, 29; Bible translation work of, 35; conversion narrative of, 31–2; and education, 36–7; as evangelical celebrity, 46; views on women and civilization, 36–7

Kalu, Ogbu, 230, 254
Kama (Xhosa chief), 110, 116
Kamastone, South Africa, 122
Kama, William, 116
Kanpur, 129
Karen (people group): relationship with Burman people, 19, 20–21, 41–2; compared to Native Americans, 25; traditional religion of, 19, 20–1, 26, 41–2; and tradition of the lost book, 19–20
Karen Christianity, 66, 103; and autonomy issues, 53–4, 84, 93–6; evangelism by, 23, 37–9, 40–1; financial issues, 95; growth of movement, 23, 39; influence on American evangelicalism, 20, 45–7, 48–55, 74, 76, 91, 99; and literacy, 39, 41, 42–3; nationalism of, 42, 94; and ordination, 51–55, 70, 259; religious zeal of, 39, 48–50; and traditional culture, 42–3, 53–4, 257–58
Karen Normal School, 71–2
Karen Theological Seminary, 70
Keswick Convention, 236, 243
Khoisa, 107
Kilner, James, 198
Kilnerton Institute, 183–84
Knapp, Jacob, 75
Knapp, Martin Wells, 236–37
Korea, 230, 242, 244
Ko Shway-bay, 26
Ko Thah-a, 51, 54
Ko Thah Byu, 257; baptism of, 21, 52; conversion of, 26, 79; as evangelist, 23, 37–8, 40–1, 60, 258; limited education of, 61, 62, 80
Krauser, Oscar von Barchwitz, 146–47
Krishnabai, 238
Kru, 210–15, 226–28
Ku Klux Klan, 180, 250
Kynett, Alpha, 135

Lamplough, Robert, 114–16, 121, 127, 197, 259
Latter Rain Evangel, 248
Lee, Jarena, 179
Leland, John, 57
Liberia, 128, 151, 154, 186–88, 192, 193, 195, 219, 247; Agnes McAllister's work in, 210–15, 256; and Amanda Smith, 226–27, 256; and William Wadé Harris, 227–30
Liberian Exodus Joint Stock Company, 186
Life of David Brainerd, 28, 254, 259, 260
Lincoln, Abraham, 170
Liverpool, 111, 193
London, 119, 140
London Ecumenical Conference, 147
London Missionary Society, 121
Lone Woman in Africa, 212
Louisiana, 162
Lovedale Institute, 199
Lubbock, John, 115
Lucknow,
Lutheranism, 169
Luther, Martin, 79

Macedonian and Home Mission Record, 93
Macomber, Eleanor, 58, 91, 92
Madagascar, 29, 240, 244
Madras, 129, 136
Mahmen-la, 37
Maine, Henry Sumner, 139
Malaysia, 29
Malcolm X, 185
Manchuria, 242
Manifest Destiny, 65–6
Manmad, 242
Manye, Charlotte, 196
Manye, Kate, 196
Marsden, George, 15, 139
Maryland, 162, 220
Mason, Francis, 80, 90; evaluations of Karen Christianity, 60–4; promotion of civilizing mission, 60–4, 69–70; views of civilization, 60–2
Massachusetts, 57, 59, 75
Massachusetts Baptist Missionary Society, 75
Massachusetts Board of Education, 78
Mau-koh, 50
Mau Mway, 50
Mauritius, 29
McAllister, Agnes, 210–15, 227, 256, 258

Index

McKinley, William, 6, 134
Memphis, Tennessee, 161
Methodism, American (*see also*, African Methodist Episcopal Church; Methodist Episcopal Church, North; Methodist Episcopal Church, South): and the American establishment, 134, 144, 165–66, 209–10; antiformalist impulses of, 112, 116, 133–34, 164–65; black Methodists, 86, 133, 163; democratization within, 12, 13, 133–34, 144, 164–65; during the early republic, 12, 111–12, 124, 133–34, 171–72, 198; during the Gilded Age, 134–35; growth of, 134; missionary efforts in American South, 87, 98
Methodism, British, 109, 112–3, 147; and the 1866 revival, 110, 114–17, 119, 120–1, 122; anxiety about African Christianity, 115, 197–200, 203–04; and civilization, 109; early mission work in South Africa, 104–5, 115; and imperialism, 120; and the native ministry, 119–21, 198–200; ordination issues, 110, 119–22, 127, 203; and race, 109, 127, 198–200, 203; relationship with Mangena Mokone, 183–84, 197, 259
Methodist Episcopal Church, North (MEC), (*see also*, Methodists, American), 111, 128, 160, 162, 216, 218, 237; creation of South India conference, 129, 131–32, 140; and the holiness movement, 145–47, 217–18, 242–43, 252; institutional system, 133–35; missionary bishop debate, 148–51; and the native ministry, 167; racial issues within, 148–51; tensions with William Taylor, 132, 133, 136, 141–42, 149–51, 154
Methodist Episcopal Church, South (MECS), (*see also*, Methodists, American), 161–62, 165, 166, 174, 177, 179
Methodist Missionary Society, 130, 132, 135–36, 141–42, 150, 152, 154–55
Mexico, 65
Mfengu: 103, 106, 110, 126; evangelism among, 104, 108–9, 114–16, 124; Michigan, 65
Miller, William, 75
Minnesota, 237
missionaries (*see also*, evangelicalism):and Bible translation, 7, 33–5, 45; discouragement from lack of conversions, 10, 30–1; perceptions of non-western cultures 24–7, 29–31, 36–7, 48–55, 60–4, 139, 233; and race, 64–9, 139, 142–44; relationship to world Christianity, 7–14, 256–60; in scholarship, 4–6; theories and theologies for, 50–1; 82–3, 90
Missouri, 162, 217
modernist Protestantism
Mok Lai Chi, 247, 251, 260
Mokone, Mangena, 183–84, 196, 197, 199–200, 203, 204, 259
Monoramabai, 234, 240, 248

Monrovia, 226
Moody, Dwight, 92, 140, 195
Moravians, 25
Morehouse College, 97
Morehouse, Henry, 98
Morgan, Thomas Jefferson, 99
Morning Star, 43
Morris Brown College, 192
Morton, Samuel George, 67
Mott, John, 45
Moulmein, 24, 26, 27, 81, 88
Moulmein Convention, 81–4
Moung Ing, 50
Moung Khway, 39
Moung Kyah, 39
Mpondo, 116, 124
Mueller, George, 246
Mukti, 3–4, 232, 236, 237–38, 239, 240–42, 243–44, 248, 253–54, 257, 258
Mumbai. *See* Bombay
Myanmar. *See* Burma
Myat Kyau, 54, 70
Mzimba, L.N., 83

Nalder, Rachel, 248
Nation, 137
National Camp Meeting Association, 146
Native Americans, 38–9; and Bible translation, 34; evangelistic efforts among, 25, 28, 56; white perceptions of, 26, 67, 137
native ministry, 103; and African Americans, 87–90, 177–78, 189; in Burma, 50–4, 69–73, 85; in China, 73; in Europe, 72–3; and race, 88–9, 93–9, 138–39, 198–200; in South Africa, 119–121, 198–200
Nazarenes, 209, 217
Negro and the White Man, 202
New Jersey, 222
New Orleans, 161
Newton Theological Institute, 61, 70
New York Baptist Union for Ministerial Education, 74
New York (city), 45, 146, 148, 220, 223
New York (state), 32, 53, 74–8, 87, 89, 138
New York Times, 138, 154
New Zealand, 111
Ngcayiya, Henry Reid, 204
Nongqawuse, 106
North Carolina, 162, 175
Norton, Albert, 242, 243
Norway, 230, 240, 242
Nova Scotia, 187

Oberlin College, 68
Ohio, 87, 121, 146
Ohio Wesleyan University, 139

Old Apostolic Faith Movement, 250
Oncken, Johann, 78
On the Origin of Species, 118, 138
Oppong, Sampson, 230
Origen, 79
Osborn, Lucy Drake, 218–19, 224, 236, 243
Osborn, William, 218, 236, 243
O'Sullivan, John L., 65

Palestine, 247
Palmer, Phoebe, 144–45, 147, 217, 223
Pamla, Charles, 103, 108, 128, 200; and the 1866 revival, 110, 116, 197, 257, 259; cooperation with William Taylor, 109–10, 114–17, 124, 152; early ministry, 104; as evangelist, 108–9, 110, 116, 121, 133, 258; negotiation of cultural differences, 110, 117–18; ordination, 120–1; and race, 117–18
Parks, H. B., 201
Parks, William, 174
Payne, Daniel Alexander, 176; and abolition, 169, 179; and African emigration, 187–88; conception of black leadership, 168–70; criticism of ring shout, 171–73; early ministry, 168–70; and female ordination, 178–79; formalist characteristics, 170–74, 189–90; and the native ministry, 189; promotion of black education, 168–70, 189, 192–93; promotion of civilizing mission, 169–70, 188–89; praise for white missionary enterprise, 188–89
Peck, Solomon, 63, 81–2, 84, 87–8
Pennsylvania, 64, 87, 89
Pentecostalism, 14, 103, 129, 155, 209, 215, 230; antiformalist impulses of, 249–52; and Chilean revivals, 242–43; and civilization, 245–57; growth of, 5; holiness roots of, 4, 236 240–44; institutional dynamics of, 251–52; and Korean revivals, 242, 244; lack of intellectuals within, 252–54; and Mukti revival, 4, 232, 240–42, 244; promotion of marginalized individuals, 247–49, 252; and the social order, 250–54; tongues question, 253–54
Pentecostal Truths, 247
Perry, R.L., 88
Persia, 219, 240
Peru, 140–42
Philadelphia, 184, 188, 192
Philippines, 6, 246
Pierson, A.T., 241
Pietermartizburg, South Africa, 116
Pilgrim Holiness Church, 217, 250
Pillar of Fire Church, 250
Plessey v. Ferguson, 181–82, 190
Poona, 231, 232, 235. 242

Port Elizabeth, South Africa, 105, 112
Portugal, 193
Powar, Soondarbai, 242, 243
Presbyterianism, African, 83, 119
Presbyterianism, American, 87, 98, 126, 165, 166, 167, 209, 219, 243, 244
Presbyterianism, Scottish, 56
Pretoria, 183, 184
Primitive Culture, 138
Prostrate South, 137
Protestant Episcopal Church, 211, (*see also*, Episcopalianism)
Pune. *See* Poona
Puritanism, 37, 55, 57, 78, 172
Pyongyang, 242

Quakers, 167, 218, 219
Quarterly Review, 57
Queenstown, South Africa, 201

Race: and African-American evangelicalism, 159–60, 168–70, 179–82, 184–91, 194; and American Baptists, 88–9, 93–9; in antebellum America, 64–9; and civilization, 64–9, 142–44, 199, 205; in Gilded Age America, 97, 137–40, 177–78; and the holiness movement, 223, 238; and the Methodist Episcopal Church, 142–44, 149–51; and the native ministry, 88–90; and Pentecostalism, 249–50; in Progressive Era America, 6; in South Africa, 117–19, 122, 126, 183–84, 197, 199, 205; theories of, 64–9, 93–9, 137–40, 199
radical holiness. *See* holiness movement; Pentecostalism
Ramabai Association, 235, 236, 244
Ramabai, Pandita: conversion to Christianity, 231, 236; evaluation of Mukti revival, 241, 253–54; fame among Pentecostals, 248–49, 260; and gender issues, 233–35; Hindu upbringing, 231, 234; and holiness spirituality, 235–36; relationship with Minnie Abrams, 237–40, 259; relationship with Sister Geraldine, 231–34, 239; role in Mukti revival, 3, 232, 240–42, 243, 246
Rangoon, 29, 31, 35, 38, 40–1, 49, 92
Reconstruction, 88, 98, 137, 164, 166, 167, 168, 180, 186, 190
Republican Party, 97–8, 137, 161
Revivalist, 236–38
Richards, John, 112–13
Richmond Institute, 93
Ridgel, Alfred, 192
Robbins, William E., 135
Robert, Dana, 58
Rochester, New York, 74–8

Rockefeller, John, 98
Ryan, M.L., 251, 252

Said, Edward, 246
Sandoway, 49, 51-2
San Francisco, 111, 121, 143
Sanneh, Lamin, 15, 43, 124, 257, 258
Santiago, 243
Sau Nga-tau, 62
Scott, Thomas J., 139
Scribner's, 137
Sears, Barnas, 169; debate with Wayland, 78-81, 85, 192; perceptions of Karen Christianity, 79; role in missionary movement, 78
Second Anglo-Burmese War, 41, 49
Second Great Awakening, 75, 164, 205
Serampore College, 50
Seymour, Horatio, 138
Seymour, William, 250
Shandong, 242
Shank, David, 229
Sharada Sadan school, 235, 236
Shway Meing, 52
Shway Sah, 50
Siam, 20-1, 38, 54
Sierra Leone, 187, 193, 195
Simmons, James, 88-9, 93
Sister Geraldine, 231-34, 239
slavery: 13, 64-5, 67-8, 85-6, 188, 202; and American evangelicalism, 12, 33, 86, 163-66; black evangelicalism during, 164-66, 168-69, 174, 175, 176; as a form of religious establishment, 88, 165-66; Smith, Amanda Berry, 220-28, 235, 243, 247, 256
Smith, Florence, 243
Smith, James, 220
Smith, Sir Henry, 105
Social Darwinism, 138, 199
Soga, Tiyo, 119-20, 123
South Africa, 151, 244, 256, 258, 259; and the 1866 revival, 103-5, 108-17, 119-22, 125-7, 152, 197, 257; AME church within, 184-5, 200-06; British imperialism in, 105-7, 126-27, 199; and the Ethiopian movement, 183-5, 196-201; racial dynamics within, 118-20
South Carolina, 85-8, 162, 174, 178, 187
South India Conference, Methodist Episcopal Church, 131-32, 140, 144, 149, 151
Spelman College, 97
Spencer, Herbert, 138
spiritualism, 75
Sri Lanka. *See* Ceylon
Stanley, Henry Morton, 153
Stanton, Elizabeth Cady, 75
St. Louis, 175
Stocking, George, 29

Sumner, Charles, 176
Sun Ju Kil, 244
supernaturalism, 3-4, 232, 241, 242; among African-American evangelicalism, 172; disbelief in, 61-2, 232, 242; and disenchantment, 10-11, 44, 146; in the holiness movement, 219, 237, 239-40; among the Karen, 44-5; missionary beliefs in, 6, 9, 112, 125, 215, 242; and Pentecostalism, 215, 240, 242, 244; and William Wadé Harris, 229-30; and world Christianity, 44-5, 215, 240, 241, 244; among the Xhosa, 105-8, 125
Swatson, John, 230
Sweden, 239, 240

Talented Tenth, 98-9
Tanner, B.T., 191, 192
Tappan, Arthur, 68
Tappan, Lewis, 68, 169
Tavoy, 19-20, 24-5, 27, 29, 38, 40
Taylor, Hudson, 246
Taylor, William: 14, 103, 195, 219, 225, 227, 256; and the 1866 revival, 110, 116, 127, 133, 197, 241, 259; antiformalist characteristics of, 112, 116, 119, 122, 126-27, 152; and civilization, 119, 122-23, 137, 153, 189; cooperation with Charles Pamla, 109-10, 114-17, 124, 152; critique of missionary system, 123, 128-29, 141-42, 151-52; and democratization, 114, 121, 131, 136-37; early ministry, 110, 111-12; election as bishop, 148-51; establishment of South India Conference, 131-32, 140; evangelism in India, 129-32, 143, 154; evangelism in South Africa, 112-17, 124-25, 154; and the holiness movement, 145, 147; influenced by African Christianity, 110, 127, 128; and the native ministry, 123-24, 127; perceptions of nonwestern cultures, 123-25, 130; and race, 117, 119, 122, 137, 140, 142-44; recruitment of missionaries, 132, 135, 141, 146-48, 154, 210, 218, 242; self-supporting mission plan, 135-36, 141, 148, 151-54, 155, 211, 243; in South America, 140-42; tensions with missionaries in India, 129-31; in west and central Africa, 151-54
Tennessee, 88
Ten Years of Self-Supporting Missions in India, 142
Texas, 162
Thailand. *See* Siam
Thembu, 116, 124
Thirteenth Amendment, 137
Thoburn, James, 129, 130, 143, 225
Three-Self Theory of missions, 83
Toro, Guillermo, 243
Triennial Convention, 267 n. 54

Trust, 248
Tule, John, 200
Turner, Henry McNeal: 256; antiformalist impulses of, 176–77; black nationalism of, 185–86, 193; and civilization, 161, 175, 177, 181–82, 194, 196; early ministry, 174–75; and emigration to Africa, 186–88, 194; establishing AME churches, 162, 180; and female ordination, 178–79; and higher education, 192–93; influenced by African American Great Awakening, 174, 191, 193; and Mangena Mokone, 184; as missionary in Africa, 184, 193–6, 200–01; as missionary in American South, 160–63, 174–77, 187; and the native ministry, 201, 202; ordination of African-American preachers, 168, 177, 178–79, 259; ordination of African preachers, 194, 201; perceptions of Africa, 187, 193–96, 203; political activities of, 180; promotion of foreign missions, 186–88, 191–93, 194; and race, 185–86, 193–96, 200–01; view of ordinary African Americans, 175–77
Tway Poh, 54, 70
Tyler, E.B., 138

Uganda, 240
Union Missionary Training Institute, 218–19
Unitarianism, 87, 167, 235
United States, dominant cultural trends of, 6, 32–3, 58–9, 189, 243–46, 259; evangelicalism in, 53, 58–9, 75–8, 128, 163–65; racial theories in, 64–9, 93–9, 137–40; imperialism of, 246
Universalism, 87, 167
University of Rochester, 99
Upper Room, 247

Valparaiso, 242
Van Meter, Henry, 44
Vassar College, 99
Venn, Henry, 83
Vermont, 148
Vinton, Calista, 58, 91
Vinton, Justus, 84
Virginia, 95, 111, 116, 143, 162
Voice of Missions, 191–92, 194, 195, 196, 200, 201

Wacker, Grant, 146
Wade, Deborah, 58, 91, 92, 256
Wade, Jonathan, 31, 51
Waller, J.C., 154
Walls, Andrew, 15, 36, 43, 125, 186, 258
Wanigasekera, D.E. Dias, 247–48, 260
War of the Ax, 105

Washington, D.C., 70, 111
Waterhouse, Lelia, 148
Waugh, James, 130
Wayland, Francis: 92, 123; as biographer of Adoniram Judson, 32, 77; debate with Sears, 74, 76–81, 85, 192; development of missionary theory, 77–8, 80–3, 88, 91, 96; perceptions of Karen Christianity, 77–8; role in missionary movement, 77; views of culture, 82; views of seminary education, 77–8
Way of Holiness, 145
Weber, Max, 10
Weld, Theodore Dwight, 68
Welsh revival, 240–41, 242, 243, 246
Wesleyan Missionary Society (*see also* Methodists, British), 104, 119, 198–200
Wesleyan University, 148
Wesley, John, 108, 109, 115, 130, 144
Whig Party, 59
White, Alma, 250
Whitefield, Annie, 219
Whitefield, George, 226
Wigger, John, 226
Wilberforce University, 169, 191, 192, 195, 196, 201
Wilkins, Andrew, 87
Willard, Frances, 145, 235
Wilmot, David, 64–5
Woman's Baptist Foreign Missionary Society, 90
Woman's Home and Foreign Missionary Society, 191, 194
Woman's State Temperance Society, 75
Woman's Work for Woman missionary theory, 90, 216, 219, 223
women. *See* gender
Women's Foreign Missionary Society (WFMS), 216–17, 219, 238
Women's Parent Mite Society, 194
Wood, Betty, 163–54
Worcester, Samuel, Dr. (ABCFM official), 56–7
Worcester, Samuel, Rev. (ABCFM missionary), 57
world Christianity (*see also,* Karen Christianity; Xhosa Christianity; Ethiopian movement; Liberia, and William Wadé Harris), 5–15, 83, 93, 210; African-American Christianity, as variation of, 159–160, 171–73, 185; in Burma, 23, 41, 74; democratized impulses within, 8–9, 256–57; impact on American evangelicalism, 4, 9–12, 20, 74, 83, 97–9, 103–4, 127, 210, 240, 242, 244, 259–60; relationships of power with missionaries, 254–60; relationship to evangelicalism, 256–60; and Pentecostalism, 129, 155, 232, 236, 240, 244, 254–55; in South Africa, 103, 125–27, 185, 205–06
World's Columbian Exposition, 194

Xaba, Jacobus, 200
Xhosa, 103, 126; and British imperialism, 105–7; cattle-killings, 105–7, 123; evangelism among, 104–5, 114–16, 124, 154; traditional religion of, 105–8
Xhosa Christianity, 203; and the 1866 revival, 105, 108–9, 126, 197; characteristics of, 109, 114, 115, 126; influence on British missionaries, 109–10, 120–21; influence on William Taylor, 127

Yale College, 70

Zulu, 104, 106, 110, 116, 124, 126, 198, 203

Printed in the USA/Agawam, MA
May 24, 2013

575596.006